D0209815

93, RUE DE VARENNE
TEL: SAXE 06-13

HENRY JAMES AND EDITH WHARTON
Letters: 1900–1915

OTHER BOOKS BY LYALL H. POWERS

Henry James: An Introduction and Interpretation

Henry James and the Naturalist Movement

Faulkner's Yoknapatawpha Comedy

AS EDITOR

The Portable Henry James, rev. ed.

Studies in "The Portrait of a Lady"

Henry James's Major Novels: Essays in Criticism

The Complete Notebooks of Henry James (with Leon Edel)

Leon Edel and Literary Art

HENRY JAMES
and
EDITH WHARTON

Letters: 1900–1915

EDITED BY
LYALL H. POWERS

CHARLES SCRIBNER'S SONS
New York

Copyright © 1990 by Lyall H. Powers

All rights reserved. No part of this book may be reproduced or transmitted in any form or by any means, electronic or mechanical, including photocopying, recording, or by any information storage and retrieval system, without permission in writing from the Publisher.

Charles Scribner's Sons
Macmillan Publishing Company
866 Third Avenue, New York, NY 10022
Collier Macmillan Canada, Inc.

Library of Congress Cataloging-in-Publication Data
James, Henry, 1843–1916.
Henry James and Edith Wharton: letters, 1900–1915/
edited by Lyall H. Powers.
p. cm.
ISBN 0-684-19146-6
1. James, Henry, 1843–1916—Correspondence. 2. Wharton,
Edith, 1862–1937—Correspondence. 3. Authors, American—
20th century—Correspondence. I. Wharton, Edith, 1862–
1937. II. Powers, Lyall Harris, 1924–
PS2123.A48   1990
813'.4—dc20   89-36809   CIP
[B]

Macmillan books are available at special discounts for bulk purchases for sales promotions, premiums, fund-raising, or educational use. For details, contact:
Special Sales Director
Macmillan Publishing Company
866 Third Avenue
New York, NY 10022

The photograph of Henry James in the frontispiece is from Culver Pictures, Inc.

Design by Janet Tingey

10 9 8 7 6 5 4 3 2 1

Printed in the United States of America

To Leon Edel

I speak of him, and can only speak, as a man
of his own craft, an emulous fellow-worker,
who has learned from him more of the lessons
of that engaging mystery than from any one
else, and who is conscious of so large a debt
to repay that it has had positively to be dis-
charged in installments; as if one could never
have at once all the required cash in hand.

Contents

Illustrations

(*frontispiece*)
Henry James and Edith Wharton

Acknowledgments

I AM GRATEFUL for a fellowship from the John Simon Guggenheim Memorial Foundation that enabled me to do much of the research and writing for this volume. I would also like to acknowledge the financial assistance given me by the office of the Vice-President for Research at the University of Michigan and by the English department of that institution.

I am pleased to acknowledge permission from Alexander R. James to include here the Henry James letters. The letters of Edith Wharton to Henry James and to Theodora Bosanquet are included by the kind permission of William Royall Tyler, owner of the Edith Wharton estate; my thanks go also to Gloria Loomis, literary agent of that estate.

Dr. Patricia C. Willis, curator of American literature in the Beinecke Rare Book and Manuscript Library of Yale University, has given me permission to publish the James, Wharton, and Bosanquet material from that library. I am grateful to Dr. Willis and her staff for their help. I would also thank Dr. David E. Schoonover, former curator of American literature at the Beinecke, for cordial and unstinting assistance over a period of years. Mr. Rodney G. Dennis, curator of manuscripts in the Houghton Library of Harvard University, has given me permission to publish the Wharton letters to Bosanquet in this volume; my gratitude for kind assistance goes to him and his staff—especially to Jennie Rathbun, who has been exceptionally generous and efficient in her dealings with me. Finally, my sincere thanks go to Saundra Taylor, curator of manuscripts in the Lilly Library, Indiana University, for permission to publish a letter from James to Wharton from the Wharton collection there.

Leon Edel had provided guidance and inspiration for this as for other work of mine; he generously read the manuscript of this volume and offered much helpful commentary. Like all Jamesians, I am deeply indebted to him; and I am most grateful for his sage counsel and his permission for several items of illustration I have used here. Susan B. Whitlock was for many months my editorial assistant; I was very fortunate to be able to rely on her intelligence, initiative, and diligence in the preparation of this correspondence.

In the early stages of preparing the manuscript much help was given me by Sir Brian Cook Batsford, artist and sometime occupant of Lamb House, Rye, and by Geoffrey Spinks Bagley, artist and honorary curator of the Ypres Castle Museum, Rye; I am pleased to express my thanks to them for their aid and their permission to use photographs of Henry James and of Rye. I would also gratefully recognize the kindness of the late Dr. H. Montgomery Hyde, an earlier occupant of Lamb House—both his hospitality to me in Rye and his permission to use here a photograph of Henry James. In Saint-Brice-sous-Forêt, France, M. Jacques Fosse, sometime Président de l'Association des Amis du Vieux Saint-Brice, was a cordial and generous host and a fund of information and anecdote; I am grateful to him for his generosity and his permission to include some photographs of Edith Wharton. I am also indebted to the Hotel del Coronado, Coronado, California, for use of a 1905 picture of the hotel.

I acknowledge my indebtedness to Mary L. Pitlick for her information on Edith Wharton and Robert Norton, and especially for sending me a James letter to Wharton that she discovered; and to Marion Mainwaring for information on Edith Wharton and William Morton Fullerton and related matters. I owe a special debt of gratitude to the artist and Jamesian amateur Fran Wright.

I am pleased to thank my colleagues Alan Howes and William Ingram for helping me identify some quotations from English and American literature; Ralph Williams for identifying some Italian literary allusions and for translating some Italian colloquialisms; Peter Bauland for clarifying some German items; and Jean Carduner, Ernst Pulgram, and especially Marcel Muller for help with some French locutions and literary quotations. I must add a special word of thanks to the Proust scholar Philip Kolb, professor emeritus of the University of Illinois, for his response to my queries.

I take particular pleasure in thanking my editor, Erika Goldman, for her informed assistance, her resourcefulness, and her general humane charm. And I gratefully acknowledge the aid of the informed and perceptive attention of Sam Flores, who read the manuscript so astutely and made many helpful suggestions.

Finally, I am exceptionally fortunate to have had the advice, sound judgment, and encouragement of Loretta Powers throughout the preparation of this volume. To her I am most grateful.

HENRY JAMES AND EDITH WHARTON
Letters: 1900–1915

Introduction

AN OBVIOUS JUSTIFICATION for publishing the letters exchanged between Henry James and Edith Wharton is that the correspondents were both important professional literary artists. Beyond that, however, lies the story of a fruitful, fascinating relationship between two principally expatriate American writers that spanned the first fifteen years of the twentieth century. The period is itself interesting and not without relevance to the relationship in question: it began with the final flowering of Victorian England and ended with the cataclysm that effectively lowered the curtain on the Empire. It was not yet time for the United States to enter the world arena and confront with some reluctance the responsibilities soon to devolve upon it as a growing international power, although the stage was already being set for that entrance.

An unlikely pair, James and Wharton, to foster a relationship worth more than cursory attention, for they would seem at first glance to have little in common beyond nationality and profession. By the turn of the century James was a quietly settled cosmopolitan, an Anglicized American artist approaching the end of an extensive and productive career. Wharton was no longer in her first youth but was twenty years his junior; she was rather well traveled but not yet by any means the cosmopolitan Europeanized American she was to become. Her future lay largely before her, and while her literary career finally extended well beyond James's death, it was at that moment merely beginning. James was financially comfortable, at the upper end of the middle class; he had a convenient London "perch" at the Reform Club and the handsome Georgian dwelling Lamb House in Rye, Sussex, with three or four servants to see to his needs. Edith Jones Wharton was quite well-to-do, a woman of substantial independent means, a member of the old New

York aristocracy and descendant of Gallatins, Joneses, Ledyards, Pendletons, Rhinelanders, and Schermerhorns. The ingredients of such a relationship appear unpromising, yet it developed into a warm and mutually rewarding friendship.

Their shared interest in the literary profession accounted for the beginning of their association, which was due in part to their common friendship with the French writer Paul Bourget. Yet the actual beginning was twice postponed, twice frustrated by crossing paths that might have brought them together. It might have occurred in 1885 when James was forty-two and Wharton twenty-three. In her memoirs *A Backward Glance* (1934) she recounts being at a dinner party with James at the Edward Boits' in Paris, "probably in the late eighties."[1] James was in Paris for a month and a half (10 September–1 November) in 1885 and then visited the Boits;[2] he was not in Paris again until 1888, for the month of December, and there is no indication that he visited the Boits at that time. The young Mrs. Wharton (she had married Edward Robbins Wharton at the end of April 1885) had dressed with special care for the dinner party in the hope of attracting James's attention. He remained unaware of her presence. A second near meeting occurred, she further recalls, "in Venice (probably in 1889 or 1890)": the Ralph Curtises had extended an invitation to the Whartons and James was to be present. He was in fact a guest of the Curtises at their Palazzo Barbaro on the Grand Canal during the month of June 1890. The eager Mrs. Wharton had a beautiful new hat for the occasion and was prepared to blurt out her admiration for "Daisy Miller" and *The Portrait of a Lady*; but James "noticed neither the hat nor its wearer."[3]

1. *A Backward Glance* (New York: Scribners, 1985), 171–72.
2. Leon Edel, *Henry James,* vol. 3: *The Middle Years: 1882–1895* (Philadelphia and New York: Lippincott, 1962), 157–58 (hereafter, *The Middle Years*).
3. *Backward Glance,* 172. There is the possiblity that Wharton was, almost half a century later, confusing two visits to the Curtises, one in the early summer of 1887 and this one of 1890; James had also been at the Palazzo Barbaro from mid-May to 1 July 1887 (see his letter to Grace Norton, *Henry James: Letters,* vol. 3: *1883–1895,* ed. Edel [Cambridge, Mass.: Harvard University Press, 1980], 195). Wharton recalls that on the second near meeting James was "staying either with Curtis at the Palazzo Barbaro, or with Robert Browning's old friend, Mrs. Arthur Bronson" (172). From the end of February to the middle of April 1887, James had been Mrs. Bronson's guest at the Casa Alvisi in Venice. During their European months, February to June, the Whartons' practice was to stay mainly in Italy; see R. W. B. Lewis, *Edith Wharton: A Biography* (New York: Harper & Row, 1975), 57–58.

Her perseverance was rewarded in 1895: she sent James good wishes for the opening of his ill-fated play *Guy Domville*. On that dire afternoon of 5 January he wrote to Minnie Bourget that "at 8:30 this evening ... my poor little play will be thrown into the arena" and added: "I offer Mrs. Wharton all thanks for her sympathy."[4] Yet it was the actual exchange of their literary productions that really opened the relationship. Wharton sent him her collection of short stories *The Greater Inclination* in 1899 and her story "The Line of Least Resistance" late the following year. Wharton's former sister-in-law, Mary (Minnie) Cadwalader Jones, supplied James with two other of Wharton's works, the short novel *The Touchstone* (1900) and the collection of tales *Crucial Instances*.[5] In 1902 Wharton sent him her Italian novel *The Valley of Decision* and he reciprocated with his own novel set partly in Italy, *The Wings of the Dove*. The earliest extant letters of James to Wharton, the first two in this collection, clearly indicate the nature of the early relationship thus begun between them. In 1888 he had published his short story "The Lesson of the Master"; he was now playing the title role opposite the fledgling Edith Wharton, who came to address him almost exclusively in their correspondence as "Cher Maître" ("Dear Master"). At once he exhorted her to recognize the most appropriate subject for the exercise of her artistic talents, the American scene and specifically New York: "I value, I egg you on in, your study of the American life that surrounds you" (26 October 1900). And we will do well to recall the implicit reason for that topic—"Use to the full your ironic and satiric gifts," he urged her as though those gifts were the most apt to treat the American scene. Then further and more specifically: "Don't pass it by—the immediate, the real, the ours, the yours, the novelist's that it waits for. ... DO NEW YORK!" (17 August 1902). To Mary Cadwalader Jones, who had been his friend for some years, he confided his desire to "get hold of" Wharton and

> pump the essence of my wisdom and experience into her. She *must* be tethered in native pastures, even if it reduce her to a back-yard in New York. (*Letters* 4, 237)

4. *Letters* 3, 506.

5. *Henry James: Letters*, vol. 4: *1895–1916*, ed. Edel. (Cambridge, Mass.: Harvard University Press, 1984), 236–38.

It was as though he had freshly in mind her first published story, "Mrs. Manstey's View" (1891). They finally met in London in December 1903.

With the opening of the twentieth century their relationship grew apace. It was an important moment in the careers of both writers. James was embarking on his "Major Phase" with the novels *The Wings of the Dove* (1902), *The Ambassadors* (1903), and *The Golden Bowl* (1904); they represent the culmination of his years of experiment as a psychological novelist to give dramatic rendering of the psychological reactions of characters held in the grip of agons of anxiety, discovery, and the possibilities of love. The experiment had benefited from his compensatory discovery on the heels of *Guy Domville*'s failure in the theater, the discovery of "a key that, working in the same *general* way fits the complicated chambers of *both* the dramatic and the narrative lock"—"the divine principle of the Scenario."[6] In the fall of 1904 he returned to the United States after an absence of more than twenty years. He toured the country on his speaking tour, made notes on his impressions of home as found for *The American Scene* (1907), and contracted with Charles Scribner for a collected edition of his fiction. And he visited Edith and Teddy Wharton at The Mount in Lenox, Massachusetts.

Her career was about to take wings: with "The Line of Least Resistance" in 1900 Wharton's work of the twentieth century would seem to follow the urgent advice of the Master. During James's year in America her first really important novel, *The House of Mirth*, was being serialized in *Scribner's Magazine*. Other triumphs followed—*Ethan Frome* (1911), *The Reef* (1912), and *The Custom of the Country* (1913)—in which she treated the American Subject, and profited thereby. Wharton wrote novels of sharp social commentary, often examining the inroads of the Philistine into old New York society and also turning her searing scrutiny upon the limitations of that venerated society. It would appear, then, that she heeded the lesson of the Master, and certainly he continued to offer her advice and criticism on her work. The truth seems to be, however, that there was in Edith Wharton a fundamental lack of understanding of James's later work and a distinct failure of sympathy with his aesthetics.

---

6. *The Complete Notebooks of Henry James*, ed. Edel and Powers (New York: Oxford University Press, 1987), 115.

It has long been a commonplace of criticism, and was so during the years of their association, to observe similarities between the works of James and Wharton, and not always to her advantage: she was dubbed a James manqué, her work characterized as "James and water." She was aware of such critical attitudes, to be sure, and understandably resented them. It is quite possible that the unfavorable comparison contributed to her dislike of the Master's late fiction. In June of 1904 she wrote rather testily to William C. Brownell of Scribners:

> I return the reviews [of *The Descent of Man*] with many thanks. I have never before been discouraged by criticism, . . . but the continued cry that I am an echo of Mr. James (whose books of the past ten years I can't read, much as I delight in the man) . . . makes me feel rather hopeless.[7]

That explanatory parenthesis may have the look of "sour grapes," certainly, but another kind of light is cast upon it and reinforcement of it as something of a confirmed critical attitude is added by an earlier letter to Sara Norton in March 1901; there she says of James's just-published *The Sacred Fount*: "(I wish so fine a title had not been attached to so ignoble a book.) . . . I could cry over the ruins of such a talent . . ." (*EW Letters*, 45). In September 1902 she sent Brownell the letter from James (17 August 1902) in which he praised *The Valley of Decision* and announced he had sent her his *Wings of the Dove*; she commented pointedly, "Don't ask me what I think of *The Wings of the Dove*" (*EW Letters*, 70). She did admire his earlier work, *The Portrait of a Lady* in particular, and recognized the signal respect he enjoyed as master of his craft; she could even admire some of his late productions. The tale "Julia Bride" (1908) she found "living & vivid, all the things *you* don't," she asserted to Sara Norton. " 'Non ragionam,' for we shall never agree on the last H.J. manner" (*EW Letters*, 140). She had, furthermore, at least a hand in the creation of the essay William Morton Fullerton devoted to intelligent praise of the achievement of the New York Edition of James's novels and tales; and that is an edition strongly marked by James's revisions of his earlier work (extensive in the case of *The Portrait of a*

---

7. *The Letters of Edith Wharton*, ed. R. W. B. and Nancy Lewis (New York: Scribners, 1988), 91.

Lady) in accord with the critical eye of the sexagenarian Master. There is, finally, an interesting passage in *A Backward Glance* that suggests a mellower if not a thoroughly revised critical attitude to the work of James's Major Phase—different indeed from the sharp comments to Brownell, at least—as she expresses preference for a crucial scene in *The Golden Bowl* over the famous chapter 42 of *The Portrait of a Lady*:

> Exquisite as the early novels are—and in point of perfection probably none can touch "The Portrait of a Lady"—yet measured by what was to come Henry James, when he wrote them, had but skimmed the surface of life and of his art. Even the man who wrote, in "The Portrait of a Lady," the chapter in which Isabel broods over her fate at night by the fire, was far from the man in whom was already ripening that greater night-piece, the picture of Maggie looking in from the terrace at Fawns at the four bridge players and renouncing her vengeance.... (174)

This was a quarter of a century after the New York Edition.

For his part, James's marked preference was for Wharton's *The Reef*, although he delighted in *The House of Mirth*, *Ethan Frome*, and *The Custom of the Country*. There should be no surprise in that choice: *The Reef* is quite obviously the most Jamesian of Wharton's novels. The terms in which he chose to praise it are significant both of his approval of her achievement and also, finally, of a profound difference in artistic attitude. He called it Racinian: "Anna [Leath] is really of Racine and one presently begins to feel her throughout as an Eriphyle [*sic*] or a Bérénice ..." (4 December 1912). It is appropriate, surely, that James invoked the creator of the famous heroines Phèdre, Esther, Andromaque, and Iphigénie in addition to Ériphile and Bérénice. For one of the important features of the work of both James and Wharton is their interesting and appealing heroines: his Christina Light (*Roderick Hudson* and *The Princess Casamassima*), Isabel Archer and also Serena Merle (*The Portrait of a Lady*), Fleda Vetch and also Mrs. Gereth (*The Spoils of Poynton*), Nanda and also Mrs. Brookenham (*The Awkward Age*), Milly Theale and also Kate Croy (*The Wings of the Dove*), Maggie Verver and also Charlotte Stant (*The Golden Bowl*), and her Lily Barth (*The House of Mirth*), Justine Brent (*The Fruit of the Tree*), Fanny Frisbie (*Madame de Treymes*), Mattie Silver and also Zenobia (*Ethan Frome*), Undine Spragg (*The Custom of the Country)*, Anna Leath and also Sophie Viner *(The Reef)*. One might claim them both as *feminist* writers, and indeed "feminist critics" have claimed them for their own. The danger is, however, that those critics may be sometimes more political than literary; that is too often the case with Wharton's readers, in fact.[8] But neither Wharton nor James was ever narrowly feminist; their fiction was not polemical, and to approach it that way is to risk serious misrepresentation. A line from Andrew Holleran's essay "Cousin Henry" is simple and apt here: "Reflecting on the success James had with London hostesses, a friend wrote, 'Henry seemed to look at women rather as women look at them. Women look at women as persons; men look at them as women.' "[9] That tendency is reflected in his, as in Wharton's, fictions.

But the "feminist" aspect of Racine's creations is not the whole story, is in fact not even the main point of the story. The crucial emphasis of James's comparison falls on the *dramatic* Racinian quality of *The Reef.* He says flatly, "The beauty of it is that it is, for all it is worth, a Drama and almost, as it seems to me, one of the psychologic Racinian unity, intensity and gracility." To that he adds the grateful observation that "the whole thing, unrelated and unreferred save in the most superficial way to its milieu and background, and to any determining or qualifying *entourage*, takes place comme cela, and in a specified, localised way, in France ..." (4 December 1912). That is the sort of appreciative comment one might expect from the Master of *dramatized* "psychologic" fiction. And not only is *The Reef* dramatic, he indicates, but also spare, economical, sharply focused in its essential concerns, and "unrelated and unreferred" to the mere superficies (as James saw it) of its avowed setting. His main point is clear and suffices amply to distinguish the aesthetic view of the late James from that of Edith Wharton.

Wharton's latest commentary on the work of the Master aids in clarifying that distinction. In *A Backward Glance* she recalls James's acute sensitivity to criticism of his work, for instance a remark of hers concerning *The Golden Bowl* that in some eyes might seem, if not an example

8. One attractive exception, among others, is the young critic Julie Olin-Ammentorp: see her "Edith Wharton's Challenge to Feminist Criticism," *Studies in American Fiction* 16 (1988), 237–44.
9. *Ground Zero* (New York: Morrow, 1988), 84.

of her own insensitivity to his writing, then evidence of her opposition to the principles it depended on:

> I was naturally much interested in James's technical theories and experiments, though I thought, and still think, that he tended to sacrifice to them that spontaneity which is the life of fiction. Everything, in the latest novels, had to be fitted into a predestined design, and design, in his strict geometrical sense, is to me one of the least important things in fiction.... His latest novels, for all their profound moral beauty, seemed to me more and more lacking in atmosphere, more and more severed from that thick nourishing air in which we all live and move. The characters in "The Wings of the Dove" and "The Golden Bowl" seem isolated in a Crookes tube for our inspection: his stage was cleared like that of the Théâtre Français in the good old days when no chair or table was introduced that was not relevant to the action (a good rule for the stage, but an unnecessary embarrassment to fiction). Preoccupied by this, I one day said to him: "What was your idea in suspending the four principal characters in 'The Golden Bowl' in the void? What sort of life did they lead when they were not watching each other, and fencing with each other? Why have you stripped them of all the *human fringes* we necessarily trail after us through life?" (190–91)

James's answer, she recalled, was (of course), "My dear—I didn't know I had!"

One might almost claim that Wharton's basic position regarding the art of fiction resembled that of the callous author of *Boon*. To say so, however, is to confront the fact that she would not have stooped, as H. G. Wells did so easily in that vicious satire, and to recognize that this difference in taste, in the espousal of a theory of fiction, in no way hindered her admiration of James the man. Nor did the apparent differences hinder his profound affection for her. He could not help but envy her the popular success her work achieved, and that on top of the financial ease she already enjoyed; and that envy was aggravated by his bitter recognition of the failure of his New York Edition to awaken public interest. The strength of their relationship rested upon other foundations, other shared interests.

Prominent among those interests were other literary practitioners and other literary work, both English and French. Paul Bourget was an early friend of both, and the correspondence is full of references to him and his works. Others among the French whose names dot these letters are Henri de Régnier, Paul Hervieu, Henry Bernstein, Charles Du Bos, and André Gide; and among the English, James M. Barrie, Edmund Gosse, Mrs. Humphry Ward, Thomas Hardy, George Meredith, Percy Lubbock, and, marginally, Morton Fullerton; to those must be added the French painter-writer Jacques-Émile Blanche and the American John Singer Sargent. There are two special cases: George Sand's fiction had early attracted James's attention, but in the new century it was rather her way of life—as it included Musset and Chopin, for example—that now drew his eye, and Wharton's as well. Likewise, the life and confessions of Hortense Allart, Mme de Méritens, less than her other writings, became a fascination of James and Wharton. The dwellings of both Frenchwomen became shrines that prompted their pilgrimages.

Their shared literary interests, in fact, early and easily moved them into shared social and then personal interests. James's visits to The Mount during his year in America (1904–1905) were important in fostering the personal connection between him and Edith Wharton. Subsequently the Whartons' decision to commit themselves rather more definitely to European residence in 1906 by leasing George Vanderbilt's apartment in the heart of the old Faubourg Saint-Germain in Paris, at 58, rue de Varenne, increased the opportunity for socializing between Henry and Edith, and for some time that included Teddy as well. Tracing the activities of James and Wharton in England and France during the next few years gives us a useful introduction to the social life and the prominent figures of the Edwardian and Georgian periods.

Of course they didn't entirely leave America behind, but their American associations now tended to be with the Europeanized. Both James and Wharton counted the Charles Eliot Norton family, for example, among their lifelong friends: daughter Sara was one of Wharton's closest (and a favorite partner for discussions of Henry James), and in the last years of his life James was closely associated with son Richard in working for the Allied cause at the outbreak of the Great War. Charles's sister Grace as well was one of James's most faithful correspondents throughout his life. Walter Berry was an American but had been born in Paris and spent most of his professional career abroad. Howard Sturgis was a son of the Bostonian Russell Sturgis, whom James had known since boyhood; yet Howard was born in England and educated at Eton and Cambridge, and he made his first personal acquaintance with America in 1904, visiting at The Mount with James. An important social center for him and Wharton in England was Howard's home, Queen's Acre, commonly abbreviated to Qu'Acre by the familiars, near Windsor. The regulars at Qu'Acre included another Europeanized American, Gaillard Lapsley, then a don at Cambridge. And still another of the breed, one who played a meteoric role in the life of both James and Wharton, was William Morton Fullerton; his brief but poignant drama with Edith Wharton began not long after James's return from his year's visit in the United States and soon after Wharton's commitment to a more definite European residence.

In England, James was helpful in introducing Wharton to the beau monde of English society. They were guests together at some of the foremost houses in England. One was the London home at 52 Portland Place of Lady St. Helier: a Scottish widow, Susan Mary Elizabeth Mackenzie Stanley, who had married Francis Henry Jeune and became Lady St. Helier when he was made the 1st Baron St. Helier. She was perhaps the leading literary hostess of the period. Wharton wrote to Sara Norton (3 December 1908) of her experience at 52 Portland Place that "everybody in London passes through this house" (*EW Letters*, 167). Outside of London they visited such country houses as Stanway in Gloucestershire, home of Lord Hugo and Lady Mary Elcho; on weekends Stanway was well attended by the most prominent figures of Edwardian society. James and Wharton also frequently experienced the lavish hospitality of the Charles Hunters at Hill Hall near Epping; Mary Hunter remained a friend of both. Wharton was so taken with the setting that she pondered purchasing a property of her own in the vicinity of Hill Hall, with much encouragement from James. They visited the Thames-side country place of William Waldorf and Nancy Astor (themselves Europeanized Americans) at Cliveden, where James suffered one of the earliest warnings of heart trouble while strolling about the grounds with Wharton in August 1912. And at Ascot they were guests of Margaret Brooke, Ranee of Sarawak. A sense of the social milieu in which they moved in England is given by the little catalogue in Wharton's letter to Sara Norton mentioned above:

> I went to Cliveden last Saturday, to the young Waldorf Astors & met there a large & very charming party—Mr. Balfour, Sir Frank Lascelles, Ld Ribblesdale, Ld & Lady Elcho, Dcess of Manchester, Lady Essex [these last two also Europeanized Americans], Howard Sturgis, &c &c.

And the letter continues, listing Mr. Barrie, Mr. Gosse, Miss May Sinclair, the Duchess of Sutherland, Lady Pollock, and Sir Philip Burne-Jones—and "Dear Henry J." Such a list reminds us that one of the singular and fructifying features of Edwardian society was its cordial gathering of figures from the political, ambassadorial, literary, and artistic walks of life, and its easy mingling of English and American, aristocrat and commoner.

The same was hardly less true of the social life of the Faubourg Saint-Germain, into which Paul Bourget helped introduce Edith Wharton. The focus of this society was for her the salon of the Comtesse Rosa de Fitz-James, née Rosalie de Gutmann, a descendant of Austrian-Jewish bankers. In *A Backward Glance* Wharton remarked that "in the last ten or fifteen years before the war Madame de Fitz-James' *salon* had a prestige which no Parisian hostess since 1918, has succeeded in recovering" (265). One of the jewels in Rosa de Fitz-James's circle as James and Wharton knew it was the gently urbane and witty Abbé Mugnier, later canon of the Cathedral of Notre-Dame de Paris, whose presence further attests to the eclectic character of Parisian society of that time.

Most significant of all, however, was the ever closer personal relationship, the burgeoning friendship of the two individuals themselves. "All we knew," Edith Wharton wrote in *A Backward Glance*, "was that suddenly it was as if we had always been friends, and were to go on being (as he wrote to me in February 1910 [8 February 1910]), 'more and more never apart.' " And her reminiscence of their early years continues:

> I had found myself, and was no longer afraid to talk to Henry James of the things we both cared about; while he, always so helpful and hospitable to younger writers, at once used his magic faculty of drawing out his interlocutor's inmost self. Perhaps it was our common sense of fun that first brought about our understanding. The real marriage of true minds is

for any two people to possess a sense of humour or irony pitched in exactly the same key, so that their joint glances at any subject cross like interarching search-lights. I have had good friends between whom and myself that bond was lacking; and in that sense Henry James was perhaps the most intimate friend I ever had, though in many ways we were so different. (173)

The importance for James of his friendship with Edith Wharton was that it offered him a combination of ingredients that he had long needed and had never quite found before. During the last twenty years of his life, coincidentally perhaps from his 1895 failure in the theater, James had felt increasingly the loneliness of his existence and the need for the warmth of more intimate associations than he had known and needed in earlier years. Evidently his two return visits to the United States in 1904–1905 and 1910–1911 served to heighten his sense of alienation from his native land and the compensatory need to snuggle more cozily into his adopted England. In these years he began to seek a kind of close association with various attractive young men who admired him and whom he found bright and interesting. One of the first of these was William Morton Fullerton, whom James met early in 1890, and whose apparent sensitivity and ingratiating manner quickly impressed him. Their friendship was further sustained from 1907 partly by their shared affection for Edith Wharton. Others included the Europeanized American Jonathan Sturges, whose advice from William Dean Howells in 1895—"Live all you can!"—provided James with the germ for *The Ambassadors*; the Norwegian-born hyperbolic sculptor Hendrik Andersen; the Irish Jocelyn Persse; the poet Rupert Brooke, whom James met as a Cambridge undergraduate; and finally the budding novelist Hugh Walpole. None of these could provide James with the quality of sustained intimate friendship he needed. With Andersen, it seems, he was awakened to the physical aspect of close friendship, but whether that brought satisfactory intimacy is dubious, and had any of the young men proposed the ultimate expression of physical intimacy (as Walpole is reported to have done), James would almost certainly have spurned it.

Of the numerous women whom James knew well during the years up to the close of the nineteenth century, two demand a special word. In his youth there was his beloved cousin Minny Temple, whom James coupled with her good friend Clover Hooper to represent his ideal of young womanhood: Minny was blessed with "moral spontaneity" and Clover with "intellectual grace."[10] Minny was cut off at age twenty-five; her spirit would "haunt" James for the rest of his life; Clover soon enough became Mrs. Henry Adams. Constance Fenimore Woolson, American expatriate writer and Jacobean disciple, is the other woman who deserves a discriminating word. James came to know her rather well, and in a sense intimately (he called her Fenimore) between 1880 and her mysterious death in January 1894.[11] She seems to have offered, or demanded, a closer and more physical intimacy than he was prepared to cope with. If Minny was James's Milly Theale (as of course she was), Fenimore threatened to be his Kate Croy.

In fact, however, James's dilemma was closer to that described by James Duffy in James Joyce's "A Painful Case" *(Dubliners)*: "Love between man and man is impossible because there must not be sexual intercourse and friendship between man and woman is impossible because there must be sexual intercourse." What Henry James sought was a manageable compromise, for he clearly wanted a dash of the piquant in his relationships, an element not physical but inescapably erotic, that would have assured him the kind of intimacy he needed and so permitted the nearest to a perfect friendship that he could have wished.

What James found in Edith Wharton was a combination of the intellectual grace of Clover Hooper with something of the moral spontaneity of Minny Temple. The author who depicted so sympathetically the "virtuous attachment" of Chad Newsome and Marie de Vionnet in *The Ambassadors* was quite prepared to accept and approve of Wharton's brand of moral spontaneity. (His "Project for Novel"[12] indicates he had the details of the novel in hand in the late summer of 1900, and just a bit earlier than the first letter collected herein.) In the meeting of minds Wharton mentions as important in drawing her and James together one detects quite readily the piquant touch of the erotic that made all the difference. That necessary quality James discovered very early in the relationship, during his visits to the Whartons in 1904–1905. His letter

10. *Henry James: Letters,* vol. 1: *1843–1875,* ed. Edel (Cambridge, Mass.: Harvard University Press, 1974), 208.

11. See *Letters* 3, 523–62, and *The Middle Years,* 356–62.

12. See *Comp. Notebooks,* 541–76.

of 7 June 1905, anticipating a return visit to repeat the pleasures of the preceding autumn, employs a revealing turn of phrase: "I feel as if those days wd. be a really deep draught—of the Pagellino vintage."

The focus there is on the Whartons' automobile; the name, a diminutive of endearment, is redolent of illicit Venetian romance (or was to Edith and Henry)—a mixture of the exotic and the erotic and evocative of George Sand and Alfred de Musset in Venice in 1834. The poet was ill and attended to by Dr. Pietro Pagello; after the ailing Alfred departed, the happy Pagello replaced him as George's lover. James had early found suitable nicknames for the Wharton automobile, in which he was delighted to be carried about with Edith—the Chariot of Fire, the Vehicle of Passion—but thus far none quite so apt as the one fragrant with reference to the exciting George. The visit to Nohant which James and Wharton made together in 1907 crowned their vicarious and chaste participation in the wonderful naughtiness of Sand and her amours. As they viewed her old house at Nohant, James pondered the memories held in the various chambers where George and friends "pigged so thrillingly together . . . all the greasiness & smelliness in which she made herself (& *so* many other persons!) at home" (as he recalled it to Wharton some years later; see letter of 13 March 1912). He mused, aloud, "And in which of those rooms, I wonder, did George herself sleep." Then, with a wicked twinkle in his eye, he pursued to his companion, "Though in which, indeed, in which indeed, my dear, did she *not?*"

James and Wharton kept a sharp eye out for documentation of George Sand's personal career and eagerly informed each other of the publication of biographical volumes, collections of letters, gossip that enlightened them further on the piggery life focused at Nohant. Yet George Sand seemed at last to be surpassed in all the most interesting ways by a friend of hers, another writer and a woman of even more liberated manners than she, Hortense Allart, Mme de Méritens. In February 1908 Wharton was in Herblay looking for Hortense's house, as she had sought Sand's in Nohant. She wrote James of her experience. He was envious but ecstatic:

> I ache to have been—or not to have been—at Herblay with you & Fullerton—fancy there being a second & *intenser* Nohant! Cette douce France! The wondrous flowers of personality it throws off in its wealth!

No wonder it's miraculous & presumptuous & splendid & *insupportable*.
(11 March 1908)

Coincidentally, James had written her just four days earlier: "Read, read
(& *roar* over) Léon Séché's 2 vols on Hortense Allart—Mme de Méritens. But of course you have! What a race!" (7 March 1908). Very soon
after the Herblay report James began referring to Wharton's automobile
as "Hortense," and she picked up the practice. The masculine "Pagellino" was laid aside along with chauffeur Charles Cook's honorific title,
"Prince of Pagellists"; the gender change was appropriate.

It is to be noted that Wharton's companion on the trip to Hortense's
Herblay was none other than William Morton Fullerton, James's friend
of seventeen years and Wharton's acquaintance since the spring of 1907.
He had been a visitor at The Mount in the late fall of that year and a
close association between him and Edith had blossomed like a November cotton flower. Three days after his departure she began a private
journal addressed specifically to him, "The Life Apart."[13] By the spring
of 1908 they were lovers in the full sense of that term, or at least in the
physical sense. She kept James ignorant of the situation during his visit

13. It was once thought that this journal was addressed to Walter Berry; see Wayne
Andrews, "The World of Edith Wharton," introduction to *The Best Short Stories of Edith
Wharton*, ed. Andrews (New York: Scribners, 1958), xix–xxiii. The first published con-
jecture that it was rather William Morton Fullerton who so occupied Wharton's mind
and heart at that moment was that of Leon Edel: see *Henry James*, vol. 5: *The Master:
1901–1916* (Philadelphia and New York: Lippincott, 1972), 412, 415, 450 (hereafter,
The Master). See also *EW Biog.*, 203ff. Lewis there notes that the journal "The Life
Apart" takes its name from Wharton's translation of a phrase from Ronsard, *L'Âme
Close*, which she added parenthetically after the title. In her story of 1906, "The Hermit
and the Wild Woman," there is a somewhat prophetic passage. The Hermit has arranged the terms on which he and the fructifying Wild Woman can coexist: "At first
the Hermit, knowing the weakness of woman, and her little aptitude for *the life apart*,
had feared that he might be disturbed by the nearness of his penitent . . ."; see *The
Hermit and the Wild Woman and Other Stories* (New York: Scribners, 1908), 32 (my
italics).

Another aspect of Wharton's (and therefore James's) association with Fullerton remains unclear. The blackmailing former mistress of Fullerton (see letters of 11 January
1909, 26 July 1909, and 9 September 1910) is identified by R. W. B. Lewis as "Henrietta
Mirecourt" in his biography of Wharton (189–91 and passim), and in the edition of her
Letters (183, 325); that identification has been vigorously denied by Marion Mainwaring
in the *Times Literary Supplement*, 16–22 December 1988, 1394, 1405.

to Paris in the late spring, when he was with both of them. But that autumn she unburdened herself to him, confessing that she and Fullerton had become lovers and that her marriage with Teddy had grown increasingly disastrous. James naturally extended his full sympathy. Much must have passed between him and Wharton during her visit to England in the closing weeks of the year.

James was rather closely involved in the Wharton-Fullerton affair during 1909, more closely than his own Lambert Strether in the affair of Marie de Vionnet and Chad Newsome, though with similar sympathy. In June he dined with them at the Charing Cross Hotel, where the two lovers then spent a rapturous night together. Wharton commemorated that night in her poem "Terminus" ("Wonderful was the long secret night you gave me, my Lover, / Palm to palm, breast to breast in the gloom"), which recaptures something of the atmosphere they created at the railway hotel just a few yards east of Trafalgar Square:

> *The bed with its soot-sodden chintz, the grime of its brasses,*
> *That has born the weight of fagged bodies, ...*
> *   ... perchance it has also thrilled*
> *With the pressure of bodies ecstatic, bodies like ours,*
> *Seeking each other's souls in the depths of unfathomed caresses,*
> *And through the long windings of passion emerging again to*
> *   the stars. ...*[14]

The setting must have struck James as offering meet compensation for his missed journey to Herblay and perhaps something better than the visit to Nohant: he must virtually "have *smelt* them," as he wrote Wharton of her first visit to Sand's house (2 July 1906).

Then, after Fullerton's brief absence in the United States, the three were reunited in England. Wharton and James hatched a plan to rid Fullerton of apparent blackmailing by one of his former mistresses (see letters of 26 July and 3 August 1909).[15] James was constantly a sympa-

14. Quoted in *EW Biog.*, 259–60.
15. Marion Mainwaring has informed me that "Fullerton was not privy to the plan to pay off" the woman in question. Ms. Mainwaring adds that the woman "did demand money from him: only it isn't clear that he didn't owe her the money" (letter to me, 9 May 1989).

thetic and supportive confidant of Wharton's during the frenetic months of her affair; there weren't many, for the passion of Fullerton in such matters burned suavely hot but briefly. This liaison had run its course by the summer of 1910, and James's support accordingly shifted to focus on her marital dilemma. He continued to stand by Edith Wharton staunchly and steadfastly, offering advice and encouragement, now as another kind of Cher Maître—devoted, benevolent, almost avuncular.

Yet he was always interested in Wharton's affairs of the heart, actual or potential; and even as the Fullerton fling was achieving the acme of its excitement, she met a brace of younger men at the Elchos' Stanway, John Hugh Smith and Robert Norton. They became instant admirers of the new Edith flushed in the new femininity awakened by her affair with Fullerton. Hugh Smith at twenty-seven (Norton was forty-two) was the more aggressive, at least initially, and was with her (and James) at Sturgis's Qu'Acre in the final weeks of 1908. When James got back to Rye, he wrote immediately to Wharton for news of the warm-blooded youth: "I want to miss nothing, & am only troubled lest you shouldn't be able to tell me about John Hugh before my nephew" (16 December 1908); James was anticipating the visit of Wharton and Sturgis to Lamb House on the weekend before Christmas, and his nephew Billy James was at the moment his house-guest. On the following day James explained: "I'm of course intensely wondering if John Hugh a pu—ou a voulu s'oublier [was able—or wanted to forget himself], thinking you—so naturally—de choix [of prime choice]. You must tell me all!"

James and Sturgis were evidently amused at the young man's attentions to Wharton at Qu'Acre, and James in particular ready to twit him gently about his ardor. Hugh Smith complained that they cramped his style: "The simplicity I sought was not helped by Howard Sturgis's and Mr. James's amused though perfectly kind remarks," he wrote her; but he looked forward to smoother and unhampered progress. "In Paris," he continued, "we shall be able to go ahead and eliminate this Jacobean element in our relation" (*EW Letters*, 172).

The association with Wharton's dalliance with John Hugh Smith and later, if less obviously, with the calmer and more discreet Robert Norton clearly gave James a good deal of stimulation and gratification; it "completed" the special relationship he enjoyed with Edith Wharton. That relationship—the marriage of true minds, sympathetic companionship, frank and intimate confidence and trust—was rounded out by the safely controlled but invigorating element of the erotic. The letters collected here afford evidence of those facets of the friendship of James and Wharton.

She was grateful for his interest and encouragement during the difficult moments of her life, and she sought means to offer what return beneficence she could. Her visits to Lamb House had convinced her that James's financial status was precarious.

> At Lamb House an anxious frugality was combined with the wish that the usually solitary guest ... should not suffer too greatly from the contrast between his or her supposed habits of luxury, and the privations imposed by the host's conviction that he was on the brink of ruin. If any one in pecuniary difficulty appealed to James for help, he gave it without counting; but in his daily life he was haunted by the spectre of impoverishment, and the dreary pudding or pie of which a quarter or half had been consumed at dinner appeared on the table the next day with its ravages unrepaired. (*Backward Glance*, 243–44)

James had always been elaborately apologetic for the modest accommodations and niggardly niceties his domicile could afford and had otherwise given the impression of near indigence: on receipt of a handsome fitted suitcase lined with morocco leather from Walter Berry, James explained that he could not accept the gift because he could not live up to it, and on another occasion, accompanying Wharton to Lamb House while his houseboy Burgess Noakes was trundling her luggage up the cobblestones of West Street in a barrow, he remarked to the successful novelist that he had bought the barrow with the earnings of his last book and hoped that the earnings on his next book would enable him to have the barrow painted.

It is evident that this concern over James's financial straits was a basic motive for Wharton's attempt to secure the Nobel Prize for literature in 1911 for the Master whose works she did not particularly admire. That plan failed, but her next effort at benevolence succeeded. The following year she persuaded Charles Scribner to offer James an advance of $8,000 for "an important American novel," $4,000 on his beginning work on it and $4,000 on its completion. The money was to be diverted from Wharton's royalties from Scribner. James was understandably delighted with the offer, quite the largest advance he had ever received, and turned his thoughts to the uncompleted *Ivory Tower*. He never finished the novel, however, and never learned the true source of the advance.

Wharton saw another opportunity to provide pecuniary assistance as James's seventieth birthday approached. In March 1913 she began soliciting contributions from likely American contributors to provide a cash present of "not less than $5000." James's nephews Harry and Billy got wind of the plan and informed him; he called a stop to it. In a rather cranky letter to his sister-in-law he explained that what he couldn't accept in the plan was "the crude raked-together *offrand*[e] of a lump of money." He knew of and had agreed to the plan in England to solicit small contributions to buy a modest gift. The cash plan made him gag, but there was yet a problem of hurt feelings: he feared that he had "incurred the grave reprobation and almost resentment" of Edith Wharton:

> ... she purposely kept out of the "movement" here, in order to associate herself with the American one; ... so, though really one of the best friends I have in the world, she fails to figure in either. (*Letters* 4, 660–61)

Wharton's disappointment was short-lived, and James included her name and Walter Berry's in his public letter of gratitude for the English gift, 21 April 1913.

That was not the first test of their friendship, not would it be the last. The outbreak of the Great War caught them both and shook them, but it marvelously drew them together in their shared hurt for the rape of Belgium, the suffering of France, and the associated drain on England. They were united in their commitment to whatever war work they could manage, and again as artists in their cooperative efforts for *The Book of the Homeless*. James was, understandably, constantly chagrined by the failure of his native land to rally to the aid of his adopted home and Edith Wharton's. In midyear 1915 he decided to renounce his American citizenship and become a British subject. That action was really the culmination of a decade of growing disappointment over developments —cultural and other—in America. He had long been critical of American ways, of American material pursuits, of American manners—or lack of them. Yet he had also steadily kept faith in the American potential. The sure signs of disappointment appear, however, in his report on America revisited, *The American Scene*; reaffirmation of that feeling is given in the stories of his last collection of tales, *The Finer Grain* (1910), and in the obvious intention of *The Ivory Tower*. A passage in one of those tales, "Crapy Cornelia," distills the essence of James's regret:

> ... if people were but rich enough and furnished enough and fed enough, exercised and sanitated and manicured, and generally advised and advertised and made "knowing" enough, *avertis* enough, as the term appears to be nowadays in Paris, all they had to do for civility was to take the amused ironic view of those who might be less initiated. In *his* [White-Mason's] time, ... the best manners had been the best kindness, and the best kindness had mostly been some art of not insisting on one's luxurious differences, of concealing rather, for common humanity, if not for common decency, a part at least of the intensity of the ferocity with which one might be "in the know."[16]

Family and many friends, including Edith Wharton, were not in sympathy with James in his decision to adopt British citizenship. His letter of justification to his nephew Harry is enlivened with the deep fervor of almost religious conviction, religious *protest*:

> ... like Martin Luther at Wittenberg "I could no other," and the relief of feeling [I have] corrected an essential falsity in my position (as determined by the War and what has happened since, also more particularly what has *not* happened) is greater than I can say. I have testified to my long attachment here in the only way I could—though I certainly shouldn't have done it, under the inspiration of our Cause, if the U.S.A. had done it a little more *for* me. Then I should have thrown myself back on that and been content with it; but as this, at the end of a year, hasn't taken place, I have had to act for myself.... (*Letters* 4, 771)

He wrote to Wharton on the very day of his becoming British, 26 July 1915, yet breathed not a syllable to her of the transaction. The news

16. *The Complete Tales of Henry James*, ed. Edel (Philadelphia and New York: Lippincott, 1964), vol. 12, 348.

was evidently a shock to her when it arrived, but she was able to overcome it and before long even to sympathize with his decision. On 17 April 1916, less than two months after his death, she wrote to Barrett Wendell about his article on James for the *Boston Evening Transcript* (1 March 1916) to confess that she did not share James's view "when he took his decision, but on which the subsequent course of things at home has shed a corroborative glare.... his change of citizenship was the result of a sensitive conscience bred in the old ideals, & outraged by the divergence between act & utterance which has come to be a matter of course for the new American."[17]

Edith Wharton's willingness to do what could be done to ease James's final days, her enlisting Theodora Bosanquet again to file frequent reports on the status of his health, and her holding herself ready to rush to England if she could be of use during his final weeks of life, all that attests amply to her unflagging concern for her "Dearest Cher Maître." The continued reciprocity is laconically indicated in the salutations James chose for his final letters to his Firebird—"Dear and unsurpassably distinguished old Friend" and the simple "Dear old Friend" of the last that survives.

She wrote Gaillard Lapsley in December 1915, a couple of months before the end:

Yes—all my "blue distances" will be shut out forever when he goes. His friendship has been the pride & honour of my life. Plus ne m'est rien after such a gift as that—except the memory of it. (*EW Letters*, 365)

Perhaps her word to Theodora Bosanquet (1 March 1916), two days after James's death, sums it all up: "We who knew him well know how great he would have been if he had never written a line" (*EW Letters*, 370).

While these letters are of interest to the dedicated scholar, to the responsible critic, and to the inquisitive student for what they reveal about

17. *EW Letters*, 373. The rehearsal of her understanding of James's decision, in *A Backward Glance*, affords this amplification: "... after the 'Lusitania,' and the American government's supine attitude at that time, James felt the need to make manifest by some visible, symbolic act, his indignant sympathy with England." To that she added, "I refrained from writing to him; I regret it now ..." (367).

the two correspondents and their circle, they have much to offer the simply curious "gentle reader" as well. Edith Wharton attributed the *intimacy* of her friendship with James to their shared "sense of humour or irony." That sense lends a particular sparkle to many of the letters in this collection, especially those of James. Wharton's letters tend (the few we have) to be more direct and businesslike: their purpose is mainly to offer or seek information. And the cluster of her letters during the last year of James's life—the first full year of the Great War—are too conscious of the impending Damoclean stroke to find space and courage for humor. Her accounts of her forays to the Western Front in the spring of 1915 are, however, absolutely spellbinding and were so for James. Yet one of the earlier letters (3 September 1912) gives some sense of what has been lost to us of her part of the correspondence. She wonders what James has been doing "since my vigilant eye has been off you," and tells him that her visit to a château in the Massif du Cantal has given her "the most interesting glimpse of French 'Shatter Life,'" reproducing thus the lingo of certain denizens of Apex City or of the cousins of Daisy Miller for "Château Life." She also regales him with an account of the doings of "the Minnie Pauls," as the correspondents called M. and Mme Bourget, especially his offer to introduce her to the man "who washes our intestines and who is also gardener to the here-siarch bishop who lives opposite the hotel"; James would doubtless have relished that bizarre example of Bourget's brand of Gallic ribaldry.

The humor illustrated in the correspondence depends, as those samples indicate, fairly heavily on verbal wit—but not to the exclusion of their own delight in the ribald. The shared logophilia is responsible for the consciously orotund expression of some of James's rhetorical fandangos. His letter of 29 October 1909 opens:

> Your letters come into my damp desert here even as the odour of promiscuous spices or the flavour of lucent syrups tinct with cinnamon might be wafted to some compromised oasis from a caravan of the Arabian nights. Put instead of these the Parisian days, & you get the torment of my nostril.

That kind of ornate burlesque sometimes baffled even Edith Wharton, as surely James's elaborate apologies for the meager comforts of Lamb

House (which she accepted as signs of his imminent indigence) were of the very ilk of "promiscuous spices" and "lucent syrups" of the passage just quoted. And his shrieks of tormented apprehension at the threatened pounce of Edith the Angel of Devastation might similarly have been mistaken (although Howard Sturgis apparently received them with unruffled amusement).[18]

James also loved to string out a joke, stretch a network of allusion, develop a pun to the extent that the strain could be born—and sometimes beyond. He begins his letter of 6 September 1913 with the hope that Wharton is back from her travels and into her apartment in the Faubourg Saint-Germain, "restored to your Parisian pénates." Allusion to the Latin *lares et penates* (household gods), followed in the next sentence by reference to her returning "with no worlds left to conquer," sets up a string of classical allusions that runs throughout the letter. The second sentence continues, mildly, "You must have recoiled & rebounded, charged with booty, upon us mere comparative Latins again." He turns to other matters, her currently serialized novel *The Custom of the Country* and the visit of his niece, Peggy. Then, much later, he refers again to Wharton's world-ranging and booty-gathering as though she were a female Alexander the Great of Macedon come home finally with no new worlds to conquer, but he embroiders that reference by associating it with George Alexander, the actor-manager who had played the lead in James's theatrical disaster *Guy Domville*:

> One of the drawbacks of the recoils of Alexandrina from the pushing of her frontiers must be the sight of what we call here the hall-table, collapsing with the burden of its postal matter; & as one needn't in fact be an Alexander (even a George), to live up to one's neck in arrears, so I

18. Another possible cause for misunderstanding James's letters that has nothing to do with wit and humor is the occasional steady focus on and detailed account of his health, his attacks and discomforts, progress and relapses. He was not simply indulging himself in egoistic preoccupations: he hated being indisposed because it prevented him from working. Percy Lubbock, who was a familiar friend of both James and Wharton, has this to say: "He could never ... feel that he had reached a time when his work was finished and behind him. . . . He bitterly resented the hindrances of ill health, during some of his last years, as an interruption, a curtailment of the span of activity; there were so many and so far better books that he still wished to write" ("Introduction," *Letters of Henry James* 1, xxx–xxxi).

could weep for you & shall be full of indulgence for my hint that I must wait.

A final flicker of the trail of classical allusion ends the letter as James mentions hearing from the recuperating Howard Sturgis, who has praised the ministrations of his companion ("delirious homage to the divine William") and of the attendant nurse: "she too all but divine. It's a regular Olympus."

Occasionally James sustains such frolics beyond the limits of a single letter. In that of 13 March 1912 (quoted above) he had written to Wharton about George Sand and her friends and how "they pigged so thrillingly together." He didn't leave it at that, for two sentences later he refers to an abbreviated Frédéric Chopin and his involvement in the "pigging": "Poor gentlemanly, crucified Chop!—not naturally at home in grease. . . ." Two months later (12 May 1912) James resumes the play of piggery to extend (but not to butcher) it:

> . . . your Perigord post-picture of dear old George [Sand] nosing for the human truffle—& infallibly finding it (when il n'y en avait plus [there wasn't any more] being exactly when il y en avait encore [there still was more] in the very next jiffy!); these things, & other wandering airs, have kept the cord [*sic*] just vibrating even when not conveniently to be thumbed.

The letter moves on to other considerations but finally arrives, many sentences later, at the subject of a new play by Bourget. The echoes reverberate:

> If you want to make the chord vibrate to a mere 2 frs. 75 worth of "thumb," will you send me (excuse my voracity) the vol. (*not* the Illustration one), of Bourget's play . . . ? I like to hear of him as I do of any other bull-fight or truffle-hunt; there appearing to en être encore [be yet more] of *him* too, always, even when il n'y en a plus [there isn't any more]. Il y en aura toujours [there will always be some]—such as it is!

He not only picks up the piggery theme (reasserted in the porcine "Chop") in the truffle-sniffing of the later letter but readjusts "Chop" in the musical echo of "airs"—itself an olfactory as well as an aural signifier; he also puns within the later one on the inconsistently spelled "cord" and "chord," in a distant tribute, perhaps, to Chopin.

The easy lapsing into French is another characteristic of this correspondence. Both were fluent in French, Wharton's home for much of the period was France, and James was her guest in Paris and its environs. Yet the amount of French here is extraordinary and much of it richly colloquial. Sometimes it serves as a veil of modesty to cloak immodest behavior and avoid the comparatively bald and frank idiom of their native tongue; yet the result of such modest gestures—themselves in part burlesque—is to underscore the naughty. The double entendre of the clauses just quoted exemplify that facet. There is a good example of a brave mixture of moral outrage (with a touch of burlesqued Victorian prudery) at the failure of taste in a poem by Maurice Rostand in which he praises his mother:

> ... his *naturelle & sublime blessure* [wound] is wonderfully wide open—so that we look all the way down his throat. Quelle engeance [What a breed]!—including Sa mère aux beaux cheveux [His mother with the lovely hair]. Why not sa mère aux beaux seins or aux belles hanches [his mother with the lovely breasts or the handsome hips] at once? (16 March 1912)

There is a sprinkling of German and Italian and the occasional fillip of Latin, but French predominates. And it is often anglicized French, not simply of the "Shatter Life" sort or the "figgery-voo" (*figurez-vous*: just imagine), but a fusing of the two languages. Wharton's salutation "Cherest Maître," adding the English superlative ending to the French *Cher* (Dear), is one example. Another is James's playing unflatteringly on the name of Jacques-Émile Blanche, "with whom I lunched three days ago on a copious dish of little *blanchailles*"; the derogatory suffix "*-ailles*" turns the significance of the term into something like "platitudinous" or "blanchitudes"—*blanchailles* are also what we call "small fry." And sometimes we come upon untranslatable puns in French, as when James promises (15 July 1912) to await Wharton's arrival "de pied ferme—& de coeur ouvert," i.e., with a firm foot and an open heart; but *ferme* also suggests "closed" and thus contrasts with (and so emphasizes) *ouvert*, "open." Pointless, perhaps, but fun for the logophiliac.

James's letters are thus very often *performances* rather than just vehicles to convey or request information. Their purpose is not always to create witty amusement, to be sure; and one of the most memorable is that of 21 September 1914, which records his shock at news of the bombing of Rheims Cathedral: "the most unspeakable & immeasurable terror & infamy—& what is appalling & heartbreaking is that it's *forever & ever!*" The opening two-thirds of the letter was translated into French by a friend of Wharton's and read to the French Academy three weeks later.

The letters are, taken altogether, as complex and various as the characters of the authors. It is rather stunning to recall that James did most of his letter-writing late at night, after the day's work was done and the other social obligations satisfied; and they were obviously written very rapidly. One can only wish that there were more.

The correspondence between James and Wharton must have originally amounted to some four-hundred items—letters, telegrams, postcards— beginning at least with her message of goodwill to him as playwright in 1895. A much smaller number survive. In November 1909, in the gloom of complex depression, James made a grand bonfire of his personal papers, including most of Wharton's letters to him, down at Lamb House. And on his last brief return to his home in Rye, October 1915, he repeated the act of burning his personal papers. Fortunately Edith Wharton was not so incendiary-minded. Nevertheless, she may well have destroyed a number of James's letters to her which she felt contained matter too private to risk keeping. This collection includes all of the surviving items (as far as I have been able to discover) of that correspondence.

The letters are arranged here chronologically, James's and Wharton's together, and the collection is divided into seven sections, each with a brief headnote providing immediately relevant biographical and other information.

Material closely related to the correspondence of James and Wharton is to be found in the appendixes. Appendix A contains four postcards to James from Wharton and Walter Berry on an Italian trip together; appendix B has the correspondence between Wharton and Theodora

Bosanquet on James's health—mainly during the last weeks of his life; appendix C has two documents Wharton enclosed in letters to James.

The first important collection of James's letters was the two-volume edition by Percy Lubbock published by Scribners in 1920. It contained 27 letters to Wharton. Those letters, however, were based on typescripts provided by Wharton herself. Furthermore, the whole of the Lubbock manuscript "was carefully gone over by Harry, by Mrs. James, by Peggy, and by Harry's younger brother, Billy. The family scrutiny was thorough."[19] Those letters to Wharton are obviously incomplete, and the deletions may be due to her, to the James family, or to Lubbock. Leon Edel published complete texts of 16 of those 27 letters: one in *The Selected Letters of Henry James* (New York: Farrar, Straus & Cudahy, 1955), and 15 in the fourth volume of his *Henry James Letters* (1984), which also included another 20 letters to Wharton. Five of those 35 letters are reprinted in his *Henry James: Selected Letters* (Cambridge, Mass.: Harvard University Press, 1987). The present collection includes the remaining 131 letters of James to Wharton as well.

There remain 8 letters and 5 postcards from Wharton to James (4 of those cards are cosigned by Walter Berry); of those, 5 letters and 1 of the cards signed by both Wharton and Berry are published in *The Letters of Edith Wharton*, edited by R. W. B. Lewis and Nancy Lewis. All 13 of those items are published in the present collection.

Of the correspondence between Edith Wharton and James's last amanuensis, Theodora Bosanquet, 36 letters survive. Appendix B has 14 letters from Bosanquet to Wharton, and 16 of the 22 from Wharton to Bosanquet. *The Letters of Edith Wharton* includes 2 of Wharton's to Bosanquet.

There are in this collection, then, 167 items from James to Wharton: 163 letters (some typed by Bosanquet at his dictation), 1 fragment of a letter, 1 telegram, and 2 postcards; the earliest of these is dated 26 October 1900, the latest 22 September 1915. There are also the specified 13 items from Wharton to James, the earliest dated 10 October 1908, the latest 10 August 1915.

19. Leon Edel, "Introduction," *Letters* 4, xxi.

The letters of James to Wharton, of Wharton to James, and of Bosanquet to Wharton are in the Beinecke Library of Yale University. The letters of Wharton to Bosanquet are in the Houghton Library of Harvard University. One exception is a letter from James to Wharton, now at Indiana University. I have based my text for all of the 210 items in this collection on the original holographs and typescripts.[20] My aim has been twofold: to provide an easily readable text and to retain something of those characteristics of the manuscripts that are responsible for the peculiarly Jamesian and Whartonian "flavor."

James frequently, though not always, used the ampersand for "and" and the ampersand with "c." for "etc." except at the beginning of a sentence. In his dictated letters, of course, the ampersand does not appear. Wharton similarly used the ampersand. I have retained that usage here. He frequently used the abbreviations "wd." and "shd." for "would" and "should" and occasionally numerals instead of words—e.g., 7 for "seven." I have followed the manuscript in this practice as well, but I have not retained James's traditional spacing with a. and m. ("a. m."), i. and e., e. and g., etc. Interlinear insertions, additions in pen to typed letters, and other editorial alterations that seem of some possible significance I have identified in notes. James underlined for emphasis with one or two lines; I have indicated that feature here by using italics for one underlining, small capitals for double underlining. Of his practice with foreign words and phrases I can only say that it was inconsistent: sometimes he underlined them and sometimes not, and I have been unable to find any guiding principle there. I have not attempted to reproduce some of the manuscript features that indicate the *pace* of James's epistolary script—reversed commas (commas that curve to the left), the impatient dash of widely varying length, the trailing stroke of the unlifted pen connecting two words or extending the crossing of a *t* into a parenthesis, and so on; but on occasion I have commented in a note on such features as have bearing on the *expression* of a

20. The Beinecke Library provided me with the 167 items of James and the 8 letters and 1 postcard of Wharton plus the 4 postcards cosigned with Berry. Leon Edel specifies 177 items from James to Wharton at the Beinecke (*Letters* 4, 817); the Lewises specify "162 letters to E.W." from James in the Beinecke and "12 letters from E.W. to James" at the Beinecke; in neither case is mentioned the letter from James to Wharton (24 July 1913), which Mary Pitlick provided from Indiana University.

passage. I have silently adjusted punctuation to conform with American practice, but not the spelling, although I have corrected a few errors. And I have left untouched the titles of books, tales, and essays as they appear in the letters, except when necessary to avoid misunderstanding.

I have provided translations of most of the foreign words and phrases found here, except the most familiar. The key words and the translations appear in a paragraph following the notes for each letter. I have identified some of the literary allusions and even some quotations that dot the text of these letters.

Otherwise, the footnotes that follow the text of each letter do their usual job with as strict economy as possible, and they frequently refer the reader to other closely related letters for clarification, amplification, etc. In the notes I regularly abbreviate "Henry James" as "HJ," "Edith Wharton" as "EW," and "William James" as "WJ." I have added to those letters in appendix B that are dated in December 1915 and early 1916—the moment of James's precipitous decline and death—identification of the day of the week on which a given letter was written, to give a sharper sense of the quotidian pace of the concerns of Wharton and Bosanquet.

Rye, Honolulu, Ann Arbor, 1985–1989

1

Beginnings

LONDON AND LENOX, 1900–1907

JAMES'S RETURN to the United States in August 1904 for a year-long lecture tour marked a distinct advance in his relationship with Edith Wharton that had begun with their first actual meeting in December of 1903: it made possible the blossoming of a friendship that would endure to the end of his life. He visited the Whartons both at The Mount, their home in the Berkshires since 1902, and at their house on New York's Park Avenue.

The bond of friendship was strengthened by James's keen approval of Wharton's novel *The House of Mirth* (1905) and also by shared interests —friendship with Paul and Minnie Bourget and numerous others in England and France and a delight in the life and works (in that order of fascination!) of George Sand and, a bit later, of Hortense Allart de Méritens. The bond was further strengthened by the Whartons' definite commitment in 1906 to a European residence: they rented George Vanderbilt's apartment at 58, rue de Varenne, the heart of the Faubourg Saint-Germain in Paris.

James continued to be deeply engrossed in preparing his fiction for the New York Edition and in gathering his impressions of the United States revisited for *The American Scene*. In the spring of 1907, however, he made time for a vacation on the continent: a three-week motor tour of France with the Whartons that included a delicious pause at George Sand's last home, his own final visit to Italy, and a reunion with the Whartons in Paris. A consequent deepening of James's friendship with

Wharton is indicated by a new feature of his letters to her—the salutation "Dear Edith," first used in August.

Edith Wharton made the fateful acquaintance of James's friend William Morton Fullerton that fall; he visited briefly at The Mount in October. She thus began the most intense relationship of her life. Three
days after his departure she began a private journal, *A Life Apart*, addressed specifically to Fullerton. The year ended with the Whartons
resuming the apartment in Paris and with James taking up again the
theatrical pen he had laid aside a dozen years earlier.

Lamb House, Rye
26 October 1900

Dear Mrs. Wharton.

I brave your interdiction & thank you both for your letter & for the
brilliant little tale in the Philadelphia resrepository.[1] The latter has an
admirable sharpness & neatness & infinite wit & point—it only suffers
a little, I think, from one's not having a *direct* glimpse of the husband's
provoking causes—literally provoking ones. However, you may very
well say that there are two sides to that; that one can't do everything
in 6000 words, one must narrowly choose (& à *qui* le dites-vous?) &
that the complete non-vision of Millicent and her gentleman was a less
evil than the frustrated squint to which you would have been at best
reduced. Either *do* them or don't (directly) touch them—such was
doubtless your instinct. The subject is really a big one for the canvas—
that was really your difficulty. But the thing is *done*. And I applaud, I
mean I value, I egg you on in, your study of the American life that
surrounds you. Let yourself go in it & *at* it—it's an untouched field,
really: the folk who try, over there, don't come within miles of any
civilized, however superficially, any "evolved" life. And use to the full
your ironic and satiric gifts; they form a most valuable (I hold) & beneficent engine. *Only*, the *Lippincott* tale is a little *hard*, a little purely
derisive. But that's because you're so young, &, with it, so clever. Youth
is hard—& your needle-point, later on, will muffle itself in a little blur

of silk. It *is* a needle-point! Do send me what you write,* when you can kindly find time, & do, some day, better still, come to see yours, dear Mrs. Wharton, most truly,

Henry James

* Oh, I'll do the same by you!

1. "The Line of Least Resistance," *Lippincott's Magazine*, October 1900.

à qui le dites-vous?: to whom do you say it? (i.e., you're telling me)

Lamb House, Rye
17 August 1902

Dear Mrs. Wharton.

I have just asked the Scribners to send you a rather long-winded (but I hope not hopelessly heavy) novel of mine that they are to issue by the end of this month (a thing called *The Wings of the Dove*),[1] and I find myself wishing much not to address myself to you to that without doing so still more. This has been made especially the case, I assure you, by my lately having read *The Valley of Decision*,[2] read it with such high appreciation & received so deep an impression from it that I can scarce tell you why, all these weeks, I have waited for any other pretext to write. I think in truth I have simply because, really, your book gives one too much to say, & the number of reflections it made me make as I read, the number of remarks that, in the tone of the highest sympathy, highest criticism, highest consideration & generally most intimate participation, I articulated, from page to page, for your absent ear, have so accumulated on my consciousness as to render me positively helpless. I can't discharge the load by this clumsy mechanism. The only possible relief would be the pleasure of a talk with you, & that luxury, thanks to the general perversity of things, seems distant & dim. I greatly regret it—I seem to have the vision of our threshing out together, if chance only favoured, much golden grain. But I gather indeed from your admirable sister-in-law and niece,[3] who have been so good as to come &

pay me a little visit, that chance *may* favour your coming hitherward—within these next few months. I shall pray for some confirmation of this—i.e. for your being able to be for a little in England. Even, however, were I prepared to chatter to you about *The Valley*, I think I should sacrifice that exuberance to the timely thought that the first duty to a serious & achieved work of art is the duty of recognition *telle quelle*; & that the rest can always wait. In the presence of a book so accomplished, pondered, saturated, so exquisitely studied & so brilliant & interesting from a literary point of view, I feel that just now heartily to congratulate you covers plenty of ground. There is a thing or two I should like to say—some other time. You see what reasons I have for wishing God-speed to that talk. *The* particular thing is somehow mistimed while the air still flushes with the pink fire of the Valley; all the more that I can't do it any sort of justice save by expatiation. So, as, after all, to mention it in 2 words does it no sort of justice, let it suffer the wrong of being crudely hinted as my desire earnestly, tenderly, intelligently to admonish you, while you are young, free, expert, exposed (to illumination)—by which I mean while you're in full command of the situation—admonish you, I say, in favour of the *American Subject*. There it is round you. Don't pass it by—the immediate, the real, the ours, the yours, the novelist's that it waits for. Take hold of it & keep hold, & let it pull you where it will. It will pull harder than things of more *tarabiscotage*, which is a merit in itself. What I would say in a word is: Profit, be warned, by my awful example of exile & ignorance. You will say that *j'en parle à mon aise*—but I shall have paid for my ease, & I don't want you to pay (as much) for yours. But these are impertinent importunities—from the moment they are not developed. All the same DO NEW YORK! The 1st-hand account is precious. I could give you one, by the way, of Mrs. Cadwalader & Miss Beatrix, very fresh & accented, if it were not past midnight. We renewed & augmented our friendship & I rejoiced to see your sister-in-law always so brave & beneficent. She made me fairly feel that I *need* her here. There you have the penalty of the dispatriated. And the Bourgets[4] are paying again one of their inexplicable little visits to England—spending three or four weeks at Bournemouth. Non comprenny!—I who know Bournemouth.[5] But it gives me the chance to hope for them for a day or two here, as I should be so glad some day to hope for you. Believe me, with kind regards to your husband, yours, dear Mrs. Wharton, most cordially

Henry James

1. In 2 vols., New York: Scribners, 1902; and in 1 vol., London: Constable, 1902.
2. In 2 vols., New York: Scribners, 1902.
3. Mary Cadwalader (Rawle) Jones (1850–1935), briefly married to EW's older brother Frederick Rhinelander Jones (1846–1918); her daughter Beatrix (1872–1959) was a famous landscape gardener, and later married Max Farrand.
4. Paul (1852–1935) and Minnie (David) Bourget, friends of HJ and EW; Bourget, French novelist and dramatist, declared himself a disciple of HJ and, to HJ's discomfiture, dedicated his novel *Cruelle Énigme* (1885), to the Master.
5. "Non comprenny" is HJ's jocular anglicization of the French for "don't understand." He had often visited Bournemouth.

telle quelle: as it is, as such; *tarabiscotage:* overadornment; *j'en parle à mon aise:* I speak of it at my ease (i.e., it's all very well for *me* to talk)

Lamb House, Rye
17 August 1904

Dear Mrs. Wharton.

I feel that I shall not be able to face you, later on, in New York, unless I have with however great imperfection, made up now for my not having thanked you, more than a month ago, for the quaint & charming photographs (of this poor garden & its two poor animals) that came to me from your infallible hand[1]—together with sundry good & charming words of temporary separation after I last, & too meagerly wrote you. And then also, after that, I read the three or four *other* tales of the D of M,[2] & they confirmed me so in my strong sense of your wise & witty art & your real practice of the Mystery, that to this hour I can't tell you why a fond postscript that was always on the point of being scribbled never absolutely got itself despatched. The reason can only have been that this radiant summer (of extraordinary beauty here after you left & all these last weeks) has been at the same time a period of singular, of the acutest pressure for me in view of my finding myself ready for doing what I am now on the edge of—I embark for N. Y. from Southampton a week from today (24th), & I go up to town to-morrow afternoon & dine that evening with whom but Paul & Minnie [Bourget]?—last seen of me a fortnight ago, or almost, at 2 Folkestone Hotels (in the 24 hours I went over from here to spend near them). They are here, on vague foundations & with obscure ideals—which I think are giving way to the need to return to Paris, her mother being very ill with a "stroke." But I will tell you more of them in the hereafter. Meanwhile read *Un Divorce*,[3] the best thing P. has done for a long time, even with all its strange cart-before-the-horse-ness. Of that also we will discourse. It is delightful to be able to say these things unberufen! I go straight on arrival to spend September with my brother William at *Chocorua N. H.*, where any word will find me & I am with kindest remembrance to Mr. Edward yours very constantly

Henry James

1. The photographs were evidently taken during the brief visit of EW and Teddy to Rye in May 1904. The meager letter HJ mentions has not survived.

2. *The Descent of Man* (New York: Scribners, 1904; London: Macmillan, 1904).

3. *Un Divorce*, Bourget's topical novel of 1904: see letter of 9 September 1904 for HJ's reiterated opinion. The novel was made into a popular play in 1908; see letter of 7 March 1908.

unberufen: unbidden

Chocorua, N.H.
Sunday [4 September 1904]

Dear Mrs. Wharton.

It is indeed delightful to be in this free & easy postal relation with you—I don't know that anything has yet (since last Tuesday)[1] so contributed to persuade me that this first phase of repatriation isn't a mere lurid dream. The 1st phase, however, is rapidly passing into the second—& I am hourly in less need of consolation, so that, already, I can begin to view the prospect of seeing you as a mere luxurious treat, a part of the finer essence of the whole strange experience. You will forgive the inconsistency with which I say that I will come to you next month, any time after the 5th or so, with very great pleasure. I foresee, promptly, that inconsistencies must be my refuge on this wondrous side of the globe & become indeed the law of my life. But there is none at least in saying that I shld. like of all things to be with you at the same time as dear Howard S.[2]—& even, since you give me such license—at the same time as no one else. Kindly mention your date at your convenience, & I am meanwhile making as few engagements as possible. I shall be *here* through this month—I don't wish to budge. The conditions are very pleasant & interesting to me—the Domestic Circle blooming, for the poor celibate exile, with the rich flowers of a new generation; & all the New England beauty of forest, mountain, lake & general Arcadian ease making its own appeal to the pulses of old—very old—association, of remembered youth—when everything that is now behind was before. I am finding again my old (young) eyes & imagination, & it is rather exquisite. But we will talk of these things & others, & I shall welcome the day. I had several occasions of Paul & Minnie [Bourget] in London, at the last, before I sailed, & they always offer plenty of text. They were full of admiration for your tale in the Aug. Scribner[3] which they communicated to me *dans le détail*, before I had read it—after which—since which—I have been admiring equally for myself. Another good matter to talk about. But I am summoned to luncheon, to which the Japanese Envoy has come! I find these innocent domestic woods bloodier even (with the Russo-Jap horror)[4] than the rever[ber]ating Strand I left. The world is too small. But let it squeeze us (Howard too!) nearer. I greet Wharton very heartily & am yours always

Henry James

1. The day of his docking in New York, i.e., 30 August.

2. Howard Overing Sturgis (1854–1920), youngest son of the American expatriate banker Russell Sturgis (1805–1887)—a senior partner in Baring Brothers—by his third marriage, was educated at Eton and Cambridge, and lived in the Sturgis villa Queen's Acre ("Qu'Acre") on the edge of Windsor Great Park; he was a good friend of HJ and EW.

3. "The Last Asset," reprinted in *The Hermit and the Wild Woman* (New York: Scribners, 1908).

4. The recent outbreak of the Russo-Japanese war.

dans le détail: in detail

Chocorua, N.H.

9 September 1904

Dear Mrs. Wharton.

My post-bag today is so appallingly formidable—it seems to go *crescendo*—that I ask pardon if I respond in fewest words to your so interesting new letter. *October 15th* is a beautiful date, & I shall joyously keep it dedicated to you; hoping that Howard may be able also to make the same brave use of it. He has transmitted me a very kind invitation from Mrs. Codman[1] to come & see them at Cotuit this month—which I should like to accept; but I fear & time isn't arrangeable, so that it will be an experience—Howard (the sight of him) on Cape Cod!—that I shall have to have foregone.

As for *Un Divorce*[2] & the strange perversities of our friend's genius & system, it is a subject so fraught with possible interest—nay rapture—on the whole, l'instinct de tirer parti (and the knowing in some good ways how) of his subject. The strange thing is that *any* dramatic interest survives it. But sometimes it doesn't, alas, at all! In this last it quite remarkably *does*, however; it is his best thing since long—in spite, too, of the so large mechanical element. But *me voilà parti*! La suite prochainement of discussion, that I hate to deflower it before we meet, absolutely interesting, luminous & felicitous as your own remarks are. Cela me menerais trop loin! Yes, it is a strange foredoomedness to put the cart of the conclusion before the horse of the presentation which is one of the oddest intellectual helplessnesses I have ever known—especially in a man who still has as *much* as B[ourget] has. I am very impatient & am yours, both, all in that spirit,

Henry James

1. Lucy Lyman Paine Sturgis, daughter of Russell Sturgis by his first marriage, was Howard Sturgis's oldest half sister. In 1856 she married American lawyer Charles Russell Codman (1829–1918) in England; they had a summer house at Cotuit on Cape Cod. See letter of 5 October 1904.

2. Bourget's novel; see letter of 17 August 1904.

l'instinct . . . parti: the instinct to take advantage; *me voilà . . . prochainement:* I'm off! The early continuation; *Cela . . . loin:* That would take me too far

Barack Matif Farm
Salisbury, Conn.
5 October 1904

Dear Mrs. Wharton.

Let me delay no longer to tell you that I shall on Saturday 15th make a point of taking the 10:45 from Boston (connecting at Pittsfield &c) for *Lee*, as you so make clear the matter to me. And I shall have a very modest quantity of luggage. I spent 3 charming days at Cotuit with Howard S[turgis] a fortnight ago & respected all his formed intentions & arrangements evidently based on definite family necessities. I am here I believe on the very fringe of your country (with my Emmet cousins —& their mother Elly Hunter,[1] who used to be Temple before she was Emmet & whom I believe you anciently, or rather, infantishly, knew). It is a ravishing land, & we see your blue hills,[2] & if I "owned," as they say, a motor I would come over & pay you an anticipatory call. But *bisogno aspettare*—which doesn't mean I'm not impatient. What weather (yesterday at the really exquisite Farmington, for instance!) & what invraisemblable beauty of country. But all greetings from yours always,

Henry James

P.S.   My address always c/o my Brother, Cambridge.

1. Ellen James Temple (1850–1920), younger sister of HJ's beloved cousin Minnie, married Christopher Temple Emmet (1822–1884) and then George

Hunter (1847–1914); her daughters were Rosina Hubley Emmet, Edith Leslie Emmet, and Ellen Gertrude (Bay) Emmet, who painted HJ's portrait in 1900.
  2. The Berkshires.

bisogno aspettare: one has to wait

95 Irving St., Cambridge
18 November 1904

Dear Mrs. Wharton.

  I have really had it on my conscience not to write to you till I should have a definite presentable *occasion*—but for this occasion, & the support & colour it would afford, I have all the while fondly yearned. Your so generous & interesting letter at last makes me feel that I may emulate G.W.S.,[1] at a distance, without compunction—& indeed with some relief. For I figure to myself that your morning's work will have been spreading its wings in a stiller air than while a poor brother-author was trying so inveterately to raise the wind in a neighbouring apartment. Otherwise I should even now look toward you with a mystic finger (which you would yet understand) on my lips.—I shall rejoice to make the acquaintance of Mr. Updyke [*sic*],[2] & to any sign I shall receive from him my response will be prompt. Only I shall not be on this spot *very* greatly longer. I am trying to make it possible to be in New York by the 6th or 7th of next month (though I *may* have to return here for a single week shortly afterwards). But I shall look meanwhile for the good Updyke, of whom your account is alluring. I feel as if I had succeeded in making my days here put on a respectable imitation of interest; but *il n'y a pas à dire.* Boston doesn't speak to me, never has, in irresistible accents, or affect me with the sweet touch of an affinity. My want of affinity with it in fact is so almost indecent that I have to resort to concealment & dissimulation. I ought, normally, to have more. But I have made two or three absences, & it was on a return from four days at Newport, night before last, that I found your letter. I found Newport quite exquisite, like a large softly-lighted pearl (& with the light partly that of faraway association); also the good Augustus Jay[3] offered me a spin round the whole island, which the remains of a bad sore throat forbade my taking in the more or less icy air—this a sad sorrow to me.

But he & his wife lunched with the Masons (Ella & Ida, with whom I was staying), and Mrs. Jay was very *brave* & ornamental. We lived over again, a little, together, he & I, our wondrous Lenox day, & that makes me wonder if you have ventured to *badiner* again with "Smalley" since that so memorable collapse of *his* gallantry. I figure you rather as *revenue* from those adventures—sated & appeased even as Misa[4] with what she "leaves." In case you have any gain of leisure, at any rate, I am venturing to send you an advance copy of *The Golden Bowl*,[5] which comes out tomorrow. The Scribners have made so pretty a pair of volumes of it that I am comparatively brazen about thrusting it on people—the type & paper are so pleasing! Sustained by this sense I would in fact send a copy to Berry[6] in Washington if I had his address. Would you very kindly inscribe the same on a simple card and post it to me? And let me know, not less kindly, at your leisure, about when you yourselves expect to migrate. If you are still as hospitably minded as you were during my blessed stay with you I should be delighted to profit by it for a week or two. I have seen almost nothing of Howard S[turgis]—he is too impenetrably at Wellesley. I greet Wharton very faithfully & am yours most constantly,

Henry James

1. George W. Smalley (1833–1916), American journalist, European correspondent of the *New York Tribune*.

2. Daniel Berkeley Updike (1860–1941), Massachusetts printer and founder in 1893 of the Merrymount Press, printed a number of EW's early books for Scribners.

3. Augustus Jay (1850–1919), American secretary of legation in Paris, 1885–1893.

4. EW's Pekingese.

5. HJ's last major novel, published that month by Scribners and early in 1905 by Methuen in London.

6. Walter Van Rensselaer Berry (1859–1927), an American born in Paris, graduated from Harvard and took a law degree from Columbia. He would be appointed to the International Tribunals in Egypt in 1909, and become president of the American Chamber of Commerce in Paris (1916–1923). He was for years an intimate friend of EW's.

il ... dire: there is nothing to say; *badiner:* trifle, joke; *revenue:* returned

95 Irving St., Cambridge
20 November 1904

Dear Mrs. Wharton.

Your letter is delightful & lifegiving, & I quite effusively thank you for it. Also I rejoice more than I can say in the restored prowess of our sweet Smalley, who must then have opened the door for you to further experience, the detail of which I beg you to keep stored up for my ear. Of all these things we will talk (D.V.) by the January fire. For this is most particularly to say, in response to your immense kindness in the whole matter, that you mustn't have me on your mind or on your hands even a little till January 2nd, or about, & that if the brave Berry is with you before that, so much the better, so far as I am concerned, as I may overlap (elsewhere) with his time in N. Y., in a manner that may enable me to see him. I have promised little visits to a couple of friends, & shall pay one in the latter $\frac{1}{2}$ December[1]—but I promise *you* very cordially the month of January—the charming idea! May all be right well with you meanwhile, & Smalley continue to feed your flame!—I am immensely touched, & even a little surprised, by Minnie Bourget's so quaint & evidently *senti* tribute, which I gratefully return. How delicately & pathetically she conceives & "says"—with her nerves, the obsession of Paul, vibrating through! Exquisite, truly, as you say, the image of the little atelier boy—& most veracious, besides, in respect to her service to Paul. It is all very beautiful & helpless, & I am glad of your communication of it. Only they don't *know* ce cher Jems.[2] But that doesn't matter, & he is yours, dear Mrs. Wharton, always, & more legibly.

Henry James

1. HJ arrived in New York (after a siege with the dentist in Boston) on 20 December, and after Christmas was a guest of Mary Cadwalader Jones.
2. HJ's Francophonic rendering of "James": this dear James.

senti: heartfelt, sincere

[95 Irving St.,] Cambridge
24 November 1904

Dear Mrs. Wharton.

Infinite & beautiful your bounty & ingenuity; but I think I had better stick to my Jan. 2d date—for many reasons, & notably because a certain number of small tributes to *relationship* seem to cluster round the threshold of my time in New York, which I can deal with better at first, & outside your radius, so as to be free of them afterwards. So, at any rate, it now appears to me; if I find I need seek more promptly the shelter of your roof perhaps you will kindly permit me to let you know *then*— taking my chance of your being able to receive me. In respect to dining with you on Xmas, let me say, too, that I shall of course not dream of doing anything else if I am by that time with you, but that if I am not there will not improbably be a particular pressure to which I shall have to respond. All thanks then—& please believe I shall offer myself betimes, with alacrity, if I am free. I am having an interminable & very formidable siege with the Dentist; of so far-reaching an order that it threatens to go on till the middle of Dec.![1] I have accepted a dinner ("offert") on Dec. 8th (in N.Y.) but must be back here to attend a party at Mrs. Gardner's Palazzo[2] a few days later, & *then* the metropolis, for which I am as impatient as I am afraid of it. Yours, dear Mrs. Wharton, always,

Henry James

1. HJ wrote Edward Warren, on Boxing Day, that the "siege" extended from 10 November to 20 December.

2. Isabella (Stewart) Gardner (1840–1924), Bostonian hostess and friend of HJ's since 1880; her Venetian *palazzo* (now the Gardner Museum) on the Fenway had just been furnished and the American art critic Bernard Berenson (1865–1959), among others, was helping her to fill it with European art.

1603 H St., Washington
16 January 1905

Dear Mrs. Wharton.

If I have delayed writing to you it is in order not to resemble too much certain friends of ours who *don't*, in similar situations, delay— who send back Parthian shots after leaving you, from the very next *étape*. But there have again & again, under the pressure of events, been words on my lips for which your ear has seemed the only proper receptacle—& which for want of that receptacle, I fear, have mostly faltered & failed & lost themselves forever. Let me make it distinct, at any rate, that things have been very convenient & pleasant for me, "straight along"—the reading of *une petite cochonnerie*, as Jusserand[1] says of his successive *oeuvres*, having constituted at the too amiable Philadelphia an almost brilliant scene—600 persons listening (& to *what*, juste ciel!) like one. I felt as if I had really me révélé conférencier (to myself at least); but too late, at last, & after having lived too long in the deep dark hole of silence. I repeat the thing, at any rate, on the 19th, at the earnest Bryn Mawr—quite like a mountebank "on tour." The only drawback is that the really touching friendliness & bonhomie of all those people, their positively fantastic obligeance (it is really very special & beautiful & boring) bury one under such a mountain of decent response that the *place*, the funny Philadelphia itself, taken as a subject to play with a little, melts away from one forever. And the same, a little, with this so oddly-ambiguous little Washington, which sits here saying, forever, to your private ear, from every door & window, as you pass, "I am nothing, I am nothing, nothing!" & whose charm, interest, amiability, *irresistibility*, you are yet perpetually making calls to commemorate & insist upon. One must hold up one's end of the plank, for heaven only knows where the other rests! But, withal, it's a very pleasant, soft, mild, spacious vacuum—peopled, immediately about me here, by Henry Adams, La Farge & St.-Gaudens[2]—& then, as to the middle distance, by Miss Tuckerman, Mrs. Lodge[3] & Mrs. Kuhn; with the dome of the Capitol, the Corcoran Art Gallery & the presence of "Theodore"— Theodore I[4]—as indispensable *fond*. I went to Court the other night, for the Diplomatic Reception, & he did me the honour to put me at his table & almost beside him—whereby I got a rich impression of him & of his being, verily, a wonderful little machine: destined to be overstrained, perhaps, but not as yet, truly, betraying the least creak. It functions astoundingly & is quite exciting to see. But it's really *like* something behind a great plate-glass window "on" Broadway. I lunch with the Lodges today, I dine with the Jusserands tomorrow—he really delightful & she much better, a little "marked," but perfectly adequate, & after Bryn Mawr I go to spend 3 or 4 Philadelphian days with my old friend Sarah Wister[5] at Butler Place. To remount vers le Nord chills me in thought—this relative mansuetude of the Washington air & prettiness of the Washington light, have affected me as such a balm. But I then come back to overtake or join (probably) the G[eorge] Vanderbilts,[6] & be personally conducted by them for 3 or 4 days at the formidable Biltmore. After that I possibly join Owen Wister[7] (queerly, though I think but imaginatively & superficially blighted in health—only physical—& with a young medical attendant) at Charleston—or at any rate work down to Florida & New Orleans. Such is the only witchcraft I am being used with—for the present; though I *may* have roamed, delirious & flower-crowned, as far as the farthest West before I see you again. I seem to see patria nostra *simplify* as I go—see that the *main* impressions only count, & that these can be numbered on the fingers; which is truly a blessed vision. I hope meanwhile that the snow isn't too high by your doorstep, nor the doubt (of the human scene) too heavy on your heart. How can you doubt of a scene capable of flowering at any moment into a Mrs. Toy?[8] By that sign you shall conquer. If you have seen Mrs. Chanler[9] again she will have told you perhaps of the pilgrimage I made with her in the rain to the Washington Cemetery—for a chance *de nous soulager*, critically, unheard que par les morts. She was for those 1st days a resource—emotionally—that I greatly miss. And I miss, intensely, Walter Berry—& fear I shall continue to do so, as I seem destined to retire, sated (with everything but *him*) about the moment he comes back. But I have had from him a charming note. I hope you have the same—that is, I mean, news of cheer & comfort from Wharton. And I am wondering further what you may perhaps be learning, de plus funeste encore, from Minnie-Paul.[10] But never dream of writing to tell me, I shall hear, in time—for all the use I can be in the matter. Don't, I mean, begin to croire devoir "answer" this sprawling scribble which has really no dimensions at all—no more length than breadth or thickness. Only fight your own battle (like Prometheus—) with the elements (of civilization). We shall see them in due course somehow softened by the springtime, & shall meet again under that benediction. Believe me yours very constantly

　　Henry James

　　1. Jules Jusserand (1855–1932), French ambassador to Washington (1902–1905), diplomat and literary historian.

　　2. Henry Adams (1838–1918), American historian, long a friend of HJ's; John La Farge (1835–1910), American painter and mentor and friend of HJ's from the Newport days of 1858; Augustus Saint-Gaudens (1848–1907), American sculptor who created the granite memorial for the grave of Clover, Mrs. Henry Adams (1843–1885), in Rock Creek Cemetery, Washington, D.C.

　　3. Anna Cabot Mills Davis, wife of Senator Henry Cabot Lodge (1850–1924).

　　4. Theodore Roosevelt (1858–1919), twenty-sixth president of the United States; in a letter to Mary Cadwalader Jones (13 January 1905) HJ calls him "Theodore Rex."

　　5. Sarah Butler Wister (1835–1908), daughter of the actress Fanny Kemble and the southern planter Pierce Butler, was a friend of HJ's since his 1872 sojourn in Rome.

　　6. George Washington Vanderbilt (1862–1914), grandson of Commodore Cornelius Vanderbilt, an agriculturalist and forester; HJ describes his enormous estate Biltmore, near Asheville, North Carolina, in the letter of 8 February 1905.

　　7. Owen Wister (1860–1938), son of Sarah Butler Wister and author of the famous "western" novel *The Virginian* (1902).

　　8. The wife of Crawford Howell Toy (1834–1919), Hancock Professor of Hebrew and Other Oriental Languages at Harvard. Sir John Pollock recalled her as "a great reader of poetry, a perfect hostess, and a fine musician," in his *Time's Chariot* (London: John Murray, 1950), 187. See letter of 7 January 1908.

　　9. Margaret "Daisy" Terry (1862–1952), Mrs. Winthrop Chanler, daughter of the American painter Luther Terry, was one of EW's closest friends. The pilgrimage was a visit to Mrs. Henry Adam's grave to see the Saint-Gaudens statue of a veiled figure.

　　10. HJ continued to refer to the Bourget couple by this creation.

une ... cochonnerie: a bit of trash (lit. a little piggery); *juste ciel:* great heavens; *me ... conférencier:* revealed myself a lecturer; *obligeance:* kindness; *vers la Nord:*

to the North; *patria nostra:* our fatherland; *de . . . soulager:* to comfort ourselves; *que . . . morts:* except by the dead; *de . . . encore:* of still more fatal nature; *croire devoir:* believe you have to

Biltmore, North Carolina
8 February 1905

Dear Mrs. Wharton.

Literally, absolutely, your good letter has found me on the very point of writing to you; I should have done so today even if this consolation (to the rigour of my fate here) hadn't come in. For I have read the February morsel of the House of Mirth,[1] with such a sense of its compact fulness, vivid picture & "sustained interest" as make me really wish to celebrate the emotion. And the emotion of being here, moreover— that is another, & a very different matter—but one that put the pen, or the idea of the pen, ever so suggestively into my hand. And yet I feel that the mere pen, too, can do but scant justice to the various elements of my situation, the recent, the constant, & above all the acutely—*so* acutely!—actual, & that really to talk about them we must take some future N.Y. good fireside hour & then thresh them out and to the last straw. I arrived here (from 2 *drearissime* days at Richmond—dire delusion!) five days ago, & was instantly taken with a most deplorable & untimely little attack of gout (in my left foot—the much éprouvé on past occasions): the result of which has been that I have not once left the house, & but scantly my room. But I am sufficiently better to intend to depart, at any cost, tomorrow afternoon, for Charleston. The whole land here is bound in snow & ice; we are 2,500 feet in the air; the cold, the climate, is well nigh all the "company" in the strange, colossal heartbreaking house; & the desolation & discomfort of the whole thing— whole scene—are, in spite of the mitigating millions everywhere expressed, indescribable. There has been no one here but little pleasant squinting Mrs. Hunt, of Washington (the architect's daughter)[2] & a pleasant (also) little old British soldier-man General Sir Thomas Fraser, who departed yesterday. I am now alone with the good G[eorge] V[anderbilt]s & Huntina; & it has all been verily a strange experience.

But I can't go into it—it's too much of a "subject": I mean one's sense of the extraordinary impenitent madness (of millions) which led to the erection in this vast niggery wilderness, of so gigantic & elaborate a monument to all that *isn't* socially possible there. It's, *in effect*, like a gorgeous practical joke—but at one's own expense, after all, if one has to live in solitude in these league-long marble halls, & sit in alternate Gothic & Palladian cathedrals, as it were—where now only the temperature stalks about—with the "regrets," sighing along the wind, of those who have declined. You who have accepted, for March,[3] be careful (if I may presume, from this experience, to advise); come late in the month rather than early,—then, if there has been a real change, you will get the benefit of the place itself—which I have wholly lacked, mantled as it is in deep snow & with every distance a vast blur of sleet. In the early spring I can conceive it as admirable. And I feel that in speaking of it as I have, I don't do justice to the house as a phenomenon (of brute *achievement*). But that truly wd. take me too far! It's only as a place to live in, & in the conditions, fatally imposed, that I, before it, threw up my hands—! But we will talk of it.—All this time, since we parted, I have seen nothing but Philadelphia & Washington—but very considerably well each of them, though I am more or less committed to going back to W. (if I *can*), late in spring—very late—for 10 days—which I shall like. They really, the two places, are very much alike; I saw no very marked differences—except as I rather preferred Phila., as having rather more furnished & peopled vistas, more consoling marble stoops, & yet imposing less frequent obligation to say one rejoiced in it. Quantities of people in both, but I could see no difference in most of them, & I think I found your Mitchell and Agnes Repplier[4] as interesting as—well, I won't be too personal! I had rather a lurid 4 or 5 hyperborean days (lurid with a *polar* light) at Butler Place (Sarah Wister's), but those again must wait. Verily, I am living through much. And I am cut down to the barest ten days in Florida, having *utterly* to be with my damnable Dentist in Boston again, for 3 days, on the 24th. This will give me, when I get away from here, but bare time to rush down to Palm Beach & then *straight* back from there (with appalling continuity) to Boston—I go then from Boston to Chicago, St. Louis & California —expecting to be back "East" again by about April 20th (though my brother assures me I shan't). I have taken my passage for England on July 4th—X X X X X X X X

Since writing the above, I have been down to luncheon, & been able to see more of the house—& feel a bit shabby at failing to rise to my host's own conception of the results he has achieved. They *are*, in a way, magnificent & such a complicated costly mass has of course all sorts of splendid sides (I admire it as mere masonry), & contains innumerable ingenious features & treasures. Still, I repeat—for a tasteful Southern *home*, it merely makes me weep!—All this time I haven't expressed the smallest sympathy with your influenza—as to which you have my tender compassion. May he have left no blight behind. But I pity you still more, I think, for having had to affront the horrors of this winter in the New York streets—my own dire dismay at which had much to do with driving me away. When I get back to them for a while as I must, it will be late, & I fear—with all thanks for your renewed invitation to P[ark] A[venue], but I shall have to be there with a certain wild freedom incompatible with genteel visiting—sounding the *basfonds*, shirking the "smart set," giving decent time to a long list of good old cousins & ancient ties (I've had, after all, on American ties) wholly forsworn—to their wounded sensibility—in my last visit; & above all *working*, from a clear ten a.m. to a clear 1/30, with a dictatee & a Remington & quantities of sprawling papers, notebooks & other impedimenta that wouldn't fit in to 884 [Park Avenue].[5] But there is time to talk of this—there is so much before me in the interval, I falter, I groan at the sight—I am already tired of my adventures—or *should* be, I had better say, if I weren't sure the West *must* be more characteristic & interesting. What I have seen, since N.Y., has *not* been that—interesting: nay, not a bit! But goodnight—I must hasten to dress for dinner & an evening with my hosts & Huntina *tout purs*. Don't dream this requires the least réplique, but remember that (forgive this blank page that I just discover) my postal anchor is always 95 Irving St. Cambridge. Yours, dear Mrs. Wharton, always & ever

Henry James

P.S.   Poor Smalley—how reduced—how banished!

1. The novel ran in *Scribner's Magazine*, January to November 1905. See letter of 8 November 1905.

2. Catherine "Kitty" Morris Hunt (1868–1963), daughter of Richard Morris Hunt (1827–1895), who designed Biltmore, in 1892 married Livingston Hunt of the U.S. Navy

3. EW and Teddy spent Christmas 1905 at Biltmore; see below, letter of 18 December 1905, and her letter to Sara Norton, 26 December 1905, *EW Letters*, 100–01.

4. Dr. Silas Weir Mitchell (1829–1914), eminent neurologist at whose Orthopedic Hospital in Philadelphia EW went for treatment in 1898; he was also a novelist. Agnes Repplier (1855–1950), esteemed literary figure and cultural leader of Philadelphia society, presided at HJ's reading given at the Bellevue-Stratford Hotel in that city.

5. EW's New York address.

drearissime: dreariest (dreary plus Italian superlative ending); *éprouvé:* tested; *bas-fonds:* dregs; *tout purs:* simply, only

The Deanery
Bryn Mawr, Pennsylvania
7 June 1905

Dear Mrs. Wharton.

Your letter is beautiful & terrible—"like Michael driving Satan"[1] &c (I being Satan); & I will stay at The Mount, I promise you, as many days as I can; but I am afraid the 25th remains the 1st day I can get *to* you—the visit to Howells[2] not being the bar so much as the visit to Newport which I am really committed to, & which, I may add, I greatly desire to make. I spend 3 days there, & *must* have a day in between, at Cambridge. I give up Ashfield[3] wholly then; if we can motor over there—& to Salisbury—so much the better. As regards your kindly inviting Howells for the time, I shall have *been* for my 2 nights at Kittery[4] (all I am intending), when I see you—& I have an impression that he wouldn't prove induceable. He somehow never *is*. I will come, I mean, on the *24th*—*not* 25th—& will do my very best to be able to stay from that Saturday p.m. to the a.m. of Saturday 1st July. I have not yet told my sister-in-law[5] of this—& il y aura bien du tirage—life is complicated, as I often—too often—remark. But there we are! It will be delightful to have your traveller's tale, & I feel as if those days wd. be a really deep draught—of the Pagellino[6] vintage. I have just arrived at these exquisite—really very charming shades; I speak my little piece tomorrow a.m. Yours, dear Mrs. Wharton, always

Henry James

1. Milton's *Paradise Lost*, bk. 6.

2. William Dean Howells (1837–1920), American novelist and editor who, as subeditor of the *Atlantic Monthly* under J. T. Fields, saw to the publication of HJ's earliest fiction in the sixties.

3. Summer home of Charles Eliot Norton (1827–1908), professor of the history of fine arts at Harvard (from 1873), editor of the *North American Review* and *The Nation*, and friend and mentor of HJ's from 1864. The Whartons motored HJ to Ashfield during his visit; see letter of 8 November 1905. For Salisbury, see letter of 5 October 1904.

4. Howells's summer home at Kittery Point, Maine, where HJ spent the weekend of the seventeenth and eighteenth; he went to Newport on the twentieth.

5. WJ's wife since 1879, née Alice Howe Gibbens (1849–1922), a former Boston schoolteacher from an old New England family.

6. The adjective derives from the name of Dr. Pietro Pagello, the surgeon who attended Alfred de Musset in Venice early in 1834 and then briefly replaced him as George Sand's lover: see HJ's account in the three essays on Sand in *Notes on Novelists* (1914), reprinted in *European Writers, Library of America* (hereafter *LA*)especially pp. 744–84. The diminutive "Pagellino" is one of the names—with erotic associations—that HJ adopted for EW's various automobiles; see letter of 8 November 1905.

il . . . tirage: that will take some doing (lit. that will really be a pull)

35 West 10th St. (or better,
95 Irving St., Cambridge, Mass.)
13 June 1905

Dear Mrs. Wharton.

I approach the subject again, after your last good letter, with infinite *malaise;* but the stern reality of things presses upon me, &, in fine, Ich kann nicht anders.[1] So, I greatly fear, as the days come on & the future bristles with formidable detail of all I have to squeeze into my time between this & my departure (bristles even like the more than fretful porcupine) I shall not be able to come to you on Saturday 24th, but only on Monday 26th. Next week is a particularly difficult one for me & it is absolutely necessary that I shall put in, make *sure* of, a clear day or two of it for Cambridge. The only way I can manage this is by clutching at Saturday 24th, aforesaid, as the *least* impossible day. Be indulgent over all this & don't shoot—"I am doing my best!" On the 26th I will eagerly come & try & squeeze in all experience between that day & the following Saturday a.m. when I shall have, by the same immitigable law, to depart. This sad little story has required to be told —but "don't answer"! though I know you would with the best gentleness. Anything else wd. embitter the few remaining drops of the cup— the "America cup"—of yours not inconstantly

Henry James

P.S.   I instantly wrote to W. Berry.[2]

1. I can do no other (Luther's famous comment on his articles of protest, "Here I stand . . .").

2. EW had told HJ that Walter Berry was to sail to England but was so far "shipless"; HJ wrote (11 June) urging Berry to join him on the Cunard *Saxonia* out of Boston on 4 July. See *Letters* 4, 358.

Lamb House, Rye
8 November 1905

Dear Mrs. Wharton.

You cannot say that I have bombarded you with letters, & I should be very sorry if I had put any such statement into your power. I have had, had perhaps to excess, a conscience about writing to you, having become aware, for myself, more & more, as I grow older, of the several things—interests—that life would be more fully, more needfully applicable to, if it were not for its letters. So many of them are not *fair*! And I have wanted immensely, where you are concerned, to *be* fair. So I have measured what I was doing—as well as what I wasn't—& have said again & again "No, no—not yet!" The limit I fixed myself was when the final number of the House of Mirth should have come out: "When I've read that," I said to myself, "I'll write." Half an hour ago, or less, I laid down the November *Scribner*, & now I have no scruple. Let me tell you at once that I very much admire that fiction, & especially the last three numbers of it; finding it carried off with a high, strong hand & an admirable touch, finding it altogether a superior thing. There are things to be said, but they are—some of them—of the essence of your New York donnée—& moreover you will have said them, to a certainty, yourself. The book remains one that does you great honour —though it is better written than composed; it is indeed throughout *extremely* well written, & in places quite "consummately." I wish we could talk of it in a motor-car: I have been in motor-cars again, a little, since our wonderful return from Ashfield; but with no such talk as that. There are fifty things I should like to say—but, after so long an interval there are so many I want to, in general, & I think that my best way to touch on some of the former would be by coming back to the U.S. to deliver a lecture on "The question of the *roman de moeurs* in America— its deadly difficulty." But when I do that I shall work in a tribute to the great success & the large portrayal, of your Lily B[art]. She is very big & true—& very difficult to have *kept* true—& big; & all your climax is very finely handled. Selden is too *absent*—but you know that better than I can make you. I hope you are having a boom. Have you read Les Deux Soeurs?[1]—& have you read the amazing little Mme Tynaire's [*sic*] "Avant l'amour"?[2] You are sure to have done both; so oh, for an hour of the motor again. The French, in the Tinayre light, are *impayables*; & so is our poor P[aul] B[ourget], frankly, I think, in the *poncif* light—& even in the "Amour" light too—this Amour light of his latest manner. But as a surrender to the *poncif* in all the force of the term, the thing—his last book—is, I think, for a man of his original value, one of the strangest literary documents conceivable. Not that the poncif was not always in some degree—in a great degree—present in his fiction (though never in his criticism &c); but the way it has now invaded his "morality," as well as his form, deprives me of any power to acknowl-edge his so inveterate, & so generous, gifts of his volumes. It affects me as a painful *End*. So I have no news whatever of that couple—they haven't come (as usual) to England this summer, & the tidings you

brought home were my last.—I despatched Mrs. Jones & Beatrix back
with as much Impression as their two brief little stations in London
(during which I went up to attend them), permitted me to stuff into
them. Beatrix I thought less well than she ought to be—but every ill
would fade from her if she would give up Doctors & Waters & really
& sacrificially commit herself to the divine Fletcher[3] (who, now that I
have got back to my own good conditions, here, for worshipping him,
has renewed the sources of my life). I have made a few short absences,
but the *pax britannica* of this (to me) so amiable & convenient retreat,
awaited me, on my return from my American adventure, with such
softly-encircling arms that I have, for the most part, sunk into it deep,
& shall be here for two or three months to come. I go to spend a couple
of days, in a week or two, with Mrs. Humphry Ward[4]—& I haven't
even yet read *Wm. Ashe*, which she has handsomely sent me, as a preparation. But I have had practically to *tell* her that all power to read her
has abandoned me—though I have put it as the power to read *any*
fiction. But she will extract from me when I see her that I *have* read Mrs.
Wharton, & what I think of that—being very gentle about it, though,
for she also greatly admires Mrs. Wharton. Of this, however, you will
have personal evidence, as she appears to be really intending to go over
& see you in the course of the winter. What a prodigious drama it will
be—her tumbling herself bodily into the circus of her millions, & how
little either the millions or she will make the other party out. *Pourvu
qu'elle en réchappe!* You must give me news of the commotion into which
I foresee you inevitably dragged & engulfed. But news of Walter Berry
I greatly want too, who, after having greatly endeared himself to me,
in the summer, par son naturel, ses dons & ses malheurs, vanished from
my sight on his mad Italian errand—& has left me since a prey to
wonder & fear. I have—I *had*—heard of, & wept over, his "ill luck,"
the guignon pursuing him—but I see it now to be in the consummate
art with which he invokes that goddess. I tried to save him—hard; but
he rushed (full of fractures) on his fate—& I don't know at all what
has become of him (in what *gargote* he sank by the wayside); & I still
lie awake at night thinking of it—that being the force of the impression
he made on me.—I am very busy "in my poor way," trying to make
my 10 months in America the subject of as many *Sensations d'Italie*[5] as
possible, & finding, strangely, that I have more impressions than I know

what to do with or can account for—& this in spite of finding that, also, they tend exceedingly to melt & fade & pass away, flicker off like the shadows from firelight on the wall. But I shall draw a long breath when I have worked them off—which it looks as if it would take me perhaps *two* (separate) volumes (*of* Impressions, pure & simple) to do; whence I fear that it may be very fantastic & irrelevant stuff I am producing—for I don't see, I repeat, where it all comes from. And the queerest part of the matter is that, though I *shall* rejoice when it is over, I meanwhile quite like doing it. *Entre temps* my thoughts wing their way back to Pagello & his precious freight[6] (have you read the luridly interesting little vol. *George Sand & sa Fille*,[7] by the way?) & hover about him as he so greatly adventures & so powerfully climbs, m'attachant à ses pas, to his flights & his swoops, & even more to his majestic roll in the deep valleys, with a wistfulness in which every one of those past hours lives again. Most of all lives, I think, perversely, & even a little hauntingly, that leave-taking of ours at the Ashfield door last June—& poor dear Charles's unforgettable fixed smile of farewell (here below) to *me*, & poor Margaret's pathetic glare. But I wouldn't for anything not have had that experience, so beautiful, of our whole going & coming, or not have rendered them that visitation, & I thank you again, even at this distance of time, for having made it so exquisitely possible to me.—I know about your shock & your pang in connection with poor Miss Crane's strange & terrible annihilation, but I can't speak of it, any more than I can of those unhappy overdarkened Dixeys (with my impressions of the boy in the pride of his youth, a great ornament & *panache* to them),[8] & of their existence there, as I saw it, all of such innocent, *un*ironic comedy. Heaven help us all!—The Pagello-sense has been with me a little, here, again, this autumn—notably during 4 or 5 splendid October days spent with Ned Abbey (& his wife—R.A.!) in Gloucestershire,[9] who have a wondrous French machine & who, in the insolence of their art gains, want to buy some fine old Jacobean (or other) house & estate. I roamed with them far over the land to look at three or four, & found it a most interesting & charming pursuit; in fact, in a capacious luncheon-stocked car, the very summit of human diversion. This absurd old England is still, after long years, so marvellous to me, & the visitation of beautiful old buried houses (as to "buy"—seeing them *as* one sees them) such a refinement of bliss. Won't you come out with Pagello, & a luncheon-basket, & feign at least an intention of purchase—taking me with you to do the lying? I will show you all those the Abbeys haven't yet bought. Submit this programme to Mr. Edward, please, with my very cordial regards. I hope his health & "form" are, in all his splendid applications of them, of the best.

But it's long past midnight, while I write—past 1 A.M., & I bid you at once good night & good morning. Don't be morbid, *you*, in the matter of our postal relation, please, & believe me yours, dear Mrs. Wharton, very constantly,

Henry James

1. Bourget's short novel of 1905.

2. Marguerite Suzanne Marcelle Tinayre (1872–1948), French biographer and novelist whose novels such as *Avant l'amour* (1897) treated the theme of the emancipation of women. She was married to the engraver Jules Tinayre. See letter of 18 December 1905.

3. Horace Fletcher (1849–1919), American food faddist, recommended chewing one's food slowly and thoroughly until it was reduced to liquid. HJ adopted "Fletcherizing," as the system was called, in May 1904; he abandoned the practice in February 1910 when he discovered it was probably responsible for his digestive difficulties.

4. Mary Augusta Ward (1851–1920), popular British novelist and bluestocking; her novel *The Marriage of William Ashe* was published in 1905. HJ's visit was to the Wards' country home, Stocks; see letter of 18 December 1905.

5. Bourget's travel sketches, 1905. HJ refers to preparation of his ten sketches of America revisited, published principally in the *North American Review* and the *Fortnightly Review* between April 1905 and November 1906, and later incorporated in *The American Scene* (1907).

6. HJ refers to EW's motor and its carrying them to Ashfield to visit the ailing Charles Eliot Norton; see letter of 7 June 1905.

7. *George Sand et sa fille d'après leur correspondance* (Paris: Calmann-Lévy, 1905), by the literary scholar Samuel Rocheblave (1854–1944), examines the touching relationship of French novelist George Sand (Aurore Dupin, Baronne Dudevant [1804–1876]) and her daughter Gabrielle Solange Clésinger née Dudevant-Sand (1828–1899); their association with Frédéric Chopin (1810–1849, Polish-French pianist and composer); and the vexed and complicated marriage (1847) of Solange to the sculptor Jean-Baptiste Auguste Clésinger.

8. To his old friend Alice Mason (1838–1913)—Mrs. Charles Sumner until her divorce in 1874, after which she resumed her maiden name—HJ wrote (11

August 1905): "I was *sickened* by the news of that handsome clever young Arthur Dixey's death. I saw something of him last autumn at Lenox."

9. Edwin Austin Abbey (1852–1911), American painter and one-time president of the Royal Academy, and his wife, Mary Gertrude Mead. Their handsome residence in Gloucestershire was Morgan Hall.

impayables: priceless; *poncif:* banal, trite; *Pourvu . . . réchappe!:* If only she escape it!; *par . . . malheurs:* by his disposition, his gifts & his misfortunes; *guignon:* jinx, run of bad luck; *gargote:* dive; *m'attachant . . . pas:* attaching me to his pace

Lamb House, Rye
18 December 1905

Dear Mrs. Wharton.

Your letter gives me warrant, & I throw discretion to the winds & answer it by return of post. Besides, I must thank you very kindly, with no delay, for the so handsome photograph in which you baissez les yeux so modestly before the acclamations of the world. They are all transcribed for you, however, by the *soins* of Romeike,[1] I surely make out, in that compendium you are reading; so that you look thoroughly in possession of your genius, fame & fortune. It is a very charming picture, as charming, that is, as a picture can be, which doesn't, none the less, "do you justice." But I take it gratefully for my étrennes & place it ever so conspicuously among quaint tributes already beginning to cluster on my mantel shelf. You make me a still handsomer present, however, in your dazzling news of your (intended) February voyage.[2] This is a delight to hear, & immediately so *furnishes* for me the rather vacant prospect of the spring that I feel as if, with an empty new house on my hands & no money left to garnish it, I had suddenly inherited a "centretable" or a chandelier; & I am already, on the strength of it, excitedly moving in. This is verily a brave showing, & I can't tell you how wellinspired I think you both. I go up to town February 1st, to stay a good many weeks, & hope to learn there, promptly, of your arrival in the almost neighbouring capital. After that I shall pull on the London string as hard as I know how—to bring you over without too much delay. Would that Pagello *were* in your train, or, failing that, even Cook, prince of Pagellists[3]—it would make me believe so in the dream of a spin with you. I *have* had a few here, this autumn, & the sense of the way England *s'y prête* made my mouth water.—I can't tell you meanwhile how mighty I think it of you to be spending the Xmastide at Biltmore[4]—I myself only going to Brighton & thinking even that formidable. May those marble halls not expand, but *contract* to receive you, & may you have, as you of course will, one of the apartments of state, & not a bachelor bedroom, as I did, in a wing overlooking an ice-bound stable-yard, & that even the blaze of felled trees didn't warm. But there must be always this about Biltmore, that it thoroughly fills the mind while one is there —little as the mind can do to fill it.—Your letter opens up deeps that call unto deeps, of various sorts—& we must really do everything to make the Poncivité of Paul & Minnie [Bourget] (for *she*'s in it, much) "keep" till we meet; in company with the unattenuated Tinayre[5] & many other things besides. I must tell you a small anecdote of the un-attenuated Tinayre—culled during a Sunday spent not long since, with Mrs. H[umphry] W[ard], at Stocks. The 2 ladies had somewhat fore-gathered "morally," during Mme T's brief visit to England 2 years ago, & after François Barbazanges, sent by the author to that of Robert Elsmere,[6] the latter had written remonstrantly, pleadingly, to know whether the "facts of life" as Tolstoy & Turgénieff handled them, didn't constitute freedom enough for the novel, & whether Mme T. hadn't really better think it over. Mme T. replied that she would think it over indeed—& promised very deferentially & sympathetically—& then in due course (of a year or two) sent Mrs. W. "Avant L'Amour" with another sweet letter saying that she *had* thought it over & that this was the result. (It appears that the vol. in question is an early-published thing, out of print,—which accounts for a certain ambiguity in it—now revived, reconsidered, retouched & above all *châtiés* [*sic*]; therefore of-fered to Mrs. W. as the fruit of her example.) This Mrs. W. retailed to me with bewildered gravity, as so strange a miscalculation of the French mind! But I see it as a *calculation* (of the French mind!) altogether—with the irrepressible *malice* of the demonic little Tinayre having made all the *frais* from the 1st, & with the ineffable Avant l'Amour ("avant"!!!) re-vamped perhaps even really just *for* the trick on her correspondent. I understood it after the tone in which dear Mrs. W. mentioned to me her suggesting to her Tolstoy & Turgénieff—but Mrs. W. (she is really an absolute dear) has never understood it to this hour.—These things, however, take me too far, & make me desire that you shld. burn my letter. You will miss Mrs. Ward in New York[7]—she is definitely, I think, & quite sublimely, to go in the spring. But let not that make you change your plan. I am afraid my little mill has ground no personal news of interest since I last wrote you. I continue to sit very tight here (& I like the quiet conditions in this misty-browny-purply & essentially *toney* South of England autumn, which is far from having your Lenox &c sublimities—but which *is*, truly, tonier); having the cogent motive of the mind to put through à tout prix the squeezing-out of my American stuff, in order both to keep ahead of it before it *goes* (really an heroic feat), &, more particularly, to clear the ground of it & be free for more inspiring work. It's very good [of] you to speak of your regret at the relegation of *that*. I do myself feel it waiting at the door & scratching there, like my little hound, to be let in. But the threshing out my American matter in this form will really enable me to use some of it (I mean some of the *sense* of it) in the fictive form better. I shall read the H[ouse] of M[irth] again, over, in the "final" state. I go back with you in spirit to the little Park Avenue House,[8] of which I have, really, a thrillingly romantic recollection. I vibrated much there & got a great deal out of it. Don't "answer" this—only make me a sign when your sailing is fixed. I enclose a special benediction to Mr. Teddy, & I think tenderly of dear demented Walter B. Yours, dear Mrs. Wharton, always & ever

Henry James

1. By the aid (care) of Messrs Romeike and Curtice, a prominent press-cutting agency in London.

2. EW and Teddy did not sail from New York until 17 March 1906.

3. EW's chauffeur Charles Cook of Lee, Massachusetts, near Lenox.

4. See letter of 8 February 1905.

5. See letter of 8 November 1905.

6. Tinayre's novel *La Vie amoureuse de François Barbaȝanges* (1904) and Mrs. Ward's novel *Robert Elsemere* (1888).

7. The trip to New York was postponed because of Mrs. Ward's illness. It was not until 1908 that she was able to go to North America for four months (March through June) with her husband and daughter Dorothy—who stayed with Mary Cadwalader Jones in New York.

8. EW's New York house at 884; see letter of 8 February 1905.

baissez ... yeux: lower your eyes; *étrennes:* New Year's gifts; *s'y prête:* lends herself to that; *Poncivité:* banality, triteness; *châtié:* chastened; *frais:* gain; *à tout prix:* at all costs

The Athenaeum
Pall Mall, S.W.
22 March [1906]

Dear Mrs. Wharton.

I think you must have arrived en pays de France,[1] & I greatly desire to greet you there. I meant to be sure to have a word awaiting you— but I am on my side in *this* deuce of a country or of a city & London, for the *ahuri* rustic, when he comes up for short periods, bristles with complications & interferences. If you were either rustic or *ahurie*, you would see for yourself when you came over. And for that matter you *will.* Didn't I converse for $\frac{3}{4}$'s of an hour yesterday with Miss Mary Cholmondeley[2] (whose literary adviser dear Howard S[turgis] is) about the House of M. (dont elle raffole aussi bien que moi)—with the effect of her saying at the end of the 35th minute: "And you'd call her *subtle,* wouldn't you?" To which I replied demoniacally: "Ah, Miss M. C., there are others to whom I should so much *more* apply that sovereign last word of the higher criticism—!" Yet let me not deflower for you in advance the fresh, the tropical bouquet that awaits you here. Come quickly & bury your nose in it. I hope you arrive, & your gallant companion not less, in good health & heart & after not too much buffetting & bruising. This is a very good period here—save for too much east wind, but April is near—to blunt a little that edge. I heard yesterday that Howard had gone to meet you—& have seen him grilling, sadly, with the sense of my proved poorer style. But wait till I show you *here*! Any scrap of news from you will rejoice the heart of yours & Mr. Teddy's always & ever

Henry James

1. EW arrived in Paris on 25 March.
2. Mary Cholmondeley (1859–1925), English novelist whose *Red Pottage* (1899) was very popular. Percy Lubbock's account is that Howard Sturgis was

a most urgent "adviser" on *Red Pottage*—in his *Mary Cholmondeley: A Sketch from Memory* (London: Jonathan Cape, 1928).

ahuri: astounded; *dont . . . moi:* which she is as wild about as I am

Reform Club
Pall Mall S.W.
29 March 1906

Dear Mrs. Wharton.

I hear from Howard S[turgis] that you are on the European scene—within immediate range of his admiration & applause, & this makes me shudder over my delay (a thought of haunting abhorrence to me, hour after hour, these days, among too numerous London notes), to renew to you my affectionate welcome. (Don't let the blur of that adjective seem to you anything but the blur of the very emotion & vibration of my utterance of it.) I sent you ten days ago, or more, a word of greeting to Munroe's Bank rue Scribe—perhaps you will have found it (it being where you had originally told me to direct). Then came Miss Bahlman[n]'s[1] note, speaking of your slight illness & delay, & giving me your brother's address[2]—whose number alas I seem already, agedly & infirmly, to forget. Yet this will reach you & take you *moltissimi saluti.* I hope the New York indisposition[3] has been flung to the waves of the Atlantic, or, better still, its winds. There are winds here (of March, alas, as yet), by which I guarantee you the removal of any clinging remainder. Please believe in my intense interest in your movements & intentions—especially as I cherish the hope that you are soon moving hitherward & intending a good stay. But London will be better (for ethereal mildness—that half-hearted mildness looks like wildness: so let it stand!) in April than now; & for social wildness (or mildness) the said Easter-time will, from about the 10th to the end of the month, make a great hole, through the general absence. I myself, however, *unnatu-*rally, don't "abhor" the London vacuum—I prefer it to any other state, & shall stick on here well into May. If you come promptly, moreover, you can make the Easter visits. *Do* make them, so that we can talk about them; though I make, insistently, nowadays, none. I am writing to H. S[turgis]—how I envy you each other! If the dear Master (of the pummice-stone) is near you, do snatch that implement from his grasp! By which I mean please give him & *her*[4] (for she's a little of a *pierre-ponce*) my tanti saluti. But give them to Mr. Teddy first. Yours very constantly

Henry James

1. Anna Bahlmann, EW's German-born secretary since 1904.
2. The Paris address of EW's brother Henry Edward (Harry) Jones (1850–1922) was 3, Place des États-Unis.
3. EW had suffered from a combination of influenza and bronchitis; she left New York in the midst of a Saint Patrick's Day snowstorm.
4. That is, Paul and Minnie Bourget, who were about to introduce EW to the society of the Faubourg Saint-Germain.

moltissimi saluti: all greetings; *pierre-ponce:* pumice stone

The Reform Club
2 April [1906]

Dear Edith Wharton.[1]

I rejoice in your so interesting & auspicious letter, & make a single greedy leap to the finest point in it. *Bien sûr que* I'll meet you at Dover on the 25th[2] or anywhere in the world—*this* world—you suggest, & motor with you as long as the machine consents to resist my weight. I respond in other words to that charming idea, or to any modification of it, very heartily, & shall await, later on, your further commands. I regard it as an enchanting prospect. And *how* I want to hear about everything! our dear Névrosés,[3] the translations, the dramatizations,[4] the asphyxiating milieu of H. S[turgis] (about whose strange drop into dullness you are sadly right), the latest "returns" from the *H. of M.* & whatever else you may confide to me as we spin. I really am exquisitely grateful to both of you for the motor-chance. I have set my foot *almost* into none since I tore myself last from Pagello.[5] (I will explain the almost.) Tout à vous, Madame.

Henry James

1. HJ's first use of EW's given name in his salutation.
2. See letter of 4 April 1906.

3. The "Névrosés" (Neurotics) included probably the Bourgets and Sturgis and certainly the hypochondriac Charles Du Bos (1882–1939), a bilingual young man Bourget had selected from a number of applicants to translate *The House of Mirth*; it ran, as *Chez les Heureux du Monde*, in the *Revue de Paris* in eight installments from 1 December 1907 to 1 March 1908.

4. EW and Clyde Fitch (1865–1909)—the most popular American playwright of that time—agreed in December 1905 to collaborate on a dramatization of *The House of Mirth*; Fitch was in Paris at this moment for a brief consultation with EW. The play opened in Detroit on 14 September and in New York on 22 October 1906; its career was brief.

5. EW's automobile.

Bien . . . que: Certainly; *Tout à vous:* All the best to you

The Reform Club
4 April 1906

Dear Mrs. Wharton.

Your letter this a.m. received makes me still further rejoice. I will do my very best to be prepared with a pleasing itinerary—of the kind you have in your eye—by the date of your advent, & in fact to meet you with it at Dover on the 25th.[1] With it without it I will meet you. If we start from D. on the 26th a.m., I vote that we come southward through Kent & Sussex—we must keep south of London—and begin by lunching that day at Lamb House. In that case we might sleep at (I shld. think) Chichester, & make our way so, by Winchester & Salisbury, into the interesting Somersetshire of old houses (Montacute the beautiful!!) by *Wells*, on the way. Thence along the North Devon coast *1st*, & then across Devonshire southward to a wind up at Sidmouth on the south coast. (Ilfracombe is rather awful.) But this is a very rough hint. Don't resent the few monuments if thrown in & *met*—not sought & gone out of the way for; in this small country they come in (the occasional cathedrals &c.) of themselves. But nous causerons de cela. How much you are laying up on your side to tell me! Save every crumb—make in due course your further signals & believe me always your

Henry James

1. HJ met EW but the motor journey was postponed; the new car (a Panhard) Teddy was to bring to Dover broke down; EW went up to London alone and the Wharton tour began there. HJ joined them at Bath at the end of April for "a three days' motor trip" (see *Letters* 4, 401) and left them at Malvern.

nous ... cela: we'll chat about that

> Reform Club
> [20 (?) April 1906][1]

... written to for us. But I shall meet you with a plastic plan. I earnestly hope your domestic influenza has waned & that your Drama has waxed. The weather here is wondrous—has been so for 2 or 3 weeks; & I pray it may endure. Poor Howard [Sturgis] & his dull-sounding journey! London awaits you! & I shall be on the pier-head. I yearn for your report of the Ward-Noailles comedy—& wonder if Mrs. W. can't produce for you the terrible Tinayre. Make me a sign if I can do anything for you here en attendant, & believe me yours always

Henry James

1. The first full sentence suggests EW's arrival is still fixed but that motor-tour plans are not, and it would seem to place this fragment after letters of 2 and 4 April; the favorable weather report of the next sentence would seem to place the fragment at some three weeks after the unfavorable report of 29 March; the familiar brevity of the reference to Mme Tinayre places this after the letters of November and December 1905, and the reference to the Comtesse Anna de Noailles, to whom Bourget had introduced EW soon after her arrival in Paris, seems to place this fragment in late April. Anna Elizabeth de Brancovan (1876–1933), Paris-born daughter of a Rumanian prince and wife of Comte Mathieu de Noailles, was a successful poet and novelist.

Lamb House, Rye
[2 July 1906]

Dear Edith Wharton.

It's horrible, the tune to which I owe you a letter! But I've really been for weeks in the disabled state, with the bleeding wound in my side, produced by the Parthian shot of your own last—your fling back at me, over your departing shoulder, of your unutterable vision of the Nohant[1] that I have all these (motorless) years so abjectly failed to enlighten my eyes withal (for I am indeed convinced that it *must*, as you say, enlighten & explain). Oh, if we could only have been enlightened & explained to together! To think that that might (dreamily) have been even while we were splashing about Ross in the rain or going up & down in the hideous Malvern lift![2] I've had so, at any rate, since that baffled vision, the ache of envy & the rage of despair, that I've been fit for nothing but to write you, under my friend Pinker's[3] earnest solicitation, the letter (of recommendation of *him*—for your literary business here) which he may, or may not, by this time have sent you. Let me take occasion to say, 1° that I *meant* to write you immediately after I had given it to him, letting you know that I had done so; 2° that I hope it didn't strike you at all as an aggression (uninvited by yourself, as it were) against your customary ways; & 3° that what I said for the excellent J.B.P. was absolutely candid & sincere. He has been to me, these several years, a blessing unspeakable—I simply couldn't live without him. He had told me before that he yearned to have you for a client, & when he wrote asking me for an introduction to you, I could but give him the hearty document I did. But my intention, as I say, had been to ask your leave first. Alas, instead of this I merely lost myself still in the golden mist of your Nohant—which I'm really almost capable of rushing over to Lenox to have your story of—*more* capable than of starting next week for Dover, Paris, Châteauroux & La Châtre. To think you have seen La Châtre!—& that you might move me over to Ashfield again & tell me about it as we go! With these grimaces, you see, I try to pluck the javelin from my side. But it will really stick there, poisoning my blood, till you *write*—I mean till you PRINT, till you "do" the place, the whole impression for me under stress of imminent publication. For of course you *are* doing, you *have* done that. You can't *not*. I yearn & languish. Write to me that this act of piety is even already performed. I've no news for you comparable to that of my emotion on all that score. And there was, on my side—there *had* been before I heard from you—a strange telepathic intuition. A few days after you had sloped away to France I said to myself suddenly: "They're on their way to Nohant, d—n them! They're going there—they *are* there!" It came to me as a jealous, yet so tenderly sympathetic, conviction—out of the blue. You hadn't spoken of it. So you owe me the *récit*. There has been, you know, no *récit* (of the impression of the place) of any sort of authority or value but George's own.[4] How you must have *smelt* them all! I spent 2 nights at Queen's Acre 10 days ago—Annie Thackeray[5] being there. Poor Howard [Sturgis] is really a good deal in pieces. Apropos of pieces, too, tell me of yours—the H. of M.[6]—& how the preparations go, & comment ça s'annonce. I wish it no end of wind in its sails. I am summering ever so strictly (as regards continuity) here. I greet Mr. Edward recht herzlich, & I hope you've not wanted for the sight of Walter Berry. I send him *tout carrément* my love. And I send *you* nothing less; & am yours always & ever

Henry James

1. The Whartons spent the last two weeks of May touring France from the Channel Coast into Clermont-Ferrand; the highlight for EW (and the envy of HJ) was their visit to Nohant, home of George Sand. Châteauroux, mentioned below, is the largest town in the vicinity of Nohant; La Châtre a nearby town. EW sent the consequent travel pieces to the *Atlantic*; they were gathered into *A Motor Flight Through France* (New York: Scribners, 1908).

2. Reference to the end of HJ's brief tour with the Whartons at the beginning of May 1906.

3. James Brand Pinker (1863–1922), HJ's literary agent since 1898.

4. See *Histoire de ma vie* (1856), which contains several noteworthy descriptions of the house and grounds.

5. Anne Isabella Thackeray (1837–1919), novelist daughter of William Makepeace Thackeray and sister-in-law of Leslie Stephen, in 1877 married her cousin Richmond Ritchie (1854–1912), later permanent under secretary of state for India.

6. EW's dramatization with Clyde Fitch of *The House of Mirth*; see letter of 2 April 1906. Fitch would visit The Mount in August.

comment ça s'annonce: how it promises to turn out; *recht herzlich:* most cordially; *tout carrément:* quite frankly

The Reform Club
17 November 1906

Dear Mrs. Wharton.

I had from you a shortish time since a very beautiful & interesting letter—into the ink to thank you for which my pen has been perpetually about to dip, & now comes the further thrill of your "quaint" little picture card with its news of the Paris winter & the romantic rue de Varenne;[1] on which the pen straightway plunges into the fluid. This is really charming & uplifting news, & I applaud the free sweep of your "line of life" with all my heart. We shall be almost neighbours, & I will most assuredly hie me as promptly as possible across the scant inter-space of the Channel, the Pas de Calais &c.: where the very first question on which I shall beset you will be your adventures & impression of Nohant—as to which I burn & yearn for fond particulars. Perhaps if you have the proper Vehicle of Passion[2]—as I make no doubt—you will be going there once more—in which case *do* take me! And such a suave & convenient crossing[3] as I meanwhile wish you—such a pro-vision of philosophy laid up, in advance, for use in, & about, rue Barbet de Jouy![4] You will have finished your new fiction[5] I "presume"—if it isn't presumptuous—before embarking? & I do so for the right of the desire to congratulate, in that case, & envy & sympathise—being in all sorts of embarras now, myself, over the finish of many things. I pant for the start of that work & languish to take it up. I think I have had no chance to tell you how much I admired your single story in the Aug. *Scribner*—beautifully done, I thought & full of felicities & achieved val-ues & pictures. All the same, with the rue de Varenne &c., don't go in too much for the French or the "Franco-American" subject—the real field of your extension is *here*—it has far more fusability [*sic*] with *our* nature & primary material; between which & French elements there is, I hold, a disparity as complete as between a life led in trees, say, & a life led in—sea-depths, or in other words between that of climbers & swimmers—or (crudely) that of monkeys & fish. Is the Play Thing[6] meanwhile climbing or swimming?—I take much interest in its fate. But you will tell me of these things—in February! It will be *then* I shall scramble over.[7] I go home an hour or two hence (to stay as still as possible) after a night—only—spent in town. The perpetual summon-ses & solicitations of London (some of wh. *have* to be met), are at times a maddening worry—or almost. I am wondering if you are not feeling just now perhaps a good deal, at Lenox, in the apparently delightful old 1840 way—a good snowstorm aiding, & the Westinghouse colouring, as I suppose, a good deal blurred. But how I want to have it all—the gossip of the countryside—from you! Some of it has come to me as rather dreadful—poor young Grace Sedgwick[8] e.g.— & that is what some of the lone houses in the deep valleys we motored through used to make me think of! I wish you were bringing Walter Berry with you—he ought to exist for bringability. However, if you *do*, bring Mr. Teddy—we shall get on, & I am meanwhile yours & his very constantly

Henry James

1. EW had arranged to lease George Vanderbilt's apartment, 58, rue de Varenne—in the heart of the Faubourg Saint-Germain, the 7th Arrondissement.

2. HJ's generic name for EW's motor, which explains the various specific names with erotic associations.

3. They sailed on the *Amerika* on 7 January 1907.

4. The Paris address of Paul and Minnie Bourget.

5. The novella *Madame de Treymes* was serialized in *Scribner's Magazine* in August 1906, then published by Scribners in 1907.

6. The dramatic version of *The House of Mirth* was no longer afloat.

7. Because of EW's bout of grippe HJ did not leave Dover until 7 March. He spent two weeks in Paris (58, rue de Varenne), then, with EW and Teddy, a motor trip of "3 wks & a day" south via Nohant. See letter of 11 August 1907.

8. Grace Ashburner Sedgwick (b. 1883) was the daughter of HJ's old friend Arthur George Sedgwick (b. 1844)—long associated with *The Nation*—who had committed suicide the preceding summer.

Lamb House, Rye

11 [and 12] August 1907

My dear Edith[1] & my dear Edward.

The d'Humières[2] have just been lunching with me, & that has so reknotted the silver cord that stretched so tense from the first days of last March to the first of those of May[3]—wasn't it?—that I feel it a folly in addition to a shame not yet to have written to you (as I have been daily & hourly yearning to do) ever since my return from Italy about a month ago. You flung me the handkerchief, Edith, just at that time— literally cast it at my feet: it met me, exactly, bounding—rebounding— from my hall table as I recrossed my threshold after my long absence; which fact makes this tardy response, I am well aware, all the more graceless. And then came the charming little picture-card of the poor Lamb House hack grinding out his patient prose under your light lash & dear Walter B[erry]'s—which *should* have accelerated my production to the point of its breaking in waves at your feet: and yet it's only tonight that my overburdened spirit—pushing its way ever since my return, through the accumulations & arrears, in every sort, of absence, puts pen to paper for your especial benefit—if benefit it be. The charming d'Humières both, as I say, touring—*training*—in England, through horrid wind & weather, with a *bonne grâce* & a wit & a Parisianism, worthy of a better cause, amiably lunched with me a couple of days since on their way from town to Folkstone & so back to Plassac (don't you *like* "Plassac," down in our dear old Gascony?) the seat of M. Dampierre[4]—to whom *à ce* qu'il paraît, that day at luncheon, we were all exquisitely sympathetic! Well, it threw back the bridge across the gulfs & the months, even to the very spot where the great nobly-clanging glass door used to open to the arrested, the engulfing & disgorging Car—for we sat in my little garden here & talked about you galore & kind of made plans (wild vain dreams, though I didn't let *them* see it!) for our all somehow being together again. They appeared, that highly-civilized young couple, to the greatest advantage: a little more pedestrian & mackintoshed of aspect than under your (*pardon*—our!) gilded *lambris*, but delightfully conversible—in the key of that milieu; & she with her pretty salient eyes & her pretty salient gesture, so vague, & yet so rounded & *invoking*, all as pretty as ever. But oh, I should like to remount the stream of time much further back than their passage here —if it weren't (as it somehow always is when I get at urgent letters) ever so much past midnight. It was only with my final return hither that my deep draught of riotous living came to an end, & as the cup had originally been held to my lips all by your hands I somehow felt in presence of your interest & sympathy up to the very last, & as if you absolutely should have been *avertis* from day to day—I did the matter that justice at least. Too much of the story has by this time dropped out; but there are bits I wish I could save for you. I spent 4 or 5 days in Paris, only, on my way home (exclusive of 3 in grim Lausanne with an afflicted relative)—after leaving Milan at 3.20 in the afternoon & reaching the Hotel Gibbon door, by the wondrous Simplon Tunnel, at 10.30 that night: an *approximation* of the compatriot-poisoned Italy (of early summer, drenched by the "Southern route")—which thrilled me even through the rage of that poison. And in Paris I called rue Barbet & found Minnie [Bourget] at first alone & very charmingly *accueillante*; full of the fact that they were (the 1st week in July!) "more mondains than ever," & that Paul had dined out every night for *nine* on end; also that he wanted to spend the whole summer so & never stir from rue Barbet, never *never* again. At last Paul came in, quite "decent" & pleas-ant, but with all his usual detachment & irrelevancy of attitude, tone & direction, & with no more question of what had happened to one or where one had been & how occupied in the 2 months than if we had broken off the day before. But I must break off—it's 1.15 a.m.!

Aug. 12th I wrote you last from Rome, I think[5]—didn't I? but it was after that that I heard of your having had at the last awful delays & complications, awful *strike*-botherations, over your sailing. I knew noth-ing of them at the time, & in fact I'm not sure I *did* hear of them till Minnie P.[6] spoke of them to me on my re-passage through Paris—she told me you had been infinitely incommoded. I can only hope that the horrid memory of it has been brushed & blown away for you by the wind of your American kilometres. I remained in Rome—for myself—a goodish while after last writing you & there were charming moments, faint reverbrations of the old-time refrains—with a happy tendency of the superfluous, the incongruous crew[7] to take its departure as the sum-mer came on; yet I feel that I shouldn't care if I never saw the perverted place again, were it not for the memory of four or five adorable occasions—charming chances—enjoyed by the bounty of the Filippis.[8] For that really quite prodigious pair arrived from Paris in due course, *par monts & vaux*, by strange passes and détours, by Venice & Macerata & heaven knows what else beside, & I saw again a good deal of them —with interest, &, as regards the handsome blowsy Caroline, with a good deal of a certain dim compassion. She is happy, but has after all married a little demonic *positif* Piedmontese bourgeois—she who is of a large & free & easy transalpine & even transatlantic tradition. It tells in all sorts of ways, as one sees them more—& they are in short decid- edly interesting, & he all that you saw him in Paris, & she considerably more; but my point is that they carried me in their wondrous car (he drove it himself all the way from Paris via Macerata, & with 4 or 5 more picked-up inmates!) first to 2 or 3 adorable Roman excursions[9]— to Fiumincino [*sic*], e.g., where we crossed the Tiber on a mediaeval raft & then had tea—out of a Piccadilly tea-basket—on the cool seas and, & for a divine day to Subiaco, the unutterable, where I had never been; & then, second, down to Naples (where we spent 2 days) & back; going by the mountains (the valleys really) & Monte Cassino, & returning by the sea—i.e. by Gaeta, Terracina, the Pontine Marshes & the Castelli —quite an ineffable experience. This brought home to me with an in- timacy & a penetration unprecedented how imcomparably the old *co- quine* of an Italy is the most beautiful country in the world—of a beauty (& an interest & complexity of beauty) so far beyond any other that none other is worth talking about. The day we came down from Posi- lippo in the early June morning (getting out of Naples & roundabout by that end—the road from Capua on, coming, is *archi*-damnable) is a memory of splendour & style & heroic elegance I never shall lose—& never shall renew! No—you will come in for it & Cook will picture it up, bless him, repeatedly—but I have drunk & turned the glass upside down—or rather I have placed it under my heel & smashed it—& the Gipsy Life *with* it!—for ever. (Apropos of smashes, 2 or 3 days after we had passed the level crossing of Caianello, near Caserta, *seven* Neapoli- tan "smarts" were *all* killed dead—& this by no coming of the train, but simply by furious reckless driving & a deviation, a *slip*, that dashed them against a rock & made an instant end. The Italian driving is *crap- ulous*, & the roads mostly not good enough.) But I mustn't expatiate. I wish I were younger. But for that matter the "State Line" wd. do me well enough this evening—for it's again the stroke of midnight. If it weren't I would tell you more. Yes, I wish I were to be seated with you tomorrow—catching the breeze-borne "burr" from under Cook's fine nose! How is Gross,[10] dear woman, & how are Mitou & Nicette[11]— whom I missed so at Monte-Cassino? I spent 4 days—out from Florence—at Ned Boit's[12] wondrous—really quite divine—"eyrie" of Cernitoio, over against Vallombrosa, a dream of Tuscan loveliness & a really adorable séjour, along with poor dear Howard S[turgis] & Mildred Seymour & the Babe,[13] & 5 or 6 other waifs & strays—without counting the quite charming daughters. Howard has found a harbour of refuge there for the summer, & a much needed—for he is literally in pieces, as far as "character" goes, & I don't see his future at all. It's the strangest disintegration of a total of which so many of the pieces are so good—& produced by no cause, by no shocks, reverses, convulsions, vices, accidents; produced only by charming virtues, remarkable health & the exercise of a *cossue* hospitality. It's all irritatingly gratuitous & trivially tragic. The Babe rallies really excellently—all his friends rally. Sans ça—! But même avec ça, as I say, it seems to me an end! I spent at the last 2 divine weeks in Venice—at the Barbaro. I don't care, frankly, if I never see the vulgarized Rome or Florence again, but Venice never seemed to me more loveable—though the vaporetto rages. They keep their cars at Mestre! & I am devotedly yours both

Henry James

P.S.   Saluti affettuosissimi, please, to Walter Berry!

1. HJ's initial use of this familiar salutation; he would continue to use it.

2. Robert Marie Aymeric Eugène, Vicomte d'Humières (1868–1915), French poet and translator who aided Marcel Proust in translating John Ruskin, was a neighbor of EW's in Paris. He was killed in action in France. HJ's description, below, of the countess echoes his description of Mrs. Brookenham in *The Awkward Age* (1899).

3. See letter of 17 November 1906; HJ had left Paris on 11 May to spend three weeks in Italy. He regained Rye on 6 July 1907.

4. Jacques (b. 1874), son of Jean Baptiste Élie Adrien Roger, Marquis de Dampierre (1813–1894), author of *La Saintonge et les seigneurs de Plassac: le duc d'Épernon: 1554–1642* (Paris, 1888).

5. Such a letter apparently no longer exists.

6. The manuscript clearly has "P." HJ was likely thinking of his dual sobriquet of Minnie-Paul.

7. Tourists, especially the Americans.

8. Filippo de Filippi (1869–1938), Italian Alpinist, and his American wife Caroline; see letter of 7 March 1908.

9. HJ published his account of this trip, "A Few Other Roman Neighbour-

hoods," as one of the "passages that speak for a later ... vision of the places and scenes in question," in *Italian Hours* (1909).

10. Catharine Gross (1853–1933), EW's Alsatian housekeeper and companion.

11. EW's Pekingese dogs.

12. Edward Darley Boit (1840–1915), American painter and friend of HJ since the 1870s.

13. Mildred Seymour, daughter of Sturgis's sister, May, by her marriage to Colonel Hamilton Seymour; William Haynes Smith, Sturgis's young companion, a cousin and fellow Etonian, was known among the Qu'Acre circle as "the Babe."

bonne grâce: graciousness; *à ... paraît:* as it appears; *lambris:* wainscoting; *avertis:* informed; *accueillante:* cordial; *par ... vaux:* by hill and dale; *coquine:* rascal, rogue; *cossue:* comfortable; *Sans ça ... ça:* Without that ... even with that; *Saluti affettuosissimi:* Most affectionate greetings

Lamb House, Rye
30 August 1907

My dear Edith.

Just a word to ask you if the assertion conveyed in the enclosed *is* authentic, & not a vain imagination of the editor?[1] I only want a hint from you to the effect that he *did* gouge out of you some allusive preference for *my* ancient hand—I only want this (it will make me feel not only more inspired, but more comfortable), to proceed to my little *étude*—to bound to it as if indeed I had Cook at the helm. On that little word in short I shall be able, I think, to "picture you up" as not even he could do. And the attempt will greatly charm me. (*Me*, I say—me; I speak not of others.)

Yet forgive me so freely breaking into a house of mourning. I received the faire-part of ces messieurs & ces dames on the subject of the late venerable & lamented Jules[2] only a day or two after I had—& at some length—written you—whereby I rather hung back from a fresh effusion. But won't you kindly represent me *auprès de ces dames* especially. Nicette's sense of bereavement must lend her deportment an inimitable shade, but for Mitou I fear the morbid—the morbid being so his danger. Combat it by every art that your psychological *maîtrise* may suggest. But ce cher grand Jules—I'm sure he passed away in the grand style. Fullerton[3] goes to the U.S. for a few weeks, & I am writing him to let you know where he is. Your tout-dévoué

Henry James

1. HJ enclosed a letter from the editor of a socialist journal claiming that EW wished an article of praise from HJ on her new novel, *The Fruit of the Tree.* He was doubtful about the matter; EW denied the request. HJ did not write the article but would later embody the whole episode in "The Velvet Glove." See Edel, *The Master,* 352–59; Adeline Tintner, "James's Mock Epic: 'The Velvet Glove,' Edith Wharton, and Other Late Tales," *Modern Fiction Studies* 17 (Winter 1971–1972), 483–99. See also letters of 4 October 1907, 24 November 1907, and 9 May 1909.

2. Jules, Nicette, and Mitou were EW's dogs.

3. The American William Morton Fullerton (1865–1952), Paris correspondent of the London *Times,* friend of HJ's. In October 1907 Fullerton visited his family in Brockton, Massachusetts; he also followed HJ's urging and called on EW at The Mount, in Lenox (see letter of 24 November 1907). Within a few months he became EW's lover.

faire-part: notification; *auprès . . . dames:* unto those ladies; *maîtrise:* mastery; *tout-dévoué:* fully devoted

Lamb House, Rye
4 October 1907

My dear Edith.

All thanks for your luminous reply to my question about the "personality" paper[1]—that reply being quite what I expected.

As the matter stands, however, the seed having been dropped, by however crooked a *geste,* into my mind, I am conscious of a lively & spontaneous disposition to really dedicate a few lucid remarks to the mystery of your genius, & I am writing today to the inquirer whose letter I sent you that if he can explain his so highly imaginative statement about your expressed wish (really, evidently, a barefaced, & as I judge, common trick of the trade), I will send him 3000 words; waiting however for the appearance of *The Fruit of the Tree*[2] to do so. I trust their appearing in his organ—which I have had an opportunity of asking about (to learn that it's recognised)—won't displease you. The organs all seem to me much of a muchness. So I shall sharpen my pen. (I lost the sequences of the F. of the T. while abroad those 4 or 5 months—it was inevitable—& then decided to *wait*. And I am intensely waiting. It has been cruel.)

I am immensely thrilled by your news of your prospective repatriation *là-bas*. It affects me as a most majestic manoeuvre—displaying in fact an almost insolent *maîtrise* of life. But your silver-sounding toot that invites me to the Car—the wondrous cushioned *general* Car of your so wondrously india-rubber-tyred & deep-cushioned fortune—echoes for me but too mockingly in the dim, if snug, cave of my permanent *retraite*. I have before me an absolute year of inspired immobility—I am in short on the shelf. But, ah, how from the shelf I shall watch you on the Aubusson carpet![3] Dear old Aubusson carpet—what a more & more complex minuet will it see danced, with the rich Oriental note of Rosa[4] flashing through (doubtlessly more closely still) & binding & linking the figures! What sequels you will see to what beginnings, & into what deeper depths of what abysses will you find yourselves interested to gaze! It's all really a mighty thought & I yearn, unspeakably, over you both, but perhaps *most* unspeakably (tell him with my love) over Teddy. But goodnight. I have lately been motoring a goodish deal (in a small way—only over the so rich & charming Kentish country), with some friends—old London ones who have a wondrous Renaud [*sic*] that has the belly of an elephant & yet takes the steep hills like a swallow—& who have had for the summer Laureate Lodge, the Garden that you (are supposed to) Love. Parlez-moi de ça—tant que vous voudrez: these mild domestic pleasures. Also I spent 5 adorable days at John Cadwalader's[5] grouse-moor with Mary C. J[ones] & Beatrix & in exquisite weather—an unforgettable experience. (As M. Arnold said of the theatre: "Organize *Scotland*—Scotland is irresistible." It has so—in its own so different way—the intense classicism of Italy.) A charming melancholy word from Walter B[erry] has just come to me out of the Mount & I am writing to thank him. (Ah do indeed work *him* into the minuet —if only for the sake of my need of his news of it!) I am trying to get at Gaillard T.[6] even now—for the love of *his* actual news. I wish you Fullerton rather more than I believe in his playing up: he's so incalculable. Not so your plain unvarnished & devoted

Henry James

P.S.   Ah *do* some time tell me what you mean by Cook's[7] having become as one of the foolish! It's a shock unspeakable—that my idol has feet of clay??

1. See letter of 30 August 1907.

2. EW's novel began serialization in *Scribner's Magazine* January 1907 and was published in October 1907 by Scribners. It was not a success.

3. The drawing room of the apartment at 58, rue de Varenne featured a magnificent crimson Aubusson carpet which bulked large in HJ's jocular eye.

4. The widowed Comtesse Robert de Fitz-James (née Rosalie de Gutmann), descendant of Austrian-Jewish bankers, was a friend of the Bourgets and a member of EW's society in the Faubourg Saint-Germain.

5. Princeton graduate Cadwalader was a successful New York lawyer, and cousin of Mary Cadwalader Jones, who served as his hostess and factotum at Millden, Forfarshire, Scotland, which he annually rented from Lord Dalhousie during August and September for the shooting. See *Letters* 4, 465.

6. Gaillard (pronounced and sometimes spelled "Gilliard") Thomas Lapsley (1871–1949), American graduate of Harvard, taught at California until 1904, when he was elected a fellow and lecturer of Trinity College, Cambridge. He enjoyed an international reputation for his work in medieval constitutional history.

7. EW's chauffeur.

là-bas: over there; *maîtrise:* mastery; *Parlez-moi . . . voudrez:* Tell me about that —as much as you like

Adelphi Hotel
Liverpool
24 November 1907

My dear Edith.

Forgive this uncanny whereabouts & this paper so tainted with the same. A woeful office of friendship has dragged me hither to meet poor Lawrence Godkin,[1] arriving from New York, & proceed with him to the melancholy (& really arduous) interment of dear little lately-extinct (as you probably know) Katherine G. in the extremely out-of-the-way Northamptonshire churchyard where her husband lies—a bleak drive of 2 hours, tomorrow, from Market Harborough—to which we have 1st to get, across country, from here. They are all such old & valued friends of mine that I have found myself involved in their lives & in their deaths; but at least during this grey Sunday in this grim place I may seek the detachment of writing you these few lines too long delayed. I haven't yet thanked you for the copy of The Fruit of the Tree (admirable work!) nor told you—since indeed this has but just become apparent—that I shall probably *not* find myself at all well-advised to do that paper on your Personality for the mendacious Markeley of the "International Press Service,"[2] or whatever he calls it, whose letter of application I confided to you. He wrote me such a very lame & unattenuated explanation of his preposterous statement that you had "expressed a wish" &c, that I felt I must cause enquiries to be made about him & his mysterious periodical—as I was able to do; & these have eventuated in nothing reassuring. I don't feel that I can "enthuse" over you in a hole-&-corner publication—it doesn't seem to me the proper place for either of us. Yet—apart from this—I am embarrassed, as I am in no intimate relation at present with either the Atlantic or the N[orth] A[merican] R[eview], which latter has behaved very rudely & in fact offensively to me over the whole progress of my American papers. If Scribner had for *deux sous* of inspiration (left over from that it employs in getting you to write in it) *it* would invite me to wrestle with your Personality in the bright arena of its pages; but I am not, for particular reasons, by way of *offering* anything to ces messieurs at all. "Only," I *want* to enthuse over you, I yearn to, quite—but I must wait for the right & bright & honourable occasion for so doing. Ne craignez rien—so to speak (as if you cared!) I say to myself at least that the thing won't lose or spoil by keeping or waiting. I have read *The Fruit* meanwhile with acute appreciation—the liveliest admiration & sympathy. I find it a thing of the highest & finest ability & lucidity & of a great deal of (though not perhaps of a completely) superior art. Where my qualifications would come in would be as to the terrible question of the composition & conduct of the thing[3]—as to which you will think I'm always boring. About this side I think there are certain things to say—but as against it the whole book intensely held & charmed me, & Dieu sait si je suis (in my blighted age) a *difficult* reader (of "new fiction"). The element of good writing in it is enormous—I perpetually catch you at writing admirably (though I do think here, somehow, of George Eliotizing a little more frankly than ever yet; I mean a little more *directly* & avowedly. However, I don't "mind" that—I like it; & you do things which are not in dear old Mary Ann's[4] chords at all.) However, there are many more things to say than I can go into now—& I only attempt to note that you have to my mind produced a remarkably rich & accomplished & distinguished book—of more *kinds* of interest than anyone now going can pretend to achieve.

Fullerton was with me on his way home for just one night—from 6.30 one p.m. to 9.30 the next a.m.—& the only visit he has paid me in all these years. But he brought me indeed brave messages from you, & the beautiful Terrace photograph (elegant entirely, & stirring within me a perfect pang of memory!) together with the charming news of your final installation in the Revue de Paris[5]—in which I immensely rejoice for everyone concerned. Allons, I shall have a letter awaiting you about Dec. 12th rue de Varenne,[6] but it won't, alas, tell you that I shall be able to come to you again this year. That, painful to relate, is really de toute impossibilité—an all insurmountably impracticable thing! Forgive this horrid little crudity of statement. The truth is I shall never, never, never, cross the Channel again—but live & die henceforth a more & more encroûté Briton & your & Teddy's none the less tender'y affectionate

Henry James

1. The lawyer son of Edwin Lawrence Godkin (1831–1902), founder of *The Nation* and editor of the *New York Evening Post*, who published HJ in *The Nation*

from its beginning in July 1865 and remained his lifelong friend. Lawrence's widowed mother, Katherine, would be buried in the churchyard at Hazelbeach. See *Letters* 4, 472.

2. See letters of 30 August 1907 and 4 October 1907.

3. HJ expressed the same reservations two weeks later to Mary Cadwalder Jones: "I have read the book myself with great admiration for the way much of it is done—there is great talent all along. But it is of a strangely infirm composition and construction—as if she hadn't taken thought for that, & two or three sane persons here who have read my copy find it 'disappointing' after the H. of M. That is not my sense—I find it superior—& I think the admirers of the 'House' will stultify themselves if they don't at least equally back it up." (8 December 1907)

4. George Eliot was the pen name of English novelist Mary Ann Evans (1819–1880), later Mrs. John W. Cross, who was much admired by HJ and EW.

5. Serialization of Charles Du Bos's translation of *The House of Mirth*, a project in which W. M. Fullerton had played a helpful role.

6. See letter of 13 December 1907. Fullerton evidently brought news that EW would change her sailing from New York from early January 1908 to 5 December 1907, and, after a brief stop in Normandy at her brother's, would be in Paris "about Dec. 12th."

deux sous: two cents' worth; *Ne . . . rien:* Fear nought; *Dieu . . . suis:* God knows I am; *Allons:* Well then; *de . . . impossibilité:* quite impossible; *encroûté:* crusty

Lamb House, Rye
13 December 1907

My dear Edith & my dear Edward.

This is a mere fond vague helpless but irrepressible *geste* that I make you as you set foot on the dear old Crimson Carpet—even at the cost of seeming wantonly to remind you that *my* feet are no more to know that softness. It's a shy pale flower cast upon your path—which I hope (& feel sure) will this winter be smothered in far other sweets. You must have had a devil of a voyage[1]—I've thought of you daily, with a perpetual pang, believing even you'll have asked yourselves in great lurches why you do these things. Well, you'll do them more splendidly than ever after you've got washed, rested & fed. And of course one of those you'll do best will be, in the teaming spring, to come to England,[2] where I very, very quietly await you. Meanwhile I pray for you hard— for I feel that after all, you'll need it & am your affectionate old super- stitious islander

Henry James

P.S.   All thanks, dear Edith, for the first instalment of Charley![3] What a difficult job he has had—& comme il s'en tire!

   1. Weather on both sides of the Atlantic was severe—cold and snowy. After a week at 3, Place des États-Unis, the Whartons moved into 58, rue de Varenne—and onto the crimson Aubusson—on Christmas Eve.
   2. HJ would be in France in the spring.
   3. The beginning of Charles Du Bos's translation of *The House of Mirth* in the *Revue de Paris*.

comme . . . tire: how he succeeds

Lamb House, Rye
16 December 1907

My dear Edith.
   It is horridly painful for me to have to write you these things in return for the beautiful *bonne grâce* of your letter—& I have let a post go for the very misery of doing it. I can't leave home at present—it is *impos-sible*.[1] That ugly word says all, & I won't break it into deplorable detail. There I *am*—I can't attenuate it. Please take it from me in all patience & charity, & ask Teddy to do the same—"with all the greetings of the Season." After this it will seem to you mockery that I rejoice in your arrival effected, your journey over, your fatigues survived, your Paris at your feet. Yet I *do* these things, with a high & affectionate sense of comfort for you, & I think ever so tenderly of your glorious scene. Mine has insistently to be other—but may yours surround you all splen-

didly & à perte de vue! I shall presently write you less awkwardly & less ruefully; this is a mere dreadful little blushing *geste* from your poor hindered but devoted old friend

Henry James

1. HJ was extremely busy, not only with continued preparation of the New York Edition but with dramatization of two of his tales—"Covering End" (1898), which was originally the one-act play *Summersoft* written for Ellen Terry in 1895 but never produced, and "Owen Wingrave" (1892). See the following five letters, especially that of 7 March 1908.

bonne grâce: graciousness; *à . . . vue:* as far as the eye can reach

2
Confidences

THE HEART HAS ITS REASONS, 1908–1909

THE FIRST VOLUMES of the New York Edition had begun to appear and James's hopes for his career were buoyed up. It also looked as though his fond yearnings for success as a dramatist were about to be satisfied in 1908: he worked on the three-act *High Bid* and the one-act *Saloon* and began on the three-act *Outcry*. Wharton was also busy with her writing. Short stories "The Verdict," "The Pretext," and "The Choice" were published in 1908 as was her collection of travel pieces *A Motor Flight Through France*; and she had picked up again what she called her "sadly neglected great American Novel"—*The Custom of the Country*. Her social life flourished as well, especially in the attractive salon of the Comtesse Rosa de Fitz-James. Henry James shared in that life a little when he visited Wharton in the spring and found the countess to be delightful. He contributed in his turn to Wharton's entry into Edwardian society during Wharton's visits to England in the autumn of that year and again in the summer of 1909—e.g., Lady St. Helier's town house in Portland Place, Lord and Lady Elcho's country house Stanway in the Cotswolds, the Astors' Cliveden on the Thames.

Relations between Edith and Teddy Wharton were becoming strained and their marriage a series of estrangements and brief reconciliations. The friendship between Edith Wharton and Morton Fullerton was blooming, as James was pleased to observe when he visited Paris in April 1908, but he was unaware that they had become actual lovers by that time. She was careful to "protect" him from the knowledge: a letter to Fullerton planning an evening at Versailles cautions, "ne le dites pas à H.J."—don't tell Henry. Yet by that autumn she had unburdened herself by the double confession that marriage to Teddy was growing unsupportable and that she had accepted Fullerton as her lover. James immediately extended his full sympathy and emotional support to her in her affairs of the heart. June of 1909 drew him more intimately into the liaison as he joined the lovers for dinner at the Charing Cross Hotel on the occasion of their important tryst, which is commemorated in Wharton's moving poem "Terminus." Later that summer the three toured southern England and among them concocted a plan to free Fullerton from the clutches of a blackmailing former mistress of his.

James had been suffering from heart trouble of a different sort, and during 1909 visited the cardiac specialist Sir James Mackenzie twice and the local practitioner in Rye on several occasions. Before the end of the year his condition suffered additional aggravation from the second annual report of royalties on the New York Edition, which confirmed that of 1908: earnings were embarrassingly meager. He went down to Rye in October, depressed and pessimistic, and emptied drawers and files of his private papers—the fruit of decades of rich correspondence among them—and created a huge bonfire of the accumulated treasure. Hopes that had been so high barely two years before were sadly dashed.

Further trials lay ahead for both him and Edith Wharton.

> Lamb House, Rye
> 2 January 1908

My dear Edith.

G. T. Lapsley has gone to bed—he has been seeing the New Year in with me (generously giving a couple of days to it), & I snatch this hour from out the blizzard of Xmas & Year's End & Year's Beginning missives, to tell you too belatedly how touched I have been with your charming little Xmas memento—an exquisite & interesting piece for which I have found a very effective position on the little old oak-wainscotted wall of my very own room. There it will hang as a fond reminder of tout ce que je vous dois. (I am trying to learn to make use of an accursed "fountain" pen—but it's a vain struggle, it beats me &

I recur to this familiar & well-worn old unimproved utensil.) I have passed here a very solitary & *casanier* Christmas-tide (of wondrous still & frosty days, & nights of huge silver stars), & yesterday finished a job[1] of the last urgency for which this intense concentration had been all vitally indispensable. I got the conditions, here at home thus, in perfection—I put my job through, & now—or in time—it *may* have, on my scant fortunes, a far-reaching effect. If it does have, you'll be the first all generously to congratulate me, & to understand why, under the stress of it, I couldn't indeed break my little started spell of application by a frolic absence from my field of action. If it, on the contrary, fails of that influence I offer my breast to the acutest of your silver arrows; though the beautiful charity with which you have drawn from your critical quiver nothing more fatally-feathered than that dear little framed & glazed, squared & gilded *étrenne* serves for me as a kind of omen of my going unscathed to the end. Gilliard has come down from Trinity, very handsomely, to spend, as I say, these three nights, looking a bit wasted & overworked, & saying—(confessing, alas), that he's not well; yet less *accablé* than when I last saw him, & visibly better, I fondly fancy, than when he got here Tuesday evening. I feel sure he would have something gentil for me to send you if he were at my elbow, but I'm alone with the lamp, the fire & the sleeping stillness of this huddled little hilltop, & he deep, I hope, in restorative slumbers. He has spoken to me ever so charmingly of the felicity of his stay with you at the Mount last summer; that nothing sweeter or more sympathetic could be imagined, & was wondrously vivid, droll & discriminating today at dinner about Lily Norton,[2] Lily's *fagotage*, Lily's red nose, Lily's everything of that sort, but Lily's social serenity quand même, her "character" & fine ease about herself—which I've always thought remarkable, & rather of the "great" tradition. I admit that it's horrible that we can't—nous autres—talk more face to face of these & other phenomena; but life is terrible, tragic, perverse & abysmal—besides, *patientons*. I can't pretend to speak of the phenomena that are now renewing themselves round you;[3] for *there* is the eternal penalty of my having shared your cup last year—that I must *taste* the liquor or go without—there can be no question of my otherwise handling the cup. Ah I'm conscious enough, I assure you, of going without, & of all the rich arrears that will never—for me—be made up—! But I hope for yourselves a thoroughly good & full experience—about the possibilities of which, as I see them, there is, alas, all too much to say. Let me therefore but wonder & wish!—And only tell me *this*. The Scribners send me 2 vols. of my Revised Works (the 1st published), & tell me of a few others—other copies—to be held, throughout, at my disposition. I want you to receive the *whole* awful series (23 vols.)[4] in their gradual order as they appear; but to this end you will kindly let me know by as brief a word as may be, if by any chance *they*, the said Scribners themselves, are sending you the vols. of their own munificent movement—since I don't want you to be burdened, in your travelling trim, with duplicates. I hope heartily not, for, this being so, I will then immediately instruct them as to how to dispose, throughout, of *one* copy of my allowance of each successive book. In fact, I will, on second thoughts, do that immediately—without your troubling to say anything about the matter. (The books must be —these 2 first issued: *Roderick H.* & *The American*—only within a day or two out *là-bas*.) But it's long past midnight, & I am yours & Teddy's ever so affectionate

Henry James

1. That is, turning his tale "Covering End," which had been the one-act *Summersoft* (see letter of 16 December 1907), into the three-act play *The High Bid* for Johnston Forbes-Robertson (1853–1937), the English actor-manager, to feature Forbes-Robertson's wife, the American actress Gertrude Elliott. See letter of 23 March 1908.

2. Elizabeth "Lily" Gaskell Norton, daughter of Charles Eliot Norton.

3. One of the "phenomena" was the severe decline in Teddy's health soon after their arrival in Paris; another was writing to a potential deadline: she was working on essays on Walt Whitman and Anna de Noailles. In addition, there was her emotional involvement with Fullerton, not yet divulged to HJ.

4. On the number of volumes, see Edel, *The Master*, 321–39, and also Michael Anesko, *"Friction with the Market": Henry James and the Profession of Authorship* (New York and London: Oxford, 1986), 143–62. By the time of publication it had swelled to twenty-four volumes.

tout . . . dois: all that I owe you; *casanier:* homebody; *étrenne:* New Year's gift; *accablé:* worn down; *gentil:* nice; *fagotage:* dowdiness; *quand même:* even so; *nous autres:* the rest of us; *patientons:* let's be patient; *là-bas:* over there

Lamb House, Rye
7 January 1908

My dear Edith.

Je vous la donne, je vous la donne indeed, our *petite donnée*,[1] which I perfectly remember every word of our talk about, & which I applaud to the echo the fructification of in your rich intelligence! Sharp & vivid come back to me the crown & consummation we formulated (for the original limited anecdote); the *voyage d'enquête* of the Englishwoman relative or reporter, & the remarkable—the *startling* (they must *startle* her!) constatations she was to be led to on the spot. I think it as beautiful & *âpre* (as Bourget wd. say of your faculty for it!) a little ironic subject as ever—&, no, I *don't* feel, on interrogating myself, that there is any objection that *counts* to your using it. My sense of the whole matter is a little *coloured* to-day, no doubt, by the fact that oddly enough I am more or less surrounded (as it were) by the English actors in the affair: that is the Sydney Waterlows, Jack Pollock's brother-in-law & sister[2] have taken a house here for the winter, & Jack himself, who is most charming & sympathetic, comes down sometimes to see them—& is even soon to spend a Sunday with *me*. (I meet, at rare intervals, Gladys Holman Hunt[3] in town—the said Jack's massive Ariadne; but *her* side of the drama is less present to me.) My own impression that the "impossibility" of "Mrs. Professor Toy" (*textual*) has been in no quarter (not even by the Youth!) fully *realized*, & that the postulate of the "pretext" hasn't therefore been brought home, affords a sufficient *cover* or protection: which is still further afforded moreover by the fact that your "free hand" rests on your complete personal ignorance of every one concerned—in the midst of which you have picked-up, & been struck by, that anecdote as you'd have picked up, & been taken by, any other. It's *inevitable* of course the Youth shld. be English—& it doesn't matter! I give you all *my* "rights" in it (all *honestly* come by—not a word of authentic light from anyone, & wish you a happy issue! Art is long & everything else is accidental & unimportant.) Only give false scents all you can & *appuyez* on the English relative, who doesn't exist in the original. She might be Mary Cadwalader's acquaintance Miss Warrender (if you've seen the latter).—Ah, how I *understand* the necessity for you of a Fellow-critic! yours & Teddy's; just as I think of the wealth of your renewed material for criticism; think all ruefully & wistfully & till my mouth waters! What a pity Life is so damnably complicated! My job just finished isn't—no, the great American novel, nor anything like it, but a very different matter & meaning, for the *present* consequences of it, not more freedom, but more immediate servitude. The eventual on the other hand wd.—may—immensely promote a larger liberty. I must wait to see. Forgive my speaking in enigmas—light will dawn. I *don't* despair of coming over to you for 15 days later on (steel-plated against mondanités). It's horrible even now not to know the Minnie-Paul, the "Charley,"[4] the d'Humières & the *Fullerton-d'Hervieu* last words &c— but je me contiens: resign myself even not to knowing if you went to the Donnay reception. Rosa [de Fitz-James], I trust, really plays up— not, I mean, in special deeds, but in *character*, candour & fidelity. I seem to *feel* she does. But even this pale immersion demoralizes yours, both, all *too* exposed, ever & always

Henry James

1. The donnée led to EW's "The Pretext," *Scribner's Magazine*, August 1908, reprinted in *The Hermit and the Wild Woman* (1908).

2. Sydney Philip Perigal Waterlow (1878–1944), Cambridge contemporary of Leonard Woolf and the Bloomsbury group, later ambassador to Greece, married Alice Pollock, daughter of Sir Frederick Pollock (1845–1937), Corpus Christi Professor of Jurisprudence at Oxford, and sister to Jack Pollock, devotee of the theater. HJ saw Waterlow often in Rye, even after his divorce from Alice (1912) and marriage to Helen Margery Eckhard (1883–1973) in 1913.

3. Gladys Holman Hunt, daughter of the Pre-Raphaelite painter William Holman Hunt (1827–1910) and his second wife, Marion Edith Waugh. Gladys stood six feet one "in her stockings"—hence "massive"; from what labyrinth she rescued Pollock is unclear—perhaps she played Margaret Ransom to Pollock's Guy Davenish, but the role of Gwen Matcher remains unknown (see EW's "The Pretext"). Unless, as the subsequent sentence might seem to suggest, the labyrinth was Jack Pollock's involvement with Mrs. Toy (whom he knew in Cambridge, Massachusetts; see letter of 16 January 1905), whence Gladys Holman Hunt as actual *pretext* extricated him; and EW's story reversed the items in the donnée—which would account for the significance of HJ's subsequent reference to a "free hand."

4. Paul and Minnie Bourget; Charles Du Bos.

Je . . . donne: I give it to you; *voyage d'enquête:* voyage of enquiry; *âpre:* sharp; *appuyez:* lean on; *mondanités:* worldlinesses; *je . . . contiens:* I restrain myself

Lamb House, Rye
7 March 1908

My dear Edith!

I won't take up vital energy & golden moments (I feel them some-how *all* golden as they scuttle through my hour glass now!) with talk of why I am only now, after so many days, thanking you for your last beautiful & adorable letter which gave me pleasure as great as has *ever* been postally conveyed to me. *Ça ressortira*—all my sore hindrances—from what I shall tell you—besides which it strikes me as admirably, as ideally established between us that we may take for *granted* the exquisite reasons & the effective causes of things. I have had one stiff & constant reason for everything this whole blest winter: the fact that I am held (I am *still*) in the steel trap of my accursed Edition[1] with a grimness of ferocity with which I have never been held by anything; & that though I am out of the wood I feel the hot breath of pursuit & the rush of the whole *meute* at my heels; which will continue for 2 or 3 months yet—& then will be blissfully over. I cut out for myself a *colossal* task, really, in dealing with the mass of my productions as I undertook—all lucidly!—to do; & though I don't for a moment regret it the quantity & continuity of application required has been beyond what I had at all intimately measured. Hence a state of tension in which my correspon-dence, my freedom of movement, my *margin*, have gone utterly to the wall. And then there has been another matter of which I must tell you explicitly—as it has tended, or rather has very freely contributed, to make confusion worse confounded. It isn't, this, Dieu soit loué, that I have let myself in for a blooming bride (it *sounds* like that); it is only perhaps a complication even more grotesque. *But* I must really tell you first what pure joy & ravishment your letter gave me—in the matter especially of its so liberal & so lovely words over the P. of a L. Preface[2] & that style of thing. My effusions & lucubrations always affect me as giving forth into such a soundless void, from which no repercussion as of the stone dropped into the deep well ever comes back to my ear (& the Edition & the Prefaces & everything else about it form no apparent exception) that the hint of recording intelligence anywhere brings tears to my eyes, & that under the influence of that virtue in you so hand- somely manifested I blubbered, as I may say, long & loud. It wouldn't take much more to make me begin again! But I *won't* begin again—for I need all my presence of mind, so to speak, to put before you coher- ently that my possibility of getting over to you for a few days this month has utterly perished. Ecoutez donc un peu! When I wrote you at Christmastide that a particular pressure then glued me to my chair it had *this* meaning—that I was (Edition or no Edition!) working under a sudden sharp solicitation (heaven forgive me!) for the Theatre, & that I had, as a matter of life or death, to push through with my play,[3] or rather with my 2 plays (for I'm doing two),[4] the more important of which (though an object little cochonnerie even *it*, no doubt!) is to be produced, prudently & provincially, at Edinburgh on the 26th of this month, when I beg you to pray for me as hard as ever you can. (The other, a one-act thing, designed originally to be done—for self-respect, for a greater dignity of exhibition, *with* the 3-act—"in front of it"—is diverted from that function by excellent reasons, *time*-reasons & others, & is apparently to be given by the Independent Stage Society in April.) This affair inaugurated by Forbes Robertson & his wife (Gertrude El- liot) at their earnest & sympathetic instance, & as to which I have been governed by the one sordid & urgent consideration of the possibility of making some money (which I may go on "writing," & even editioniz- ing, without making)—this affair I say has made for some time endless havoc and ravage with my life & my precious time, & will make more before it has done with me. I began to hang about some time ago for rehearsals in London—to the virtue of which I feel I can so actively & intimately contribute & three weeks since, after delays & difficulties (of cast &c, though there are but 6 persons in the little 3-act horror & only three who count), they got started to the extent of a rather promising & interesting week—& then were interrupted by the going on Tour of my interpreters. I hurried back here to resume other desolated & blighted labours, but hurried back with an attack of influenza, which made *another* week's hole in my desperate margin. I am now better of that, but am pegging away here, that is putting in indispensable days, against my having to begin afresh, at Manchester, on the 16th & so rehearse hard till the said 26th at Edinburgh—whither we proceed— "we"!—on the 22d. These six or eight (or ten) will have [been] the only ones really to count. Forgive so vulgar a tale—but I am utterly brazen about it; for my base motive is all of that brassy complexion—till sicklied o'er with the reflection of another metal. I shouldn't have stirred if the F.R.s (it was an old question coming to life again) hadn't temptingly beset & bribed me; but now in for it, I shall try, for all I'm worth, to put it through. This *speculative* stage of a production (as you know for yourself, however) is at best a very trying one & a sad tension, & one is only sustained (at least I am), by the fact that I am playing for high stakes. I won't tell you for the moment *what* my rubbish *is*—it doesn't matter; in addition to which you know for yourself enough the "artistic basis" of appeal to the mob of the Anglo-Saxon theatre (though there are, truly, improving chances here now). But the small stuff, such as it is, is neat & light & lively, all pure comedy & irony &c, & yet concrete story; & is, furthermore, I believe, though I say it who shouldn't & my own poor hand only has touched it, quite consummately *expert*! I loathe the theatre, but the drama tormentingly speaks to me, & if it catches me up God only knows what it will do with me or I with it. Meantime it's as an extreme relief to my nerves that we are making this first "country" trial-trip (or series of such), for the production of the thing in London, in May, is wholly contingent on what it "does" in April in the country. And Edinburgh is pronounced, after London, the most tasteful public in the kingdom! But do have a mass or two said for my bedevilled soul. Pardon this long story & these "fastidious" items! It's all *wrong*, hideously & horribly, that we shouldn't somehow & somewhere have a week's talk (about Everything—plus Rosa—& no, not *minus* Paul);[5] but so the dreadful history of the time seems to be getting itself written. If you leave for Italy (as I seem to infer) on the 1st April you will go, ah (I won't pretend not to say!) quite beyond any possible present or even future swing (or spring) of your aged & impaired friend. The iron of that country (or rather of the conditions under which one now deals with it) entered into my soul last May & June—for all the beauty of 2 or 3 impressions opened to me by the *plantureuse* Caroline[6] (whom you'll see & finally *love*)—& the book is now closed for me & shelved. Vous y viendrez du reste. And meanwhile you and

Teddy, in the Pontine marshes & at Subiaco, will feel planturous & Carolinian & Philippic yourselves—even like Filippo yourselves. I don't quaver out any question so *naïf* as to ask if by any blessed miracle you should be sailing from a British port—since I take for granted you are using a Mediterranean.[7] But I don't say another word of any sort now—though there *are* such miserable oceans of the unsaid & the unasked & the unanswered & the unanswerable. I don't know whether I yearn most for the "yarns" of Rosa or the items of the *manière d'être* of Paul. His theatric triumph,[8] as I judge it, immensely interests me: ah, que n'y suis-je pas for 4 hours? only (just now) for that. And what you tell me of your seeing dear Fullerton,[9] whom I am really very fond of, gives me the greatest pleasure. Oh, the letter I owe *him*—! But very kindly give him my love, please. I hope Teddy returned like a giant refreshed from the refreshing Ralphs![10] There's another subject. Oh, the subjects—for this caged & starved animal. But I will whine at you, through my bars & out of the sawdust & orange-peel of my circus from Manchester, if not before. Believe in me still—bear with me & don't doubt of me proving myself yet again all tenderly yours both

Henry James

P.S. Read, read (& *roar* over) Léon Séché's 2 vols on Hortense Allart—Mme de Méritens.[11] But you of course have! What a race!

1. The New York Edition.
2. *The Portrait of a Lady*, vol. 3 and 4 of the New York Edition.
3. *The High Bid*; see letter of 2 January 1908.
4. The second play was the one-act *Saloon*, developed from "Owen Wingrave." The success of *The High Bid* was limited to five matinees beginning 18 February 1909 and preceded by Louis Tiercelin's *A Soul's Flight*. *The Saloon* opened on 17 January 1911, produced by Gertrude Kingston. See *The Complete Plays of Henry James*, ed. Edel (Philadelphia and New York: Lippincott, 1949), 549–53, 641–49.
5. Rosa de Fitz-James and Paul Bourget.
6. Caroline, Mrs. Filippo de Filippi (see letter of 11 August 1907), which accounts for the subsequent punning on the name; "plantureuse" means abundant or fertile—or "planturous," as HJ anglicizes it below.
7. The Italian voyage did not materialize; HJ's visit to France did.

8. *Un Divorce*, the dramatization of Bourget's novel of the same title (1904), had enjoyed a marked success since its debut on 25 January 1908.

9. On Thursday, 13 February, Fullerton lunched alone with EW; on Saturday they drove to Herblay to seek the home of Hortense Allart, Mme de Méritens (see HJ's postscript), author of erotic novels. HJ and EW soon adopted "Hortense" as sobriquet for EW's automobile; see letter of 11 March 1908.

10. From 12 to 21 February Teddy was on the French Riviera visiting Ralph Curtis (son of the wealthy Boston expatriate Daniel Curtis) and his wife, the former Lise Colt of Providence, in their Villa Sylvia at Beaulieu. (Cf. letter of 11 March 1908.) See EW's "The Verdict" for a fictionalized view of the Curtises.

11. Léon Séché (1848–1914), French literary scholar whose *Hortense Allart de Méritens* was published by the Société du Mercure de France in Paris in 1908. Hortense-Thérèse-Sigismonde-Sophie-Alexandrine Allart (1801–1879), French writer, beauty, and free spirit, was the mistress of Chateaubriand, Sainte-Beuve, Sir Henry Bulwer (1801–1872), and others and a friend of George Sand's from 1832; her marriage in 1843 to Napoléon-Louis-Frédéric-Corneille de Méritens lasted a scant year. (See her fictionalized autobiography *Les Enchantements de Mme Prudence de Saman L'Esbatix*, 1872.)

Ça ressortira: That will emerge; *meute:* pack; *Dieu . . . loué:* God be praised; *Ecoutez . . . peu:* Now just listen to this; *cochonnerie:* piece of trash (lit. piggery); *Vous . . . reste:* You will come to that, furthermore; *manière d'être:* lifestyle; *que . . . pas:* why can't I be there

Lamb House, Rye
11 March 1908

My dear Edith.

Most generous & beautiful your letter & above all most sustaining —for I am really pretty well "druv." I don't start for Manchester[1] till Monday next, & then spend 2 nights in London on the way; but I am infinitely pressed here, in view of that absence, *till* then. This is to say 2 or 3 things—in addition to how I thank you for all the comfort of your charity; but to say in particular that it looks, in the light of what *you* say, as if I really *may* be able to go over to you for a week, thank the Powers! I am full of sympathy for Edward's affliction[2]—what a devil

of a time he must have had! & easily embrace your remedial alterna-
tives. I will come whatever happens, but verily the latter ½ of April (if
you *are* still there then) will suit me better than the former—& this
even at the cost of missing Teddy. (By *that* [latter]³ time I shall, D.V.,
have shipped enough copy off to America to leave me a little more
margin.) Meanwhile would you very kindly write on a large postcard
the Countess Rosa's *address* (Mme de Fitzjames) which I have utterly
forgotten & cause it to be dropped in for me? She has sent me a pictorial
postcard—très gentiment—& I can send her nothing less than a book.
I seem vaguely to recall rue de Grenelle (?)—but unnumbered. Ah your
formidable City! (When I come I must come masked & muffled.) I *ache*
for all your new conclusions—& even for your old *potins*. I ache in
particular perhaps for some new formulations of the Minnie-Paul
Truths—& to know whether the new a little redeems or only aggra-
vates the old. I ache to hear about the Vaudeville play⁴—eke to see it
& know what figure it makes to your own view. His success ought to
gentil-ize him—& I daresay it has. I ache to have been—or not to have
been—at Herblay with you & Fullerton⁵—fancy there being a second
& *intenser* Nohant!⁶ Cette douce France! The wondrous flowers of personality it throws off in its wealth! No wonder it's miraculous & presumptuous & splendid & *insupportable*. I rejoice afresh—tell him please
—that you have dear Fullerton a little "on toast." And oh for Teddy's
Ralph-&-Lisa⁷ documents. No, I miss too much. But I shall miss more
unless I pause here. I shall manage it somehow. And I *should* like Rosa's
number. I shall indeed write you from Edinburgh on arrival there 22d
—& probably from Manchester! Do make Teddy feel how devotedly I
am *with* him. Yours & his all & always

Henry James

1. See letter of 7 March 1908.
2. Teddy had been suffering from depression since the turn of the year; his
malady was later diagnosed as gout. See letter of 29 March 1908.
3. HJ inserts this in parentheses above the line.
4. Paul Bourget's *Un Divorce*; see letter of 7 March 1908.
5. See letter of 7 March 1908.
6. Home of George Sand.
7. The Curtises; see letter of 7 March 1908.

très gentiment: very kindly; *potins:* gossip; *gentil-i*ʒ*e:* make nicer; *Cette . . . France:* This gentle France; *insupportable:* unbearable

Roxburghe Hotel, Edinburgh
23[i.e., 22] March 1908[1]

My dear Edith!

This is just a tremulous little line to say to you that the daily services of intercession & propitiation (to the infernal gods, those of jealousy & *guignon*) that I feel sure you have instituted for me will continue to be deeply appreciated. They have already borne fruit in the shape of a desperate (comparative) calm—in my racked breast—after much agitation—& even today (Sunday) of a feverish gaiety during the journey from Manchester, to this place, achieved an hour or two ago by special train for my whole troupe & its impedimenta—I travelling with the animals like the lion-tamer or the serpent-charmer in person & quite enjoying the caravan-quality, the bariolée Bohemian or *picaresque* note of the affair. Here we are for the last desperate throes—but the omens are good, the little play[2] pretty & pleasing & amusing & orthodox & mercenary & safe (absit omen!)—cravenly, ignobly *canny:* also, clearly, to be very decently acted indeed: little Gertrude Elliott, on whom it so infinitely hangs, showing above all a gallantry, capacity & *vaillance,* on which I had not ventured to build. She is a scrap (personally, physically) where she should be a Presence, & handicapped by a face too *small* in size to be a field for the play of expression; but allowing for this she illustrates the fact that intelligence & instinct are capables de tout—so that I still hope. And each time they worry through the little "piggery"[3] it seems to me more *firm*—more intrinsically without holes & weak spots—in itself I mean; & not other, in short, than "consummately" artful. I even quite awfully wish you & Teddy were to be here—even so far as that do I go! But wire me a word—*here*—on Thursday a.m.— & I shall be almost as much heartened up. I will send you as plain and unvarnished a one after the event as the case will lend itself to. Even as Edinburgh public isn't (I mean as we go here all by the London) determinant, of course—however, à la guerre comme à la guerre, & don't intermit the burnt-offerings. More, more, very soon—& you too will have news for yours & Edward's right recklessly even though ruefully

Henry James

Do telegraph him[4] too—

1. HJ probably misdated this: 23 March 1908 was a Monday, but the letter specifies "today (Sunday)." He would be less likely to mistake the day of the week than the date of the month; 22 March seems the correct date
2. *The High Bid.*
3. Literal translation of *cochonnerie*—"bit of trash"; see letter of 7 March 1908.
4. Evidently Teddy, who sailed for New York on 21 March 1908.

guignon: bad luck; *bariolée:* variegated; *vaillance:* valor; *à . . . guerre:* when at war, do as war requires

Reform Club, S.W.
29 March 1908

My dear Edith.

I returned yesterday from Edinburgh, & I have your excellent letter to acknowledge—which I do thus all briefly—in face of the scarce diminished pile of other correspondence which the last ten days of distraction have caused to accumulate. I wired you from the scene of action—& remained over a second evening, taking the midnight train to town afterwards (though one ends by *loathing* so one's stale mumming—even one's very own). As well as Provincialism can give the measure the little thing (it plays but from 9 to 11) is a confirmed success, or, so to speak, victory: but, written down to the level of the Lowest & Densest as it is, it is still a thing for London—& straight in London should have been produced, one now sees. It will probably go there about May 1st[1]—but there is time for that. Meanwhile I drink *in* what you tell me of your own situation & movements. I am glad, heartily, that poor Teddy is on his present way to healing waters[2]—may they indeed bring him grace; as everlasting as possible. On the loss of Rue de Varenne[3] I condole with you; but your brother's palazzino strikes me as the charmingest compensation. It must be *there*, I fear—though fear is a gross word—that I go to you for a few days; & for this reason. I absolutely can't leave home again without putting in immediately some quiet days at Lamb House—to which I now return—to make up for ever so many just now utterly blighted by recent interruptions. My awful Monster of the Edition is close at my heels & I *must* get off another reproducible volume or two to New York before I stir again: calamity & disgrace will overtake me unless I do. But I am nearing the end, thank God, & the work in question won't occupy me many days. I shall have to put in 2 or 3 here again with the accursed Dentist (encore!) a short time hence—but I shall be able to rush over on as early as possible a day in the *latter* half of April. Trust me absolutely for this—I throw myself on your patience & your pity meanwhile; & will write you again as soon as the prospect clears a little. Let me say, alas, that it is just those admirable & amiable inquiries for "Cher James" that profoundly terrify me in advance—I feel as if I couldn't in any degree face the Social Monster—so formidably irrelevant to me now. Let me come, please, utterly incognito & masked wholly in motor-goggles— removable for Rosa [de Fitz-James]—ever—tout au plus! Yours all constantly

Henry James

1. Jerome K. Jerome's *The Passing of the Third Floor Back* intervened in Forbes-Robertson's plans and proved so immensely popular that *The High Bid* had to wait until February 1909 for a London staging, which Beerbohm Tree gave it at His Majesty's Theatre. The play and the Forbes-Robertsons there enjoyed a *succès d'estime*.

2. Teddy went to Hot Springs, Arkansas, to take the waters for his gout. See letter of 11 March 1908.

3. The Whartons had to relinquish the George Vanderbilts' apartment at 58, rue de Varenne. They moved into the *hôtel particulier* of EW's brother Harry Jones, 3, Place des États-Unis, while he was in the United States.

tout au plus: at most

105 Pall Mall, S.W.
3 April 1908

My dear Edith.

I am in possession of two heavenly letters from you; & they have beguiled the impatience of a tiresome little enforced "wait over" in London—imposed upon me by the deadly Dentist just as I was starting for my industrious little home. I do start tomorrow, however—this *épreuve* is almost over, & these poor words are but a signal of renewed fidelity. A week at Lamb House will clear up for me much the question of the approximate day on which I shall be able to be with you. The idea of meeting you at Amiens steeps me in rapture & there's nothing I should enjoy more than a little *tournée*, under motor-goggles, in Normandy, of which blest land I am much more ignorant than I have ever liked to be. I've everything there to see—& oh, will you take me to the Croisset,[1] by Rouen, as a pendant to Nohant? (Ah, & to Herblay too please, shrine of the *inouïe* Hortense?)[2] (What shrines we *do* arrange for ourselves!) I rather think, however, that if I can "bilk" the absolute Easter outrush (a terrific current), from here & make for our tryst just as it is about to set backward, it will be better for me in all ways (of intimate *débarras* at home, of clearance of people, weather, season, roads, inns & everything. Normandy *at* Easter!) If you are to be at the Palazzino on into May I would stay with you there to that further extent *gladly*. But I shall be at home from tomorrow p.m. & there, after a little, much more master of the prospect. En attendant, tout à vous Madame et chère confrère

Henry James

P.S.   I rejoice you've met Wilfrid & Jane Von Glehn[3]—of both of whom I'm fond.

1. Home of novelist Gustave Flaubert (1821–1880).
2. See letter of 7 March 1908.
3. Jane Emmet (1850–1906), a cousin of HJ, married the painter Wilfred von Glehn, a friend of John Singer Sargent's. At the outbreak of World War I they changed their name to *de* Glehn.

épreuve: trial; *inouïe:* outrageous; *débarras:* riddance; *En . . . vous:* Meanwhile, all the best to you

Lamb House, Rye
13 April 1908

My dear Edith.

I am just hanging on here from day to day to tuck in more of my redundant bulging drapery—or papery!—& in truth much moved to let the horrible Easter Exodus (the worst—as being most compressed—of the year here, really) start without me, roll ahead of me—& then set forth myself when the tide is turning backward. This will bring me to *about* the 23d, & it will be my idea to stay with you then, if you can kindly keep me, & are to be till then in Paris, to May 6th or 7th. Thus I shall proceed if I hear nothing from you in any other sense. This quiet time here is *immensely* helping me—& the season is getting itself into happier trim. Very "fine" here, but too northwindy. The little play provincially flourishes much, but it seems the devil now to secure a *small* London theatre[1] for May–July. Everything is tied up, as yet, & we ought (F[orbes-] R[obertson] ought) to have played *earlier* a bolder game. We don't (*I* don't) believe enough in my "star." But soyez tranquille—it will bring me to you safe. Heaven speed the interval. Your devotissimo

Henry James

1. Terry's Theatre was available but not large enough for the sets of *The High Bid.*

soyez tranquille: rest easy; *devotissimo:* most devoted

Lamb House, Rye
16 April 1908

My dear Edith.

I quite see your beautiful point—& have in fact, in lucid anticipation of it, been on the extreme & dizzy verge of sending you a word to forestall the little worriment, for you, of having to *make* it. If you let our day be *Friday 24th* I can make it *absolutely* & delightfully definite. I will join you at Amiens[1] as early in the p.m. of that day as trains will serve—& that idea *& ce qui en suivra* is rapturous. I take it that we can *only* accept spending the night at A. & be very glad to do it. To see the

Cathedral in the late afternoon will be of the last refinement. And it will be *adorable* to have W[illiam] M[orton] F[ullerton]—kindly tell him, with my love, how immensely I feel this. I judge the week *end* favourable for him. I will inform you again exactly of my hour of approach to the Hotel—the name of which you will perhaps kindly let me have on a postcard. I haven't been there for years & wholly forget.—Very charming to see Clyde Fitch's[2] little hearsay tribute to the Plaything—which it was nice of him to have passed on to you. If he knew with what music falls upon my ear that *inouïe* expression "popular" in application to *anything* of your so ever constant but so long populated

Henry James

1. Plans changed: HJ went on to Paris alone and was met at the Gare Saints-Lazare by EW and the New York social journalist Eliot Gregory.

2. See letter of 2 April 1906.

& ce . . . suivra: and whatever will follow it; *inouïe:* unheard of

The Mount,
Lenox, Mass.
[10 October 1908][1]

Dear Henry James,

I have decided to sail on the Provence Oct. 29th for Havre, & I shall cross over directly from there to England, if it will be convenient for you to have me go to see you there for a few days.—

Yrs. afft. Edith

Oct 11th. / over

Send me a line to meet the steamer, Care of the Cie. Générale Transatlantique, Havre.[2]

1. The envelope is clearly postmarked "Oct 10/ 12 30 P/ 1908." EW probably wrote this note on 9 October and added the postscript the next day, mistakenly dating it the eleventh, before it was taken to the post.

2. See letters of 13 and 15 October 1908.

Lamb House, Rye
13 October 1908

My very dear Friend!

I cabled you an hour ago my earnest hope that you *may* see your way to sailing with Walter B[erry] on the 20th[1]—& if you *do* manage that this won't catch you before you start. Nevertheless I can't not write to you—however briefly (I mean on the chance of my letter being useless) after receiving your two last, of rapprochées dates, which have come within a very few days of each other—that of Oct. 5th only today. I am deeply distressed at the situation you describe[2] & as to which my power to suggest or enlighten now quite miserably fails me. I move in darkness; I rack my brain; I gnash my teeth; I don't pretend to understand or to imagine. And yet incredibly to you doubtless—I am still moved to say "Don't conclude!" Some light will *still* absolutely come to you—I believe—though I can't pretend to say what it conceivably may be. Anything is more credible—conceivable—than a mere inhuman *plan*. A great trouble, an infinite worry or a situation of the last anxiety or uncertainty are conceivable—though I don't see that such things, I admit, can explain *all*. Only sit tight yourself *& go through the movements of life*. That keeps up our connection with life—I mean of the immediate & apparent life; behind which, all the while, the deeper & darker and the unapparent, in which things *really* happen to us, learns, under that hygiene, to stay in its place. Let it get out of its place & it swamps the scene; besides which its place, God knows, is enough for it! Live it all through, every inch of it—out of it something valuable will come—but live it ever so quietly; &—*je maintiens mon dire*—waitingly! I have had but that one letter, of weeks ago—& there are *kinds* of news I can't ask for. All this I say to you, though what I am really hoping is that you'll be on your voyage when this reaches the Mount. If you're not you'll be so very soon afterwards, won't you?—& you'll come down & see me here & we'll talk à perte de vue, & there will be something in that for both of us—especially if we are able then in a manner to "conclude." Believe meanwhile & always in the aboundingly tender friendship—the understanding, the participation, the *princely* (though I say it who shouldn't) hospitality of spirit & soul of yours more than ever

Henry James

P.S.   I can't tell you what hearty joy I take in Walter B's beautiful appointment.[3] I delight—I revel, in it—& I infinitely desire to see him. I expect to be in London for a few days from Nov. 3d or 4th. If you can only be there then too!

H.J.

1. They sailed together from New York on 30 October (*EW Biog.*, 239); but see letter of 10 October 1908.

2. EW's double confession of the desperate disintegration of her marriage and the burgeoning affair with Morton Fullerton.

3. Berry's appointment to the International Tribunal in Egypt.

rapprochées: near; *je . . . dire:* I stick to what I have said; *à . . . vue:* till the cows come home

Lamb House, Rye
Thursday [15 October 1908]

My dear Edith.

I have your telegram & I am sorry, but would the 5th or the 7th do you any good?—by which I mean enable you to do *me* any—in the Barrie affair.[1] I shld. be able to manage *them*—but not, I fear anything else. (I think by the way you *did* say the 7th, alas, is taken. I might strain a point for the 8th—with your company for my guerdon. Voilà —& we shall at any rate meet on the 30th.) The day is lovely here— & even arrears mountain-high don't block it out as I sit, *all* the length of it, attablé. But I yearn over your adventures. Have all you can, & believe me with love to you [&] ces messieurs[2] all affectionately

Henry James

1. Sir James Matthew Barrie (1860–1937), Scottish novelist and playwright, was planning a London repertory theatrical program with the backing of the American producer Charles Frohman (1860–1915). Invited to participate, HJ prepared *The Outcry*. See letters of 21 November and 16 December 1908, and 2 March 1910.

2. "These gentlemen" are EW's dogs.

Lamb House, Rye
21 November 1908

My dear all-wondrous Edith!

I have two all-gracious notes from you & I have just written both to Barrie & to Howard [Sturgis]—to the former most rejoicingly over the invitation to the Savoy grillroom dinner antecedent to the Play on the 7th &c,[1] & to the latter not less responsively over the question of dining & sleeping at Quacre[2] on the 5th. I am entangled, however, over the 6th, the Sunday[3]—& please ask Howard to read you what I have said to him thereanent. We shall have a chance to deal with it, however—you & I—on the 30th. René Bazin[4] has written me from Paris—as to whether I shall be in London precisely on that 6th—& unfortunately I had fallen into the trap—for a reason!—before the Quacre question had come up. But *he* may fail of it! I gather from Howard that you are making as many *gestes* as possible, for which I heartily applaud & commend you, & only wish I could make more of them with you. Keep at them, keep at them, & when you've made a great, *great* many—well, you'll see! So I rejoice that circumstances make for the multiplication of them. Before such phenomena as the sending of that paper &c, I lose myself, I lose myself! *There* is a geste, *par exemple*, of a truly indescribable sort!—I am making all the diligence I can, here, these next days & all the week, in order to be able to come up on the 30th. Do keep, if possible, the *morning* of the 1st, in order to go somewhere with me where we can talk—if only to the National Gallery or the British Museum, or the New South Kensington! I shall have to return hither in the p.m. You'll have already then such lots to tell me; & *how*, all week, I shall see you gesticulating! I'm so glad you're in the dear old country where is so much pretext for that & yet so little other, or *concurrent*, practice! But *I* shall gesticulate immensely on your being again beholden of yours all constantly

Henry James

1. EW, HJ, and Sturgis were Barrie's guests at the Savoy and at the performance of his *What Every Woman Knows* featuring Gerald Du Maurier.

2. Sturgis's home at Windsor.

3. HJ had arranged to go to the Haymarket Theatre to see *The Last of De Mullins*, a new play by St. John Hankin (1869–1909).

4. French novelist (1853–1932).

Lamb House, Rye
16 December 1908

My dear Edith.

It is delightful that you can come & that Howard can[1]—as I have already more concisely signified to you, & je rêve already over your presence & hold out my now empty cup—scoured quite clean of baser matter—for whole rich & thick flowing reports of everything. It will take you at least all Sunday, I feel, to do justice to John Hugh[2]—therefore I am greatly hoping you will stay over that day. The only thing is that I fear I shan't be able to put up Gross, as my young Oxford nephew (aet. 17)[3] will then be in possession (with the 2 interposing doors barred & padlocked) of the room beside yours. *He* has not been affected (that I know of) by foreign precedent; but *you* have. I seem moreover to discern that you are probably sending Gross straight on to Dover—& we shall all be, here, at your intimate service. *I* only claim to be préposé aux paillettes—je m'y entends. Give my tender love to Howard, & please say to William [Haynes Smith], for me, that if my nephew weren't here, & the capacity of the house thus filled out, I wouldn't hear of *his* not coming. Let me live with you again over Stanway[4] & Chipping C[amden] (I know it well!) & Gloucester—I won't say how well I know *it*. I want to miss nothing, & am only troubled lest you shouldn't be able to tell me about John Hugh before my nephew. We will appoint at any rate a motor-run for the purpose, & I am all impatiently & constantly yours

Henry James

P.S. Please don't let Howard doubt of my joy in receiving him. I rejoice infinitely they can do the foreign run with you.

1. HJ anticipates a visit for Saturday, 19 December, from EW and Sturgis, and EW's staying over Sunday the twentieth.

2. John Hugh Smith (1881–1964), prosperous young English banker whom EW had just met at Stanway, would become one of her keenest admirers; see letter of 17 December 1908.

3. Alexander (Aleck) Robertson James (1891–1946), WJ's youngest son.

4. The handsome Gloucestershire home of Lord Hugo and Lady Mary Elcho; he was the son of Francis Charteris, 10th earl of Wemyss.

je rêve: I dream; *préposé . . . entends:* in charge of the spangles—I know my way around with them

Lamb House, Rye
Thursday p.m. [17 December 1908]

My dear Edith.

I just got your letter. I shall be delighted to see Gross, for whom there is ample room now[1]—& who will be installed beside you absolutely as before. I shall be delighted if you can get here by luncheon, but frankly don't expect it—& if you don't we shall [have] a most conversational tea. No nephew till 7 o'clk. Love to Howard & buonissimo viaggio!

I'm of course intensely wondering if John Hugh [Smith] a pu—ou a voulu s'oublier, thinking you—so naturally—de choix! You must tell me all! Ever,

Henry James

1. See letter of 16 December 1908.

buonissimo viaggio: have the best of voyages; *a pu . . . s'oublier:* could—or wanted to forget himself; *de choix:* of prime choice

Lamb House, Rye
11 January 1909

Dearest Edith.

Your word of today (Mon) gives me a world of satisfaction. I feel a good deal like dear old "Sainte-Beuve"[1] (in the 'thirties or whenever) between interesting Her & interesting Him[2]—yet with a highly appreciative sense of having still finer material to deal with. Immensely relieved & fortified am I at any rate that what I felt from far back—viz: that the darkest enigma would get light if you could only travel on to the possibility of a *talk* has justified that constant conviction. I couldn't put it to you more definitely, for I hadn't the right, & I was indeed myself not a little puzzled & at a loss; but *en somme* I was sure—& couldn't accept at all the possibility of a non-clearance—from the moment a *meeting* remained possible or could again become so. But this I had very much—like a tactful old Sainte-Beuve—to keep to myself. (I doubt if he would in fact at all have equalled me.)—Of course I hadn't expected you would now *tell* me anything beyond your simple allusion to Morton's hell of a summer; & my question for myself has only been as to what may have been going on since. I knew everything up to last May or June—but have practically not heard from him since then—any more than you had, for the greater part; & I most intensely wish he could make it possible to get over to me here for three days during these next weeks. The thought of the tune to which he must want a holiday is heart-breaking to me—& a poor enough snippet of one would that be; but it would be something, & I am presently writing to him in that sense, & on, I fear, the bare chance. Glad as I am that we "care" for him, you & I; for verily I think I do as much as you, & that you do as much as I. We can help him—we even can't *not*. And it will immensely pay.—I thank you most kindly for Bourget's play.[3] I am intensely occupied & haven't had much of a go at *it*—but it strikes me as a bit heavy & not void of original sin (by which I mean, inevitably, of course, his particular one—in which it had its origin). What interests me I confess more is dear Howard [Sturgis]'s having given you that chance for him in Paris[4]—which must have turned out to him a big thrill & joy & treasure *so* laid up at Quacre. And how delightful for you to have had him—so genuine & special & charming a social value, & all "our own"—to produce in a society so deeply sentient of such values. I back dear little Rosie[5] not to have been au dessous the sense of him indeed. So bless you both—& all. Burgess[6] awaits my letter— ce détail will speak to you, & I am your ever so *dis*tormented & recon- soled

Henry James

1. The French critic Charles Augustin Sainte-Beuve (1804–1869).
2. HJ alludes to Sainte-Beuve's affair with the wife of Victor Hugo, but also to the situation of EW's lover, Morton Fullerton. Katharine Fullerton (1879– 1944), Morton's cousin and fiancée, in England during the summer and fall of

1908 on sabbatical leave from Bryn Mawr, was plaguing the inattentive and evasive Morton with her demands that he clarify the status of their engagement. Further demands on Fullerton were being made by the most aggressive of his former mistresses.

3. *L'Émigré*, published in November 1908.

4. Sturgis had left on 21 December with EW for France, traveled rapidly to Dijon and Avignon, then back on New Year's Eve to 58, rue de Varenne (recently restored to her) whence she proceeded to introduce him to the society of the Faubourg Saint-Germain.

5. The Comtesse Rosa de Fitz-James.

6. Burgess Noakes (1884–1975), HJ's valet.

au dessous: beneath

Lamb House, Rye
31 January 1909

My dear Edith.

It is dreadful for me to have to write you in these terms of impracticability—you to whom nothing is impracticable—but it won't be possible or *thinkable*, as it were, for me to come to you—& I've been putting off these 3 days the pain & the *laideur* of telling you so. But here at last it has to come—& *I* have not to. I can't go into explanations & reasons—they are dreary & thankless things; but it is *vital* for me not to leave home & I mustn't attempt it. You won't understand the "Vitality" of my languishing in this hole—as against what you offer; but my hole is my present condition of existence—there it is. Don't curse, & don't even miss, me; for you wouldn't find me good company at all—though I shall be better (company) when you yourselves come over after Easter, as we absolutely count on your doing. Forgive this language of violence. I have been rather worryingly unwell,[1] I am sorry to say; but am distinctly better, & shall go on. But I am not a fit visitor in any brilliant house—or shouldn't be one even in an *habitation lacustre* or otherwise primitive place of hospitality. Such is my unamiable story. And the worst is that I have nothing amusing or interesting or *émotion-*

nant, thank God, to tell you. Je ne bouge pas d'ici (I don't count a few days in London next week),[2] but the winter slips terribly away none the less, & things I had determined I shld. see done are scarce getting done at all. I am very, very sorry for Teddy's bad moments[3]—but if you're having in Paris anything like the beauty—bland, radiant—of the Season here—he will soon respond & give himself up to joy. I send him my best love & a kiss—even two—inert lump of a friend as he may be moved to pronounce me. I infinitely grieve over poor Cook's accident, which sounds most evil, & should like to send him mille voeux & devoted sympathy. It heartens me a little to think of the art & affection with which you must all be missing him. What fell things can happen in the *grande vie*! I snuggle into my hole the more abjectly as I think of them. I hope you are reading "Tonay-Bungay,"[4] [*sic*] for the immense life & "cheek" of it; but the barbarous want of art & of real doing isn't, to me, forgiveable. That periodical in fact is a poor show for English letters. I have heard a little from Morton, to my exceeding consolation; but I believe in his really coming to me here for 3 or 4 days as an incident of his American journey[5]—& I can't exhibit myself to him, & to Paris into the bargain, now. Be easy with me, dear Edith, be easy—my days are over for the *grande vie*; I should have been caught younger & must crawl very quietly at best through what remains to me of the *petite*. We shall have more of *that* together, & I shall be to the end your devotissimo

Henry James

1. Theodora Bosanquet's diary entry for 17 January 1909: "Mr. James unwell (heart trouble)"; and for 19 January 1909: "Mr. James better but still avoiding morning work." HJ wrote for advice to the famous Canadian-born physician Sir William Osler (1849–1919); Osler had treated WJ. See letters of 14 and 19 April 1909.

2. HJ went up to London for the matinee performances of *The High Bid* during the third week of February 1909.

3. Since his arrival in Paris on 18 January 1909, Teddy had continued to suffer from melancholia, which the diagnosis as gout and the "cure" at Hot Springs had not alleviated.

4. *Tono-Bungay* (1909), a novel by H. G. Wells (1866–1946).

5. HJ's hopes of this visit were disappointed.

laideur: ugliness; *habitation lacustre:* lakeside cottage; *émotionnant . . . d'ici:* moving . . . I don't budge from here; *mille voeux:* best wishes

Lamb House, Rye
14 April 1909

My dear, dear Edith.

Hideous & horrible has been my long silence, but there have been inevitabilities in *its* depths of inevitability—that have just mercilessly (mercilessly to *me*) brought it about, & that you will believe in without any étalage of them, on my part, before you—from the moment I, 1st, give you my foi d'honnête homme for them, & 2d, tell you I'm unspeakably sick of them. Fortunately I am gradually surmounting them[1]—but *all* my correspondence, now for a long time past, has utterly gone to pieces; I have had to accept the ignominy, & much of it I shall never pick up again. But I love you all the while as much as ever, & there hasn't been a day when I haven't hung about you in thought & yearned over you in spirit, & expended on you treasures of wonder & solicitude even as I have seen the hours & the days & the weeks go by. It has been so confirmed to me that I mightn't budge from here that even making you the commonest sign seemed a flying in the face of the rather grim providence quite inexorably appointed me. So I've had to live my life without any echo of yours—save the faintest & most roundabout. I have known Teddy has been much éprouvé—& imagined you thereby scarce less so—& yet my sense of these things has been compatible with my deep inaction: judge therefore how my own fate has, in its obscure & désobligeante fashion, ridden me. Believe at the same time with this that my interest & affection & tenderness haven't all the while abated one jot—& I suffer almost to anguish for the darkness in which I sit. I haven't for a long time known as little of you as these weary weeks—in fact *never* known as little probably in proportion to what there is to know. You must have been living very voluminously in one way & another—& however right it may serve me not [to] possess the detail of that I have to invoke a terrible patience—which precludes no gnashing of teeth. You *are* coming to England for the summer—& from an early date—are you not? I expect to go up to town on May 1st for some five weeks—it hasn't been possible before this for more than a few days. I beseech you to give me your news to *that* extent. But good night—this is my limit. You see how little you've lost by the suppression of *such* postal matter. I greet Teddy very very kindly & helplessly & am yours, my dear Edith, all constantly

Henry James

1. On 25 February 1909, following the recommendations of Sir William Osler, HJ visited the eminent heart specialist Sir James Mackenzie (1853–1925), who pronounced his heart quite sound for a man in his mid-sixties. See letters of 31 January and 19 April 1909.

étalage: spread; *foi . . . homme:* word as an honest man; *éprouvé:* tested; *désobligeante:* disobliging

Lamb house, Rye
19 April 1909

My dear Edith!

I thank you very kindly for your so humane & so interesting letter, even if I must thank you a little briefly—having but this afternoon got out of bed to which the Doctor three days ago consigned me—for a menace of *jaundice*, which appears however to have been, thank heaven, averted! (I once had it, & *basta così*); so that I am a little shaky & infirm. You give me a sense of endless things that I yearn to know more of, & I clutch hard the hope that you will indeed come to England in June. I *have* had—to be frank—a bad & worried & depressed & inconvenient winter—with the serpent-trail of what seemed at the time—the time you kindly offered me a princely hospitality—a tolerably ominous *cardiac* crisis—as to which I have since, however, got considerable information & reassurance—from the man in London[1] most completely master of the subject—that is of the whole mystery of heart-troubles. I am definitely better of that condition of December-January, & really believe I shall be better yet; only that particular brush of the dark wing leaves one never quite the same—& I have not, I confess (with amelioration, even), been lately very famous;[2] (which I shouldn't mention, none the less, were it not that I really believe myself, for definite reasons, & all intelligent ones, on the way to a much more complete emergence—both from the above-mentioned & from other worries). So much mainly to explain to you my singularly unsympathetic silence during a period of anxiety & discomfort on your own part[3] which I all the while feared to be not small—but which I now see, with all affectionate participation, to have been extreme. Poor dear Teddy, poor dear Teddy—so little made, by all the other indications, as one feels, for such assaults & such struggles! I hope with all my heart his respite will be long, however, & yours, with it, of such a nature as to ease you off. Sit loose & live in the day—don't borrow trouble & remember that nothing happens as we forecast it—but always with interesting &, as it were, refreshing differences. "Tired" you must be, even you, indeed, & Paris, as I look at it from here, figures to me a great blur of intense white light in which, attached to the hub of a revolving wheel, you are all whirled round by the finest silver strings. "Mazes of heat & sound" envelope you to my wincing vision—given over as I am to a craven worship (*only*, henceforth) of peace at any price. This dusky village, all deadening grey & damp (muffling) green, meets more & more my supreme appreciation of stillness—& here, in June, you must come & find me—to let me emphasize that—appreciation!—still further. You'll rest with me here then, but don't wait for that to rest somehow & somewhere en attendant. I am afraid you won't rest much in a retreat on the Place de la Concorde.[4] However, so does a poor old croaking barnyard fowl advise a golden eagle!—You are a thousand times right to allude on a note of interrogation to Morton's article[5]—& no note is sharp enough to pierce, I fully see, the apparent obscurity of my behaviour. All will be well, but there is a special explanation of—reason *for*—my having, lash myself as I would, been inevitably paralysed (that is embarrassed—up to now—fairly to anguish) over it. But that explanation I shall immediately, I shall in a day or two, make to him, if you will meanwhile lay me, all grovelling & groaning at his feet. Kindly assure him of my absolutely consistent affection & fidelity & ask him to have a very small further—a scrap of divine—patience with me. I plead—I plead; also I bleed (with—attenuated—shame). Everything shall still be right & I am, dearest Edith, all constantly & tenderly yours

Henry James

1. Sir James Mackenzie.

2. HJ has anglicized the French *"fameux"*: "not . . . lately feeling very well."

3. EW had whisked Teddy away in early February 1909 on a ten-day motor trip through southern France in an effort to distract him and relieve his melancholia—without effect. Teddy left, mid-April 1909, for the United States.

4. The lease of 58, rue de Varenne having ended, EW moved temporarily into the Hôtel de Crillon.

5. Fullerton's article "The Art of Henry James," praising the New York Edition, finally appeared in the *Quarterly Review*, April 1910.

basta così: that is enough; *en attendant:* meanwhile

Lamb House, Rye
9 May 1909

Dearest Edith!

Your letter gives me extraordinary pleasure—for my poor efforts don't meet with universal favour. Two American "high-class (heaven save the mark!) periodicals" declined poor John Berridge & the Princess[1]—which was a good deal comme qui dirait declining *you*; since bien assurément the whole thing *reeks* with you—& with Cook, & with *our* Paris (Cook's & yours & mine): so no wonder it's "really good." It wd. never have been written without you—& without "her."[2] At any rate, as I seem to be living on into evil days, your exquisite hand of reassurance & comfort scatters celestial balm—& makes me de nouveau believe a little in myself, which is what I infinitely need & yearn for. While I *do* the Velvet Gloves I quite succeed in believing—but at all subsequent stages, when they are done, everything seems to address itself to dispelling the fond illusions (one amiable friend—"lady-friend"—said to me of the V. G. just after its appearance: "I *can't* say I think it's up to your usual mark!"); so that in short, dearest Edith, you are a direct agent of the Most High for keeping alive *in the me* the vital spark. You've blown upon it so charmingly to-day that it's quite a brave little flame again. Add to that I've just lately begun to believe again that I shall "recover my health to some extent"—& that the day here is most exquisite—divine & windless for a change—& you may feel that you've done a good stroke of work. But oh how I want your news, the real, the *intime*—how I want it, how I want it! I have been intending a movement on London for some days—but many things have conspired to delay it: however I do, I believe, absolutely go up for a while on the 12th, though with such country-*douceur* breaking out all about us here I ask myself how I can think of Pall Mall. If I think too much ill I shall retreat again. At any rate I go down to Howard from Saturday to Monday next.[3] Comme vous nous manquerez—but how we shall jaw about you! I shall then perhaps hear a little when you are "due"—if the influences contribute as I infinitely supplicate the gods to make them. I mean by this if they will only leave poor dear Teddy a little in peace.—I wrote a few days ago to Morton & shall very soon be writing him again—will you kindly mention to him on the first occasion, with my love? En voilà un a little of whose news—real & intimate—I should also like! But the things, the things, the things—i.e. the details—I yearn for—! Never mind; I believe I *shall* see you a bit effectively. And meanwhile I am ever so gratefully & tenderly & revivingly yours

Henry James

1. John Berridge and Amy Evans—here "the Princess"—are in HJ's "The Velvet Glove," *English Review*, March 1909. The story involves an extended motor run through Paris; hence the allusions to Cook, EW's chauffeur. See letter of 30 August 1907.
2. EW's automobile. HJ inserted this sentence between the lines.
3. HJ stayed with Sturgis at Qu'Acre 15–17 May 1909.

comme . . . assurément: as who should say . . . most assuredly; *de nouveau:* once again; *douceur:* sweetness; *Comme . . . manquerez:* How we shall miss you; *En voilà un:* Now there's one

Queen's Acre, Windsor
16 May 1909

Dearest Edith.

Howard [Sturgis] offers to "frank" me, & I just scrawl this line to add to your "realizing sense" that we are here together in a Quacrey bliss from which you are absent, but which consists of our dragging you in a very great deal—though that process is a poor substitute for drawing you out. We are planning for a better—& not distant—time when we *shall* be able to draw you out to the very end of your reel; so much do we depend on you to have tightly wound up & tucked away for us. This moment here is lovely—though a little cold; the splendid freshness of the mighty Windsor umbrage is a spectacle apart. I have your beautiful letter of 3 days ago—& shall respond to it in a better form than this poor word at the corner of a table round which coughing & wheezing & even wailing hounds (for poor little hysteric thing now *wails*) are competing with after-luncheon Sunday scrappiness of talk to interfere with the concentration que je vous dois. May Falle (ex. Seymour) & he[1] for whom she fell are here, & with no one else but the Babe it isn't furiously folichon. But Howard is in excellent & charming form & has been apparently having of late a much less put-upon life than for a long time. We are starting on a Park walk together—en attendant Elle et Lui[2]—et vous, Madame à bientôt donc, from your tout-dévoué

Henry James

1. Howard Sturgis's sister, May, married first Colonel Hamilton Seymour and second Sir Bertram Falle.
2. HJ uses the title of George Sand's novel *Elle et Lui* (1859)—a thinly veiled fictional account of her affair with Musset—to refer to May and Bertram, but couples them with EW and, by implicit extension, Fullerton.

que . . . dois: that I owe you; *folichon:* amusing; *en . . . tout-dévoué:* while awaiting Her and Him—and you, Madame, let's see you soon, . . . all devoted

Lamb House, Rye
26 July 1909

Dearest Edith.

I could really *cry* with joy for it!—for what your note received this noon tells me:[1] so affectionate an interest I take in that gentleman. How admirable a counsellor you have been, & what a *détente*, what a blest &

beneficent one, poor tortured & tattered W[illiam] M[orton] F[ullerton] must feel! It makes me, I think, as happy as it does you. And I hope the consequence will be an overflow of all sorts of practical good for him—it *must* be. Of course I shall breathe, nor write, no shadow of a word of what I have been hearing from you to him—but if he should in time—& when he *has* time (he can't have now), the pleasure I shall take in expressing my sentiments to him will be extreme.

Your telegram arrived in time to keep me from writing Macmillan otherwise than in the sense it expressed; but I have now written him in *this* sense: that I am aware of matters (I named them a little)[2] in Morton's situation that make me think a sum of money will be highly convenient to him, & that if M. writes to propose an advance I shall like greatly to send them, the Macmillans, a cheque for £100 that they may remit him the amount of as from themselves, I remaining, & wishing to remain, wholly unmentioned in the affair. But send me no cheque, please, not only till I have let you know what reply I have had from Macmillan, but till Morton tells you he *has* made the request.

I hope the sum he has to pay to the accursed woman isn't really a very considerable one, or on which the interest for him to pay will be anything like *as* burdensome as what he has been doing. And 53 rue de Varenne?[3]—But you will tell me of that at your leisure. I'm delighted you're to have Miss Bahlmann with you. Paul Harvey[4] comes to me here for the night, & I think will be able to give me some news of Walter B[erry]. I am greatly touched by your so gentil little *envoi* of the étude of the Praslin story. I haven't immediate time to master it, but have sampled it a little, & have known it more or less before. I remember Mrs. Deluzy-Field in the U.S., & her coming one day to see my mother when I was there—a very impressive & demonstrative white-puffed person, impressing *les miens* as a Frenchwoman of the most insinuating & dazzling manners. She was a méridionale Protestant (of origin), I think—& that worked badly for her relations with the Duchess &c. But how when we were *tout-jeunes* in Paris the closed & blighted & *dead* closed hotel P[raslin] used to be pointed out to us as we walked in the Rue St. Honoré.[5]

Ever & always yours
H.J.

1. EW's note evidently confirmed Fullerton's willingness to participate in the plan she and HJ concocted en route to Chichester, 13 July 1909, to pay off the former mistress (the "accursed woman" of paragraph 3), who was blackmailing Fullerton. The plan was to get Frederick Macmillan (1851–1936), head of the publishing firm, to invite Fullerton to write a book on Paris and offer an advance of £100, the £100 to be paid by EW via HJ to Macmillan's. See *The Master*, 416–18, and *EW Biog.*, 263–64, for a full account of the plan.

2. This brief clause is an interlinear insertion in the manuscript to follow "convenient to him," but since it obviously refers to "matters," I have relocated it here and added the parentheses. See *Letters* 4, 529.

3. EW's new home in the Faubourg Saint-Germain.

4. Harvey (1862–1948), later Sir Paul, was the son of Edward de Triqueti (a painter) and an English governess, and the nephew of Mrs. Edward Lee Childe (formerly Blanche de Triqueti). HJ knew Paul as a child in 1876 when he visited Edward Lee Childe (1836–1911) and his wife on their estate in France. Harvey was in the British diplomatic corps and in 1909 serving as financial advisor to the khedive of Egypt—where Walter Berry was sitting on the International Tribunal. Harvey spent the night of 26 July 1909 at Lamb House.

5. Leon Edel explains: "Mrs. Wharton had sent HJ an account of the celebrated murder in which the Duc de Choiseul, Charles Laure Hugues Théobald Praslin (1805–1847), stabbed his Duchess, Altarice Rosalba Fanny Sebastiani, to death. Mrs. Deluzy Field was the former Henrietta Deluzy-Desportes, a governess in the Duke's household, who created the friction between the ducal pair that ultimately resulted in the Duke's using three knives to dispose of the Duchess. The crime occurred in 1847, and the James family, in Paris in 1855, still heard echoes of it. HJ remembers the Hôtel Praslin, winter home of the family, in the rue du Faubourg St. Honoré. The Duke committed suicide after the crime; Mlle Deluzy was arrested as an accessory but was released. She married an American, the Reverend Henry M. Field, and became renowned in New York as hostess and conversationalist. Mrs. Wharton toyed with the idea of using the story as a novel; a descendant of Mlle Deluzy, Rachel Lyman Field, wrote a successful novel based on the family history, *All This and Heaven, Too* (1938)." See *Letters* 4, 528.

détente: release; *les miens:* my kinfolk; *tout-jeunes:* youngsters

Lamb House, Rye
3 August 1909

Dearest Edith.

Deeply interesting your letter this a.m. received, & in nothing more so than in its wonderful & beautiful account of the change wrought in Morton by recent events, & which it verily enchants me to hear from you. It brings home to me with a force under which one fairly winces as for pain, the degree of the pressure of the incubus under which he had so long been living[1]—& which one knew & infinitely pitied him for, with the sense that the normal & possible expanding & living man was lost in it, lost to himself & lost to *us*. Now that we have got him —& it's *you*, absolutely, who have so admirably & definitely pulled him out—we must keep him & surround him & help him to make up for all the dismal waste of power—waste of it in merely struggling against his (to put it mildly) inconvenience. You speak of his having "recovered the possessions &c" of his own that she had in detention; but will you (at your leisure—when you write) mention whether she has surrendered the papers, letters, scraps of writing containing references to people &c, which he mentioned to me, originally, that, as they were private things all, she threatened to make God knows what injurious & public use of? Those, I imagine, were what it was most essential to his tranquillity that he *should* get back. But I indeed infer from what you say that his recovered tranquillity means precisely that he *has* got them. They are—they *must* be—*le plus clair* of the real finishing of the affair.

As for your proposition of lending him the sum you mention, through me (if he can't manage to arrange it otherwise), I can only accede to the beautiful, the noble beneficence of this on your part, with an extreme appreciation of all it represents—& even though it puts *me*, poor impecunious & helpless me, in the ridiculous nominal position of a lender of de fortes sommes! That, however, is la moindre des choses; so please consider that I will play my mechanical part in your magnificent combination with absolute piety, fidelity & punctuality—if it shld. *come* to the combination. That he will *let* you do it will seem in that case almost as beautiful as that you should do it; & of the beneficence of it, in converting a stricken & comparatively sterilized life into a life worthy of his admirable intelligence & capacity, I can't speak in terms adequate—or without emotion. Therefore I regard it as *all* worthy of three children of light & of honour. You will let me in time, if necessary, hear more about it.—Kindly meanwhile say to Morton that I did receive his Boulogne letter & am still belatedly replying to it. I want to write him *now*—ever so discreetly & *generally*, but ever so attachedly. My delay was inevitable at the time—through my immediately hearing from you of the tension of the situation in Paris that at once set in, & that made everything (nominally) outside mal à propos for the moment.—You rejoice me further by what you tell me of Walter B[erry] & of his of course coming on from you to England. I shall have a letter waiting for him by the 15th—& I have *de plus* my little vision. You will probably motor him to Boulogne—after which why shouldn't you let him ferry *you* over? With which you would both come *here* to me for two or three days[2]—& I would (at your convenience) go back with you—to Folkestone (and all this even if Walter *is* straining the leash to rush to the arms of Lady G.). You will tell me about this—j'y compte. It's horribly cold & damp here now—Novemberish altogether; but the other scale must come up—or go down; & we shall have good times yet. Poor dear worried Teddy—I think of him ever so kindly. But it's a normal anxiety—& so far almost a good one. All & always yours

Henry James

1. See letter of 26 July 1909.
2. The envisioned visit did not materialize; see letter of 15 August 1909.

le ... clair: the clearest sign; *de ... sommes:* substantial sums; *la ... choses:* the least of our worries; *mal à propos:* inappropriate; *j'y compte:* I count on it

Lamb House, Rye
15 August 1909

Dearest Edith.

A letter in the admirable sense you indicate[1] goes to our friend by this post—& I have made the appeal emphatic & urgent; have said "You will give as much pleasure by accepting as you can have done by any act of your life." This is about true, isn't it?—& at any rate he will have given as much to *me*! However, it is easy to *me* to speak—& I can only do profound homage to the splendour of your impulse. Of course he will *interpret*—my overture—but, frankly, I venture to hope & believe that he will, after the first step back, see the thing in a *light*—in the light in which it will have been presented. And if he does that I shall rejoice, & I am sure you deeply will. For it will mean the release of his mind, his spirit & his beautiful intelligence from a long bondage. And they are worth releasing.—I congratulate you *de coeur* on Walter B's arrival—or imminent one, & I shall immediately write to him. I foresee that par le temps qu'il fait (torrid, but exquisite here!) he won't come to England; & I can't, absolutely can't, dearest Edith, come to France. Everything in my present situation & circumstances conspires against it. I won't go into details, but only offer you the rueful assurance of my complete & quite unheroic inability. I am tied by tight cords.[2] I hope Paris isn't proving for you too agitated a frying-pan—even though the metal be enamelled gold. "She"[3] must create a frequent breeze for you—bless her! But Teddy has my continued & intimate commiseration. He is passing a terribly *mauvais moment*. May it not too dreadfully drag out.—I will do whatever you instruct me, to the letter, in the above matter—& hold myself all at your disposition. What a harsh task master is the Times![4] Tout à vous toujours

Henry James

1. See letter of 3 August 1908.
2. HJ's diary for August 1909 records an extremely full calendar of social engagements in and around Rye; see *Comp. Notes*, 306–7.
3. EW's automobile.
4. A reference to Fullerton's demanding position as Paris correspondent for the London *Times*.

de coeur: heartily; *par . . . fait:* with the weather we are having; *mauvais moment:* bad time; *Tout . . . toujours:* All the best to you always

Lamb House, Rye
[20 August 1909]

Dearest Edith.

Your letter is full of news—of the very mixed human sort. Poor Mrs. Wharton![1]—what a difficulty in laying down her long burden, & what a strain so long & helpless a watching of it. But I quite understand what you mean by its doing Teddy good; through being a very big normal & natural experience & taking him so much out of himself. But what a new start in life now devolves upon his sister—to which, however, she will be, I shld. suppose, highly adequate! I am very sorry about Walter [Berry]—with the clearer element of holiday cut so short for him & the same ordeal perhaps awaiting him. But I hope he will be back with us presently to better purpose. I shall take an immense interest in No. 53 —which if the numbers are pairs & impairs (though I think you've told me & I've frivolously forgotten), must be on the other side of the street from 58.[2] But I shall perhaps some day see—if I ever, yes *ever*, "go abroad" again—as I on the whole greatly doubt. You ask me, kindly, to vous toucher un mot of my health; & the word most veracious seems to me to be that my holding at all together of the few feeble remnants of it that I have managed to save depends essentially on my *not* going abroad at all, at all, & of hugging tight the policy de ne pas courir les aventures in general & that one in particular. I react violently against the great globe, to which is now being added the air, or "firmament" life of my contemporaries. But on that basis I don't despair of working out my salvation. I had the adventure a day or two ago pourtant— though neither globular nor aerial—of a lovely run hence, in a charming Napier, ma foi! to Hurstmonceau[3]—pronounced Hurstmon*soo*; which made me furious that *we*, the worthier we, had never taken it. Well, we must do Hurstmonsoo (which is admirable, & beyond what I knew) on the very most prochaine occasion.—I appreciate every word that you tell me of Morton—& especially the sovereign truth of its being a good thing for him to have the Paris book there to get itself written. It will help him so that among other helps it will help him to write it—& he will help it to write *him*; which he hadn't for a long time been able to help anything sufficiently to do! If he has another address—or *when* he has another—than the Times office, I shall ask you to let me know of it en passant. It's meanwhile a real luxury to me to remember de temps en temps that he hasn't Rue Fabert. But good-night—if one may predict good of *this* "dead unhappy night, when the rain is on the roof"—& almost through, in fact, into the room. What a season again! I made this afternoon a solicited pilgrimage over to the high parts of the Old Town of Hastings to have tea with a petite vieille, Miss Mathilda Betham-Edwards,[4] who used to write novels—"Kitty" & "Doctor Jacob"—& I used to read them, when I was young, & who is now an octogenarian officier de l'Instruction publique (rather an awful thing to be) from having lived long in France & which country she has written about & adores: a very gallant little mid-Victorian relic. How like her I feel myself now—in the Old Town of Rye. Get me the *order*, you & Morton!

H.J.

1. Teddy's widowed mother died on 17 August 1909 in Lenox, Massachusetts, leaving his sister, Nancy, alone and in charge of affairs. That the consequent sense of release might be "doing Teddy good" was an idle hope: his behavior became a kind of frantic exultation that worried his physician.

2. No. 53 is on "the other side of the street," the south side, and just a few steps eastward from No. 58.

3. HJ consistently misspelled Herstmonceux (although he got the pronunciation right); he drove to the castle—which is near Hastings—on 17 August 1909 in the "charming Napier" with Mrs. Richard Hennessy, a Rye neighbor, "of the Brandy family."

4. Miss Betham-Edwards (1837–1919), the "little old lady" *(petite vieille)*, was a popular English novelist (of part French ancestry) who lived in Villa Julia, 1 High Wickham Terrace on the heights of Hastings.

vous . . . mot: give you a word; *de . . . aventures:* not to embark on adventures; *pourtant:* however; *ma foi:* my word; most *prochaine:* nearest; *en passant:* in passing; *de . . . temps:* from time to time

Lamb House, Rye
23 August 1909

Dearest Edith.

What I hear from you today is exactly what I feared was hanging over our poor friend, but what I hope will be almost immediately averted by your further magnificent energy. The thing won't surely have been brought so far, the vessel, I mean, almost have reached port

& the cargo been landed, to encounter dangerous, really dangerous, weather at that stage. Evidently no—with such a pilot as you have on board. But he will, le cher homme, have been tormented—as he will also, D.V., have been redeemed! I shall draw a long breath when I get your final news. The purpose of this is only to give you that very obvious assurance & to say I understand everything—which is an obvious assurance enough too. I had a charming droll note from Walter —expressing in vivid figures how he had offered, or has the occasion of the offering of, the last violence to Hortense[1]—unprecedented violence I gathered, though I don't quite identify the scene, or the scenes, of the outrage. It is enough for me to feel that she will after a brief *recueillement* throw it off & recover her happy tone; elle n'aura donc pas à redouter, here, the particular Monsoo that the Home of the Hares[2] will expose her to. Lady Ottoline & an American[3] friend come down from town tomorrow to luncheon & tea—& you must figure me affably conversing with them from about 1.30 to 7.30—when they take their homeward train (for an American motor—of the friend's—has somehow failed them); unless they too will consent for a part of that time to se recueillir—for which I pray. It rains here overmuch—& yet the days melt away as never yet. An intensity of (difficult) work solicits & absorbs me; that is both the blest & the curst reason. I am exceedingly interested in it—& shall be, I foresee, more & more so. And now, in spite of the hour, I must write to poor dear Howells at Carlsbad—he having travelled thither from Kittery Point, N.H.,[4] *d'un trait*, to learn from his Doctor that "he needn't have come." The luxury of woe—or of weal—of you great magazinists! When the Minnies[5] arrive won't you very kindly beseech them to make some sign of their English date, or dates, a little in advance? I am booked, too uncannily to explain, to go to the Hereford Musical Festival (to stay in other words at the Deanery there),[6] from the 6th to the 9th, and there are other September complications—but I want a lucid relation with *them*. Felicissima notte!

Ever your
    H.J.

1. "Hortense" had become the name of EW's automobile.
2. "Monsoo" is HJ's jocular anglophonic rendering of "Monsieur," and may refer to the chauffeur of John Hare, veteran London actor-manager who was

proposed for the cast of HJ's *Outcry* for the 1910 repertory season planned by the American producer Charles Frohman. See letter of 25 October 1911.

3. Lady Ottoline Violet Anne Cavendish-Bentinck (1873–1938) in 1902 married Philip Morrell (1871–1943), soon a Liberal M.P.; she was an eccentric popular English hostess at this time entering the precincts of the Bloomsbury group, and was intimately associated with Augustus John, Bertrand Russell, D. H. Lawrence (who based his Hermione Roddice of *Women in Love* on her), and others. She came down to Lamb House with a Mrs. Kaerner (see *Comp. Notes,* 307).

4. HJ's geographical error: Kittery Point is in Maine.

5. Minnie and Paul Bourget.

6. The dean of Hereford, the Honorable and Reverend James Wentworth Leigh, was married to Frances, the youngest daughter of HJ's old friend the actress Frances Anne "Fanny" Kemble (1809–1893).

recueillement: moment of meditation; *elle . . . redouter:* she will certainly not have to fear; *se recueillir:* gather themselves together; *d'un trait:* non-stop; *Felicissima notte:* Happiest good night

Lamb House, Rye
[8 October 1909][1]

Dearest Edith,

I was obliged to make you yesterday my feeble little telegraphic wail, but today I am (since noon) sitting up tant bien que mal, & can do myself, & above all you, & your blest news, a little less "mean" justice. Besides which your second note (the Moberley Bellina one—poor, *poor* dear Morton, the prey of such *grues!*) gives me a further lift in the right direction. How long I've, as it were, owed you a letter! I came home but a week ago (a week tomorrow) from five weeks' absence[2]—I had let the Paddingtonia[3] (for one among several reasons) take a long flight—& was kind of waiting for the calmer hours of home to commune with you again properly. Then, immediately after my return, dear Gilliard [Lapsley] absolutely held me absorbed for 48 hours—after which I tumbled into bed with a most deplorably unprovoked & unearned attack of gout. It has not, thank heaven, however, been the worst I am capable of, & I seem really to have entered into the phase of relief.

I can say at the best, none the less, little of what I want, but please take it from me in this poor form, even, that your news about the comparative *apaisement* of Morton's horrible haunting crisis pours balm upon my spirit & makes me for the moment indifferent to almost everything else. I can't tell you how I feel it & what a difference it makes to me; & I only want your testimony, later on, to the difference you see it makes to *him*, & to the practicable & sensible taking effect of his liberation. Ah, how I agree with you—if certain things, blest things, for him, *could* happen! But perhaps they may—as they are not all essentially impossible. Meanwhile is his Paris book turning out a really attaching matter to him—does it actually draw him on & beguile him? Tell me of this at your full leisure—& anything more there is to tell about him. And let him know how I—in thus appealing to you—yearn over him. Not, however, that he is to have me the least scrap "on his mind."—Gilliard was all delightful: what a beautiful, charming & interesting being! He *looks* so magnificent that he inspires one with a kind of confidence—or wd. do so if he didn't somehow suggest (physically—*so* only) a sort of very exquisite & expensive or rather fallacious *carton-pierre*—as used by Nature for the fine handsome effect of him.

What you tell me of your St. Martin's summer of a time with Paul [Bourget] infinitely diverts & attaches me (à vos pas, in the matter); & oh how I wish I could go with you to the repetitions![4] Also to all the jobs about 53. I *am* a participator—& drink in all you me mandez.— Florence La Farge (& Grant)[5] are very briefly in England, but after her holding out hopes I see I shall wholly miss her.

Ever your
H.J.

1. HJ's diary entry for 2 October 1909: "Returned Rye 4.25." See fourth sentence of this letter.

2. HJ's diary lists numerous social engagements for September that drew him away from Rye, including a long weekend at Overstrand discussing with Frederick Macmillan a projected book on London. See *Comp. Notes*, 273–80. The book was never written.

3. Mrs. Paddington—"a pearl of price," HJ called her—was his housekeeper until 1912.

4. HJ's anglicization of *rèpètitions:* "rehearsals."

5. Grant La Farge, the son of the American painter John La Farge (1835–1910), and his wife, the former Florence Bayard Lockwood.

tant . . . mal: indifferently; *grues:* whores; *apaisement:* easing; *carton-pierre:* papier-mâché; *à . . . pas:* to your pace; *me mandez:* send me word of

Lamb House, Rye
29 October 1909

Dearest Edith.

Your letters come into my damp desert here even as the odour of promiscuous spices or the flavour of lucent syrups tinct with cinnamon might be wafted to some compromised oasis from a caravan of the Arabian nights. Put instead of these the Parisian days, & you get the torment of my nostril. Vous m'en direz tant!—it *is* the Grande Vie, led by you with a Maenad motion, that you cause so to glitter before me; & which, mark you, I'm enchanted you should lead, for the sake of the paillettes I pick up. These are pretty well all I do pick up in such a deadly season—one which puts to the strain a little even *my* remarkable constitution for supporting, in fact enjoying, deadly seasons. I hang about you in dreams, & you open up vistas to me in letters—never was a happier adjustment. I yearn, of course I yearn—*après* you all; but I'm just hell on vain yearning, & it suits me down to the ground. There is only a certain bitterness in having to make our heroic Walter B. a subject of the same—if I were only young & gracile, like himself & yourself, only inkless & faithless & tactless, I would dog his very steps before I would let him return to the shining East alone. I hoped for him here on his way & have been feeling for him in darkness & storm, please tell him, with a fear that he would pass & deny me. However, I daresay that he passed 500 miles off, & I only miss him & admire him & bewail him. You tell me otherwise too the most interesting & thrilling things, but if I were to take them all up, they would carry me far. Morton's *pacte* with his fiend sounds grim, but I refuse to believe that before that time is out vengeful Fate won't have once for all turned against her. Bien des choses may have happened. It isn't quite for me to goad him about his book—but if I could only get nearer to him (which everything seems to prevent), I would urge him not to wait for any ideal *readiness* to begin it, but to let a beginning *make* that readiness, which I shall defy him then to distinguish from the ideal. But over him too do I vainly yearn—please tell him so while I gnash my teeth. But it won't be so always—nor very long. I have desperately little news for you. My simplified—yet so subtilized!—existence slips horribly along —I mean with a sense of melting in my grasp—as if our torrential rains were washing it away & away. No report of any sort has come from Gilliard [Lapsley]—dear, lofty *fronton*, whom one seems to see at moments almost laugh himself down; but I imagine him still in England, at Cambridge or wherever, with his decision in the balance. I should suppose this damnable autumn (endlessly drenching here) extremely bad for him. From Howard & Quacre I've had no glimmer for months —but the silence is only like all the congestions of Quacre, the spell of Berlin wool, or the repleteness *before* (even) dinner, or the wallowing of Misery on the Sofa—& doesn't affect me as momentous or sinister. Lady Jeune[1] has written her Memoir, which I haven't read, but which seems to me rather to resemble Bernstein's duel,[2] as if she had longtemps cherché some untried form of activity pour se *re*poser. That formula of Bernstein's expositors shines far over the society in which you live. Well, nothing shines over us, & a million duels wouldn't pose us. Goodnight dearest Edith. I owe you a better communication. Delightful your news of the Quartiere. I have *been* in worse form than now.

    Ever yr.
        H.J.

1. The Scottish Susan Mary Elizabeth Mackenzie, widow of Colonel Stanley of the Coldstream Guards, married Francis Henry Jeune, later the 1st Baron St. Helier; her grandniece Clementine Hozier became the wife of Winston Churchill in September 1908. Lady Jeune's *Memories of Fifty Years* (1909) makes no mention of HJ or EW.

2. Perhaps an allusion to the violence of the plays of French dramatist Henry Bernstein (1876–1953).

Vous ... tant: You will tell me so much about them; *paillettes:* spangles; *gracile:* slender; *Bien ... choses:* many things; *fronton:* façade; *longtemps cherché:* long sought; *pour se reposer:* on which to resettle herself

Lamb House, Rye
24 November 1909

My dear Edith.

Yes, Bernard Harrison *is* of Frederic's[1] offspring—though I had for-gotten meeting him at Stocks. I know him slightly otherwise, & he is a very excellent though slightly colourless youth; but attached to Paris by a long "art" residence & devotion, & a very refined & rather skilful & interesting painter of French landscapes &c, things that (as I remember them) might be of a good French hand. He has a very nice & charming mother ("c'est le père qui n'est pas bien"!) long known to me, & to whom I think it would give much pleasure could you in any way be-friend the youth.—Ceci dit, it is dreadful how I have for the moment to postpone still a little "answering" your rich & delightful letter of 4 or 5 days since. I am under pressure of a very urgent & difficult task[2] —just approaching more or less its practical completion—& it leaves me spent & timeless, & with letters difficult, so that I have to throw myself on your mercy, *pour l'heure*; till the beastly little tension, on behalf of which I blush to make such a solemn & particular plea, is over—as it soon will be. Before it is I am obliged to go up to London on Friday[3] (taking, however, my work with me), when I expect to see Blanche,[4] who writes me he is there & asks when he can urgently see me, as he leaves on Sunday; only then to leave unanswered these 24 hours the prepaid telegram in which I at once replied with an eye to my own arrangements. Ces aimables français in the midst of which you live— ils n'ont d'yeux décidément que pour les "vies de femmes," les veuves tragiques & les mères émues (& qui devraient bien l'être). Your be-stowal of the so vivid report of that delicious woman's pleasant motor-day I immensely thank you for—it makes me live as much with *you*, in the spirit, as with her. What a 1st class "show" perpetually surrounds you, what a ceaseless circus, & how you are in the 1ères loges for assisting at it. I ache with all I have to ask you—but no more tonight; except my very tender benedictions to Teddy.[5] Yes—a thousand thanks!—I *wd.* come & occupy my *quartierino* with great pleasure; but it can't be till after March 1st. Poor *poor* Walter B.—quel acharnement du sort. I wish I could somehow aid & abet him against it. I greet Miss Wharton with effusion. Read Walkeley [sic][6] on the New York plays in the Times. Ce New York! It's Morton, I suppose, I read on "Sire"[7] in the same sheet—which I find very prettily—I mean for *him*—charmingly done. But he should—or *might*—have spoken of the early Lavedan novel of the same name from which it's *tiré*—for the curiosity of the way in which the tirage has been operated. Or rather no—ça n'a pas d'importance. And I am your

H.J.

1. Frederic Harrison (1831–1923), English historical and literary essayist. Stocks was the Humphry Wards' country place.

2. HJ had been asked to examine some of the letters and private papers of Lord Byron by Lady Lovelace, widow of the poet's grandson (see *Comp. Notes*, 110).

3. Completing his play *The Outcry*; see letter of 23 August 1909.

4. Jacques-Émile Blanche (1861–1942), French painter who, at EW's instigation in 1908, had painted HJ's portrait (now in the National Portrait Gallery, Smithsonian Institution). EW had visited him briefly in October 1909 at Offranville, near Dieppe.

5. Teddy had returned to Paris at the beginning of November 1909, accompanied by his unmarried sister, Nancy "Nannie" Wharton.

6. Arthur Bingham Walkley (1855–1926), drama critic of the London *Times*.

7. Morton Fullerton had reviewed favorably the five-act play of Henri Léon Émile Lavedan (1859–1940) based on his novel of the same title (1883) for the *Times* of 23 November.

c'est . . . bien: it's the father who isn't any good; *Ceci dit:* Having said that; *pour l'heure:* for the time being; *Ces . . . français:* These amiable Frenchmen; *ils . . . l'être):* they positively have eyes only for "lives of women," tragic widows and mothers who are disturbed (and who very well should be); *quartierino:* little corner; *quel . . . sort:* what tenacity of fate; *tiré:* taken; *ça . . . d'importance:* that is not important

Lamb House, Rye
13 December 1909

Dearest Edith.

I'm horribly in arrears with you & it hideously looks as if I hadn't deeply revelled & rioted in your beautiful German letter[1] in particular —which thrilled me to the core. You are indeed my ideal of the dashing

Woman, & you never dashed more felicitously or fruitfully, for my imagination, than when you dashed at that particular psychologic moment, off to dear old rococo Munich of the "Initials"[2] (of my tender youth) & again of my far-away 30th year.[3] (I've never been there depuis.) Vivid & charming & sympathetic au possible your image & echo of it all; only making me gnash my teeth that I wasn't with you, or that at least I can't ply you, face to face, with more questions even than your letter delightfully anticipates. It came to me during a fortnight spent in London—& all letters that reach me there when I'm merely on the branch succeed in getting themselves treasured up for better attention after I'm back here. But the real difficulty in meeting your gorgeous revelations as they deserve is that of breaking out in sympathy & curiosity at points enough, & leaping with you breathless from Schiller to Tiepolo—& through all the Gothicry of Augsburg Würzburg und so weiter. I want the rest, none the less—*all* the rest, after Augsburg & the Weinhandlung, & above all how it looks to you from Paris (if not Paradise) regained again—in respect to which gaping contrast I am immensely interested in your superlative commendation of the ensemble & well-doneness of the 2d play at Munich (though it is at Kabale und Liebe[4] that I ache & groan to the core for not having been with you). It is curious how a strange deep-buried Teutonism in one (without detriment to the tropical forest of surface-&-half-way-down-Latinism) stirs again at moments under stray Germanic *souffles* & makes one so far from sorry to be akin to the race of Goethe & Heine & Dürer[5] & *their* kinship. At any rate I rejoice that you had your plunge—which (the whole pride & pomp of which) makes me sit here with the feeling of a mere aged British pauper in a workhouse. However, of course I shan't get real thrilling & throbbing items & illustrations till I have them from your lips: to which remote & precarious possibility I must resign myself.

Blanche has been here (in London—he lunched with me) yes—& was very genial & intelligent & gentil; though impressing me more than ever with his genius for pushing his fortune par toutes les voies (we surely aren't *in* it with the French there!) but I fear I didn't do anything else very amusing in town except have a turn of gout again, in bed & in my unhappier foot; & see the Russian actress, Princess Bariatinsky,[6] in private & in public (very expert & artful, but not very interesting or rare); & attend the 1ère of L'Oiseau Bleu at the Haymarket in Madame Maeterlinck's[7] box—& sup with her (& him & a few others!) afterwards. I vulgarly liked Georgette, & found the accommodating Maurice shy & sympathetic—being accommodating myself; though I didn't probe either of them to disgraceful depths. And now I am back here for—I hope—many weeks to come; having a morbid taste for some, even most—though not all—of the midwinter conditions of this place. Turkeys & mince pies are being accumulated for Xmas, as well as calendars, penwipers & formidable lists of persons to whom tips will be owing; a fine old Yule-tide observance in general, quoi! A lonely stranded friend[8] who is *mal* with his wife (she having retired overseas), & who rather bores me, comes to spend the 3 or 4 days with me; & my amanuensis Miss Theodora Bosanquet, with a pal[9] & second-self of hers (a lady-pal) has been secured for dinner. I can't say fairer than that, foul as it will doubtless all appear to you in the lurid light of your meilleur monde. While I was in London I had a yearning cry from Howard [Sturgis], whom I haven't seen for months, & arranged to go out to him for tea & dinner; but on the eve came a telegram putting me off by reason of such bad news that he couldn't see me. The bad news proved to be that his nephew Dick Seymour[10] had been operated for appendicitis at Berlin & that his state caused some anxiety; but he is now rapidly recovering, & I didn't therefore get to Howard, who wrote me afterwards that he "couldn't at that time have received even the Angel Gabriel"; but that also, fortunately, the Babe had been a "perfect tower of strength & support!" I felt that with the towering Babe my visit might have been possible, but enfin il n'y a que lui, poor dear Victim of consanguinity, for being so prostrated by the inevitable accidents of a numerous, too numerous, circle. That Walter B[erry] is with you again, after quelle odysée, I know by a couple of charming signals from him—this a.m. received, & which I shall immediately acknowledge. I sit & wonder at such heroic oscillations. Il paraît qu'on y survit pourtant. I hope Teddy feels firm on his feet & that the long épreuve of the Crillon[11] draws to an end. I think 20 times a week of W. M. F[ullerton], and wish it could make some decent difference to him. But good night—tanti saluti affetuosi [*sic*].

Ever your
   H.J.

1. EW and Anna Bahlmann went to Germany when the manic Teddy and his sister took a motor trip to Pau.

2. A novel by Baroness von Tautphoeus (Jemima Montgomery) describing German life, a childhood favorite of HJ.

3. With sister Alice and Aunt Kate HJ had been in Germany and Austria for ten days in September 1872, and HJ was then not favourably impressed with Munich.

4. A 1784 play by Johann Christoph Friedrich von Schiller (1759–1805) about corruption in German aristocratic circles.

5. Johann Wolfgang von Goethe (1749–1832), German writer; Heinrich Heine (1797–1856), German poet; Albrecht Dürer (1471–1528), German painter.

6. HJ met the Polish actress Lydia Yavorska (d. 1921) at a luncheon at Sir Frederic Pollock's (5 December 1909); she was in London to play in Ibsen's *Hedda Gabler* and would remain with her husband, Prince Bariatinsky, in British exile.

7. On 9 December 1909 HJ attended the English premiere of the symbolist play *L'Oiseau Bleu* by the Belgian Maurice Maeterlinck (1862–1949), Nobel laureate of 1911; "Madame Maeterlinck" was the former actress Georgette Leblanc (1869–1941), Maeterlinck's companion (not wife) from 1895 to 1918.

8. The British journalist T. Bailey Saunders.

9. Ellen "Nelly" Bradley.

10. Dick Seymour, son of Howard Sturgis's sister, May, by her first marriage—to Colonel Hamilton Seymour.

11. The trial (*épreuve*) of the Hôtel de Crillon, place de la Concorde, into which EW moved when her lease at 58, rue de Varenne ran out in April.

depuis: since; *und so weiter:* and so on; *Weinhandlung:* wineshop; *souffles:* puffs of air; *par . . . voies:* by all means; *quoi:* eh wot; *meilleur monde:* better world; *enfin . . . lui:* finally there is no one like him; *Il . . . pourtant:* It seems, however, that one survives it; *tanti . . . affettuosi:* all affectionate greetings

Lamb House, Rye
Christmas Eve, 1909

Dearest Edith.

Your beautiful sad letter reached me yesterday—such a melancholy Christmas tale[1]—but the storm & stress of this crisis here, & the simultaneous arrival for a few days of a lone & stranded old friend,[2] who has required a good deal of slightly dreary attention & converse, have delayed my writing to you for 24 hours. And indeed, a good deal, your startling revelations knock me out & leave me sans le souffle—the more that I ask myself all woefully what the shock of them (though a little "led up to," I infer) must not have been for yourself—with their dreadful eye-opening force. However, I applaud still more the gallantry & serenity and lucidity with which you state them to me, & am infinitely touched by the confidence with which you let me participate. I scarce know how, for that matter, to tell you that all the while, these many months past, & without warrant or license or definite data (the *shadow* of them) to go upon, I've been uncannily *haunted* in respect to your situation (that is on the side of Teddy's absence, his condition & the conditions over there &c) with something or other in the way of an apprehension or a malaise, an apprehension or divination of evil, & that would at any time, with the faintest "jog," have made me break out "Il y a quelque chose, il ya a quelque chose!" Admire my devilish super-subtlety—for all the good it could have done you—or me. And nothing will do you, or *can*, any good now but the passing of a few weeks of time—which will clear up many things for you; that is from the moment of course you are able not to be *too* appalled at the quantity of depredation wrought. With my own poor measures of debit & credit the existing depredation looms huge & dreadful, & you have my deepest & tenderest sympathy in all the pain & horror & inconvenience. What I immensely hope at any rate is that the inconvenience isn't likely to prove practically intolerable or unmanageable—in relation for instance to your "taking up" your new apartment[3]—since you must have a home & a basis of settlement for work & peace & readjustment, & couldn't probably—could you?—have a more practicable one, taking all things together. But I suppose you don't fully *know* yet, or see your way, & are still hanging more or less on the cable or the post. Please don't become unconscious of how exceedingly & intimately I am with you & how infinitely desirous of any further news, especially if there be any comfort in it—that you may be able to give me. What I don't understand is Teddy's état d'âme over it all—if his âme, that is, hasn't ceased to palpitate at all, hasn't gone to the bottom altogether. It must be for him, in presence of the whole business, a different state of aberration from any he has had before; since if he was in dismay then over losses that hadn't taken place he can now de gaieté de coeur, "go in" for them—for disasters—without dismay. Is he absolutely *bien malade* (to account for such a turn), or is he only unexpectedly selfish & perverse? I feel indeed as if I oughtn't to put such questions to you—things take such endless qualifying & explaining; but the questions are only the worriments of my interest & the helplessness of my wonder. I read you over again—I keep re-reading you; but mainly with the effect of my feeling how anxious & troubled the whole autumn you must have been, & how acutely distressing it must at last have become. The great thing I hope is—& seem to infer from you, isn't it?—that he can do—can intervene & bedevil—no more, & that as co-Trustee with your Brother he *has* to liquidate.[4] But I shall learn more from you—at your convenience—as you see further yourself. I devoutly rejoice that you are not deprived of Miss Bahlmann for the present. And Morton, bless him—though I think of him as chronically accablé—must have devotedly rallied. Your little word about him—& about his not writing, & the way he's driven to death—aren't needed to make me ache with all his aches and bleed with all his wounds. I'd write to him for ten years without counting, if it were necessary—I mean if it were to do him any good to keep twitching his sleeve and *seeming*, even, to jog his elbow—& beg you to please tell him with my love that I am as much in his skin as he is himself; & that my idea of a proper affection for my friends is to *be* to that degree in their skins (with my faculty of dédoublement not exhausted by the above feat I am really at present as much in yours), without being in their way.—I had a telegram from Howard yesterday, $\frac{1}{2}$ an hour before your letter arrived, to inquire whether you were yet rue de Varenne or still at the Hotel. I answered that I *thought* you didn't move till sometime early in the New Year. I don't know what his question portended—but I hope my answer to it still represents more or less what may be about to take place. Today here is a warm shining sunburst in endless tropical rains—the dampest damnedest winter. But may the New Year give us—& you in particular—some sort of leg up!

Ever, dearest Edith, your
Henry James

P.S.   I blindly skipped this page[5]—& I just use it to add that I am, thank goodness, decently well, if I take care, & immersed in a fresh recrudence of occupations; having, among many things, just settled to a "shortish" novel[6]—which has got to be done, for serialization—in 8 numbers—very, very soon; & this with the question of London "rehearsals"[7] surging over its head. Touchez-moi a word, when you next have a free enough mind, of Bourget's play![8]

1. On his return from Pau to the Hôtel de Crillon in Paris on 8 December 1909, Teddy announced to EW that during the summer he had converted some of the holdings in her trust fund into cash and bought an apartment in Boston in which he installed (1) a young woman as his mistress and (2) a number of chorus girls. The full story was, if slightly less lurid, more substantially vexing in its details: Teddy's "depredations" on EW's funds amounted to more than $50,000, and the apartment in Boston proved to be a parcel of land with buildings in one of the choice sections of town—on Mountfort Street near Beacon Street. EW's decision was that Teddy return to the United States (he did so just before Christmas) and make appropriate restitution.

2. See letter of 13 December 1909.

3. At 53, rue de Varenne in Paris.

4. Henry Edward "Harry" Jones was cotrustee. Teddy inherited ca. $70,000 and some property on his mother's death.

5. The complimentary ending and the last four and a half sentences of the letter—from "rue de Varenne or still at the Hotel"—are written up the left margin and across the top of the first page of the letter. This postscript is written on the back of p. 7 (the fourth sheet) of the letter.

6. In response to a request from Harper's for a novel, HJ began early in December 1909 to make notes for *The Ivory Tower*; see *Comp. Notes,* 256–60.

7. Of *The Outcry*.

8. *La Barricade*, the first play of Bourget's not drawn from one of his novels, was scheduled to have its premiere 7 January 1910 at the Vaudeville in Paris.

sans le souffle: breathless; *Il . . . quelque chose:* Something is going on; *état d'âme:* state of mind; *de . . . coeur:* lightheartedly; *bien malade:* really ill; *accablé:* worn down; *dédoublement:* playing a double role

Lamb House, Rye
26 December 1909

Dearest Edith.

Your letter of 3 or 4 days [since][1] (or which I answered then) *would* have been fautif (or *ive*) if it hadn't seemed to you to make its occasion for the sequel yesterday received. For that postscript is in a manner relieving, as showing me what excellent aid & council you have to depend upon for the right information & assistance. May these beneficent friends, brother or cousin, straighten out the tangle effectively. But the more I think of it the more I feel what an infernal time of worry you must have been through. What a melancholy dismal Christmas! I, even, am struggling with the contrast between the perfunctory forms of the ponderous British revel, & the real state of one's physical & spiritual "in'nards" at almost any time. My depressed & not folichon friend is still with me—the end is not yet. But the woeful matter is our worst foe—however, this isn't meant for a wail. It's a quite other *geste*, really —an absolute attestation of my faith in your quick emergence from the shock of tant d'ennuis all at once. You will feel tout autre as soon as you're housed & settled. And I wish you such a bonne année. And oh how I wish Morton a better one! I have still 90 letters to write. Your fedelissimo

Henry James

1. See letter of Christmas Eve 1909.

fautif (masc.), *fautive* (fem. to agree with fem. "letter"): faulty; *folichon:* amusing; *geste:* action; *tant d'ennuis:* so many worries; *tout autre:* quite different; *bonne année:* happy new year; *fedelissimo:* most faithful

Lamb House, Rye
30 December 1909

Dearest Edith!

I am not very famous[1] today, as I had to take to my bed yesterday with (saving your presence) a *mal d'intestins*; which however I think I know the cause of (*cela rentre* into categories of a lifelong familiarity, really, I think); a fact that almost always makes me as elate over an uncanny (as at 1st it may have appeared) physical visitation as if I hadn't had it. I am on my feet again this afternoon & definitely relieved & reassured—so in the flush of reasserted vitality I can't not let you know of all the interest & emotion & devotion with which I've read & re-read your so luminously explanatory letter of Sunday last. It over-whelms me indeed—with a sense of the elements you've been having to deal with—& of the wonder indeed of the whole unspeakable story.[2] Vous en doutiez-vous?—of his being of that degree & perfection of detrimental energy? I confess *I* didn't dream of it—but of course I had comparatively few data to go upon; even though these were in some degree suggestive. His "Just my luck!" over his clothes for New York is one of those *cris* (of character) that make the despair of possessors of the creative imagination even of the *envergure* of you & me. It's the old story—of people being so much more like themselves than any possible forecast we can make of their likeness; but the general blackness & frivolity of it—I mean of the *whole* history—doesn't unfortunately com-mend itself the more for the beautiful consistency of the parts with each other. *That* they may clearly, in the case, always be trusted to achieve. He may, under stern *sommation* from your Trustees, repair his dilapi-dations, but who or what will repair *him*, poor insensate man?—& yet what but inconvenience can there be in your having a personage so helplessly out of gear in your existence at all?—inasmuch as I am afraid I don't see him as capable of any real virtue of contrition. I shall sound to you like Rosa [de Fitz-James] & the Bourgets—suggesting the gros moyen which is indeed winged so on Paul & Minnie's lips by the irony of fate: what a wonderful & beautiful case of it & what a proof of how much easier people really are than their opinions! What a pity Teddy's views aren't opinions—so that he might conveniently deviate from *them*! It does me great good to hear that Walter B., as well as your Brother, was able to be of light & guidance to you—& how I wish it were possible for me to stand in any degree just now in a pair of shoes like theirs. The fact with me, however, is verily that I'm not at present fit or apt in any degree for any *adventure*, & Paris, for me is ever an im-mense one. I haven't just now the 50th of an inch of margin for anything save sticking tight in my socket, so long as that socket itself will hold me. Later on we will make it up handsomely, & I don't despair of being less useless then. But *knowing*, now—knowing, I mean, so far as I may, what the days & weeks bring forth for you—this gives me, I confess, the illusion rather less than more—& you mustn't think I make *too* easy terms for myself if I say that it will be much more of a blessing to hear from you after than not. I'm convinced that when once you get into your apartment, meanwhile, you will feel your feet comparatively on a rock. Therefore I'm delighted to hear that you soon expect to do so. But my interest attaches itself to every detail—such as the question of whether White[3] is available for you in Paris, or whether Teddy monopolises his graceful attentions. With the absence of "clothes" for New York these may be less urgent over there. Forgive my levity—it's only that my imagination & wonder play so fondly over the whole subject.

I hope you have Miss Bahlmann as long as you want, & I bless her name as I think of her attachment. In what état d'âme must you not have made that escape to Germany[4]—& what a splendid victory of the finer appreciation *that* makes of your beautiful letter to me thence. Well your finer appreciations will float you through *all* deep waters—& they'll become finer & finer than anything but my own appreciations *of* them! Tell Morton how I go on appreciating—àpropos of such beautiful processes—*him*: & requiring no aid from anything at all except the pleasure que j'y trouve. I've got so much work to do that the plot thickens about me, & my one thought is to keep somehow—everyhow, rather—in such form as to carry it through. But bonsoir, Madame—with every pious invocation on your beautiful head. We shall go in together for an ever so much better year—which will make me, among its happy strokes, even still more & more yours

Henry James

1. HJ uses the anglicized "fameux"—"I'm not great." In addition to the intestinal problems, HJ had just suffered two serious attacks of gout, and there would be further complications in the coming weeks; see letter of 17 January 1910. The whole was aggravated by his burgeoning depression over the financial failure of the New York Edition of his works.

2. Teddy's behavior. See letters of Christmas Eve and 26 December 1909.

3. Arthur White, a Cockney, had joined the Wharton household as butler in 1888.

4. See letter of 13 December 1909.

mal d'intestins: intestinal trouble; *cela rentre:* that leads; *Vous en doutiez-vous?:* Did you suspect it?; *cris:* cries; *envergure:* scope; *sommation:* legal summons; *gros moyen:* vulgar means; *état d'âme:* state of mind; *que j'y trouve:* that I find in that

3

Slings and Arrows

JANUARY–AUGUST 1910

AT THE BEGINNING of the year Wharton moved into her new apartment at 53, rue de Varenne and sold her New York home at 884 Park Avenue. James began the year by dictating what would be his last notes for *The Ivory Tower*; he then gave Theodora Bosanquet a holiday. He was suffering from digestive disorders and "food-loathing" brought on not only by his practice of "Fletcherizing"—chewing one's food until it is reduced virtually to liquid—but also by his continuing depression; that had worsened to such an extent that brother William sent his son Harry over to England at the end of February. Harry took his uncle up to London in mid-March for a thorough examination by Sir William Osler. Osler found nothing organically wrong with James but set up a strict regimen for him to follow.

Edith Wharton's situation suffered the aggravation of Teddy's return to Paris in March seriously ailing. She crossed to England to visit Howard Sturgis at Qu'Acre and James in London at Garlant's Hotel. She found James at first rather perky but the next day in the depths of despair and having fantasies of suicide. Wharton concocted the plan of bringing Teddy over to Folkestone (medical authorities had given permission) and shuttling between there and Rye to keep an eye on both sufferers until the arrival of William and his wife, Alice. She sketched her plan to Fullerton and added, "But what a strange situation I shall be in, entre mes deux malades [between my two patients]!" (*EW Letters*, 206). At the end of May Teddy entered a sanatorium at Kreuzlingen in Switzerland.

139

William James, in failing health, planned to take the cure at Bad Nau-heim, Germany; he and Alice arrived in England in early April and Henry seemed to be buoyed up by this respite from the comparative solitude of Rye. Furthermore, Edith Wharton provided a car and an English chauffeur from Folkestone so that James and his brother and sister-in-law could enjoy a brief interval of motoring. Misfortune struck a blow to James's morale with the news that the death of Edward VII meant cancellation of the repertory theater plan, which was to include *The Outcry.* William diagnosed his brother's fluctuating health as a con-sequence of psychological as well as physical stress.

After William's departure at the beginning of May for Bad Nauheim, Henry and Alice enjoyed a month of social distraction in London and at the Charles Hunters' Hill Hall; then they joined William in Germany. By the time of their return to London in July both brothers were decid-edly ill. Coincidentally Edith Wharton was facing the crisis of Teddy's release from the Swiss sanatorium. Berry came to her aid; he had re-cently resigned from the International Tribunal and installed himself in Wharton's guest suite at 53, rue de Varenne. She managed a few days in England in August to see both Sturgis and James. As James saw her off at Folkestone, he felt distinct trepidation about her future with the unsettled Teddy.

James decided to give up his perch at the Reform Club in London and to let Lamb House in order to accompany William and Alice back to America. They reached Chocorua, New Hampshire, on 19 August; William died on 26 August.

The correspondence shows that both novelist-friends have reached distinct crossroads in their lives. They will face them together and apart, on both sides of the Atlantic.

Lamb House, Rye
17 [14]¹ January [1910]

Dearest Edith.

I have had beautiful & interesting & thrilling letters from you & yet have been silent, which means, however, only that I have been for many days quite boringly & "beastly"—that is most inconveniently, unwell

—& scarce fit even for the scrawl of a rare pencil note. Within 24 hours I am markedly better—though I *had* a marked improvement a week since & then a depressing little *rechute*. However, this time I think I am really out of the wood, & the more so that I am more or less able to believe that I have mastered a miserable obscurity & perversity in my condition—which was about the worst of it. I am still not at all famous[2]—but I am improving, &, yes, shall improve further. But when such states settle on me—an utter inward & stomachic collapse, the sombrest[3] *sickness*, with a complete loathing for food & a consequent deep inanition & depression & disqualification (for everything—but the tomb); I can but crouch in my corner & cling to it, viewing with dismay any thought of ever leaving it while such liabilities attend me. (It's their so *prolonging* themselves I resent.) I am wriggling back to beef tea & wine-jelly—but Mrs. Paddington[4] still enjoys long leisures; all of which I regale you with that you may simply know *why* I am, or have been, so little à la hauteur. Don't, none the less, I beseech you, worry over me—or *it*; I am working out my salvation, & am nothing if not almost uncannily patient. I wasn't at all famous even when I wrote to you last, but have had a more dismal épreuve, & a more mysterious, than I expected. I am delighted, all the same, to find I can in a manner drive the pen, for I've lost precious days at a moment when I can ill afford it. And yet after all I must stop here this p.m. (Friday 14th); [&] see if it shan't be a better one. I hope you are—now chez vous[5]—at comparative peace. Love to Morton. Ever your

H.J.

1. The letter is clearly dated "17 January," obviously a slip of the pen that is corrected in the closing lines of the letter.

2. In the sense of the French *fameux*, i.e., I am not feeling great.

3. The manuscript has "sombreest"—the British spelling plus a superlative ending.

4. HJ's housekeeper.

5. EW moved into 53, rue de Varenne, Paris, at the beginning of the year —hence "chez vous" or at home.

rechute: relapse; *à la hauteur:* up to the mark; *épreuve:* trial

[POSTCARD]   L[amb] H[ouse], [Rye]
                                                    21 January [1910]

Am worrying slowly through very tiresome & depressing stomachic
crisis, with return of appetite and power to eat (more than a very little)
much hindered and delayed. I have better hours & days & then dis-
couragements; but no complications of any sort and excellent care. Am
not in bed, but mostly in my room, & go to bed early and rise late.
This noon I was out in sun an hour & $\frac{1}{2}$. It is all a question of chronic
sickishness (not active) & food loathing. But I shall beat it!

H.J.

P.S.   All "work" of course dismally *stopped*!

                                                    L[amb] H[ouse], [Rye]
                                                    Sunday [23 January 1910]

Dearest Edith.

One can't "thank" for such things—& this isn't for that: that acknowledgment must wait. This is only to say that I am doing very well.
Till 3 days—or 4—ago I had been fighting in the wilderness & by the
fallacious light of nature, by which I mean trying to take care of the
doctor rather than let him do so of me.[1] But now that I am continuously
in bed, prostrate & already mending, with Nurse only mercifully triumphant & feeding power coming definitely back, I [am] all your & Morton's thoroughly improving & returning

H.J.

1. Dr. Ernest Skinner of Mountsfield, Rye. Theodora Bosanquet, idled as
amanuensis by HJ's illness, was sending bulletins to EW (at her specific request) and other friends and to HJ's family. On this date she wrote to EW; see
letter of 23 January 1910 in app. B.

[POSTCARD]   L[amb] H[ouse], [Rye]
                                              25 January [1910]

Your beautiful letter this a.m. welcomed.[1] I am doing admirably,
mending fast, though sitting up but an hour for the 1st time (these
several days) this afternoon. Beseech you to kindly send me Tales of
Men.[2] I want so awfully to see how you do it. More very soon. Am
forbidden "style." Yours

H.J.

P.S.   All my sympathies in your immersion[3]—which must be grand
& horrible.

1. See EW's response to Bosanquet, this date, in app. B.
2. EW's collection, *Scribner's*, October 1910.
3. On 23 January Paris suffered its worst flood in a century and a half; the
Faubourg was seriously smitten but the area of 53, rue de Varenne was virtually untouched.

                                              Lamb House, Rye
                                              2 February 1910

Dearest dearest Edith!

My progress is but very gradual & I am as yet but a poor incommoded thing; though sitting up awhile today for the 3d successive time
(day). However *eppur' si muove*! This is a most baffled scrawl to tell you
how *divine* I hold your 2 letters (the one of yesterday & the previous
message through Morton's heroic medium); but that really I am not—
absolutely & positively not—in need. I am on a very decent & easy
financial basis with a *margin* of no mean breadth, a most convenient
balance at my bank, & a whole year quite provided for even if I shld.
do no work at all. You see I have my modest "independent" income
(my share of our—my father's—patrimony)[1] *and* this house; which con-
stitutes here a real aisance! Moreover it so happens that I have definite
arrangements for this year (on the basis of production) which will
represent—from the moment I get to work again—a bigger budget than
I have *ever* been in for.[2] And slowly, but sensibly, I *am* coming round. I

am sitting up today for the 3d time; 4 to 5 hours yesterday—6 today—
& feel within, with slow but sure distinctness, that the worst is well
over. Absit omen!—I shall be at work again by—as before—the 1st of
next month; & *never* has the fire of genius burned more luridly or impatiently within me. So, I *supplicate* you, don't have these lurid fears &
soothe your angelic spirit to rest & confidence. Your general conditions[3]
have been as a nightmare to me—a real impediment to recovery; but
the beginnings of the latter have come with the appearance that your
worst is over. Tragic munificent Paris—always the Heroine, always en
scène—not to say en Seine! And now for God's sake do let me know
what has been decided about Teddy & about your going over.[4] This
latter image is too deplorable, & I hope & pray it is to be the other
way, without knowing, however, how, in so bad a business, you yourself see it. What dire complications—& you knocking off "sellers" in
the midst of them! You are prodigious & magnificent & that I am[5] more
& more your devoted old

Henry James

1. Income from Syracuse real estate, which HJ shared with brother WJ,
originally yielded ca. £20 or $100 per month, but reorganization of the prop-
erty by nephew Harry and a rise in rents had increased the income over the
past two years to ca. £51 or $250 per month.

2. His income for 1910 would be ca. £1820 or $9100, whereas his income
for 1909 was ca. £1480 or $7400.

3. HJ refers to her problems with Teddy, details of whose capers were still
flowing in. The previous day HJ had written to Howard Sturgis about EW's
"inconveniences & complications about Teddy (who has had no 'melancholia'
but on the contrary excess—queer—demented excess of levity & gaiety which
has translated itself into incongruous & extravagant forms & consequences)."

4. Among various solutions to Teddy's dilemma, EW offered to send the
butler White over to the United States to bring Teddy back to Paris or to go
over for that purpose herself. She did neither (see letter of 5 February 1910),
and Teddy came back at the beginning of March.

5. HJ evidently had two grammatical constructions in mind as he hurried his
letter to its close.

eppur' si muove: it moves nevertheless (Galileo's famous insistence); *aisance:* ease;
en scène: on stage

Lamb House, Rye
5 February 1910

Dearest Edith.

Your touching letter of yesterday makes me feel as [if] I had, vulgarly speaking, a little "wounded," or a bit unduly disconcerted you by my poor (as yet) embarrassed & clumsy form of response to all your good-ness;[1] but you will of course really all the while be allowing for the halting gait of a still much-retarded convalescent (who feels even yet—though better, yes *better*, so beastly sick & blue most—or much—of the time), & won't be hard on his artless accents. They shall become aw-fully artful with you yet, & I vow to you on my sacred honour that in the *event* of any trouble or worriment, this year, of the kind in question I will hurl myself upon you with the fullest, frankest force of my need. What you have written is meanwhile a beautiful treasure of my soul. Meanwhile too, at the same time, I can't take any interest in my own case at all—*that* is the difficulty in presence of what your letter tells me of your developing situation—all the circumstances of which (& with Morton's thrown in) have haunted me, the last horrible 3 weeks, like a prolonged nightmare. Dismal enough the case looks—though it may easily put on a more practicable face when it comes to be taken in its piecemeal & from day to day actuality. I wish I could help you other-wise than by my poor impotent sympathy & vain fond thoughts. But I *shall*, somehow or other; I'll be hanged if I don't. Do be conscious meanwhile of how deeply I yearn over you—& find in it an earnest of something better to come. I thank the Powers (or the brothers, or the doctors, or whoever) that you are not starting for the dire N.Y.—hor-rible wd. be the thought. And aren't you glad you have at this crisis a kind of a sort of *fester Burg* of a home even in the ravaged & desolated Paris?[2] But of the tragic city itself I can't yet make bold to think.—All thanks for the Scribner[3] & the Deshabillage of poor Aimée,[4] whom I haven't had time to get in range of yet—but which I mean to do. It is most happily *right* & tender—& personal, & impersonal, enough—& with some of your quoted instances altogether fine & beautiful. It hor-ribly renews my sense of the stupidity of his extinction. How much mightn't one have still been going to enjoy him! But one mustn't think. What an ineffable blessing you must be—you in your embrowned saloon—to the harassed Morton, to whom I send my impotent homage—& of whom I feel that without you I shouldn't just now have courage to think at all. I'm sure you must have added a livelier iris—even—to the burnished Artist! I see it shine from afar. I beseech you to let me know what further happens, & to love me still—as your faith-fullest old

Henry James

1. Her offer of financial aid; see letter of 2 February 1910.
2. The serious flood of 23 January 1910; see letter of 25 January 1910.
3. *Scribner's Magazine* published EW's tribute "George Cabot Lodge" in its February number. "Bay" Lodge had died the preceding August at age thirty-six.
4. The stripping *(déshabillage)* of Aimée refers to a volume of letters from Alfred de Musset (1810–1857), *Lettres d'amour à Aimée d'Alton,* edited by Léon Séché, which had just been published by Mercure de France. The letters were deposited in the Bibliothèque Nationale in 1880 by Aimée (1811–1881), via Jules Troubat, but forbidden to the public for twenty years. The affair lasted a scant two years, 1837–1838; four years after the death of Alfred she married his elder brother, Paul (1804–1880), who acquiesced fully in her deposition of the letters and who in fact helped Aimée "edit" them somewhat, as Séché indicates. The years of that affair, Séché points out, were among the most productive of Musset's brief career. But see letter of 8 February 1910.

fester Burg: mighty fortress

Lamb House, Rye
8 February 1910

Dearest Edith—

I am in receipt of endless bounties from you & dazzling revelations about you: item: 1st the grapes of Paradise that arrived yesterday in a bloom of purple & a burst of sweetness that make me—while they cast their Tyrian glamour about—ask more ruefully than ever what porridge poor *non*-convalescent John Keats must have had: 2d: your exquisite appeal & approach to the good—the really admirable—Skinner,[1] who has now wrung tears of emotion from my eyes by bringing them to my knowledge: 3d your gentle "holograph" letter, just to hand—which treats *my* stupid reflections on your own patience with such heavenly gentleness. When one is still sickish & shaky (though that, thank goodness, is steadily ebbing) one tumbles wrong—even when one has wanted to make the most delicate geste in life. But the great thing is that we always tumble together—more & more never apart; & that for that happy exercise & sweet coincidence of agility we may trust ourselves & each other to the end of time. So I gratefully grovel for everything—& for your beautiful & generous enquiry of Skinner, in the midst of all your own importunate images & aches, more than even anything else. The purple clusters *are*, none the less, of a prime magnificence & of an inexpressible relevance to my state. This is steadily bettering—thanks above all to 3 successive morning motor-rides that Skinner has taken me, of an hour & $\frac{1}{2}$ each (today in fact nearly 2 hours) while he goes his rounds in a fairly far circuit over the country-side. I sit at cottage & farmhouse doors while he warns & comforts & commands within, &, these days having been mild & grey & convenient, the effect has been of the last benignity. I am thus exceedingly sustained. And also by the knowledge that you are not being wrenched from your hard-bought foyer & your neighbourhood to your best of brothers.[2] Cramponnez-vous-y. I don't ask you about poor great Paris—I make out as I can by Morton's playing flashlight. And I read Walkley on Chanticlere [*sic*]—[3] which sounds rather like a glittering void. I have now dealt with Alfred & Aimée[4]—an unprofitable pair. What a strange & compromising French document—in this sense that it affects one as giving so many people & things away, by the simple fact of springing so characteristically & almost squalidly out of them. The letters in which Alf. arranges for her to come into his dirty bedroom at 8 a.m., while his mother & brother & others unknowingly *grouillent* on the other side of the cloisons that shall make their *nid d'amour*, & *la façon dont elle y vole*[5]—react back even upon dear old George [Sand] rather fatally—à propos of dirty bedrooms, their cloisons & the usual state of things, one surmises, at that hour. What an Aimée & what a Paul & what a Mme Jaubert[6] & what an everything! Ever your

Henry James

1. Local physician.
2. Harry Jones had evidently been a great source of aid and comfort to EW in this time of difficulty over Teddy.

3. *Chantecler*, the second great dramatic success of Edmond Rostand (1868–1918), had its debut on 7 February 1910.

4. Musset's letters to Aimée d'Alton; see letter of 5 February 1910.

5. Before he could afford a temporary love nest for them, behind the Madeleine, Musset invited Aimée to come "between 7 and 8 in the morning" to his room—even though "the apartment is not very large, and inside are my mother, a sister, a brother, and three servants." Aimée came often. The other details are from HJ's imagination.

6. Paul de Musset and Aimée's cousin, née Caroline d'Alton, who introduced Aimée and Alfred in 1835.

Cramponnez-vous-y: Hang on to that; *grouillent:* swarm; *cloisons:* partitions; *nid . . . vole:* love nest, & the way she flies there

Lamb House, Rye
16 February 1910

Dearest Edith.

This very hour—as I sit here solitudinous—there has dropped upon me a basket, or casket, of celestial manna that can only have been propelled to its extraordinarily effective descent by the very tenderest & firmest, most generous & most unerring hand in all this otherwise muddled world. You are truly of a gorgeousness of goodness—& the *vermeil* clusters again reflect the splendour of your spiritual complexion. I bow my head even while I open my mouth—& I listen to my heart, agitated to its rich maximum, even while I undisguisedly gloat. No, however, I can't "thank"—not that for the present. But the score piling up for you to face will be heavy—after a little. Meanwhile exquisitely addressed to my case is the juice of the grape. This would be perhaps still even more to the case were my case not now so definitely & charmingly improving. I am distinctly, unmistakably better; having excellently rallied from a collapse, a rechute, brought on by too rude a push forward. The venturing forth for 3 or 4 brief motor-flights[1] proved a delusion & a snare; & I paid for them by a tumble back into bed & a return to the 1st principles & the regime of an undesired small sop of something every hour or two. But that passed—& I have really taken a good straight forward step. I sit up practically all day again—& feed more introspectively & in larger sops. It is beastly solitudinous—but the days go & go, & the situation is in every way clearer & brighter. I wish I could have some sign from you that yours is half as good—or at least of how yours is promising to work out, if promise can be predicated of it. My illness, with its large element of black depression, had made me frightfully pusillanimous—abjectly so—about surrounding Trouble; but [I] can't be a hunted ostrich forever—& at least I am trying to flourish a little my tail-feathers. (Pardon this graceless metaphor—a convalescently feeble best.) At any rate I can't even face thinking that you may be having another flurry of apprehension on the flood question—too damnably sick does it make [me] again when I want to be up & doing, helping, saving, subsorbing [?][2] or something or other. However I refuse to believe that your worst isn't absolutely over. And do you know what would help *me* more than anything else? Why, the booming ghost-story,[3] for which je languis, je brûle. Yesterday I even corrected a proof of my own—for the English Review;[4] but a thing that will be half murdered by my having to consent to divisions of its noble unity into the April & May nos. I lay the most clutching hand on Morton & am your fedelissimo

Henry James

P.S. I've never thanked you for the wondrous theatrical paper with its glowing & nombreux tribute[s] to B's piece[5]—as to which I'm delighted to infer a big success.

1. With Dr. Skinner; see letter of 8 February 1910. For "automobile journey" HJ has borrowed a term from the title of EW's travel book *A Motor-Flight Through France* (New York: Scribners, 1908).

2. The word is crammed hard against the right-hand margin and the first syllable is difficult to read; the next two are clearly enough "sorbing"; evidently a Jamesian coinage.

3. Perhaps EW's "Afterward" *(Century,* January 1910), in *Tales of Men and Ghosts,* October 1910.

4. "A Round of Visits," published in October 1910 in *The Finer Grain*; this was to be his last published short story.

5. Bourget's latest play, *La Barricade,* was enjoying great acclaim after a month's run in Paris.

vermeil: ruby-red; *rechute:* relapse; *je . . . brûle:* I languish, I burn; *fedelissimo:* most faithful; *nombreux:* numerous

Lamb House, Rye
2 March 1910

Dearest Edith.

I am capable of a very scant script—but I must "thank" you for your endless bounties. I am having a bad & difficult time, as I wired you—& though flares & glimmers of greater ease occur they don't *last* alas (more than 24 hours), & *rechutes* seem, with me, more & more to rule the day. I blush to say that I have got at last rather demoralized—in the sense of feeling blighted beyond my power to throw if off; but I probably am not really so at all, & will—with time & some turn as yet incalculable—wear out my curse before it wears *me.* Meanwhile it isn't gay—& when I say to myself that I'm a beast thus to wail & whine to you I reply, cogently, that if I make a hollow show of that which isn't I shouldn't at all be able to live up to it & the grimacing mask wd. drop of itself. The arrest of work is hardest to bear—& the probable lapse (for the present Season) of my Repertory play[1] & its advantages through my inability to be participate in Preparations &c. It isn't "due" till some time after Easter, but the time shrinks space. Meanwhile my "blest" Nephew's, Harry's, arrival[2] (how *choisie* your letter to him!) is indeed an immense alleviation & support. He is a most admirable & valuable youth (of 30!) & of excellent wisdom & counsel. He went today up to town for 48 hours—& there is a possibility of my being somehow able to see the grand Osler[3] for a 1st class "opinion" & a superior, a supreme, light, next week. It will depend on how we can work it. Also I take great comfort in the fact that my Brother & Sister-in-law[4] (I extraordinarily value *her*—as well as him!), who have been at any rate planning to spend the coming summer in Europe, may not improbably start at no distant date in order to be with me—she, & my niece, of whom I am very fond, in particular. To these props & cheers I confess (I am past all *attitude* now) je me cramponne quite abjectly. Think of them for me to ease off that admirable sympathy of your own my consciousness of which, & of your generous tenderness, as a back-ing, an inspiration & a hovering presence, is of the deepest, the fondest, dearest Edith, & the most sustaining intensity. My sense of Morton's abiding affection—as expressed, e.g., in his exquisite letter of the other day, of which he shall have on the 1st possible occasion *almost* adequate acknowledgement—is another intimate & vivid luxury.—In the midst of all of which me voilà tout étourdiment neglectful of my greatly relieved sense of the terms in which you speak of Teddy's actual condition[5] & quietude & of my wish to offer him even this far-off quaver of a welcome. Please give him my love & tell him I pat him most fraternally (& yet ever so much more gently than most brothers do that sort of thing) on his perfectly-proportioned back.—I shall take the greatest interest—I need scarcely remark—in what Dupré[6] may say of him.—I have greatly appreciated your gentillesse in sending me 2 so accomplished notices of Bataille's play,[7] & above all your statement of what befell you & Morton at Chantecler. The latter circumstance intensely interests me—it floods the subject with light—& above all with the particular light that in the midst of my troubles I have been *sourdement* invoking. I was sure it was like that—& to have your demonstration of it makes me owe you both a thousand effusive thanks. Ouf!— Most able & artful & doué must Bataille be, & I shld. like immensely to read La Vierge Folle; the great hitch & stumbling-block for *our* emulation of such abilities & arts & *dons*, however, being in the postulates & concessions such a situation primarily requires: the eminent lawyer, with an admirable wife, enlevé—by his consent, by the charming daughter of the most high-toned house in which he honourably visits & with his interest for us positively placed on the ground of his having made her his mistress. We are so abjectly wedded—& have to be—to the idea of the gentleman-when-it-comes-to-the-test; to say nothing of that of the lady equally incommoded! If it weren't for that what a theatre we—even we—might still have! But we—or *they*, our possible objects of reference—are too incommoded.—Let me add that I am better—feel better—at the end of this scribble than I did at the beginning; which I regard as of such good omen. Perhaps my cure would be to write you perpetual letters—all day. But what mightn't become then your disease? See at any rate the endless quantity of blessing that you 1st in one way & then in another (those last grapes were royal, as some American "lady-herald" has proved Miss Elkins to be; but *voyons*!) shed on your devotissimo

Henry James

1. Not HJ's persistent ill health alone, nor the additional pain of the revisions (mainly cuts) in the text of *The Outcry*, but finally the death of King Edward VII on 6 May 1910 dictated the lapse—not only of HJ's play but of the whole of Frohman's repertory program. HJ received £200 forfeit fee and reclaimed rights to the play, which he turned into a successful novel. Theodora Bosanquet typed a restored version of the play, but it was not produced during HJ's lifetime.

2. The family's concern over HJ's health prompted them to dispatch his eldest nephew to look in on him. Harry arrived at Lamb House on 27 February 1910.

3. Harry secured an appointment with the physician Sir William Osler for 14 March 1910; see letters of that date and 21 March 1910.

4. WJ and Alice.

5. A much quieter, chastened, and guilt-ridden Teddy arrived back in Paris at this moment.

6. Dr. Dupré, a specialist in nervous diseases, would soon be predicting that Teddy was a likely suicide. Dr. William Sturgis Bigelow, a friend of the Lodges, interested himself in Teddy's case and saw clear signs of mental illness as did the eminent Parisian nerve specialist Dr. Isch Wall.

7. *La Vierge Folle* by French dramatist Henry Bataille (1872–1922) had its premiere in Paris on 25 February 1910.

rechutes: relapses; *choisie:* choice; *je me cramponne:* I clutch; *me . . . étourdiment:* here I am quite thoughtlessly; *sourdement:* dully; *doué:* gifted; *dons:* talents; *enlevé:* carried away; *voyons:* come now; *devotissimo:* most devoted

> Garlant's Hotel
> Suffolk St., Pall Mall S.W.
> 14 March [1910]

Dearest Edith.

I think I shall wire you tomorrow but I want you to have at any rate this more explicit account of my marked & prompt improvement in consequence of my having on Saturday,[1] my gallant Nephew aiding, broken by departure the evil spell & the vicious circle that has held me tight for so long at Lamb House. The mere getting away, by whatever effort, began immediately to help me on, & this a.m. in this place an extraordinarily reassuring & cheering & even inspiring interview with Osler (cher grand homme who came up from Oxford *apposta*) set the seal on my sense of being really on the way to (with a certain decent patience & care) straight & complete recovery. Osler "examined" me more thoroughly & nudely than I have ever been examined in my life & the account he gave me of my general machine was good enough to have *pâti* even as I have done to get it. His opinion & advice are of the highest value to me—I am exceedingly glad I saw him. But he wants me to come to him for Sunday next at Oxford (chez lui with my nephew), so as to have me for 24 hours under his close observation.[2] I *feel* now that I am getting well—& all very quickly & almost suddenly (after doing nothing but *constater* during 7 weeks in particular, between the good Skinner[3] & the grim Nurse that I was steadily getting worse). It is an unspeakable blessing—& I probably shall be able to stay on in London & after a little go back to my Reform Club quarters—I mean feel it quite safe to do so. Meanwhile the idea of seeing you here within a few days is a great joy—it will give me an immense further lift. How wonderful & beautiful that you are able to come. I am not yet good for more than this scrawl—but I am another creature from the one who even on Wednesday last lay in bed in a blue funk & a cold sweat (*where he had lain for so many days of repeated rechute—that* was the demoralizing thing) at the idea of getting up & travelling & throwing himself on the terrible London. I am already told I scarce look as if I had been ill—& I am "filling out." My Nephew is an angel—& an *able* angel. So congratulate me. I feel as if I were *flaunting* fairly now my advantages—as against the carking cares which perhaps occupy your consciousness —but for every item of which I have dearest Edith the great yearning of your

H.J.

1. That is 12 March, with nephew Harry.
2. There was evidently a change of plans. HJ saw Osler briefly in the morning of Saturday, 19 March, and returned to Lamb House that afternoon.
3. Dr. Skinner was present at Osler's examination of HJ.

cher . . . homme: dear great man; *apposta:* especially; *pâti:* footed the bill; *chez lui:* at his place; *constater:* taking note of the fact; *rechute:* relapse

[TELEGRAM]   Post Office Telegraphs, Rye
                                              9:41 a.m., 21 March 1910

Wharton
Queens Acre, Windsor[1]

Did journey successfully better yesterday[2] less well today but home
helpful

James

1. A distressed Teddy had reappeared in Paris. EW made plans for him to
undergo a rest cure at Neuilly, which his sister scotched. Their Parisian physician gave permission for light travel in England. EW had evidently told HJ
they would visit Howard Sturgis at Queen's Acre.

2. HJ sent the message to EW, evidently before receiving the invitation from
her from Folkestone; see letter of 21 March 1910.

                                              Lamb House, Rye
                                              21 March 1910

Dearest & noblest Edith.

This is brave & beautiful news—having you at Folkestone; though I
must rather ruefully add that Osler's explicit instructions to Skinner
have but just now come—& are on a "rigid" *rest cure* (in open air—
open windows) basis, under a Nurse[1] & seem to involve an all day
coucherie with massage & feeding [&] packing.[2] It is only, yet, a question
of finding the right man (or more probably—he being an animal very
difficult & rare—the right woman). This doesn't fall in with excursions,
but it permits I hope & pray visitors (that is you & Teddy)[3] and at any
rate doesn't prevent the daily increasing devotion of your

H.J.

1. Nephew Harry brought a Nurse Barnes down to Lamb House from London on 23 March.

2. HJ had written "massage & packing," then inserted "feeding" with a caret
in the space before "packing." This is a letter vexed with numerous such
insertions—a reflection of his health.

3. EW and Teddy motored over from Folkestone to visit on 27 March, Easter Sunday.

coucherie: confinement to bed

Lamb House, Rye
14 April 1910

Dearest Edith.

Don't wince at these pale characters again—for they still come easier to me; & I am still *climbing* my steep & interminable ascent—I am not yet at the top or on the high level plateau. But I am much more on the way. My sister-in-law[1] wrote to you yesterday—was very glad to do so, & I rejoice in it; but she was doubtless cautious & guarded. My history is that I had for more than 15 days after I last saw you here the longest & clearest steady progress I have had. I kicked absolutely against the maddening massage &c, but kept the nurse, though absolutely declining it & the "hydrotherapy" I had, in all, 3 weeks of rest-cure & air-bath, with resolute & successful feeding, which saw me further on than anything has done. It's my doom, however, always to have accidents & *rechutes*—from what I call medical interference—& I have had over the last 4 days—out of which I am struggling even as I write. They are shorter than before & I come out of them more easily & further on. Really 6 days ago I seemed pretty *near* being well—& shall feel so again, feel nearer. I am "up & dressed" again—from 10.30 or so to 9 or so—& generally am much more confident. Ci vuol' sempre pazienza—an heroic amount; but I shall still find it. The presence of my brother & his wife is still—or much—more vivid of my supreme tenderness of affection & remembrance. I can't write yet to Morton—but ça viendra. My companions think I look extremely better than they expected. Ever your

H.J.

1. WJ and Alice arrived at Lamb House 7 April 1910—twenty-four hours after Nurse Barnes had left.

rechutes: relapses; *Ci . . . pazienza:* It always takes patience; *ça viendra:* that will
come

Lamb House, Rye
16 April 1910

Dearest Edith.

William wrote to you, expressing, besides all his own, a part of my
deeply-stirred emotion, yesterday; but I am now, thank heaven, sufficiently *raffermi* to follow up without more delay that assurance of my
ineffable appreciation of the exquisite ingenuity, the truly divine subtlety
of your letter. Il n'y a que vous, verily, for such refinements of art &
such inspiration of charity—one can scarce say which phase or element
of the heavenly amalgam prevails—& I can only bow my head & bend
my knees in the intensest grateful assent to your magnificent offer. I
have become these last days not *afraid* to say that I am daily gaining
ground &, to put it grossly, getting better (&, more or less, *well*) &
my sense of what the sister, "she" (& the brother Morgan)[1] would
contribute at this juncture to that process of benefit to the world (&
incidentally to myself), deprives me of the power of anything but abject,
greedy, grasping response. Let them, Her & Him of Folkestone, arrive
then at their 1st convenience—but on the explicit understanding that
their Garage & bed & board expenses here (for their coming to & from
Folkestone would represent the wear & tear of some 40 or 50 miles a
day) shall be met, please, by your so cheeringly convalescent benefici-
ary. I feel that they will *complete* the admirable process that the delayed
whole rupture with sick-room discipline lately began. After I saw you
last I assured the Doctor & the "specialist" Nurse that if I was *touched*
again for maddening massage & water-cure "packing" I would throw
myself out of the window upon the flags of the court, & that stopped
that, with prompt alleviation. But the authoritative 6 times a day feeding
punctually to the minute, willy-nilly, with Nurse standing over me like
Queen Eleanor over the Fair Rosamond with the cup of cold poison,
continued, for I tried to keep up the tradition of it for myself some 4
days or so after my Brother & Sister arrived & Nurse departed. Then
it came over me (under a sharp little *rechute*) that just *that itself* was doing

me the harm & leading me nowhither but to nervous fear of the consequences of not submitting—while it was exactly in not submitting
(my brother strongly backing me) that recovery would lie. So I again
rebelled, & I am now therefore free as air, going out walking (petitement), eating as when inclined (which always sooner or later comes)—
& getting well. So there we are. Skinner has taken it beautifully. We
are not good—I mean I am not good for much penmanship yet, as you
can see—but everything is coming—& I shall go to meet it $\frac{1}{2}$ way in
the Daimler. Don't worry about the London play-question—I shall only
go near it—& I needn't till about *May 5th*—if the absolutely right thing
has happened meanwhile. Teddy has my close accolade—Morton has a
distinct one all himself (I quiver & almost quibble over the imminent
Quarterly)[2] & for you, dearest Edith, are reserved the deepest devotedest abasements of your faithfullest old

Henry James

1. "She" is EW's motor and Morgan is the English chauffeur; EW had kindly
made them available to HJ et al. at this juncture. But see letter of 25 April
1910.
2. Morton Fullerton's essay on the New York Edition; see letter of 19 April
1909.

raffermi: strengthened; *Il . . . vous:* There is no one like you; *rechute:* relapse;
petitement: moderately

Lamb House, Rye
25 April 1910

Dearest Edith.

I am writing you but a lame & limp letter—because things have
again not been well with me. I am sorry—I am deeply grieved—to say
that on further experiment the beautiful motor & the excellent Morgan[1]
prove too much for me—I am not up to them. My bad nervous state is
alas, a stern reality & I come back from the "spins" overstrained &
overdone. I am afraid it will be a long time before I am in any condition
for this particular pleasure. I took 4 runs (with my brother & sister) &

the last, on Saturday settled the question, I think, for me. I skipped yesterday to see the effect of omission & try once again this afternoon, if possible (I write you at 11 A.M.) but it is best the car should *end* its visit today at any rate, returning to Folkestone tomorrow. This will have made the series of days from Wednesday 20th to Monday 25th, inclusive (6 days in all)—for which I am, *we* are, deeply indebted to you. My brother & sister have immensely enjoyed. I am heart-broken at having again to report myself as so much *abattu* & able to *stand* so little—after telling you last of my sensible gain. But I seem deplorably at the mercy of accidents—& scarce see the end! Forgive my woeful wail again—which shows the vanity of all one's reports *one* [?] of one's state at a given moment. The one comfort of my situation is the presence—so beneficent—of my companions; without whom I should, frankly, go under. Will you please give my most particular love to Morton—to whom my last wire said (I think) I would write. I can't now—I am too down; but the bounty of the article is a joy to me & I am yours, dearest Edith, not less tenderly than ruefully

Henry James

P.S.   The going up to town is smash for the time again—God only knows what the effect of my impotence in the matter will have on the production of my play![2]

P.S.   The expenses of car & Morgan *here* of course are paid.

1. Which EW had lent HJ and WJ and Alice; see letter of 16 April 1910.
2. See letter of 2 March 1910.

abattu: beaten down

Lamb House, Rye
13 May 1910

Dearest Edith.

I have been hideously silent—but it has had to be—even after your priceless letter about my tale in the blue Review[1]—& all your other beautiful bounties since. My situation remains very difficult & my demoralization great. Yet I am *slowly, slowly* less bad—that I think I can measure. I cling like—or with—frenzied terror to my blest sister-in-law; alone it would all come to an end. (My brother is still abroad.)[2] Even I am making the colossal effort to go away with her for a few days to a friend's (Mrs. Charles Hunter's)[3] in Epping Forest—so intensely does the sameness & staleness of this long prison press on me, & the sense of the possible value of change, *as* change, increasingly work in me. Yet my nervous uncertainty & abjectness are great, & I take my courage in both desperate hands. I have never anything but recurrent *tracasses*[4] here—even after comparative little improvements. Forgive these poor weak words & oh, be sorry for me. Howard S[turgis] writes me that you & Teddy go to Lausanne.[5] All my blessings on it. My own yearning is to be well enough to stay away from here—somehow, in town, preferably, it may be, for some time; yet with someone of my own to cling to &—I blush to confess it—*cry* to! But it is very problematical. Still, I am fighting hard & I think just microscopically gaining. Ever your devoted (with all tenderness to Teddy)

Henry James

1. "A Round of Visits"; see letter of 16 February 1910.

2. WJ, with a severe heart condition, had gone on to Bad Nauheim in Germany to take the "cure."

3. Mary (1857–1933), wife of Charles E. Hunter (d. 1916). The Hunters had recently acquired the substantial country house Hill Hall; see letter of 21 May 1910.

4. Although almost illegible, the word is evidently some form of *tracasser* (to trouble, worry, annoy)—e.g., the nouns *tracas* and *tracasserie*—quite possibly anglicized (a common enough practice of HJ's), as it is in this text, "annoyances."

5. Seeking a solution to Teddy's problems, EW had taken him to Lausanne to see an eminent neurologist—to no avail.

Hill Hall
Theydon Bois, Epping
21 May 1910

Dearest Edith.

No, I *must*, write & thank you for all your generosity & bravery & patience—I am too "sorry," all the while, for you & Teddy not to. In spite of my strange whereabouts—a most beautiful & vast old "Jacobean" house lately acquired by the Charles Hunters in Epping Forest —I am having much of a devil of a time, through the formidable nervous aggravations which are with me more often than not—& with me *here* most direfully. Mrs. C. H. is divinely kind—& *such* a nice & wondrous woman, & I suffered myself to be urged by my advisers (*Dr.* mainly) to come away from home "easily" for the vital test of "change of scene," air, diet &c. It has worked with painful complications—I haven't responded &c; but I hang on till Monday,[1] when I probably seek my lair again with a drooping wing & much uncertainty for the future. I cling hard—utterly—to my blest sister-in-law (my brother is at Nauheim) & have a term of solitude while utterly unfit for society. Adventures of any kind terrify me—& the future looks uncertain. There is a plan of our joining William at Nauheim,[2] but that undertaking fairly appals me. So everything is mixed & dark! Your own possibilities seem not much easier or brighter—& it is all a mauvaise passe; but I cherish your affection more than ever & think with ineffable kindness of Teddy, as of one who suffers. Yours then more tenderly than ever.

Henry James

1. HJ left on Wednesday, 1 June, for London to book passage for himself, WJ, and Alice for the United States.
2. See letter of 10 June 1910.

mauvaise passe: difficult situation

Bittongs Hôtel Hohenzollern
Bad Nauheim
10 June 1910

Dearest Edith.

Your kindest note met me here on my arrival with my sister last evening. We are infinitely touched by the generous expressions of it, but there had been, & could be no question for us of Paris—formidable at best (that is in general) as a place of rapid transit. I had, to my sorrow, a baddish drop on coming back from high Epping Forest (that is "Theydon Mount") to poor little flat & stale & illness-haunted Rye —& I felt, my Dr. strongly urging, safety to be in a prompt escape by the straightest way (Calais, Brussels, Cologne & Frankfort) to this place of thick woods, groves, springs & general *Kurort* soothingness where my brother had been for a fortnight waiting us alone. Here I am then, & having made the journey, in great heat, far better than I feared. Slowly but definitely I *am* emerging—yet with nervous possibilities still too latent, too in ambush, for me to do anything but cling for as much longer as possible to my Brother & Sister. I am wholly unfit to be alone—in spite of amelioration. That (being alone) I can't even as yet think of—& yet feel that I must for many months to come have none of the complications of society. In fine, to break to you the monstrous truth, I have taken my passage with them to America by the Canadian Pacific Steamer line ("Short sea") on August 12th—to spend the winter in America. I must break with everything—utterly—of the last couple of years in England—& am trying if possible to let Lamb House for the winter—also am giving up my London perch.[1] When I come back I must have a better. There are the grim facts—but now that I have accepted them I see hope & reason in them. I feel that the completeness of the change là-bas will help me more than anything else can—& the amount of corners I have already turned (though my nervous spectre still again & again scares me) is a kind of earnest of the rest of the process. I cling to my companions even as a frightened cry-baby to his nurse & protector—but of all *that* it is depressing, almost degrading to speak. This place is insipid yet soothing—very bosky & sedative & admirably arranged, à l'allemande—but with excessive & depressing heat just now & a toneless air at the best. The admirable ombrages & walks & pacifying pitch of life makes up, however, for much. We shall be here 2 or 3 months longer (I seem to entrevoir) & then try for something Swiss & tonic. We must be in England by Aug. 1st.—And now I simply *fear* to challenge you on your own complications. I can *bear* tragedies so little. Tout se rattache so à *the* thing—the central depression. And yet I want so to know—& I think of you with infinite tenderness, participation—& such a bare & helpless devotion. Well, we must hold on tight & we shall come out again face to face—wiser than ever before (if *that's* any advantage!). This address I foresee, will find me for the next 15 days—& we might be worse abrités. Germany has become *comfortable*. Note that much as I yearn to you, I don't nag you with categorical (even though in Germany) questions. I affectionately greet Minnie & Beatrix[2]—out of my dumbness—& of Morton [Fullerton] I ache always & habitually to think. Ever your unspeakablest, dearest Edith,

Henry James

1. At the Reform Club, 105 Pall Mall, overlooking Carlton House Terrace.
2. Mary Cadwalader Jones and her daughter.

Kurort: health resort, spa; *là-bas:* over there; *à l'allemande:* in the German fashion; *entrevoir:* foresee; *Tout . . . à:* everything is so tied to; *abrités:* sheltered

Bad-Nauheim
21 June 1910

Dearest Edith.

To have heard from you again meets, within me, a deep conscious yearning. I am haunted by speculation about you, & you give me something to go upon. But what a tension must be unbrokenly yours & with what intimate participation do I consider it. How I wish you *were* going over to the Mount in August—capable as I am of beginning to dream now that I might come to see you there—She, the great She,[1] becoming again des nôtres—to say nothing of the great Morton too, since he is again going over. For my process of gradually working from under the nightmare of the last 6 months, seems, thanks to the merciful powers (if there be such!) to go quietly on here (where most, though not all, of the conditions are favorable). I eat, I walk, I *almost* sleep—& what I shall most have done, if things go on as I hope, will be to have walked myself well. I thank you ever so gratefully for seeing an enlightened sense in my going back for a while to America. I hold it of vital importance that I shall not inhabit L[amb] H[ouse] again for a year (I want to break as completely as possible with the sinister sense that my squeezed-in & boiled-down life there insidiously put on for me these last 2 years & $\frac{1}{2}$ in particular); & a series of months là-bas will help to this more than anything. Besides: other reasons conspire strongly; preeminently that my brother & sister, who have been such angels to me, have asked me to come, for a long visit to *them*, & that to be for a time with my brother, in his own home, invalidical as he is, is a call to a chance that pulls at my heart-strings coercively. And there are other grounds still. Meanwhile I am not at all trying to let L.H. now for next winter—have taken & am taking no steps for it. A sort of contingent offer was made me 4 weeks ago, & I then *generally* assented, but nothing more has come of that since, & as I have nothing to do with agents or such-like, I am strongly convinced the place won't let at all. Houses let badly, & at the best for very small returns, during the winter—at Rye, I mean. We stay here till the end of this week—or till Friday, & then *probably* go on to Munich & the Bavarian Highlands—though it will depend on the Doctor's last word after my Brother's last bath. We have turned against stale Switzerland. We expect to be in Geneva for a week the last thing before returning to England (my sister gets her & my niece's *clothes* there!), & shall have to be in England some ten days before sailing (on Aug. 12th). So the time to dispose of otherwise is not very considerable.—I rejoice in what you tell me of the Americanization of Morton's article[2]—& of the Roosevelt achievement[3]—what a heavenly Providence you are to him! And I don't know what strange & impertinent comfort I take in Miss Katherine's [*sic*] marriage[4]—lifted above the tremor of a mere engagement! At all events these things are an occasion for my sending him my most devoted assurances. Forgive this waggly-wobbly scrawl. I am not back to the act of writing at all yet—or even to my loose apology for a hand. The II *Got*, like the 1st,[5] interested me much (he was a tremendous *character*); & I am beginning to read again—for weeks & weeks it was dismally impossible. But I cling to you, dearest Edith, through thick & thin, & believe that we shall find ourselves in some secure port together yet. Meanwhile how your noble image is cherished by your affectionate old

Henry James

1. EW's auto.

2. Fullerton's article on the New York Edition (see letter of 19 April 1909) was reprinted in Boston's *Living Age*, 11 June 1910.

3. Theodore Roosevelt's speech (23 April 1910) at the Sorbonne, "Citizenship in a Republic," observing that socialism "would spell sheer destruction; it would produce grosser wrong and outrage, fouler immorality, than any existing system," etc., provoked a May Day demonstration in Paris.

4. Morton's cousin Katharine Fullerton, to whom he was "engaged" as late as November 1909, became engaged in February 1910 to Gordon Gerould, an instructor at Princeton, and had just married him.

5. Edmond Got (1822–1901), of the Comédie Française; his son Médéric had just published the *Journal de Edmond Got* in two volumes with a preface by Henri Lavedan. In 1877 HJ had called him "the first of living actors."

des nôtres: one of us; *là-bas:* over there

Lamb House, Rye
29 July 1910

Dearest Edith.

It's an intense joy to hear from you, & when I think that the last news I gave you of myself was at Nauheim (it seems to me, with the nightmare of Switzerland that followed—"Munich & the Tyrol &c" which I believe I then hinted at to you proved the vainest crazy dream of but a moment) I feel what the strain & stress of the sequel that awaited me really became. That dire ordeal (attempted Nach-Kurs for my poor brother at *low* Swiss altitudes, Constance, Zurich, Lucerne, Geneva &c) terminated however a fortnight ago—or more—& after a bad week in London we are here waiting to sail on Aug. 12th. I am definitely much better, & on the road to be *well*; a great gain has come to me, in spite of everything, during the last 10 days in particular. I say in spite of everything, for my dear brother's condition, already so bad on leaving the treacherous & disastrous Nauheim, has gone steadily on to worse—he is painfully ill, weak and down, & the anxiety of it, with our voyage in view, is a great tension to me in my still quite *struggling* upward state. But I stand & hold my ground none the less, & we have really brought him on since we left London. But the dismalness of it all—& of the sudden death, a fortnight ago, of our younger brother in the U.S., by heart-failure in his sleep[1]—a painless, peaceful, enviable end to a stormy & unhappy career—make our common situation, all these months back & now—fairly tragic & miserable. However, I am convinced that his getting home, if it can be securely done, will do much for William—& I am myself now on a much "higher plane" than I expected a very few weeks since to be. I kind of *want*, uncannily, to go to America too—apart from several absolutely imperative reasons for it. I rejoice unspeakably in the vision of seeing you & Walter[2] here— or even in London or at Windsor—one of these very next days. I think I should be able to get in the course of the (of *next*) week a couple of nights in town & could come out to a tea or lunch, or even a dinner, with Howard [Sturgis]—especially if *She*[3] should be with you & open her arms & wings to, &, for, me. I might manage it for Tuesday & Wednesday—or for Wednesday & Thursday—especially (again) if you should motor over from Folkestone & pick me *up* here & take me.[4] *Don't* fail of this. I might manage that last even if you come, as I hope & pray, *Monday*. But I hurry this off to the post. You tell me nothing of Teddy—but you *will*. I send my unstinted love to Walter—brazen that thus out in spite of being abjectly in his debt. But I shall address him the "Strike but hear me!"[5] in a way to bring the house down. Come from Folkestone to tea or lunch at *any* rate. Monday, only remember, is Bank Holiday—but that doesn't matter for Her the least little bit. Ever your all-affectionate, dear Edith,

Henry James

1. Robertson James (b. 1846), HJ's youngest brother.

2. Walter Berry had resigned, as of 20 June 1910, his position with the International Tribunal in Egypt.

3. EW's auto; also "Her" at the end of the letter.

4. EW and Berry picked HJ up on Friday, 5 August, and motored to Sturgis's for an interrupted long weekend; EW drove Berry to Southampton on Saturday; HJ and EW motored to Folkestone on Tuesday, 9 August; HJ returned to Rye by train.

5. The response of Themistocles (c. 525 B.C.–c. 460 B.C.), Athenian statesman and naval commander, to Eurybiades, commander of the Spartan fleet, when the latter raised his staff as though to strike him.

Nach-Kurs: after-treatments

Lamb House, Rye
31 July 1910

Dearest Edith.

I have your good (or bad) wire this A.M.,[1] & am waiting for your letter—but am meanwhile thrusting myself on your great charity for a small material service. While in Geneva 3 weeks ago my brother & I left 3 gold watches with Messrs Vacheron & Constantin there (admirable watchmakers & the author of their—the watches'—being), to be cleaned, regulated & sent us back hither. I hear from V. & C. today that great difficulties have arisen about sending gold watches to England without the English hall-mark, & that if some friend can *bring* them to us that will be the best way. It never takes much to make my thoughts revert to *you*, & at any rate this awkward news has sufficed on the present occasion. I have therefore let them know—in fact I wire them, though I've already written, tomorrow, that if they will instantly send the small articles by post to you (for *France* there are no difficulties) you will be so good as to bring them to us. We shall be intensely grateful —& I just hurry off this word. I am getting on excellently & my brother is a little better. Ever your faithfullest

Henry James

1. Evidently informing HJ that she would not arrive in England until Thursday, 4 August, and so not arrive at Lamb House until Friday morning; see letter of 29 July 1910.

4

At the Crossroads

SEPTEMBER 1910–DECEMBER 1911

IN AUTUMN 1910 James was still in America and ailing rather seriously, in part as a result of his brother William's death. Yet he roused himself in October to visit the temporarily reconciled Whartons at the Hotel Belmont in New York. In a whirlwind three-day interval Fullerton arrived, Teddy left to go round the world, and Berry, Fullerton, James, and Edith Wharton dined together at the Belmont. She left the next day for Paris and suffered a brief nervous collapse on regaining 53, rue de Varenne.

In early 1911 James spent two months in New York with Mary Cadwalader Jones. The visit was interrupted by his medical appointments in Boston and Cambridge—with the Freudian psychiatrist Dr. James Jackson Putnam and with his dentist Dr. Roberts—and by his sitting for his portrait to nephew Billy James and to Cecilia Beaux.

Edith Wharton in Paris resumed work on her novella *Ethan Frome*, as she had begun it in June 1910, under the favorable circumstances of Teddy's absence. Its publication in August coincided with that of James's final novel, *The Outcry*. Teddy's return to Paris typically provoked in Edith an asthmatic attack and sent her flying off to the spa at Salsomaggiore and then to New York and Lenox. John Hugh Smith, Gaillard Lapsley, and James joined her at The Mount for a few days in midsummer. The abrupt arrival of Teddy on 13 July scattered the guests after a violent scene in which he demanded control of his wife's finances. From Nahant, Massachusetts, where he was a guest of old friend George

A. James, James wrote to urge her to take a double decision forthwith: get rid of The Mount and separate from Teddy.

For her part, Wharton had been for some months working to enlist the aid of influential people like Edmund Gosse and William Dean Howells in her campaign to secure the Nobel Prize for literature for James. The campaign failed in the end: the prize was awarded to the Belgian Maurice Maeterlinck.

James and Wharton found themselves restless on their return to Rye and to Paris in the later months of 1911 and sought relief in travel. James went off to Scotland and visited in and around London. Wharton went to Italy with Berry (James had to refuse her invitation to join them) and later alone to England. She was back in Paris by the end of December. James had determined to stay in London and found suitable working quarters adjoining Theodora Bosanquet's flat in Chelsea; there he began work on the autobiographical *A Small Boy and Others*. Henry and Edith anticipated beneficial alterations in their lives and careers as 1911 bowed out.

Chocorua, N.H.

9 September 1910

Dearest Edith.

Your letter from Annecy—you poor dear goaded wanderer!— touches me, as I sit here stricken & in darkness,[1] with the tenderest of hands. It was all to become again a black nightmare (what seems to me such now) very soon after I left you, to these days of attempted readjustment of life, on the basis of my beloved brother's irredeemable absence from it, in which I take my part with my sister-in-law & his children here. I quitted you at Folkestone August 9th (just a month ago today—& it seems six!) to find him, at Lamb House, apparently not a little eased by the devoted Skinner, & with the elements much more auspicious for our journey than they had been a fortnight before. We got well enough to town on the 11th, & away from it, to Liverpool, on the 12th, & the voyage, in the best accommodations &c we had ever had at sea, & of a wondrous lakelike & riverlike fairness & brevity, might if he had been really less ill, have made for his holding his ground.[2] But he grew rapidly worse again from the start & suffered piteously & dreadfully (with the increase of his difficulty in breathing); & we got him at last to this place (on the evening of the Friday following that of our sailing) only to see him begin swiftly to sink. The local (8 miles away) physician here was really good, his son a very intelligent & modern young Doctor too, was immediately installed in the house & was a most blessed resource, & we quickly managed to get up from Boston, even in the vacuity of August, a man of high & special reputation there. (It is wonderful here now what the ubiquitous telephone & the extraordinarily multiplied motor together achieve.) But it was in spite of everything a heartbreaking unforgettable week—he suffered so & only wanted, wanted more & more, to go. The sight of the rapidity of it at the last was an unutterable pang—my sense of what he had still to *give*, of his beautiful genius & noble intellect at their very climax never having been anything but intense, & in fact having been intenser than ever all these last months. However, my relation to him & affection for him, & the different aspect his extinction has given for me to my life, are all unutterable matters; fortunately, as there would be so *much* to say about them if I said anything at all. The effect of it all is that I shall stay on here for the present—for some months to come (I mean in this country); & then return to England never to revisit these shores again. I am inexpressibly glad to have been, & even to be, here now— I cling to my sister-in-law & my nephews & niece: they are *all* (wonderful to say) such admirable, loveable, able & interesting persons, & they cling to me in return. I hope to be in on this spot with them till Oct. 15th—there is a great appeal in it from its saturation with my brother's presence & life here, his use & liking of it for 23 years, a sad subtle consecration which plays out the more where so few other things interfere with it. Ah, the thin, empty, lonely, melancholy American "beauty"—which I yet find a cold prudish charm in! I shall go back to Cambridge with my companions & stay there at least till the New Year—which is all that seems definite for the present.

I am afraid you are having little rest in your dragging of your car up hill—by which I don't mean at all "her," but only & emphatically *him*.[3] But I hope your beautiful high Reposoir has brought a remedy at least to your hay fever. It's a sorry picture, your being driven to such restless repose. But most distressing to me [of] all, I confess, is your account of

Morton's treatment, after his long & admirable career, by that brutal slut & those vulgar & odious people.[4] All my feeling about it gathers itself into the intense desire to see him—though, in spite of having had a telegram (cable) from him I don't know where to address him. I shall, however, risk a word to Hotel Vouillemont, begging for news of his sailing hither, & then keenly watch for him. From Walter B. I have also had a kind wire, but all addressless, save that he seemed to be at Newport—& I don't know at all how to get at him. *Cambridge, Mass.* will steadily find me here. All devotedly yours, dearest Edith,

Henry James

1. WJ died just before 2:30 p.m. on 26 August 1910.
2. For HJ's account of the crossing, see *Comp. Notes*, 318–19.
3. Teddy.
4. Evidently the blackmailer had resumed her harassment of Fullerton. The "odious" people may be her abettors or perhaps the new directors of the London *Times*.

Chocorua, N.H.
25 September 1910

Dearest Edith.

Your news (of the 15th)[1] is most touching & thrilling, but that is the case with the generality of your newses. I fear you have been having a most troublous time—your heroic step sufficiently points to us. May this, scrawled here of a rainy Sunday a.m., with the mountains & forests all sheeted with dense white wetness, find you with your foot planted (temporarily!) on our queer American earth. May it just at once meet & greet & comfort & even beguile you a little, in fine; till we make out what is possible in the way of closer communication. I'm afraid you will have left before receiving my letter[2] posted to you a few days—very few—after my receipt of your cable on my brother's death—I wrote you then at considerable length. My news since then, at any rate, is of the smallest—save in so far as it's "small" to have been living here more & more *into* the difference in the world & the whole aspect of life [made] by the extinction of his so cherished & dominant presence. But that belongs to the unspeakable—only that I am staying on here, & shall stay on (on this particular spot), for the intimate desire of being as long as I can with his wife & children, who cling to me as I to them. The length of our stay longer will depend on the season, temperature, weather—but is all unlikely to exceed Oct. 15th, & may anticipate it. When I hear from you, in however few words your pressure may restrict you to, I can give thought to the arrangements we shall make for meeting. My own general plan is to be at Cambridge (95 Irving St.) for November, December & whatever more. Anything to this place till Oct. 12th or so will be safe—& *always* everything safe to the Cambridge address as above. I'm afraid you will immediately be full of trouble & anxious preoccupations & tensions over what shall be found best for Teddy & I cling to the hope that the Morton Johnson (or vice-versa) motoring plan[3] may be workable. Heaven send it, or something as presumably propitious. All thanks for W. M. F[ullerton]'s date here—at the beastly *Times*![4] Most absolutely we must meet together, & oh how I want to see you both. But I think of *you* just now with most suspense. All affectionately yours

Henry James

P.S. I am motoring "some" here—with immense benefit & help. The *big* beautiful—rudely, crudely appealing country! for it!

1. Announcing plans to arrive (with Teddy) in New York about 21 September and to be situated in the Hotel Belmont.

2. See letter of 9 September 1910.

3. Johnson Morton, sometime editor of the *Youth's Companion*, was a writer and a social worker among the poor of Boston. The projected autumn tour that EW proposed he and Teddy take to the Rockies and into California was expanded into a world tour to begin in mid-October. See letter of 30 September 1910.

4. Fullerton was about to sever his connection with the London *Times*; see letter of 9 September 1910.

Chocorua, N.H.

30 September 1910

Dearest Edith.

I received your 2 letters last night both together, in spite of their difference of dates, & I address myself at once to sympathetic response. I deeply grieve over your immediate disconcertments & their effect on Teddy—but I hope more light & a better connection with your Doctor has come. Likewise I am staggered by your mere quinzaine of a projected stay here—it seems so scant a value for so long a reach. You may say that *any* stay, no matter how long, in our unspeakable country is a scant value—though, just now, in this gorgeous & so native weather with the great chamber of nature hung about as with some embossed & gilded & crimsoned & purpled cuir de Cordoue, to say nothing of bigger crackling & snapping fires than ever Cordoue could show (let alone the motoring some, or the sum of motoring), just now, I say, I feel kind of resigned & friendly to this particular aspect of it all (dread whole!)—with other very persuasive elements added. However, the great matter is that if you really *are* to sail on the deplorable Oct. 15th[1] we absolutely must meet before. I much desire to cultivate on my own side, by very practical art, that ideal. I *think* I shld. be able to come to New York for 2 days on the 10th or the 11th—spending the said 48 hours there: that is the 11th & 12th or the 12th & 13th; perhaps even the 14th. Will you kindly let me know whether (as I fully take for granted) those days wd. find you "in the city." In that case I wd. go down to Boston from here on the 10th or the 11th & take the night-train (oh this execrable native blotting paper!) to N.Y. (I did that, 6 years ago here, 4 or 5 times & found it, with a good "stateroom," the least fatiguing course). In this case I shld. go to the big hotel opposite the big (Grand Central?) station—of which I forget the name, but which was large & easy & plantureux. So beautifully make me the sign. May some good development befall you meanwhile—for this I earnestly, devoutly, pray. Alas I saw no scrap of Gilliard [Lapsley] whatever—only heard from him soon after I arrived & while my trouble was of the darkest. My beloved brother's death has cut into me, deep down, even as an absolute mutilation; but I hold up my head, nevertheless, partly because I feel that I am mastering more & more, through every-thing, the damnable difficulties of recuperation heaped on me by last winter & spring & all the early summer. I am getting away & away from that dismal time. My sister & nephews & niece, to whom I fondly cling, beautifully help. But make me the sign. Ever your

H.J.

P.S. *Such* a letter, just to hand, from Bourget—absolutely indecipherable, among other things!—When "Hotel Belmonts" are gîtes, surely, que faire en un gîte à moins que l'on ne paie!²

1. Fullerton arrived in New York on 15 October; Teddy left on his world tour with Morton on the 16th; EW, HJ, Fullerton, and Berry dined at the Belmont on the 17th; EW sailed on the 18th. HJ had arrived on the 12th; he lingered at the Belmont until Saturday the 22nd before returning to Cambridge.

2. HJ's adaptation of the opening of La Fontaine's fable of "The Hare and the Frogs": "A Hare was dreaming in his lair, / (For what else would one do in a lair except dream?)"—i.e., *Car que faire en un giste, à moins que l'on ne songe?*—substituting "paie" (pay) for "songe" (dream).

quinzaine: fortnight; *cuir de Cordoue:* Cordovan leather; *plantureux:* plentiful, ample

95 Irving St.
[Cambridge, Mass.]
2 November 1910

Dearest Edith.

Very relieving, in a manner, your vivid signal from your further shore—relieving, I mean, as to speed & an early port. Still, it must have been rather a nightmare—& know how I ache over you! But may a period of peace succeed.—Morton comes here tonight from Brockton, to dine & sleep. I haven't seen him since the Thursday after your embarkation¹—when he came & dined with Lawrence G[odkin] (with Minnie J[ones]) & "captured" Lawrence (not that the latter can help him!).² He tells me he sails on the 16th or 17th. I remained in N.Y. only to the Saturday—being much less well as soon as I had lost you, & in fact had a pretty bad Thursday & Friday—after which I tumbled into the train & returned here. Since then I have been remarkably better till yesterday, when I had a bad *accès*—to the effect of which, still rather abiding, please attribute the weakness of these lines. I have these accursed depressing little relapses[3]—I say "little" for they tend to be shorter. *E pur' si muove*; & I shall more or less hold up my head for Morton tonight, he comes presently, at 5. I can *only* be here for the present (at Cambridge); but oh the American melancholics! Ever your

H.J.

1. That is, 20 October.

2. Having broken with the *Times*, Fullerton was seeking to establish himself as a freelance writer in New York.

3. The relapse continued through November and into the new year; see letter of 9 February 1911.

accès: attack; *E . . . muove:* and yet it does move (Galileo's insistence)

95 Irving St.
Cambridge [Mass.]
9 February 1911

Dearest Edith.

Hideous & infamous, yes, my interminable, my abjectly graceless silence. But it always comes, in these abnormal months, from the same sorry little cause, which I have already named to you to such satiety that I really might omit any further reference to it. Somehow, none the less, I find a vague support, in my consciousness of an unsurpassable abjection (as aforesaid), in naming it once more *to myself* & in putting afresh on record that there's a method in what I feel might pass for my madness if *you* weren't so nobly sane. To write is perforce *to report of myself* & my condition—& nothing has happened to make that process any less an evil thing. It's horrible to me to report darkly & dismally—& yet I never venture 3 steps in the opposite direction without having the poor effrontery flung back in my face as an outrage on the truth. In other words to report favourably is instantly—or at very short order—to be hurled back on the couch of anguish—so that the only thing has, for the most part, been to stay my pen rather than *not* report favourably. You'll say doubtless: "Damn you, why report *at all*—if you are so crassly superstitious? Answer civilly & prettily & punctually when a lady (& 'such a lady,' as Browning says!)[1] generously & à 2 reprises writes to you—without 'dragging in Velasquez' at all." Very well then, I'll try—though it was pretty well poor old Velasquez who came back 3 evenings since from 23 days in New York, & at 21 East 11th St.,[2] of which the last 6 were practically spent in bed. He had had a very fairly flourishing fortnight in that kindest of houses & tenderest of cares & genialest of companies—& then repaid it all by making himself a burden & a bore. I got myself out of the way as soon as possible—by scrambling back here; & yet, all inconsequently, I think it likely I shall return there in March[3] to perform the same evolution. In the intervals I quite take notice—but at a given moment everything temporarily goes. I come up again & quite well up—as how can I not in order again to re-taste the bitter cup? But here I *am* "reporting of myself" with a vengeance—forgive me if it's too dreary. When all's said & done it will eventually—the whole case—become less so. Meanwhile, too, for my consolation, I have picked up here & there wind-borne *bribes*, of a more or less authentic savour, from your own groaning board; & my poor old imagination does me in these days no better service than by enabling me to hover, like a too participant larbin, behind your Louis XIV chair (if it isn't, your chair, Louis Quatorze, at least your larbin takes it so). I gather you've been able to drive the spirited pen without cataclysms, & that Teddy's tremendous tour (let alone his companion's)[4] does follow, heroically, the greater curve of the globe. I take unutterable comfort in the thought that two or three months hence you'll probably be seated on the high-piled & *done* book[5]—in the magnificent authority of the position: even as Catherine II on the throne of the Czars. (Forgive the implications of the comparison!) Work seems far from *me* yet— though perhaps a few inches nearer. A report even reaches me to the effect that there's a possibility of your deciding, on Teddy's return, to come over and spend the summer at the Mount,[6] & this is above all a word to say that in case you should do so at all betimes you will probably still see me here; as though I have taken my passage for England my date is only the 14th June.[7] Therefore should you come May 1st— well, Porphyro[8] grows faint! I yearn over this—since if you shouldn't come then (& yet shld. be coming at all), heaven knows when we shall meet again. There are enormous reasons for my staying here till then, & enormous ones against my staying longer. Such, dearest Edith, is my meagre budget—forgive me if it isn't brighter & richer. I am but *just* pulling through—& I am doing *that*, but no more, & so, you see, have no wild graces or wavy tendrils left over for the image I project. I shall try to *grow* some again, little by little; but for the present am as ungarnished in every way as an aged plucked fowl before the cook has dealt with him. May the great Chef still see his way to serve me up to you some day in some better sauce! As I am, at any rate, share me generously with your I am sure not infrequent commensaux Walter B. & Morton F., & ask them to make the best of me (an' they love me—as I love *them*) even if you give them only the drumsticks & keep the comparatively tender, though much shrivelled, if once mighty "pinion" for yourself! Morton is much—immensely—on my mind, but I escape from that into the golden chambers & corridors, the prospective ones at least, of his Paris book.[9] I hope Walter, whom I embrace no less, is engaged in as noble an architecture. I saw no one of the least "real fascination" (*excusez du peu* of the conception!) in N.Y.—but the place relieved & beguiled me—so long as I was *debout*, & Mary Cadwal & Beatrix were as tenderest nursing mother & bonniest soeur de lait to me the whole day long. I really think I shall take—shall risk—another go of it before long again, & even snatch a "bite" of Washington (Washington pie, as we used to say); to which latter the dear H. Whites[10] have most kindly challenged me. Well, such, dearest Edith, are the short & simple annals of the poor! I hang about you, however inarticulately, de toutes les forces de mon être & am always your fondly faithful old

Henry James

P.S. I presently go out, through deepish snow, to call on Miss Longfellow[11]—"sweet Alice"—so to speak, comme qui dirait, the children's hour. I shld. say "without ambiguity"—didn't this perhaps seem to make it a little worse!

   1. "A Toccata of Galuppi's," stanza 5.
   2. Home of Mary Cadwalader Jones, where HJ arrived on 18 January; "Velasquez" was one of her nicknames for HJ.

3. HJ came to New York on 15 March and remained until 20 April; during that time he sat for the portrait by Cecilia Beaux.

4. See letter of 25 September 1910.

5. *Ethan Frome* (1911).

6. Teddy arrived in France in April; EW left for New York on 24 June.

7. See letter of 4 May 1911.

8. Chaste lover of maid Madeline in Keats's "The Eve of St. Agnes"; see l. 224.

9. Fullerton's book on Paris that he had agreed to write in return for the advance from Macmillan arranged in the summer of 1909 by EW; see letter of 26 July 1909.

10. Henry White (1850–1927), American diplomat under five presidents and most recently (1907–1909) ambassador to France; his wife, née Margaret Rutherford, was a friend of EW's from their girlhood days at Newport.

11. Alice Mary Longfellow (1850–1928), second daughter of American poet Henry Wadsworth Longfellow (1807–1882) and his second wife, née Frances Elizabeth Appleton (1817–1861); she was herself a writer of modest reputation. Longfellow's poem "The Children's Hour" mentions "Grave Alice."

à 2 reprises: twice over; *bribes:* scraps; *larbin:* flunkey; *commensaux:* table companions; *excusez du peu:* excuse the paucity; *debout:* on my feet; *soeur de lait:* foster sister; *de . . . être:* with all the strength of my being; *comme qui dirait:* as who should say

95 Irving St.
Cambridge, Mass.
4 May 1911

Dearly beloved Edith.

On the blessing of your news of an hour ago—by which I mean the balm & bounty of hearing your voice across the waste of ocean! It isn't that what you tell me is so intrinsically *folichon* as that we directly communicate & that, that warm consciousness restored, one wonders (at least *I* do) how I have languished through the cold interregnum. And yet it has been "all right" & inevitable & accordant—involved intimately in your situation, *de part & d'autre*, & now the blest renewal has come precisely at its hour. Many days before you get this, moreover, that renewal will have been intensified by the cable I shall have sent you this afternoon to the effect that I have shifted my sailing from June 14th to August 2d. I must absolutely go on this later date—but I now must most advisedly & desirably stay *till* then. In fact even if this hadn't within these last few days become clear I would certainly have decided for the wait on receiving your news of this morning. Even if you don't sail till June 15th (& I assume this as, by the trick of the gods, most probable because least delectable), I shall still be "round" for 5 weeks or so after you arrive, & we can in that time cut some ice. Es wird doch "schön" sein, in a measure, all the same. And may the Salso cure[1] meanwhile be as a heavenly dew & a new birth for you. Only what a devil of a journey for you par monts & par vaux—by dusty plains & bristling frontiers. Unless indeed "she" takes you on her back—which is more than probable, or even certain, after all. I even wildly dream of hearing the divine whirr of her wings myself—though let me not presumptuously anticipate.—I stay my hand from speaking now & here of the questions that mass themselves round Teddy, or encircle him with their devils' dance & the whole matter will stand ever so unfailingly to our earliest meeting. And meanwhile as I understand from you that he is sailing—or *has* sailed[2]—I shall perhaps find myself in touch with him here—& shall do my best that that touch be on my part as soothing as possible. (If he comes to Boston I shall meet him doubtless at the Somerset Club—as I have the convenience of going there.) I lately came back from 5 weeks with Mary Cadwal. in New York—weeks of a heavenly benevolence on her part, but of an unthankful interruptedness of physical equilibrium on mine—which ended in my abrupt flight back here. (I am at this present writing better—very much better again; better than at any time for long months & months past. Confidence & reassurance begin again to attend me.) I *appear* to be going at last about the middle of the month to spend a belated week with the Harry Whites in Washington; but it may still fail[3]—so many things have been against it all winter; though largely her own long & very beneficial séjour at Aiken, S. C., which has fanned the flame of her patriotism, I infer, as well as healed the wounds & ills of her beautiful person. This later evolution of hers is of the most charmingly weirdest—as they are building a house in Washington; of all of which I am sure I shall enjoy a nearer view.—What you tell me of our Morton, to whom I send heartiest love, interests & appeals to me deeply, & I shall write to George

Prothero,[4] on the matter of the "Quarterly" Article, by this very same post. I am very well placed for doing so, & though I can answer for no *absolute* result I am sure I shall be able to make a considerable impression on him. I shall at any rate make the strongest appeal. Recommend me *caramente* to Walter B[erry]. Oh how I want a thousand particulars, lights on the true inwardness, of everything & everyone (& especially of E.W.) from you! I, in my poor way, have much to tell you—such a nosegay of the flowers of my desert, that is, to offer you! May all your gifts & graces & genius now serve & support you—I mean bear you bravely to within hail of your fondly faithful & faithfully fond old

Henry James

1. An attack of "hay fever," typically provoked by Teddy's arrival and brief sojourn in Paris in early April, had sent EW south to Salsomaggiore, the Italian spa.

2. Teddy had sailed for Boston, after a couple of weeks spent visiting London tailors, before the end of April.

3. It failed.

4. George Walter Prothero (1848–1922), Cambridge historian and president of the Royal Society of Literature as well as editor of the *Quarterly Review*; he and his wife, Fanny, were near neighbors of HJ in Rye.

folichon: amusing; *de ... d'autre:* on both sides; *Es ... sein:* It would really be lovely; *par ... vaux:* by hill and dale; *séjour:* sojourn; *caramente:* affectionately

Lowland House
Nahant
27 June 1911

Dearest Edith.

Your beautiful letter of the 8th has been with me for some days "to warn, to comfort & command";[1] & I scrawl you this fond response & account, that it may meet you in New York, while my own decks are still comparatively clear—since from tomorrow on they will be for some days considerably encumbered. Please thus feel my arms open at their very widest to receive you & then close about you at their very tenderest! I have been at the tip end of this austere promontory for the whole of this month almost—though indeed tasting on this particular spot, with my extraordinarily kind old friend of long years back George A. James[2] (very widowed, of Lily Lodge, Cabot's sister, & very deaf, now; but always profusely florid & floral & wonderfully sea-girt & gardened & groved here) the breeziest & easiest & sweetest side of it; a situation which, for many reasons, has been a great cool, comfortable blessing & independence to me. I go up to Cambridge tomorrow—by the aid of *une d'Elles*,[3] but a mere venal beauty, of promiscuous favours, this time—to receive at Harvard Commencement an Honorary Degree (Oxford had offered me one,[4] too late for personal presence, on the same date); dont je n'ai que faire, but to which I bow a patient & weary head; then come back here for 2 nights, after which, on Friday 30th I go up to New Hampshire to stop over July 4th with some friends at Intervale[5] & proceed on the 5th to my sister at Chocorua. The stay I must absolutely make there before leaving the country can only *begin* then—all our movements, relations, & possibilities having been dislocated & put out of tune by my poor young Niece's long & grave illness,[6] which has made the flight to the country (planned for June 1st) impossible till now (Peg., convalescent, goes with her Mother & Nurse on the 1st), & has on the other hand made me for many weeks past (1st in Connecticut & afterwards here) keep at a respectful & considerate distance from the Cambridge household of doctors, nurses, anxieties & hot weather. My last séjour with les miens has thus suffered extreme frustration & contraction & has to be put in so far as there is still a margin; which means, alas, in respect to your roseate July 8th at the Mount, that I shan't be able to come to you there till the 15th or even the 17th.[7] Then I shall be able to stay, however, till 3 or 4 days before my New York sailing (Wednesday Aug. 2d. I shall have to go back to Cambridge, worse luck, for 36 hours, to do sundry urgent material things—& thence to N.Y.). But these details are grossiers & premature—the essence of the matter is that I will come to you at the very first hour I can compass it. I wish you meantime all possible firm ground to rest on or move on—yet feel helpless & of poor dim counsel to you. I am of no validity to speak of even for myself in these days—& only unutterably yearn to get out of "American conditions" at large & back to the air & *ambiente* that I believe will still show themselves workable. But goodnight now & a hundred thousand welcomes. Another 100 000 to Walter B[erry], if he is with you, as I fondly infer. I have been talking of you with beautiful brave Bessie Lodge[8] here—interesting & touching creature. I hope you haven't been sea-worried—that lion so dormant here. *Chocorua, N. H.* will postally serve, & I am yours all & always

Henry James

1. Like Wordsworth's phantom of delight: "A perfect Woman, nobly plann'd, / To warn, to comfort, and command. . . ."

2. George Abbot James, classmate of HJ at Harvard, had married Lily, sister of Senator Henry Cabot Lodge.

3. Following his custom of referring to EW's auto as "She," etc., HJ here indicates a mere hired car— "of promiscuous favours."

4. See letter of 29 June 1912.

5. He interrupted his sojourn at Intervale to visit Alice at Chocorua; he went to EW at The Mount until 13 July.

6. Margaret Mary "Peggy" James (1887–1952), WJ's daughter; her recovery from an appendectomy was vexed and slow.

7. HJ actually arrived on 7 July; EW and Cook drove him from Springfield. Teddy's sudden appearance at The Mount on 13 July precipitated a domestic crisis. HJ returned to George James's at Nahant and remained there until the thirtieth. On 1 August he went to New York and sailed the next day on the *Mauritania*.

8. Elizabeth "Bessie" Frelinghausen Davis, the widow of George Cabot "Bay" Lodge. See letter of 5 February 1910.

dont . . . faire: for which I have no use; *séjour . . . miens:* sojourn with my kinfolk; *grossiers:* rough

Lowland House
Nahant
19 July 1911

Dearest Edith.

No, I am not "magnificent" here—though your letter is. I have become—if that is the word—rather inconveniently unwell again (dropped, I mean, to a pretty woefully lower level with the confinement & contraction into which one inevitably sinks at the bottom of this so long-necked & stoppered Boston bottle). The craziness & beauty of our peninsula-tip is great, but it's a queer piazza-prison & it paralyses me somehow to sickness—which tells on my poor organs. However, I shall hold on & worry through, counting the hours & the days, checking them off till the end of next week—when I get into motion (motion is above all remedial for me), for New York & the ship. Forgive meanwhile a sorry & seedy letter. I understand every word of your actual, dreadful history[1] (the question of what terms you *can* make with such abysmal insanity)—I take it intimately home. But 2 things surely emerge clear: 1st that it's vital to get rid of the absolutely unworkable burden & complication of the Mount; & 2d that with the recurrence of scenes of violence you must insist on saving your life by a separate existence. You must *trancher* at all costs. Those scenes are by the nature of the case recurrent—& on that you must take your stand. But settle the Mount question first, & the rest will offer itself in much simpler form on that terrain déblayé & with that precedent established. I rejoice immensely to hear of the new possible purchaser, & of Walter B[erry]'s approach. Only these things—& everything—make me feel woefully abject, helpless & feeble. I can so for the moment but just steer my own boat.—Yet your brave words about my old stuffs[2]—such faded shelved Tapestries as they seem for me now—give me a glow of pleasure: as at the sight of you taking them down & unrolling them, & making them hang & shimmer (finding they still *can* a little); with the tender sigh for the "short length" of poor Julia[3]—tragically sacrificed to the effort to make a snippet of a short story of her, to meet a request (*then* made once in a while) by Alden[4] of Harper's. I had embarked on her to do her in 6 or 7 thousand words (the man had asked for 5000!) & though he took her at her mutilated length he kept her a year before publishing & only grumbled at her being what she was. Of course she is a brave little shortish novel lost—& I wish I could take her up again. I probably can't. However these are thin false notes amid your realities—in your so otherwise complicated concert. Yet I shall write again. Yours all & always

Henry James

P.S.   I am struggling over George Meredith again, & find Harry Richmond[5] of a badness almost incredible & unreadable: the *cheap* (for a rich man) let loose as never!

1. Teddy had returned, physically chipper but in mind depressed and vindictive, to demand the right to control EW's finances and charge her with cruelty to him. HJ had already given her the advice repeated in this letter. See Lewis, *EW*, 304–8.

2. HJ's novels and tales of the New York Edition (1907–1909), the apparent failure of which had much depressed him. The "stuffs" were freshly in EW's mind: she had endeavored, with the aid of Edmund Gosse (1849–1928)—essayist, biographer, and librarian of the House of Lords—in England and William Dean Howells in America, to get the Nobel Prize for literature that year awarded to Henry James. It was given to the Belgian Maurice Maeterlinck.

3. HJ's short story "Julia Bride," *Harper's Magazine*, March-April 1908, reprinted in the New York Edition, vol. 17; Harper then published it separately in 1909.

4. Henry Mills Alden was editor of *Harper's New Monthly Magazine*.

5. George Meredith (1828–1909), English poet and novelist and a friend of HJ's since 1878; his novel *The Adventures of Harry Richmond* (1871).

trancher: make a break; *terrain déblayé:* cleared ground

> [Lowland House]
> Nahant
> 21 July [1911]

Dearest Edith.

Beautiful & generous & almost reassuring your letter—but, alas, I mustn't embark on a new move now, do you mercifully see? On one of the last days of next week—probably Friday—my blessed sister comes down from N.H. to render me certain definite aids & comforts, during 2 or 3 days, before I depart—& I must go to Cambridge to be with her; besides that, though the time draws near, not one of my preparations for departure or for winding up my year's stay here has been made (beyond my having paid my passage); & there are urgent things I must do in Cambridge & Boston, the former especially, as soon after Monday next as possible. I brought such impedimenta with me from England that merely packing, or seeing it properly performed, is formidable—but from *this* near a workable basis the thing is possible. Only I am too out of sorts to "fly round" or bustle, & must manage as I can, & not soon go up from here for the day *till* next Monday—when leaving for an absence wd. be impossible to me. In short—but I am already breath-less; I can't, dearest Edith, write more! It is only that I can't put distance again, during this last shortening time, between my languid powers (which will revive, I feel confident, as soon as I get well away from our fatal shores) & the complicated businesses I must attend to. My host here,[1] moreover, has been as a ministering angel to me & *counts* on me in his utter solitude. I can't well break away from him after having come back with pledges & assurances— In short, in short! But how good you are to me all the same—! Lovely your remarks about these ancientries;[2] you make me believe & hope again, & recall, as with hallucination, my doing them. Read over, if you can, dans le même genre, the brief "Gre-ville Fane"[3]—& see if that does at all still, as for a certain vivid close compression. Embrace Gilliard [Lapsley] for me—& rejoin *me*, both of you au plus tôt. I took away D'Annunzio & Tolstoi[4]—you shall have them back. I've read *Le Tribun*[5] & do justice to the earnest effort. But the elaborate *lourdeur*, the ponderosity of method, the large queer as-sumptions, with the cartload of explanations dragged along & the gen-eral absence of wit & of the flashlight, make me wonder—! But you & Gilliard will say I'm at the Katherine business again—! Well I *do* be-tween the 2 authors see a similarity—! There! Yours, dearest Edith, till better days,

Henry James

1. George A. James.
2. The New York Edition.
3. HJ's short story "Greville Fane" (1892), reprinted in the New York Edi-tion, vol. 16.
4. Works by the Italian writer Gabriele D'Annunzio (1863–1938) and the Russian novelist Count Leo Nikolaevich Tolstoy (1828–1910).
5. A play by Paul Bourget that had its premiere in Paris on 15 March 1911.

dans ... genre: in the same genre; *au plus tôt:* as soon as possible; *lourdeur:* heaviness

95 Irving St.
Cambridge Mass.
Sunday p.m. [30 July 1911]

Dearest Edith.

I am in the last throes of preparation for flight from these shores—it has been a most difficult & even desperate week—& yet must scrawl you this word of gratitude for the sweet generosity of your letter. I came finally up from Nahant but this morning—though I had to spend three separate days of last week here & in Boston; & Bessie Lodge & I yesterday broke our hearts over the failure we had each heard from you of your having met in your attempt to get *at* us by telephone. It is horrible, for there we were *in* the Boston book—*G. A. James, 37 Lynn* —Lynn being the terra-firma headquarters for all such approach to the Nahant Peninsula. Bessie L., has I suppose, a similar emblem, & in short we should have leaped at your signal, awaited you with ecstacy, & made you come straight to Lowland House for the night. There were empty rooms gaping for you, the place is really elegant (& also beautiful),—George James was inconsolable for what might have been but wasn't—yesterday—on receipt of your letter. Such is our (or at least your) stormy destiny. I can't write much—I can only make you this sad, faithful tender sign. I shall not be fit for anything but weary worry till I am off—then I shall really pick up. I can't write you of your affairs—or your Affair: I don't know where you *are*—I walk in darkness & hold on, all round, as I can. I yearn to see Walter [Berry], to whom I owe a fond sign; but there is a complication about Tuesday p.m. at the Belmont (I don't get there till dinner time) which *may* prevent.[1] However, I *hope*. I wait for you là-bas. Do come soon & come to England. Ah so all devotedly yours

Henry James

1. HJ dined at the Belmont on Tuesday, 1 August; Berry called at 10 p.m.

là-bas: there

The Athenaeum
Pall Mall, S.W.
7 September 1911

Dearest Edith.

I write you under difficulties, but still I write you, just a little word to break the *laideur* of my long silence & tell you that I, as ever, all helplessly & wonderingly & above all tenderly think of you. That's all it comes down to—all that is possible, or that will be until these evil conditions of this perfect nightmare of a summer abate & I get the benefit, in some degree or other, *of* the abatement. I left America sadly spent with the long *épreuve* offered us there for so many weeks, but I returned here only to a renewal of the same, with fresh afflictions & alarms added—as everything, simply, since my arrival, has made for deep discomfort. No rain has fallen, in this part of the land, for an unprecedented time, & everything is more red-hot & dried-up than in all my long years here I have ever known it. I went straight down to Lamb House on reaching town from New York[1]—the thermometer that day in London was 97°; but the hot glare of the South Coast, my parched & blighted garden & the sight of all the young sheep & lambs languidly prostrate & starving, dying, in the Marsh, drove me away, under solicitation, to umbrageous Essex—where I remained captive at spacious & splendid Hill Hall (the Charles Hunters') in Epping Forest,[2] & benefitting not a little by the fact of "three motors kept." I broke away from there after 16 days, & as I go tomorrow to Norfolk (Overstrand),[3] for 4 in all, I have waited over in London (from the 4th) & been thereby caught in this oven-trap. The thermometer is now only in the eighties, but the eighties in London are hellish. On the 14th I go to Scotland for 5 days—spending them in Forfarshire with John Cadwal. & Mary of that ilk.[4] Both in Norfolk & there I shall reach out for "tone"—against the couple of days (at most) I am pledged to spend at Quacre on my way back home[5]—where if I do reach out for it I shall reach in vain. Howard [Sturgis] is in Scotland with the Eshers[6]—where I have heard from him with the last perfection of Howardry. But we shall at last meet—after my failing to go [to] him on my way to Hill, even under the bribe of the offered Blair Fairchilds (or at least of *her*), as an inducement to my visit then—& so I prate of my poor affairs, dearest Edith, just by reason of my dread of prating too vainly & mainly about yours. I send this forth toward you, but am far from sure of its finding you still at the Mount.[7] Yet I got a couple of days since a letter from Gilliard [Lapsley] (promptly answered), in which he spoke of having just left you there—so this may be in time; all the more that he testifies to nothing settled or conclusive in your actual situation.[8] There it *is*—how can I talk to you, under these frustrations & limitations, of *that?* Deeper & deeper your dilemma, I know—with the way twist is added to twist in it & tangle to tangle. You'll disembroil it all—you've only to sit tight & live outside of it as much as you can. There I am—talking what must seem to you mere amiable ineptitude! Well, I can only hang about you by the power of participation supersensual & devotional—can only wish for some return of that age of fond faith in which one could really pray for those one would fain help. I can't but believe in some practical subsidence—by the "operation of circumstances"—of the *worst* acuteness of your question. May the Fates more & more *determine* that process!—I have seen nobody & nothing here to report you of—with the desolation of London nobody was at Hill, to speak of, but we motored 40 miles one day to Audley End (owned by Lord Braybrooke, but let to Lord Howard de Walden, who, absent, had kindly ordered tea for us with the Housekeeper!). It's lovely-coloured & low & vast—though but a fragment of the original house; & is on the whole rather a disappointment. Still, vous me manquiez for the relish of it—& even more for that of Weald Park, a still more interesting, a very beautiful, smaller & obscurer house nearer to Hill. Well, see what we might do. I yearn over you & await you, & in spite of everything do pray for you. Yours, dearest Edith, all & always

Henry James

1. HJ disembarked in Liverpool on 8 August and was in Lamb House for luncheon on the ninth.

2. From 19 August to 4 September.

3. The country home of publisher Sir Frederick Macmillan.

4. HJ was at John Cadwalader's until the twenty-first, briefly in Edinburgh, and back in Lamb House by the twenty-sixth.

5. HJ means "back home" from Overstrand: he was at Sturgis's 12–14 September, where the ironic "inducement" was Sturgis's cousin Edith, Mrs. Blair Fairchild from Paris; see letter of 13 September 1911.

6. Reginald Baliol Brett (1852–1930), 2nd Viscount Esher, later governor of Windsor Castle, and his Belgian wife (since 1879) Eleanor, née Van de Weyer.

7. EW sailed from New York on this very date.

8. Teddy now had power of attorney in matters including The Mount. He sold it in June 1912, EW reluctantly cosigning.

laideur: ugliness; *épreuve:* trial; *vous me manquiez:* I missed having you

> Queen's Acre
> Windsor
> 13 September 1911

Dearest Edith.

Ah, que n'êtes-vous assise à l'ombre des forêts![1]—by which I mean these dear familiar forests in which Quacre so sociably nestles. The first rain I have assisted at for long months—a blest steady downpour—is descending at last on this scorched & famished land & keeping us in-doors, &, Edith Fairchild, the other Edith, your hated & dangerous rival,[2] both as to the intellect & the affections (your strongest points—& *hers!*) having gone to town for the day, dear Howard & I have had a free field for talking of you, in one fond unarrested flood, ever since luncheon—& it's now much past tea. I have been able to tell him rather more of your recent history than he has had wherewithal to match it—& thus even though your most recent is still inevitably so shrouded from me; but between us we have kept the game bravely up, & the effect of it is to make me thus yearn to reach out to you as you swim again into our comparative ken—& all the more that I ruefully think of the letter I addressed you at the Mount some five or six days ago[3]—a sweet wasted letter that will have missed you there by a week. (My belief had been that it would *about* catch you—though you would prob-ably be leaving that complicated scene within the month.) Two days ago, at Overstrand, where I spent 3 days, Fredk. Macmillan mentioned to me that he had had occasion to hear from you & that you were sailing—*would* have sailed, on Saturday last,[4] though (not unnaturally) but for France. Filled with the emotion of this I came down here last evening for 2 nights, & hence it is that I make my poor thin fond geste of wide arms of welcome. Of course I have been dismally silent—as with the instinct of holding my breath (since my return to England) before the stress & strain, & even storm & sorrow, of the last act of your personal drama at & anent the Mount.[5] I wish to goodness I had sent you my wandering letter—which will come back from there but so belatedly—ten days or so sooner; but, as I have intimated, everything intrinsic & extrinsic made for the hush of sympathy & anxiety—& I'm conscious of a certain violence & grossness in thus making free with you, after all your presumably stiff last *épreuves* even now. But I want to make you the sign of fond fidelity, deeply & inevitably in the dark though I may be—I want you to feel that I wait & watch for you. I go back to town tomorrow—& on that evening up to Scotland to spend 4 or 5 days with John Cadwalader & Mary C., who depart (for home) I believe on the 28th. May your journey have been commode—& may, above all, the air of your situation be clearer & more benign. I put you in your fatigue & exhaustion no question—I only, for the time, circle about you on tiptoe & with all the tenderest consideration & divination of your faithfully fond old

Henry James

P.S. I go straight back to Lamb House from Scotland. Dear H[oward] si doux et si faible!

1. "Ah, why are you not sitting in the shade of the forests!"—HJ's appropriate adaptation of the words of Phaedra in Racine's play *Phèdre* (1687), act 1, sc. 3, l. 24: *Dieu! Que ne suis-je assise à l'ombre des forêts!* (God! Why am I not sitting in the shade of the forests!)

2. EW would have caught HJ's ironic designation of this "rival." HJ described Mrs. Fairchild to his niece Peggy in a letter of this same date as "a very pleasant, uninteresting honest little lame (very lame) lady."

3. See letter of 7 September 1911.

4. "Saturday last" was 9 September; EW had sailed on Thursday, the seventh.

5. See letter of 7 September 1911.

épreuves: trials; *commode:* comfortable; *si . . . faible:* so sweet and so feeble

Millden Lodge
Edzell, Forfarshire
19 September 1911

Dearest Edith.

Your postcard from the Provence, with its mention of a constantly vitreous Sea, gives me infinite comfort—the particular comfort that feeling your presence in this more select of the 2 hemispheres alone can confer. Having you nearer again seems always a kind of blest approach to having you *near*. You will have found a letter from me awaiting you at rue de Varenne, & will thereby have learned that I had delusively written you at the Mount just in time not to catch you before your sailing thence. *That* letter will perhaps even turn round & follow you across the sea again; it was a poor thing but mine own, & will give you a little more of my earlier news. I have been invoking all the voices of the air for such scraps of yours as they might vouchsafe—you will have seen that I even laid Fredk. Macmillan under contribution, to say nothing of Edith Fairchild at Quacre, sweet Edith if not with "golden hair"[1] at least with the fond fiction (passed on to her, I believe, by, or through, "Mrs. Walter Maynard")[2] that you had wound up, before leaving, the great business of parting with the Mount.[3] Beatrix [Jones] has heard from you here since my arrival & that illusion is again demolished for me. I heave a gros soupir as I think of your having still to present "shoulders atlantean to the too vast orb"[4] if not of your "fate" at least of your New England home. But it all must have been as it *had* to be, & *how* wearily & repeatedly in those weeks after I left you, you must have swung all round the circle! You will tell me of these things, & I shall breathlessly follow them, when you pay us all a pious visit here in November or par là,[5] as I so fondly count on your doing. (For *me*, my piety is to consist henceforth, I intimately see, in never again quitting this distracted island.) I came up here on the 15th (arriving that a.m. early) to admirable weather—allowing for the cruel desiccation; awfully apparent & ugly in England; but much less disfiguring on the braes & by the burns. It's a house of bloody shooters, & even Trixy's [Beatrix's] hands are imbrued—but of great domestic amiability; god-fearing plain men, with no flirt of petticoat save Mary C.'s or Trix's very well-"draped" ones since Mrs. "Tommy" Hastings[6] carried away hers—on *such* a pair of straddling legs (though convergent feet!) 36 hours after my arrival (to my regret, for I liked her). Mary C. is again the soul (& the brain) of pure benevolence to me, but is having I fear a season rather starved of any pleasant bit [of] final London margin— they sail on the 28th in the Cedric, with John C[adwalader], & go to town but a day or two before. The moorish air does me meanwhile great good—even though I inhale it as the very mildest & most un-armed of Brahmins. In 2 or 3 days more, however, I shall turn my face homeward—I long for my humble home & for conditions again pro-pitious for calling on the Muse (to see whether she will heed me. It's open to me again to get more good from her company, I think, than from that of any but 2 or 3—who are *both* muses & mortals!) It was at rather melancholy Quacre I think that I wrote you my few lines the other day—melancholy from poor dear Howard [Sturgis]'s having at last so *franchi le pas* to old-ladyhood. It will be but a farther step now from his knitting exquisite shawls & making beautiful caps to his set-tling down to wear them—he really scarce emerged, while I was there —emerged as to mind & brain & *geste*—from his circumjacent billows of lovely, fluffy "stitch." His billows are all pillows, alas, & his field of battle more & more the work basket. Even Edith Fairchild & poor I were determined characters beside him, & *she* went up one afternoon to a matinée in the Strand. But we must still pull him round—& part of the piety of your November visit to us must be for that purpose. May Salso meanwhile wash away all your aches—Italian Lick operating to that effect while the French variety[7] does so not less happily (I devoutly trust) for Teddy. What resources our great country seems after all to hold for your situation!—I think of that even while I think of that gorgeous millstone of the Mount—hanging about your atlantean neck, yet helping too it would after all seem to turn the wheel of poor Teddy's fortune. Ainsi soit-il. I am struck with the resources too when I read, as I have been doing with great admiration & applause, such a matter as the 2 first parts of your Berkshire tale in Scribner[8]—so beautifully done, so *soutenu*, such a feat of artistic & imaginative projection. It will be a triumph—since clearly you will have held the note to the end; Mary Cadwal & I are equally struck with it. Ah, may you but get back to work! And Morton—???? I yearn over him—he *must* (if he is now in

America) stop at my door on his way back. My best address is always Rye. Ever, dearest Edith, your devotissimo

Henry James

P.S.   Scotland is exquisite—in this weather: an almost incomparable little country.

1. See Longfellow's "The Children's Hour": "And Edith with golden hair." See letters of 7 and 11 September 1911.

2. EW's friend Eunice Ives married Walter Maynard (1853–1907), director of a New York publishing house, in 1903; the Maynards were Lenox friends of EW from 1905.

3. HJ did not know of the apparent reconciliation of EW and Teddy in August, which halted plans to sell The Mount, until informed by Beatrix; see letter of 7 September 1911.

4. Cf. Milton, *Paradise Lost*, bk. 2, ll. 306, 1029.

5. The visit was paid in December, still "par là" or "thereabouts."

6. Helen R. Benedict of New York, wife of Hastings (1860–1929), an American architect with McKim, Mead, and White.

7. EW spent a few days at the spa Salsomaggiore for asthma or hay fever treatment before embarking on a motor tour of north-central Italy with Walter Berry. "French variety" is HJ's jocular reference to the spa French Lick, Arkansas, which Teddy visited in October; HJ turns Salsomaggiore into "Italian Lick"—to set up his joke.

8. *Ethan Frome*; see letter of 9 February 1911.

gros soupir: huge sigh; *franchi le pas:* crossed the threshold; *geste:* motion; *Ainsi soit-il:* so be it; *soutenu:* sustained; *devotissimo:* most devoted

Lamb House, Rye
27 September 1911

Dearest Edith.

Alas it is not possible[1]—it is not even for a moment thinkable. I returned, practically, but last night to my long-abandoned home, where every earthly consideration, & every desire of my heart, conspires now to fix me in some sort of recovered peace & stability; I cling to its very doorposts, for which I have yearned for long months, & the idea of going forth again on new & distant & expensive adventures fills me with—let me frankly say—absolute terror & dismay—the desire, the frantic impulse of scared childhood, to plunge my head under the bedclothes & burrow there, not to "let it (i.e. *Her!*)[2] get me!" In fine I *want* as little to renew the junketing & squanderings of exile—*time-*, priceless time-squanderings as they are for me now—as I want devoutly much to do something very different,[3] to which I must begin to address myself—& even if my desire were intense indeed there would be gross difficulties for me to overcome. But enough—don't let me pile up the agony of the ungracious—as any failure of response to a magnificent invitation can only be! Let me simply gape all admiringly, from a distance, at the splendour of your own spirit & general resources—or rather let me just simply stay my pen & hide my head (under the bedclothes before-mentioned). My finest deepest sense of the general matter is that the whole economy of my future (in which I see myself reviving again to certain things, very definite things, that I want to do) absolutely lays an interdict (to which I oh so fondly bow!) on my *ever* leaving these shores again. And I have no scruple of saying this to you—your beautiful genius being so for great globe-adventures & putting girdles round the earth. Mine is, incomparably, for brooding like the Hen, whom I differ from but by a syllable in designation; & see how little I personally lose by it, since your putting on girdles so quite inevitably involves your passing at a given moment where I can reach forth & grab you a little. Don't despise me for a spiritless worm, only *livrez-vous-y* yourself (& livrez-y Walter [Berry], to whom I am writing) with all pride & power, & unroll the rich record later on to your so inevitably deprived (though so basely resigned) & always so faithfully fond old

Henry James

1. EW had invited HJ to join her and Walter Berry for a five-week motor trip through northern Italy. EW and Berry sent HJ a series of postcards from Italy; see app. A.

2. EW's automobile.

3. His planned biographical memorial of WJ, which soon developed into his autobiography.

livrez-vous-y: give yourself up to it; *livrez-y:* deliver up

[POSTCARD]   Verona[1]
                                                   9 October 1911
Henry James
Lamb House
    Parma, Sabbioneta, Mantua—and *this!*—Just off to Vicenza now. I hope the Neo-Paddington[2] surpasses the original as far as the new 50 h.p. Mercedes excels our old plodding Hortense.[3] Come & see!!!—

    E.W.

    1. This is the first in a series of cards to HJ; see letter of 27 September 1911, and app. A.
    2. Preparing to leave for the United States with WJ and his wife, HJ had dismissed his housekeeper, Mrs. Paddington, on 28 July 1910; her replacement on his return to Rye was Joan Anderson.
    3. EW's automobile.

                                          Lamb House, Rye
                                          25 October 1911
Dearest Edith.
    All thanks to M. de Ségur, to the yearning niece, & to yourself, très-chère Madame. Poor D.M.—or poor D——mn!—has been translated (to the complete sacrifice of all her small pinch of substance or sense) by Mme Pilon [*sic*], the wife of an old philosopher-friend of my brother's—twenty years ago.[1] I think we don't want 2 of them—& will you kindly *remercier*, with all my acknowledgments? You will see by the enclosed (isn't it sweet of dear Jacques?)[2] what IS, *auprès de moi*, the real chance of the Translator—& will find the volume itself on your table when you reach home. At least I so gave directions for it; kindly tell

me if it delays. It is of course nothing but my Barrie-&-Frohman comedy, "The Outcry"³ of 2 years ago (*just* that now), then never acted,
through general collapse, simply *printed*, a little misleadingly—with such
a running comment as merely represents decent interpretation & expression. But I wince a little at your reading it after Blanche's fine hyperbole!
You must indeed have had a Bacchic Tuscan time—but oh for the details! Don't dream, however, that I "*might*" have come—I so utterly
mightn't! I went to Howard [Sturgis] for 36 hours—& it's deplorable
(& *superfluous*) comme il baisse. A little more at this rate & il n'en restera
plus rien. You really must come over & we'll see about it together. I
go up to town tomorrow (& proceed with him, for 2 days, to the
Wilfred, the "Clare," Sheridans').⁴ But I spend, practically, the winter
in London, most decidedly; the era of Rye hibernations is definitely
closed. London, & London alone, is now excellently good for me—
better than any other place in the world.—I exceedingly admire, sachez
Madame, *Ethan Frome*. A beautiful art & tone & truth—a beautiful artful
kept-downness, & yet effective cumulation. It's a "gem"—& excites great
admiration here. Nous en causerons. I could wail over Walter [Berry]
—buffetted prey of the gods! But he'll "come out all right!" I calculate
that this will find you at the Plantier⁵—& meet you there; & beg that
if it does you will assure Paul & Minnie of "my faithful & affectionate
remembrance—all my sympathy & *mes voeux*"—I leave nothing, you
see, to your discretion; it wouldn't be fair; if I began that I should have
to leave so much—*all*. Apropos of whom I vainly watch for the *Tribun*
done by Morton [Fullerton] into Alexandrines.⁶ Où en est that undertaking? Oh the unutterable Theatre! I only hear that Alexander, with
Oscar Wilde for a stopgap (the doddering rococo & oh so flat "fizz"
now of "Lady W[indermere]'s Fan"!)⁷ has "gone to Germany to look
for a play." And Morton—whom I eternally fail to see? His Gil Blas
&c is nice—but not up to his best mark. He is, I hope, pushing forward
with his *Paris*. But I shall very soon write him—& I draw breath. Make
me, do, a sign from Paris—& believe me yours all affectionately

Henry James

1. A request was extended via EW from the Marquis de Ségur and his niece
for a French translation of HJ's tale "Daisy Miller: A Study" (1878). HJ refers

to the French translation made by Mme F. Pillon of "Daisy Miller," "An International Episode," and "Four Meetings," published in 1886.

2. HJ enclosed a favorable commentary on his newly published novel *The Outcry* by Jacques-Émile Blanche.

3. See letter of 15 October 1908.

4. Clare (1885–1970), daughter of Morton and Clara Jerome (aunt of Winston Churchill) Frewen, talented sculptor, had married Wilfred Sheridan (descendant of the Irish playwright Richard Brinsley Sheridan), who was killed in the Battle of Loos, September 1915.

5. Le Plantier, villa of Paul Bourget at Costebelle, near Hyères, in the south of France.

6. Fullerton was making an English translation of Bourget's play *Le Tribun* (see letter of 21 July 1911) and had also translated Lesage's picaresque novel *Gil Blas de Santillane* of 1715–35. Macmillan had given him an advance for a book about Paris (see letter of 26 July 1909).

7. He had seen it six days earlier in London with Jocelyn Persse.

très-chère: very-dear, dearest; *remercier:* extend my regrets; *auprès de moi:* with me; *comme il baisse:* how he is declining; *il . . . rien:* there will be nothing left of him; *sachez:* I want you to know; *Nous en causerons:* We shall chat about that; *mes voeux:* my good wishes; *Où en est:* Where has it got to

[The Reform Club][1]
19 November 1911

Dearest Edith.

There are scarce degrees or differences in my constant need of hearing from you, yet when that felicity comes it manages each time to seem pre-eminent & to have assuaged an exceptional hunger. The pleasure & relief, at any rate, 3 days since, were of the rarest quality—& it's always least discouraging (for the exchange of sentiments) to know that your wings are for the moment folded & your field a bit delimited. I knew you were back in Paris, as an informer passing hereby on his [way] thence again to N.Y. had seen you dining at the Ritz en nombreuse compagnie, "looking awfully handsome & stunningly dressed." And Mary Hunter, ces-jours-ci had given me earlier & more exotic news of you, yet coloured with a great vividness of sympathy & admiration.

En voilà une who will be "after you" dès votre arrivée—& with whom you will really always find, I think, a good relation immensely easy & pleasant. But I feel that it takes a hard assurance to speak to you of "arriving" anywhere—as that implies starting & continuing, & before your great heroic rushes & revolutions I can only gape & sigh & sink back. It requires an association of ease—with the whole heroic question (of the "up & doing" state)—which I don't possess, to presume to suggestionise on the subject of a new advent. Great will be the glory & joy, & the rushing to & fro, *when* the wide wings are able, marvellously, to show us symptoms of spreading again—& here I am (*mainly* here, this winter), to thrill with the 1st announcement. London is better for me, during these months, than any other spot of earth, or of pavement; & even here I seem to find I can work—& n'ai pas maintenant d'autre idée. Apropos of which aid to life your remarks about my small latest-born[2] are absolutely to the point. The little creature *is* absolutely of the irresistible sex of her most intelligent critic—for I don't pretend, like Lady Macbeth, to bring forth men-children only. You speak at your ease, chère Madame, of the interminable & formidable job of my producing à mon âge another Golden Bowl—the most arduous & thankless task I ever set myself. However, on all that il y aurait bien des choses à dire; & meanwhile, I blush to say, the Outcry is on its way to a fifth Edition (in these few weeks) whereas it has taken the poor old G.B. 8 or 9 years to get even into a third. And I shld. have to go back & live for 2 continuous years at Lamb House to write it (living on dried herbs & cold water—for "staying power"—meanwhile); & that would be very bad for me, wd. probably indeed put an end to me altogether. My own sense is that I don't want, & oughtn't to try, to attack ever again anything *longer* (save for about 70 or 80 pages more) than The Outcry. That is déjà assez difficile—the "artistic economy" of that inferior little product being a much more calculated & ciphered, much more cunning & (to use your sweet expression) crafty one than that of five G.B.'s. The vague verbosity of the Oxus-flood (beau nom!) terrifies me—*sates* me; whereas the steel structure of the other form makes every parcelle a weighed & related value. Moreover nobody is really doing (or, ce me semble, as I look about, *can* do) Outcries, while all the world is doing G.B.'s—& vous même, chère Madame, tout le premier: which gives you really the cat out of the bag. My vanity forbids me (instead of the more sweetly consecrating it) a form in which you run me so close. Seulement alors je compterais bâtir a *great many* (a great many, entendez-vous?) Outcries—& on données autrement rich. About this present one hangs the inferiority, the comparative triviality, of its primal origin.[3] But pardon this flood of professional egotism. I have in any case got back to work—on something that now the more urgently occupies me as the time for me circumstantially to have done it wd. have been last winter when I was insuperably unfit for it, & that is extremely special, experimental & as yet occult.[4] I apply myself to my effort every morning at a little *repaire*[5] in the depths of Chelsea, a couple of little rooms that I have secured for quiet & concentration—to which a blest taxi whirls me from hence every morning at 10 o'clk, & where I meet my amanuensis (of the days of the composition of the G.B.) to whom I *gueuler* to the best of my power. In said repaire I propose to crouch & me blottir (in the English shade of the word, for so intensely revising an animal, as well), for many more weeks; so that I fear, dearest Edith, your idea of "whirling me away" will have to adapt itself to the sense worn by "away"—as it clearly so gracefully will! For there are senses in which that particle is for me just the most obnoxious little object in the language. Make *your* fond use of it at any rate by first coming away & away hither. I yearn for news of what is taking place over the *Tribun*[6]—so mystified am I by the fact that Alexander is announcing (for a few days hence) a dramatization of our Hichens[7] (—yours & mine, the one we back so against Lady True Benson), just at the moment I have been hoping that the version of Bourget would bring Morton [Fullerton], & par la même occasion sympathetic *you*, to just round the corner here. Your allusion to your having lent a hand in Paris reassures me, however; a reassurance confirmed by [Jacques-Émile] Blanche— with whom I lunched three days ago on a copious dish of little *blanchailles*;[8] he telling me that you have "written in a love-scene." I yearn most of all then for *your* Alexandrines—or rather I yearn for them next after the passion with which I yearn for Morton's personal advent in the interest of his own is spent. Please give him my fond love. Yours & his all & always

Henry James

P.S. This was begun 5 days ago—& was raggedly & ruthlessly broken off—had to be—& I didn't mark the place this Sunday a.m. where I took it up again—on p. 6th.[9] But I put only today's date—as I didn't put the other day's at the time.

1. He had been back in Rye less than two weeks, and black days of depression had descended. He went up to London to the Reform Club, and for his work used the "little *repaire* in the depths of Chelsea." See letter of 25 October 1911.

2. His novel *The Outcry*; see letter of 25 October 1911.

3. *The Outcry* was originally a play; see letter of 25 October 1911.

4. His autobiography, begun as a memorial biography of WJ.

5. The den where he worked on his autobiography with typist Theodora Bosanquet. Women were not allowed in rooms at the Reform Club. Actually Mary Weld (d. 1953) had typed *The Golden Bowl*, listening to HJ "gueuler"— the term Flaubert used to describe his *bellowing out* his own prose.

6. See letter of 25 October 1911.

7. The novel *Bella Donna* by Robert Hichens (1864–1950) was dramatized and produced on 9 December 1911 by the popular actor-manager Sir George Alexander (1858–1918), who had produced and played the lead in HJ's *Guy Domville* in 1895.

8. A pun on the name of J.-É. Blanche with a derogatory suffix—"ailles"; perhaps "blanchitudes." Further, *blanchailles* are little fish called small fry in the United States and whitebait in England.

9. He seems to have resumed the letter with the sentence beginning "And I shld. have to go back & live for 2 continuous years . . . ," the fourteenth sentence of the letter.

en . . . compagnie: with a large party; *ces-jours-ci:* recently; *En . . . une: There* is one; *dès . . . arrivée:* from the moment of your arrival; *n'ai . . . idée:* have now no other intention; *à mon âge:* at my age; *il . . . dire:* there would be much to say; *déjà . . . difficile:* difficult enough as it is; *beau nom:* handsome name; *ce me semble:* it seems to me; *vous . . . premier:* you yourself, my dear Madame, first of all; *Seulement . . . bâtir:* Except, now, that I would count on constructing; *entendez-vous:* do you understand; *données autrement:* data (ideas) otherwise; *me blottir:* nestle; *par . . . occasion:* by the same opportunity

The Reform Club
30 November 1911

Dearest Edith.

Going out in a few moments, I shall probably wire to you; but I reinforce my telegram with this, which must for the moment figure poorly instead of a *begun* letter of 4 or 5 days ago, in the style of our inimitable Anticipator of Scenes & terminator, in lassitude, of *rendezvous*, & substitutor of parentheses for the baptismal font; but which under the strain & stress of the labyrinthine London I have had to lease a more mild small fragment, & which now rests on my table, far upstairs, while I scribble or gabble (say *scrabble*) this feverish word here below. Howard [Sturgis] is *impossible* to me for Saturday-Monday,[1] because I have promised, up to me eyes, to go to Mary Hunter, at Hill, for that occasion, & because she intensely wants me to induce you to come. I forwarded you a letter from her this a.m. (sent to receive your *number*), & I have promised to do what I *can* so to move you. It will be very pleasant, with a good many people, I infer—& I am absolutely booked for it. I will go with you to Howard for the following week-end[2] (I can't go for the week-middle) with all the pleasure in life. So it *has* to be—I am working intently every forenoon—10.30[3] to 1.30 (I have a little repaire in Chelsea[4] for the purpose); though if you must put in intermediate days with Howard I could on one or two come down to tea & dinner, returning by the last p.m. train. The great thing is that you do, please, *please*, PLEASE, come down to Hill on the 9th. It would so facilitate everything—with Howard's beloved man's[5] general accessibility. I thrill at your approach—I revel in the dawn of you; & I have read with a horrid sense of pain & almost of humiliation that awful little pamphlet on the hustling, the devastating Curie.[6] Oh "divine" passion of love, what a lot of ugly faces you have to show! But nous en causerons—& of everything. I wish you *such* a convenient coming. Ever yrs.

H.J.

1. The weekend of 9–11 December; see below. This rendezvous was kept; and on Monday 11 December HJ and EW went to see *Kismet*, a dramatization by Edward Knoblock of the novel by "George Fleming"—HJ's old friend Constance Fletcher (1858–1938).
2. HJ went down to Sturgis's Queen's Acre to join EW and Logan Pearsall Smith (1865–1946), American essayist and linguist, on Friday 15 December.

3. The manuscript has "1.3"—obviously a slip of the pen.

4. See letter of 19 November 1911.

5. William Haynes Smith, "the Babe."

6. HJ probably refers to Gustav Téry's article "The Sorbonne Scandal" in the Paris magazine *L'Oeuvre* for 23 November 1911, which included long extracts from letters by Marie Curie (1867–1934) to French physicist Paul Langevin (1872–1946); they had been friends and possibly lovers since the death of her husband, Pierre (b. 1859) in 1906. Téry's article unjustly blamed Mme Curie for the breaking up of Langevin's marriage and briefly inflamed nationalist sentiment against the Polish-born physicist. A month later she received the Nobel Prize for chemistry, becoming the first scientist to be awarded two Nobel prizes.

repaire: den; *nous en causerons:* one shall speak of that

The Reform Club
2 December 1911

Dearest Edith.

Poor dear little world-worn Mitou,[1] qui avait vu tant de choses with those wise, those so disillusioned old eyes of his—& hadn't a single illusion left—unlike Nicette, who has that of her successfully *affecting* to have them. What a little past-away Person!—& what a little personal loss. They are intense personal losses. But what a charming death—for *him*! Be assured of all my participation. Enfin!—*Don't* bring the Motor, dearest cunning cosmopolite, no matter what lassitudes, of the ends of —anything, or even of all things, you may foresee; for it is absolutely impossible your poor Jemmes[2] should return to Paris with you: he has such overwhelming reasons for sticking fast here—dut-il (or dut-anyone else!) en mourir! But it isn't a question of dying; sticking fast is what helps him exactly to live—that & that only. You won't miss the car at all—the taxis here are as excellent as they are numerous, & if you will trust me I will *take* you on Saturday to Hill.[3] I will dine with you on Wednesday 6th[4] with great joy, & will breathe no word that may reach Lady St. H[elier].[5] Yours all & always

Henry James

P.S.   I won't come to meet you—I *think*.

1. Mitou and Nicette were EW's Pekingese dogs.
2. HJ's jocular rendering of the French pronunciation of "James."
3. See letter of 30 November 1911.
4. They dined at the Berkeley Hotel on Thursday 7 December.
5. See letter of 29 October 1909.

qui . . . choses: who had seen so much; *Enfin:* Now then; *dut-il . . . mourir:* even if he should die of it

> The Reform Club
> 20 December 1911

Dearest Edith.

Your letter is delightful, but Sargent *postpones* the portrait (that is the sitting) till after the 15th of Jan.[1] It is inevitable—the mornings here are of black darkness, & he wrote me at the 11th hour (I had written proposing today), asking me to wait a little, or till after the New Year. I go down to L[amb] H[ouse] on the 28th or 29th, desiring to stay, if I find that possible, a fortnight—& that makes the larger (though still not very large, n'est-ce pas?) delay. I will arrange to have my sitting ready the very instant I come back, & though I shall thus be growing older & more battered every hour, I beg you to possess your soul in patience; it's a question only of about 3 weeks, & every justice will doubtless be done to my *then*, as God shall will, aspect by the lightning artist. Let the aspects of your favourite city, the fascinating (to those of your temperament) Paris meanwhile sustain your spirits. The aspects here are as of smeared soot, & we wallow, drenched, on a thick mud paste. My *repaire* in Chelsea & my love of syntax alone console me; but the *repaire* comes high when syntax butters no parsnips, or, as you say in Paris, cuts no ice. However, I must push ahead as I can, & do as soon as possible another *Outcry*, this one, I fear, having done now all it's going to. A dismal document from the Scribners flanked by an appalling one from the Macmillans this a.m., tells me that the sales of my Edition, on which I counted for the bread of my vieux jours, is rapidly

& hopelessly falling to derisive figures[2]—Golden Bowl, my dear, & all. However, I shall get on if I can only keep a series of Outcries[3] before me as lodestars. What it means, what it stands for, as you say, again, &c, is that my letters must be short now—however my affection itself lengthens & lingers. I congratulate Norton[4] on the plums you'd put into his Xmas pudding, & am yours all stoically

H.J.

P.S.   I don't feel as if I had spread enough—half—on your generous, your angelic visit, but you saw how I liked it!—& I see how I did!

1. EW had commissioned a charcoal drawing of HJ from John Singer Sargent. HJ would be at Sargent's Tite Street studio on 24 January, 1 February, and 13 March 1912. The result was initially a disappointment to all concerned; Sargent did a second drawing, which is now at Windsor Castle in the Queen's collection of portraits of recipients of the Order of Merit.

2. According to "Cash Accounts" HJ kept in his diaries, the New York Edition brought him for the years 1909–1911 about $2,000.

3. *The Outcry* is the last work of fiction HJ completed.

4. EW's friend, the Englishman Robert Norton, a half-dozen years her junior, was educated at Eton and Cambridge, established himself in the British Foreign Office, and then served as private secretary to Lord Salisbury until the latter's death in 1903, when Norton went into business in London; he was an amateur painter.

n'est-ce pas: is it; *repaire:* den; *vieux jours:* old age

The Reform Club
[22 December 1911]

Dearest Edith.

Mille fois merci for the colossal petit Larousse[1]—it is indeed *Kolossaal*, judging from the survey of all the knowable that even $\frac{1}{2}$ an hour of it has enabled me to take. It will nourish the Outcries to come & make them shine with a specious culture. Evan Charteris[2] ought to have a copy before he again meets you, & *mine* only alas came too late for my

meeting Lady Gosford (at Mildred Acheson's[3] at lunch, with her so dear
& so pathetic parents overwhelmed by their disponibility, 2 days since).
In short it begets a social confidence that I have never known—even if
it isn't characterised—materially—by the svelte élégance of Lucien
Daudet's novels.[4] Well, I perpetually stagger under the burden of my
debt to you—& a 100 kilos or so the more or the less—! But I grieve
at your lassitude as an effect of our devotion here, a cruauté tendre
beyond what we intended. I "took up my life" (as Marie Sturgis[5] told
me *she* did, quand même, when she found how long her father was to
be ill)—took it up as I could after your departure—even to the tune of
meeting Lady Ripon & Mary Hunter & Ribblesdale, our vieille garde,
2 nights ago at Lady Charles B[eresford]'s.[6] I dine tonight at Violet
Ormond's,[7] where I shall probably see Sargent—as to whom there is
no danger that we shan't, sous peu, bring our job greatly off. I stay on
here over Xmas, & go home on the 29th for 10 or 12 days—& on Feb.
1st Bill arrives at L[amb] H[ouse] with his bride.[8] It rains & it rains here
to sick satiety, & if I hadn't the little Chelsea temple,[9] with its Egeria,
to actively ignore such matters in for a few hours each day, I couldn't
answer for my not being consentingly washed away. Take refuge in
your like Tabernacle when Teddy comes[10]—which I am very sorry to
hear of. However, the case will settle itself—there must be so few *questions* now—save only the final or conclusive one; & you need lose no
inch of the ground you have gained. I rejoice in Miss Bahlmann[11]—&
am perpetually grateful to her; & am yours so tenderly without a grain
of cruelty

Henry James

1. A "concise" French dictionary.
2. Evan Charteris (1864–1940), sixth son of the 10th earl of Wemyss, biographer of Edmund Gosse (1931).
3. Lady Louise Augusta Beatrice Montagu in 1864 married Archibald Brabazon Sparrow Acheson (1841–1922), 4th earl of Bosford; their son Archibald
Charles Montagu Brabazon Acheson (1877–1954) married Mildred Carter in
1910.
4. Lucien Daudet (1883–1946), son of Alphonse Daudet and himself a novelist and editor and a friend of Marcel Proust.
5. Marie Eveleen "Riette" Sturgis, daughter of the English poet and novelist

George Meredith (1828–1909), in July 1894 at age twenty-three married the widower Henry Parkman Sturgis, age forty-seven, eldest brother of Howard Sturgis. Meredith was under Riette's care for several months during the last six years of his life.

6. Gladys, Marchioness of Ripon, at whose Coombe Court in Surrey both HJ and EW visited, was a patron of the arts and, with the Princesse Edmonde de Polignac (née Winaretta Singer), especially Nijinsky and Diaghilev's Ballets Russes. Mary Hunter is Mrs. Charles Hunter of Hill Hall. Thomas Lister (1854–1925), 4th Baron Ribblesdale, master of the Queen's Buckhounds, Liberal whip in the House of Lords (1896–1907), was Margot Asquith's brother-in-law. Mina Gardner in 1878 married Admiral Charles William de la Poer Beresford (1846–1919), 1st Baron Beresford.

7. Sargent's sister.

8. WJ's youngest son and the former Alice Runnels; see letter of 24 February 1912.

9. HJ's study at 10 Lawrence Street adjoining the flat of his amanuensis Theodora Bosanquet—his "Egeria."

10. Teddy Wharton, diagnosed as psychotic, had just announced his intention to cross to France for the holidays. EW had sent the butler Arthur White to accompany him. At the last moment Teddy changed his mind.

11. Anna Bahlmann, Ew's longtime secretary and companion.

Mille . . . merci: A thousand thanks; *cruauté tendre:* affectionate cruelty; *quand même:* in spite of all; *vieille garde:* old guard; *sous peu:* shortly, in a bit

Oil portrait of Henry James, 1900, by his cousin Ellen "Bay" Emmet Rand
Leon Edel

James in the garden of Lamb House, 1901. *H. Montgomery Hyde*

Peggy James, William (her father), Henry (her uncle), and Alice (her mother), at 95 Irving Street, Cambridge, Massachusetts, 1905 *Leon Edel*

Hotel del Coronado in Coronado, California, as it was when James was a visitor there in April 1905. *Hotel del Coronado*

Edith Wharton, c. 1905, in a photograph by Miss Ben Yusuf

The High Street, from the bottom of West Street, Rye, c. 1907. *Rye Museum Association Photographic Collection; Geoffrey Spinks Bagley, Honorary Curator*

West Street, leading to Lamb House *(right)* and the Garden Room, c. 1907. *Rye Museum Association Photographic Collection; Geoffrey Spinks Bagley, Honorary Curator*

Interior of the Garden Room of Lamb House; it was destroyed by enemy bombs in 1940. *Rye Museum Association Photographic Collection; Geoffrey Spinks Bagley, Honorary Curator*

William Morton Fullerton at
his desk in Paris, 1907
Leon Edel

Edith Wharton, Henry James, chauffeur Charles Cook, and Teddy Wharton in
the Wharton auto—"the Chariot of Fire" or "Hortense"—in Paris, 1907
Leon Edel

James as he posed for his bust by sculptor
Derwent Wood, June 1913. *Sir Brian Cook
Batsford*

James as he posed in profile for the sculptor
Derwent Wood. *Sir Brian Cook Batsford*

Billy James and his bride, Alice, on their honeymoon, in the garden of Lamb
House, Rye, 1912. *Rye Museum Association Photographic Collection; Geoffrey Spinks
Bagley, Honorary Curator*

Wharton at the beginning of
World War I. *Jacques Fosse*

Wharton and her
housekeeper-companion
Catherine Gross in the South
of France, not long after
James's death. *Jacques Fosse*

Two pages of James's letter to Wharton, 21 September 1914, on the bombing of Rheims Cathedral. *Beinecke Library, Yale University*

Two pages of Wharton's letter to James, 11 March 1915, on her visit to the front lines at Verdun. *Beinecke Library, Yale University*

Fresh Woods, New Pastures

JANUARY 1912–APRIL 1913

THE NEW YEAR found Edith Wharton in Paris, ill and still embroiled in drastic crises with her husband, and Henry James determinedly in London after a brief visit with newly wed nephew Billy James and his bride, the former Alice Runnels, at Lamb House. He had given them the house for the first half of the year as a wedding present.

February saw the arrival of Teddy Wharton in Paris. Walter Berry, new head of the American Chamber of Commerce in Paris, rallied to Edith's support as he had under similar circumstances in June 1910: he moved into the guest suite of 53, rue de Varenne. The Whartons' trip together to Madrid over Easter was a typical gesture of reconciliation. Teddy returned to the United States in May, and Edith began five months of restless travel on the continent and in England interrupted by brief intervals in Paris. Berry joined her at Salsomaggiore; their tour—Florence, Rome, Venice—afforded them some escapades on mountain roads and at least one automobile accident in June before they got back to the rue de Varenne.

At the beginning of February James sat to Sargent for a portrait commissioned by Edith Wharton; it really satisfied none of them, and now hangs in the gallery of Windsor Castle devoted to recipients of the Order of Merit. James clung to London but retreated to Rye when his health demanded; the visits there with Billy and Alice were augmented by his taking them round to the Hunters at Hill Hall and even up to London on occasion—e.g., to see Nijinsky and Diaghilev's Ballets Russes. He read his address "The Novel in *The Ring and the Book*" at the Centenary Celebration of Robert Browning's birth held by the Royal Society of Literature. In June the young honeymooners left Lamb House and James went to Oxford to receive an honorary degree.

In July Wharton's peregrinations led her to England. She spent a weekend at Lamb House; then she and James visited Sturgis at Qu'Acre, Lady St. Helier at Newbury, the Ranee of Sarawak at Ascot, and the Waldorf Astors twice at Cliveden. During the second visit at Cliveden James suffered a "pectoral attack"; Wharton took him off to Qu'Acre and then had him driven to Lamb House in the care of her chauffeur. She checked in on him en route back to France.

James had been busy in his "den" in Chelsea dictating his autobiographical *A Small Boy and Others* to Theodora Bosanquet. She took a holiday when he went to Rye in July; he tried, with Lois Barker as her replacement at the Remington, to push the *Small Boy* to completion. Miss Barker did not suit, seemed "to be without everything, and especially any degree whatever of speed" (he noted on 17 July). Understandably, then, James's frustration in this is reflected in the epistle to Sturgis headed "Reign of Terror ce vingt juillet [20th]," warning him of the imminent advent of the Angel of Devastation: Edith Wharton was coming. Nevertheless James did move ahead with the autobiographical volume, and Wharton did complete her novel *The Reef*—James's favorite —that August.

Her experience of James's domestic arrangements at Lamb House (she returned to Rye again in the autumn) convinced Wharton that his financial status was unstable. She persuaded Scribners secretly to divert funds from her royalties so as to offer James an advance of $8,000 for "an important American novel." He was delighted to accept his largest advance ever; he never learned its true source and unfortunately never completed *The Ivory Tower*. Here was a kind of compensation for her failure to secure the Nobel Prize for the Master.

The autumn descended with a blow on James and Wharton alike: he suffered a severe attack of shingles and she the disturbing news that Teddy's riotous Boston life-style had been extended to France and Monaco. By the end of the year, however, promising changes occurred for both, as James had found a comfortable flat at 21 Carlyle Mansions in Chelsea where Miss Bosanquet could take his dictation, and Wharton had at last begun plans to divorce Teddy.

Edith Wharton's gestures of benevolence continued as the new year opened: she provided a nurse for the ailing mother of James's house-keeper Minnie Kidd, thus relieving Minnie of the responsibility of caring for her mother and enabling her to continue at the Chelsea flat as James's shingles persisted. Then Wharton began her plan for a substantial gift ("not less than $5000") for James's birthday that April. Her plan was frustrated when James got wind of it and demanded it be stopped. A disappointed Wharton turned to Italy with Walter Berry.

A successful birthday plan in England (Wharton's had been for American donors only) directed by Lubbock, Gosse, and Hugh Walpole led to purchase of a silver gilt porringer—a "golden bowl"—for James, a portrait of him by Sargent and a bust by Derwent Wood, and a dinner engagement at No. 10 Downing Street. Thus James celebrated his 70th birthday, a significant milestone, on April 15. April 16 marked a significant milestone of another sort for Edith Wharton: her divorce from Teddy was decreed.

105 Pall Mall, S.W.
26 January 1912

Dearest Edith.

Deep calleth unto deep, & my temporary indisposition greets yours. Mine is only a poisonous bad cold (the 1st one I've had for the last five years), but it makes me rather sick & sorry, & you must forgive me the dimness of these few lines. That dimness indeed flushes into rich sympathy over your accès de vertige;[1] but still the expression is poor compared with the felt tenderness, & I must wait a little to talk to you better. Don't let the *idea* of them aggravate the fact—which has nothing in it [at] all infrequent or insuperable. I had them constantly for some five years, long ago—from about 1881–2 to 1886–7, & they finally went off entirely & have never again given me news—& it was during a certain longish stay in Paris[2] that I remember them as worst. You'll find, of a sudden, the right thing to do *or* not to do—& then they will drop like a wounded bird. I haven't *dreamed* of your writing—you need never dream that I do, blessing the chance windfall, but never *shaking* l'arbre aux pommes d'or. Gilliard [Lapsley] a good bit since gave me your fresh message, put me in possession of certain facts, & that was something to go in with. I welcome what you further give me, & I await Walter B[erry] with impatience. If he is right about that matter (of his own)³ it will do us all almost as much good as if we had a finger in the pie—as morally & affectionally we *have*. We live under water here, & that does us *no* good, now that it's up to our necks. I lately spent 15 days at Lamb House,⁴ but London is again inexpressively better for me than *that*. I get on excellently on *this* basis—& that of my small cabinet de travail in Chelsea. I see no friend of yours—but mean soon to put my hand on Robt. Norton. Here endeth *this* lesson. I am only fit for bed & giving up. But ça passera vite. There are many dodges now. You will find that—you will find that more & more. Therefore tout en vous soignant bien—well remember that you'll do it best with confidence. Have much of that in your fondly faithfully old

H.J.

P.S.   Paul on Eugène-Melchior, in the Revue,⁵ rings all the changes on poor E.M.'s "race" as if he had never otherwise known a Gentleman, & couldn't get over it!—I hear dear little Percy⁶ is having an operation—to something in his *forehead*—ces jours-ci.

1. EW began suffering the attacks of vertigo shortly after the beginning of the year; they were diagnosed as an otic problem associated with anemia.

2. The sojourn from 10 September to 1 November 1895.

3. Berry was appointed head of the American Chamber of Commerce in Paris.

4. From 30 December 1911 to 14 January 1912.

5. Bourget's "Eugène-Melchior de Vogüé" appeared in the *Revue des Deux Mondes* for 15 January 1912, pp. 241—65; his praise has a heavy Tainesque dependence on "l'empreinte ineffaçable de la Race et du Sol"—"the ineffaceable imprint of Race and Land." The Vicomte de Vogüé (1848–1910), diplomat, novelist, and literary scholar, had been a member of the Académie Française since 1888; his study of the Russian novel (*Le Roman russe*, 1886) was very influential in France.

6. Percy Lubbock (1879–1966), British critic and biographer, edited *The Letters of Henry James*, 2 vols. (1920).

l'arbre . . . d'or: the tree of the golden apples; *cabinet de travail:* study; *ça . . . vite:* that will quickly pass; *tout . . . bien:* while you are looking after yourself; *ces jours-ci:* one of these days

The Reform Club
2 February 1912

Dearest Edith.

Will you very kindly forward or deliver the enclosed? I have our admirable friend's address in the form of the "rue St. Guillaume"[1] only, without a number—& am afraid to launch into such vagueness anything possibly precious. Walter [Berry] was beautifully with me on Wednesday night & gave me the latest new fact about you. Don't let that fact unduly agitate you—for it will "shape" as a small & short & feeble fact, a fact of mere restlessness & inanity, & will have *spent* all its impact in 3 quarters of a minute. *Then* it will be a simple bankrupt little fact— which you will again have to give credit to, certainly—but which *on* this credit will go forth again to seek fresh adventures—such as will much less closely concern you. Against his restlessness *rest*—you, simply; & that will be to you as a *fester Burg*. One defies him to have anything to *propose*—& without that he will presently evaporate. This is a short vain word—I am in the midst of rather thick temporary complications here which render me postally breathless. It was an immense [word omitted][2] to me to see Walter under so apparently auspicious a star reflecting the pearly light, from his own handsome surface, in such exquisite iridescent ways. I am to write to him as soon as the rue St. Guillaume materialises by another point or two. Enfin he will help *me* a little to materialize—heaven knows *j'ai de quoi*—to your great charity & patience; as they have never yet failed yours, dearest Edith, in constant participation,

Henry James

1. Evidently Walter Berry's Paris address. But almost at once Berry moved into EW's guest suite at 53, rue de Varenne on news of Teddy's arrival. See letter of 5 February 1912.

2. HJ clearly intended a word like "joy," "pleasure," "delight."

fester Burg: mighty fortress; *Enfin:* Then; *j'ai de quoi:* I have means

The Reform Club
5 February 1912

Dearest Edith.

I don't know indeed how I came, so stupidly, not to mention that I have already sat *twice* to the great man,[1] & am as soon as possible to sit again—to sit in fact till the thing rightly shapes. It proved, the 1st time, not to be a matter of the famous "one" impressionistic sitting at all—& he finds me difficult, perverse, obscure—quite as if I were a mere facial Awkward Age or Sacred Fount.[2] The end of the 2d séance left us rather off & away—& if the next one doesn't bring us back & more into line again I think he will make a new start—on a clean slate. He will do it—he clearly *knows* he will, & greatly wants to, & it is only a question of a little patience. Count on me for all the case shall demand, chère Madame & grand confrère; only I shall have to take it a little easy—as *he* seems to feel he must too—as regards intervals & continuations: I am apparently to give him a 3d pose toward the end of next week.[3]

I can't tell you how I am with you over Teddy's reappearance. But *do*, yes, bear in mind that all these phenomena essentially contain the germ of their own rapid evanescence, & if he comes but to destroy he destroys his own duration, his own application, his own continuity or consistency even more than anything else. Il fait ici un froid de loup & I am able to bear it, I am sorry to say, only like a lamb. But it's very "fine" & dry & rosy-morning'd & evening'd; & we must all sit tight. It will pass—even à la Teddy. Walter [Berry] was adorable—but I owe him such a letter. He shall have it—& you shall still have a better than this, though sadly congealed is the flow of your never very fluvial—yet still so tortuous—

Henry J.

1. HJ sat for Sargent on 24 January and 1 February 1912.
2. HJ's novels of 1899 and 1901.
3. HJ fell ill on 7 February and went down to Rye.

il . . . loup: it is wickedly (wolfishly) cold

The Reform Club
24[–25] February 1912

Dearest Edith.

It isn't to harass you with correspondence, Dieu sait, but because I want, as it were, & speaking vulgarly, to squeeze your hand, & that your so "thoughtful" envoi of Mme de Loynes[1] gives me a pretext for the same—Mme de Loynes dont j'ai vécu the last day or two very much as she did originally at least on ces messieurs, though with the difference qu'à mon tour, hélas, unlike her, je ne fais vivre personne. I have found her most interesting & d'un documentaire in respect to the life & moeurs of that incomparable people which is only equalled perhaps by all the edification & haute moralité qui s'en dégagent in the hands of M. Arthur Meyer—though in directions in which one would mostly so little expect them. How full of information, all round, the sweet volume,—for spirits like you & me—& dear Walter [Berry]! And how interesting & curious the illustration of the way the French can dispose with the *lady*—socially & in widening circles—by kind of "faking" so good a substitute for her—whereas on the other hand they don't seem to get an equal substitute for the gentleman at all. But what an intelligent sort of confession in it for them all that they don't deserve or need a more essential lady than the Dame aux Violettes, who could collaborate so with the Academy & with the relèvement de son pays. But this just to pass the time of day with you & to tell you how I participate.[2] I think of you at every hour, & am hoping that you as much as possible let everything *liquefy*. *Keep* it all fluid—au risque de vous y noyer, you'll say; but you *won't* drown at all. Don't let it harden or stiffen, & so you'll float & float till the current takes you into port.

Feb: 25th I had to break this off yesterday a.m.—to scramble away & try & put in some sort of morning's work before coming down here for Sunday—here being "Hill," where we had that observational week-end together the other month,[3] & whither I have come now, for the 36 hours, just to befriend & accompany my Nephew & Niece,[4] whom Mrs. Hunter has kindly asked & who have come up from Rye for the purpose. (They wouldn't have come save in my company—that is to join me, for this, in town—& it amuses & interests them, & the party is small homogenous & easy. They go back to L.H. I hope, for a number of weeks still.) I heard a few days ago from Walter [Berry]—not quite in the tone of a reckless gaiety, but that is so little the tone of any of us in these days that any pretence to it would shock like the presentation of a forged cheque. I had lately a baddish "relapse"[5] into my old back-wardness of recuperation (from my illness of 1910); & had to go, twice over, down to L.H. & put myself to bed for a while; but it was most superficial & came after a longer—much longer—interval than any other had done; & I have now returned apparently to the main road—to tread it again as long as possible for the present. Stay you *there* too, dearest Edith,—don't deflect into by-paths or wander into wilds—stick to the firm Macadam & the firm Macadam will stick to *you*—save in so far as Gross[6] can brush it lightly off. What has Teddy to *propose?*—which isn't a fair question, however, when I didn't mean to put you *any*. If he has nothing better to propose than your proposing to be quiet, one seems to make out that that itself must minister to quietude. You will say that j'en parle à mon aise: still, hold out, hold out—hold on, hold on.—There is nothing here of any actuality save the great looming coal strike—which really quite blackens all the sky & is in fact the most appalling of prospects; *so* appalling however that I can't believe the *general* national energy won't avail somehow to avert it. On the other hand we may be on the edge of evil days. Mrs. Hunter looks older than even a couple of months ago—alas for us all; but she fights the good fight & is very wonderful. Think a little that, or *how*, I think of you; & believe me your devotissimo

Henry James

1. Jeanne (Detourbay), Comtesse de Loynes (1837–1908), is the focus of *Ce que je peux dire* (1912) by Arthur Meyer (1844–1924), *royaliste* writer and director of the journal *Le Gaulois*.

2. EW's situation with the volatile Teddy continued to worsen. HJ informed Howard Sturgis, 22 February 1912, of Berry's report on Teddy from Paris: ". . . that with his restlessness he can't 'endure,' so on the other hand, & from the same cause, he can't be endured, or scarcely; & that he does last long enough, each time, to make one feel that there's no issue, & that with these renewals he may go on & on. It sounds rather bad. . . ."

3. HJ and EW were guests of Mrs. Charles Hunter at Hill Hall on December 9–11, 1911; see letter of 30 November 1911.

4. Billy James and his bride Alice, honeymooning at Lamb House; they left at the end of June 1912.

5. See letter of 5 February 1912.
6. Catharine Gross, EW's housekeeper.

Dieu sait: God knows; *dont ... vécu:* on whom I have lived; *ces messieurs:* these gentlemen; *qu'à ... hélas:* for my part, alas; *je ... personne:* I enliven no one; *d'un documentaire:* documentary; *moeurs:* manners; *haute ... dégagent:* high morality that emerges therefrom; *relevement ... pays:* recovery of her country; *au ... noyer:* at the risk of drowning in it; *j'en ... aise:* it's all very well for me to talk about it; *devotissimo:* most devoted

Reform Club, Pall Mall, S.W.
13 March 1912

Dearest Edith.

Just a word to thank you—so inadequately—for everything. Your letter of the 1st infinitely appeals to me, & the 3d vol. of the amazing Vladimir[1] (amazing for *acharnement* over her subject) has rejoiced my heart the more that I had quite given up expecting it. The 2 first vols. had long ago deeply held me—but I had at last had to suppose them but a colossal fragment. Fortunately the whole thing proves less fragmentary *than* colossal, & our dear old George *ressort* more & more prodigious the nearer one gets to her. The passages you marked contribute indeed *most* to this ineffable effect—& the long letter to sweet Solange[2] is surely one of the rarest fruits of the human intelligence, one of the great things of literature. And what a value it all gets from our memory of that wondrous day when we explored the very scene where they pigged so thrillingly together.[3] What a crew, what moeurs, what habits, what conditions & relations every way—& what an altogether mighty & marvellous George!—not diminished by all the greasiness & smelliness in which she made herself (& *so* many other persons!) at home. Poor gentlemanly, crucified Chop![4]—not naturally at home in grease—but having been originally *pulled* in—& floundering there at last to extinction! Ce qui dépasse, however—& it makes the last word about dear old G. really—is her overwhelming *glibness*, as exemplified e.g. in her long letter to Gryzmala [*sic*][5] (or whatever his name) the one to the 1st page or two of which your pencil-marks refer me, & in which she "posts" him, as they say at Stockbridge, as to all her amours. To have such a flow of remark on that subject, & everything connected with it, at her command helps somehow to make one feel that Providence laid for the French such a store of remark, in advance &, as it were, should the worst befall, that their conduct & moeurs, coming *after*, had positively to justify & do honour to the whole collection of formulae, phrases &, as I say, glibness—so that as there were at any rate such things there for them to inevitably *say*, why not simply *do* all the things that would give them a *rapport* & a sense? The things *we*, poor disinherited race, do, we have to do so dimly & sceptically, without the sense of any such beautiful *cadres* awaiting us—& therefore poorly & going but half—or a tenth of the way. It makes a difference when you have to invent your suggestions & glosses all after the fact: you do it so miserably compared with Providence—especially Providence aided by the French language: which by the way convinces me that Providence thinks & *really* expresses itself only in French, the language of gallantry. It will be a joy when we can next converse on these & cognate themes—I know of no such link of true interchange as a community of interest in dear old George.

I don't know what else to tell you—nor where this will find you. In what case you will be found is another matter, & I scarce dare to advance to the threshold of speculation. I kind of pray that you may have been able to make yourself a system of some sort—to have arrived at some *modus vivendi*. The impossible wears on us, but we wear a little here, I think, even on the coalstrike & the mass of its attendant misery; though they produce an effect & create an atmosphere unspeakably dismal & depressing; to which the window-smashing women[6] add a darker shade. I am blackly bored when the latter are at large & at work; but somehow I am still *more* blackly bored when they are shut up in Holloway & we are deprived of them. Mary Hunter's sister, Ethel Smythe [*sic*],[7] has just been condemned to two months' hard labour there—M.H.'s depressed & *ob*sessed sense of her cold, her inanition (very little food & practically no fire) & her isolation is somehow aggravated by her thinking she really quite deserves it. A propos of whom, M.H., I am to sit tomorrow to Sargent for the 3d time (& I surmise, & hope, she will be there—for she really helps the sitter). I have a certain amount of impression that he may sacrifice the work of the 2 other sittings[8] & make a fresh start. If he does he will probably, over the known, the learnt, ground, go much straighter. *But* he may pick himself—or *me*—up, & dash along as it is.

—I rejoiced in your comparatively bright evocation of Morton [Fullerton]—as if he were engaged for the moment almost in a gay Nijinski[9] *pas*. DO be so far as possible his Lady Ripon[10] in any such performance. I hold my breath over Walter [Berry]—he might be able to bear a mécompte—but *I* shouldn't. But n'en parlons pas de ça. It ravished me to hear that Rosa, the Charleys,[11] the Bourgets &c, "abound in their sense" more & more; Paul, above all, can never do so enough for me—for what a comfort it adds to life when you feel you can absolutely count on such aboundings! Keep him at it—don't let him *faiblir*. But I hear you say "Pas de danger qu'il faiblisse," & it's du pain sur la planche! when so much round about us fails. *You* don't fail— *you're* a store on the shelf; but then in another cupboard altogether! Yours all & always, dearest Edith,

Henry James

1. Wladimir Karénine, *George Sand: sa vie et ses oeuvres, 1804–1876*, vol. 3 *(1838–1848)* (Paris: Plon, 1912). The pen name covered the identity of the Russian critic Varvara Dmietrievna (Stasova) Komarova (1862–1942). HJ's review of the volume was published in the *Quarterly Review* for April and the *Living Age* for June 13, 1914, and reprinted in his *Notes on Novelists*. See *LA* 3, 775–90. The earlier volumes—1 *(1804–1833)* and 2 *(1833–1838)* (Paris: Plon, 1899)—covered only the first thirty-three years of the life. A final volume—4 *(1848–1876)* (Paris: Plon, 1926)—completed the biography. HJ's review was published in the *North American Review* for April 1902 and reprinted in *Notes on Novelists*. See *LA* 3, 755–75.

2. George Sand's daughter; she married the sculptor Auguste Clésinger (see Jean-Baptiste letter of 8 November 1905), whom Sand could not abide; a rift ensued and Solange complained of mistreatment by her mother. The "long letter to sweet Solange" (HJ's irony) of 25 April 1852 (Karénine, *George Sand*, vol. 3, pp. 611–16) is full of dispassionate rejection of her complaints about the bed she has made and of sound moral advice.

3. HJ and the Whartons were at Nohant on 20 March 1907.

4. Chopin sustained an affair with George Sand from 1836 to 1847.

5. Count Albert Grzymala, Polish exile, a friend of Chopin's. (HJ had written "Gry," crossed it out, then boldly resumed that spelling.) Sand's letter to Grzymala, 12 May 1847 (pp. 570–72), includes passages omitted by Rocheblave

in his *George Sand et sa fille*, 1905 (see above, letter of 8 November 1905), that refer to her affair with Chopin: e.g., "For seven years I lived like a virgin with him and others, I've grown old before my time ..." (p. 571; my translation).

6. Suffragettes.

7. Dame Ethel Smyth (1858–1944), composer and conductor, was a leader of the women's movement.

8. There were no further sittings for this portrait. The finished drawing was delivered to Lamb House on 26 March; see letter of 29 March 1912.

9. Vaslav Nijinsky (1890–1950), renowned premier dancer of the Ballets Russes. The manuscript rather clearly has "gay Lejinski *pas*"—as though HJ had been thinking "gay *leger* (light) Nijinsky *pas*."

10. See letter of 22 December 1911. Lady Ripon was involved in numerous extramarital affairs!

11. Charles Du Bos and his wife, Zezette.

acharnement: tenacity; *ressort:* reemerges; *moeurs:* customs; *Ce qui depasse:* What tops it all; *cadres:* limits; *mécompte:* miscalculation; *n'en ... ça:* let's not talk about that; *faiblir:* weaken; *Pas ... faiblisse:* No danger of his weakening; *du ... planche:* money in the bank (bread on the shelf)

The Reform Club
16 March 1912

Dearest Edith.

Maurice[1] is indeed a sweet little flower of *snobisme*, & his *naturelle & sublime blessure* is wonderfully wide open—so that we look all the way down his throat. Quelle engeance!—including Sa mère aux beaux cheveux. Why not sa mère aux beaux seins or aux belles hanches at once? However, they are made for our delectation—& what on earth should we do without them? When coal & trains & other supplies fail, as here, they at least are toujours là. So I thank you for these unfailing recalls to them. I wrote you 2 or 3 days ago,[2] & this was at any rate to have been a postscript. I have sat again to Sargent with complete success, & he has made an admirable drawing. He kept on with the work of the 2 previous séances—& brought it round, beautifully developed, & redeemed & completed it. It's a regular 1st class living, resembling, enduring thing. Now he wants to know if: 1st he has your leave to have it, for safety, *photographed*, in one or two copies. 2d. If he shall then send it to you to Paris—or if it shall await here—in his hands—your next possible, & it is hoped probable, coming.[3] He is all at your orders, as is your all devoted

H.J.

P.S.   He will have the thing at any [rate] glazed & framed—so as to guard against rubs of the charcoal &c.

P.S.   Perhaps you will write J. S. S[argent] a word to himself—31 Tite St. Chelsea. S.W.

1. Maurice Rostand (1891–1968); HJ refers to his poem "A ma mère."
2. See letter dated 13 March 1912.
3. EW began a five-month tour of Italy, England, and France in May; she did not reach England until late in July 1912.

blessure: wound; *Quelle engeance:* What a breed; *Sa . . . cheveux:* His mother with the lovely hair; *sa . . . hanches:* his mother with the lovely breasts or the beautiful hips; *toujours là:* always there; *séances:* sittings

The Reform Club
[29 March 1912]

Dearest Edith.

I understand some of your reserves about the brilliant image[1]—which I greatly admire myself; but I am moved to distress as well as to the deepest confusion & anxiety by your offer to me of so valuable a trophy, your disposition *de vous en défaire* for my benefit. Your grand manner of munificence again deeply touches me—in how many forms have I not known it?—but I am now beseeching you to just consider a while longer without—or before—making me a party to the transfer. Keep it on near you for a certain time, the so interesting if not exhaustive (!!) thing, & then see how you are affected. Wait, in short; *wait*, WAIT! We will then talk of it again, if you are freshly moved—& meanwhile, after your return from Spain[2]—a good while after—I will broach the question to you, carrying your lavish, your more than generous, *procédé* in my heart. It may interest you to read my Nephew Bill's impression of it[3]—from the photograph which by your indulgence I was able to send him; his letter came in to me tonight with yours. Don't, please, return the torn-off sheet I send you.

May your "fugue" with Rosa [de Fitz-James] bring you (*be* for you) a big diversion & refreshment; & after that the better months come to you promptly. I almost envy you—but only almost. The thought of a déplacement is utterly impossible to me.—We continue here up to our ears in our crisis, though a light does seem at last dimly to break. I am with the Government wholly—& shld. even go farther. But good night—it's just tomorrow. It's a pang to me not to hear that Walter [Berry] has now *positive*—! Basta—pazienza! Yours all & always

Henry James

1. The Sargent drawing; see letters of 5 February and 13 March 1912.
2. EW planned to take Teddy to Madrid at Easter.
3. Billy's letter of 28 March 1912 announced, "The Sargent drawing came day before yesterday," and continues: ". . . considering the greatness of the man who did it I must admit a certain disappointment. There are certain perfectly palpable refinements and finesses in your face which I supposed Sargent would have inevitably taken his stand on, but they are ignored, passed over. Not one feature—not even the eyes which are the best of it, I think—is just right even from the point of view of construction, which would make it 'feel' right and look right in a mirror. . . . Sargent seems to reveal himself as one who takes a running start and gets across with what he can carry. That's just like Bay Emmet. . . . how much may not Sargent's flying start manner of work account for his being the great painter that he is?"

de . . . défaire: to get rid of it; *procédé:* proceeding; *Basta—pazienza:* Enough—patience

105 Pall Mall, S.W.
12 May 1912

Dearest Edith.

I have your beautiful letter, & am as a result of it even more *émotionné* than you can probably conceive. The mere hearing from you at all deeply moves me—oh all the past impossibilities, & the almost equally intense present difficulties, have been but too vivid & lurid to me. We communicate as through black darkness & over sheer abysses, & it's all a bad time to pass; even though we don't ever, I feel, wholly not communicate. Your beautiful envoi a few days since of the 2 lemon-coloured volumes, Loti & Lemaître,[1] which I am so gratefully ravished to have (the eternal readability of everything about Chateaubriand—he, of old, so admirably constructed & elaborated to be endlessly & richly unexhaustedly *exposed*!) shines with a still ampler grace than what, in it, meets the mere eye, or even the mere mind. And then your Perigord post-picture of dear old George [Sand][2] nosing for the human truffle— & infallibly finding it (when il n'y en avait plus being exactly when il y en avait encore in the very next jiffy!); these things, & other wandering airs, have kept the cord [*sic*] just vibrating even when not conveniently to be thumbed. In addition to which your good letter does thumb it—with such breadth!—for the whole packed fulness of which I tenderly thank you. It might indeed have diverted you to be present at our Browning commemoration[3]—for Pinero[4] was by far the most salient feature of it (simple, sensuous, passionate—that is artless, audible, incredible!) & was one of the most amusing British documents we had had for many a day. He had quite exhausted the air by the time I came on—& I but panted in the void. But dear Howard [Sturgis] & dear Percy [Lubbock] held each a hand of me—across the width of the room—& I struggled through. (My stuff is to be published in the Quarterly, & I will send it to you.) I seem to get the side-wind of great adventures, past, present & to come, from you, tout de même—not counting the chronic domestic one; which keeps my heart in my mouth. "And did you see Shelley plain?"—and did you three times go to Nohant ("coloured"?),[5] retour d'Espagne too? all of which plunges me into yearnings & broodings ineffable, abysses of privation & resignation. It's all right for you to go—by which I mean it's all right for *me* not to; but it's all wrong for me not otherwise to participate—& I shall sit gaping, watch in hand, till I do. And you go to Salso again[6]—& you "motor in Italy"—& you're ready for anything prodigious; as such *are*, obviously, the sublimities of the sublime. It is the grande vie, don't deny that—for which I was so little framed, ever—& am so much less so than ever now. I hear from Mary Hunter, hoping for you at Salso—but she will be back in England for Whitsuntide by the time you get there. I don't presume to speak to you of eventualities—we are all in the lap of the gods. What are they by this time doing for Walter[7] there?—but let me not put questions, especially as to things as to which I literally shouldn't be able to bear or survive the possibly (absit omen!) wrong answers! If you want to make the chord vibrate to a mere 2 frs. 75 worth of "thumb," will you send me (excuse my voracity) the vol. (*not* the Illustration one), of Bourget's play,[8] if it comes out before you leave? I like to hear of him as I do of any other bull-fight or truffle-hunt; there appearing to en être encore of *him* too, always, even when il n'y en a plus. Il y en aura toujours—such as it is! I am staying on in town till about June 12th;[9] I like my little Chelsea *repaire* so for work—& my young relatives[10] are, for that matter, to my great joy for them, still a month more in possession of Lamb House. I probably spend 2 or 3 days at Hill at Whitsuntide—but without the attrait that the mistress of it will have lately seen you. However, she did as she went out—& I shall grasp at that. I am really finding I can work again—& it will be all my *avenir*. My voracity for it is almost indecent—though I have to gratify that but in my still small way. What I mean is that it *goes*. Over *your* preventions I weep all the larmes de mon corps. Howard appears to have been of late extraordinarily sound & serene—& is always the dearer when he *is* so. Good-bye, dear grande viveuse. Keep rising above (you do it so splendidly); yet drop *some* day again even to your faith-fully-fondest old

Henry James

1. Jules Lemaître (1853–1914), French literary critic and dramatist; his *Chateaubriand* (1912). Pierre Loti (pen name of naval officer Julien Viaud, 1850–1923), French novelist; his *Un Pèlerin d'Angkor* (Paris: Calmann-Lévy) had just been published.

2. EW's leisurely return from Madrid with Teddy included a visit to George Sand's home at Nohant.

3. At the centenary celebration by the Royal Society of Literature, HJ read his paper on "The Novel in *The Ring and The Book*." The revision was published in the *Quarterly Review*, vol. 217 (July 1912), and in *Notes on Novelists* (1914); see *LA* 2, 791–811.

4. Arthur Wing Pinero (1855–1934), British playwright.

5. The slight misquotation of the first line of Browning's "Memorabilia"—"Ah, did you once see Shelley plain"—seems doubly appropriate in a letter that describes HJ's performance at the centenary celebration and also delights

in the continued eagle flights of EW: the last stanza of the poem recounts, "I picked up on the heather . . . an eagle-feather!" EW had been to Nohant in May 1906 with Teddy and a second time in March 1907 with HJ.

6. EW did go south to take the waters at Salsomaggiore in Italy after Teddy's return to the United States.

7. Berry was suffering from fatigue and enteritis.

8. *Le Tribun*, which HJ had asked about in the letters of 25 October and 19 November 1911.

9. HJ did not get down to Rye until 11 July.

10. Nephew Billy and his bride, Alice.

il . . . plus: there wasn't any more of it; *il . . . encore:* there was again more of it; *tout de même:* just the same; *en . . . encore:* be some still; *il . . . toujours:* there isn't any more of it. There always will be some; *repaire:* den; *attrait:* added attraction; *avenir:* future; *larmes . . . corps:* tears of my body; *grande viveuse:* high liver

The Athenaeum, Pall Mall, S.W.
15 May 1912

Dearest Edith.

But what an *Apache*[1] side, tout de suite, under all their easy intelligence & pretty play—the ferocious impudence or insolence that leaps to its feet at the 1st lapse of guard! (You see what a wide mouth I make for the least wandering air that has past by you—so as to compass some small & shrunken reciprocity!) It's the Apache even if Guitry's[2] every wondrous word is true—as (heaven forgive me!) I even feel it can't possibly not be. It's very odious for Paul even if toutes ces dames, the fine Françoise,—in spite of her lassitude!—& the whole Academy & the *Figaro* &c, do rally to him—though what *their* Apache side may make them do who knows after all? And I who was all the while *envying* poor dear Paul the *amenity*—aesthetic & other—of his relations with such an interpreter, producer & confrère! The atmosphere of art! Amenity?—where on earth is it left, what with Roosevelt-Taft,[3] or Taft-Roosevelt, chez nous, that sort of adventure chez Minnie & Paul, almost everything everywhere indeed! I really think we are *on the whole* better here; our bêtise has really some better *dessous* than these awful ones of their genius. But this is only a weak word. London is charming just

now—wondrous weather, & the green country a dream. Still, no muf-
fles (or mufles, I believe) of any envergure worth speaking of, & no
Minnie-Paul *blottis* in a divine Versailles! What I live without! You, tout
d'abord. But do send me the suite prochainement—there must be a
suite! I shall write to Walter [Berry]. I lose myself over Morton [Fuller-
ton]! I am dining out tonight for the 1st time for 3 months.[4] *Judge* of the
emotion of your ever constant

H.J.

1. A colloquial French term for a Parisian thug.
2. A dispute between Bourget and the French actor Lucien Guitry (1860–
1925) over rights to the dramatization of Bourget's novel, *L'Émigré*, which was
a success in 1908 with Guitry its star. When Guitry wanted to remount the
play in 1912, Bourget refused and appealed to the commission of authors for a
ruling; they supported him, and Guitry aired his grievance in a letter to Paris
newspapers.
3. Theodore Roosevelt and William Howard Taft (1857–1930), twenty-sev-
enth president of the United States (1909–1913). In 1912 these two contended
once again for the Republican presidential nomination in a vicious mudslinging
campaign. Taft won the nomination but lost the election (November 1913) to
Democrat Woodrow Wilson.
4. An exaggeration: he had dined out ten times since mid-February. On this
date he dined with John W. Cross (1840–1920), husband and biographer of
George Eliot.

tout de suite: suddenly; *toutes ces dames:* all those ladies; *chez nous:* with us; *bêtise:*
stupidity; *dessous:* bottom, foundation; *mufles:* cads; *envergure:* extent; *blottis;* snug-
gled; *tout d'abord:* first of all; *suite prochainement:* rest soon

[The Reform Club]
29 June 1912

Dearest Edith.
(Forgive this vulgar paper which chance thrusts under my hand as
most convenient for the moment.) Je vous laisse deviner what it *means*
for me, as they say in Boston, to have a *real* little letter from you, as
they also say in Boston (they say so much in Boston!) & this even
though I have known that the deeper currents (Boston again!) *couldn't,*

all these months, sit to an easy interchange between us for reasons too conceivable; & though, further, even what I have from you today is but the pale ghost & the meagre ash of the grand manner d'antan. However, it is *you* (*kind* o' you), & this is kind o' me, & my pen kind o' moves on a kind o' paper; so here goes for a kind o' spurt. I have a plain fact or two about you—if such recorded, & transacted, items as your biography yields are not always, rather, of the very essence of ornament—for a lady's life; & I grasp it, the authentic bristling nettle, even if its points *are* of sharpest gold tipped with finest enamel. Poor dear Walter's misadventure & distress[1] are indeed wretched news; & yet, even there, when you soar so high & spread your wings in such pride, the nearer you get to the sun (in *his* pride) the greater your risk of melting for a drop! However, it must all have been very brave & beautiful (for natures of your *trempe*), & I measure the disconcertment & depression of so irrelevant a check. May honest Walter find at Plombières the right wash for his wounds. I sit writing this while I await a taxi-cab that is to convey me this p.m. to Hill[2] for two nights. I have been offered as a seduction thither the Princess Teano & Jacques Blanche, & am not sure that the prospect of his remarks about her (which I forecast simply as, in the way of Blanchissage,[3] inevitable) has not had much to do with my embracing the opportunity. However, it will be also a goodbye to the mistress of that house, whom I must all the more take leave of for a long parting if your bright vision (in the sense of a brightness to *us*) really is to veil itself as thickly as your letter portends. I mean of course your vision of August here—or a part of it; which I hang my head at your giving up—little as I can enter into any of those colossal considerations: questions of the eagle-flight or the trapeze-spring, that is to say, in connection with a given gyration, the more or the less. I don't live, you see, or think, or feel, *in such terms*—& fall so altogether beneath the free use of the globe that they all, & all the while, take for granted, that I can only offer myself, in the whole connection, as relatively abject & inane. As one *is* those things, so one mustn't be presumptuous—& therefore I have no inch of ground under my feet for beckoning you on hither *quand même*, or for not bowing a sad old head to your not coming. I shall immensely miss you, that's all; & I feel as if I had scarce even the right to *mention* that when it's so forbidden to me to mention even that I can't *girare* myself. It is written, dearest Edith (& I have myself written it twenty times, I think), that I shall never (D.V.) again leave the shores of this island; which makes, I agree, a dismal enough prospect in respect to seeing you again. I can't appeal against [it], on the one hand—& to accept it at all is to accept it with an all but mortal pang on the other. There it is, however; the Continong[4] is an utterly & finally closed chapter: that book sharply & inviolably padlocked, stands now[5] on the very highest thinkable shelf, far out of my reach. Some day you *will* come over, I believe; for you will always *girare*, & certain inevitable gyrations simply involve the en-counter of the spatial mass (such as it is) dont je suis. If this may, by your rejoinder, be long hence let the fact, or the possibility, figure (by mine) as horrible—yes; but such is our mortal lot, & such the infirmi-ties, the necessities, the deficiencies, the perversities, if you will, of your fellow-mortal. There we sadly are! I hope indeed you *will* go over & see Mary Cadwal[ader Jones]—so vivid an impression did I lately get from her here that she greatly hopes for you & counts on you some-where. She was a week in town, in excellent "shape" & most gentle to me; in which coin, seeing her repeatedly,[6] I paid her unstintedly back. She could do without the Continong, I think, almost as well as I must— & do; but her fate seems to lead her more captive. Anything nobler or more exquisite than Oxford last Wednesday,[7] grey-greening it for me so harmoniously round my personal (& even facial) scarlet relevé with silvery dove-colour, no word of mine can tell. The Continong has noth-ing more to my purpose—by extreme good luck under all the circum-stances. Howard [Sturgis] I haven't seen for many weeks, but he appears to have been all winter in confessed & approved & even flaunted good health. I shall go down to him for a Mrs. Lees evening before I return to Rye on the 11th. There I again resume residence till about December, I surmise. I groan for the verisimilitude of it when you tell me that Morton [Fullerton] the book-maker *défaillit*. There it deplorably is—that he isn't,—won't be, probably *can't* be—a book-maker. And his intelli-gence has such perversities! What is to be done about it? Oh if we could talk! I shall tell Mary Hunter that you prefer Thuringia[8] to Yorkshire (small blame to you) & she will wail, for she has been living in some confidence. However, these confidences are monstrous things, & *I* am all sadly & stoically heroically yours

Henry James

1. Still plagued by enteritis, and exposed to a hair-raising drive up a steep and winding trail to the monastery at La Verna, Berry then "developed an agony of inflammation in a tooth" that sent him hurrying toward Paris; en route to Milan he and EW were involved in a rather serious automobile accident (see EW to Berenson, 29 June 1912, *EW Letters*, 272–74).

2. The Charles Hunters' Hill Hall.

3. HJ's bilingual pun on Blanche's name and the French noun for "laundry."

4. HJ's rendition of the stereotypical Briton's rendering of the French *continent*.

5. The manuscript quite clearly reads "not"—an obvious slip of the pen.

6. HJ saw Mary Cadwalader on three days of her week in London.

7. HJ was in Oxford to receive, on 26 June (the Wednesday), his honorary degree of doctor of letters.

8. The resort area of the Thuringian Forest in eastern Germany (as it then was); EW had invited HJ to accompany her on a motor tour through Germany.

Je . . . deviner: I leave it to you to imagine; *d'antan:* of yesteryear; *trempe:* temper (as of steel); *quand même:* even so; *girare:* spin, gyrate; *dont je suis:* of which I am part; *relevé:* set off; *défaillit:* fails

Lamb House, Rye
15 July 1912

Dearest Edith.

I just got your wire—& I welcome it with effusion, by which I mean rather that I shall welcome *you*, for Friday & I hope Saturday & Sunday.[1] This particular Coming of Edith is marked with even more than the normal beauty & bravery of the great phenomenon in general. The temperature is high—it must be mountains high in Paris; & I have a fear it will last a little. That however may very well be only till your arrival. I await you at any rate de pied ferme—& de coeur ouvert.[2] Such treasures of history as you'll bring! I saw Berenson in town before leaving—& he gave me a little apparently sound news of you. What a concentrated little commentator! I also dined at Quacre—Howard [Sturgis], Percy [Lubbock] & Babe[3] (la vieille garde!)—& marvelled again at the "Protean" forms of poor dear Howard's occasional noncerebration—when he has a kind of freshness of death! But go to see him—he isn't buried! Hasten (slowly) then, & be assured of the fondest accueil of your faithfullest old

Henry James

1. EW's visit at Lamb House extended from Sunday, 21 July, until 11:00 a.m. Tuesday, 23 July.
2. That is "with a firm stance—& an open heart"; here is an untranslatable pun with *ferme* (firm) suggesting "closed" as opposed to *ouvert* or "open."
3. Sturgis's companion William Haynes Smith.

la . . . *garde:* the old guard; *accueil:* welcome

Lamb House, Rye
Saturday [3 August 1912]

Dearest Edith.

This is but a word to say that it all went beautifully,[1] as you will have heard from Cook, & that I am ever so much better in consequence; quite a different man. I tumbled straight into bed—where I still am, to keep perfectly quiet till tomorrow a.m.—I shall then I think have regained my permitted normal. Let this condense my brevity. Your loan of the motor was a sovereign benevolence—it made the whole thing possible. I really enjoyed the run, & the renewed beauty of the day, & the wondrous splendid land, & the ideal virtue & beauty of Cook, who insisted on returning to you in the evening—we got here at 6.30. Embrace & caress Howard [Sturgis] for me please, & let him, not less for me, embrace & caress you. You shall presently hear further, & I am your devotedest (both yours)

Henry James

1. HJ was with EW from Thursday, 25 July, until noon Friday, 2 August—visiting Sturgis at Qu'Acre, the Ranee of Sarawak at Ascot, and the Waldorf Astors twice at Cliveden. During the second visit to Cliveden HJ suffered a "pectoral attack" while walking with EW after lunch, and another after dinner.

On the following day, 2 August, EW put her automobile and chauffeur, Charles Cook, at HJ's disposal and sent him to Qu'Acre and then on to Lamb House.

Lamb House, Rye
6 August 1912

Dearest Edith.

Do come for tomorrow night or for *Thursday* p.m.[1]—since it seems to me that this howling gale must give you pause. It *has* been, & still *is*, very bad here—it comes home to us from the distracted Sea's nearness. I think of dear Mary Cadwal[ader Jones] in it—& devoutly hope she hasn't been crossing today. Wait *you* until the whole thing abates—the Channel will be a bad place even *after*, till it has had time to subside. Come Wednesday p.m. (tomorrow) or Thursday or Friday—only let me know a little before. Don't repine (as in your *douce* letter today rec'd.) over the Cliveden crisis; it was très-particulier, & not at all brought on by the walks there *in themselves*—THEY, I am convinced, were purely beneficial & informing—Tuesday & Wednesday p.m. & Thursday a.m.[2] showed it. But there was something in the conditions of excitement & tension, of having to reckon simultaneously with the whole time-scheme & social chaos, & also with the very *emotion*—of our impressions, that for the hour tipped the balance the wrong way. I had another small accès yesterday afternoon—after being in-doors here (& largely in bed), since the moment Cook deposited me, that was thus not brought on by movement, but by its very absence: partly owing to my first *seeking* to be quiet, & then to my *having* to be, through this prohibitive out-of-doors tempest; which has raged 3 days. I have seen Skinner twice, last night & this morning (when he looked me thoroughly over, cardiacally &c),—& he is of very good counsel & comfort. He finds me "a very good heart," & with no *cardiac* justification for my pectoral passages. He believes altogether in all quiet walking for me that is not *at the time* persistently painful—& would have had me yesterday afternoon, after ½ an hour's rest from my access,[4] carry out my plan of going out with a lydy[5] (I was just preparing for it here—as on Thursday with you & Spencer S.),[6] only taking a tabloid of nitro-glycerine (trinitrin), if the accès had declared itself again. So, he believes (& so I really, but too timidly felt), it would have been bettered more than by a mere return to immobility. Unfortunately I didn't see him till *too much* after —7 o'clk.; & meanwhile my own confidence (without the trinitrin & *with* the wind), had too much failed me. Now I am absolutely suffering from too much immobilization, & feel certain that even a Cliveden walk (without any of ce monde-là waiting for me) wd. do me nothing but good. But forgive this flood of demonstration—it's only in answer to your unqualified verdict on our beautiful meanderings. I absolutely refuse to take that Wednesday raid upon the Disboroughs' soil as anything but a proof of validity. But I must catch the post. Mille tendresses to Mary Cadwal—when she comes. I await you here—& am your faithfullest old

H.J.

1. EW arrived at teatime on Thursday, 8 August, and left Lamb House about twenty-four hours later for Folkestone.

2. That is, 30 and 31 July and 1 August; see letter of 3 August 1912.

3. HJ comments in his diary that the attack was due to "too much hurry and tension on slopes and staircase" (see *Comp. Notes*, 365).

4. HJ uses the literal English equivalent of the French *accès*, meaning "attack."

5. HJ's cockney phonetic rendering of "lady."

6. The manuscript clearly reads "Spencer S.," but HJ's diary entries for Wednesday, 31 July, and Thursday, 1 August, refer to Spencer Lyttelton; the "S" is obviously a slip of the pen for "L." The Honorable George William Spencer Lyttelton (1847–1913) was assistant private secretary to Gladstone between 1871 and 1894.

douce: sweet; *très-particulier:* most peculiar; *accès:* attack; *ce monde-là: that* lot; *Milles tendresses:* A thousand tender greetings

Château de Barante
Dorat, Puy de Dôme
3 [–4] September [1912]

Dearest Cher Maître,

How are you & what have you been doing since my vigilant eye has been off you?[1] I am in the château of Prosper de Barante, the friend, lover, cousin, correspondent (or all four) of nearly everybody in the de Staël-Récamier group, & spent all last evening reading Récamier, de Staël, Châteaubriand [*sic*], and Joubert letters, not to speak of earlier and later ones of equal interest, from Rousseau to Mérimée.[2] How I did want you to be here!—

(Continuation next day, from Vic-Sur-Cère, in the Massif du Cantal) —I had to dash down early yesterday morning to see my host's first editions (in a library of 50,000 volumes!) & look again at the family portraits & the miniatures of the irresistible Prosper's loves, from Corinne to Caroline Murat[3]—& after that it was time to jump into the motor & start; so my plan of telling you all about Barante was broken in two. It is a wonderful place, about 30 miles from Clermont Ferrand, in an immense English-looking park, with big oaks & cattle, &, from the house, incomparable views over the whole Puy de Dôme region, the Monts Dores, & this Massif du Cantal that we're now in. Mr. de Barante is a Paris friend who had always adjured me to come to Barante whenever I was in Auvergne, & who is really worth seeing there, under Grandpa's out-spread glory, every little sparkle of which he zealously polishes up every morning. It's altogether the most interesting glimpse of French "Shatter Life"[4] I've ever had.

Well—to revert.—I left Paris about a fortnight ago, & went for a week to be with the Minnie Pauls[5] at Pougues les Eaux, a vile place where, in a sinister little mouldy villa, they lived (!) as Paul says: "Comme des cloportes sous une pierre."

I "mealed" with them, but enjoyed the relative advantages of a clean room & a bathroom at the neighbouring hotel. We roamed the country in the motor, & I tried to coax them to come off with me for ten days (with their own motor, which they had there). Minnie was very anxious to come, & *he* wanted to, but couldn't make up his mind what day he would start; so after a week I departed without them. My old friend Marion Richards[6] was villégiaturing[7] with the Jusserands in J's "maison familiale," in the Lyonnais (such a dear old XVIII maison bourgeoise, in a garden full of clipped bpx, looking over the plain of the Lyonnais & the mountains); & I picked her up there & spent an hour or two with the Js. It was a refreshing atmosphere after the drug-dreariness in which the M. P.s are sunk to their chins. (Paul's first remark on my arriving at Pougue [sic] was: "Ah, je vous ferai voir l'homme qui nous lave les intestins, et qui est en même temps le jardinier de l'évêque hérésiarch [sic] qui habite en face de l'hôtel." That really boxed his compass!)

Well—we went from the Jusserands' to Vichy for a day or two, then to Barante, & now we're here in this primitive pleasant mountain place, where we shall "lay" for a day or two more before going on to Vernet & the Eastern Pyrenees. The sun is out at last, & we are going to follow it south for another week or ten days, possibly over the edge of Spain.—I shall be back in Paris toward the 20th of September for a few days, & after that I'm uncertain.—Teddy seems to be really better, & quite relieved of the pain in his face, since his teeth are gone. He announces his intention of sailing for England at the end of the month.

Marion is a perfect traveller. Everything interests & amuses her, & as she had never been in Auvergne the Romanesque churches are quite new to her, & she knows enough of architecture to be aware of what they "stand fer," as we say in Boston.—

Don't write me,[8] but keep well, & think of me very often—

Yr devoted Edith

P.S.   Walter cabled me last week that he had hopes of a prompt settlement.

1. See letter of 3 August 1912.

2. Guillaume-Prosper Brugière, Baron de Barante (1782–1866), literary critic and historian, was in his youth a lover of Mme de Staël, Germaine Necker (1766–1817), who in 1786 became the Baronne de Staël-Holstein; she was the center of an important literary-political salon in Paris and author of the influential novel *Corinne, ou l'Italie* (1807). The affair between Prosper and Germaine blossomed during composition of that novel (1805–1807), and they are readily identifiable as its hero and heroine, Oswald and Corinne. Mme de Staël's closest friend was Jeanne-Françoise Récamier (1777–1849), whose literary salon fea-

tured François-René, vicomte de Chateaubriand (1768–1848), author of *Le Génie du christianisme* (1802), and Benjamin Constant (1767–1830), political writer and author of *Adolphe* (1816) and sometime lover of Mme de Staël. The other letter-writers are Joseph Joubert (1754–1824), lecturer on spiritual philosophy; Jean-Jacques Rousseau (1712–1778), influential social reformer and author of *Confessions* (published posthumously, 1781)—whose granddaughter was the wife of the Baron de Barante; and Prosper Mérimée (1803–1870), versatile writer and author of important novellas such as *Carmen* (1845) and short stories such as *Mateo Falcone* (1833) and *La Vénus d'Ille* (1837)—both of which HJ translated as a youth in Newport and the latter of which strongly influenced his tale "The Last of the Valerii" (1874).

3. Prosper de Barante came to call Germaine de Staël by the name of her famous heroine, Corinne. Caroline (Bonaparte) Murat (1782–1839) was queen consort of Joachim Murat, king of Naples.

4. HJ-EW satiric Americanese for "Chateau-Life."

5. The Bourgets.

6. Sister of Elise, Mme Jusserand.

7. "Holidaying"—EW turns *villégiature* into an English gerund by the "ing" addition.

8. HJ disobeyed: see letter of 6 September 1912.

Cher Maître: Dear Master; *Comme . . . pierre:* Like wood lice under a stone; *maison familiale:* family home; *maison bourgeoise:* a substantial residence (not a castle or château) that may be divided into apartments to let; *Ah . . . l'hôtel:* Ah, I will show you the man who washes our intestines, and who is at the same time the gardener of the heretic bishop who lives opposite the hotel

Lamb House, Rye
6 September 1912

Dearest Edith.

Very beautiful & wonderful, very splendid & *interesting*, your letter, the behest of which not to write I am obeying, you will see, by writing so microscopically little (though not "small")[1] que ce sera tout comme. I do rejoice that you're leading the great life in your great way, for the mere rushing side-wind of it enlarges for the hour the horizon of one who seems more & more condemned to a mere fine far-scanning wistfulness. I have been having difficult days pretty steadily since your departure, physically speaking—quite *chronically* afflicted have I been, in the manner that I gave you some exhibition of. I mention this for simplification's sake—I can't pretend to do as if I were really free & easy. Everything tends to show that my botheration is 9 tenths digestive & stomachic deviltry to 1 tenth any other—but the effect of the disturbance is none the less an inconvenience. With it all I am considerably able to work,[2] thank the Lord (otherwise—!) & to enjoy the pleasures of the mind: which is why your vivid & admirable Baranteries,[3] to the conception & vision of which I so gratefully rise, really help to keep me going. Ayez-en le plus possible, & if ever in doubt have one for me, at a venture—even, I mean, when not sure for yourself. I really *ought* to have looked out with you on the Massif Central. I *always* wanted to handle that massif—& shall never again come so near it. And the M[innie] P[aul]s & the Jusserands—what commerce & visions altogether! How amazing Paul's failure to decide to see a little country with you! If he had my "intestines" I can imagine the incompatability; but doué comme il est it was surely designated. I'm glad you've had such a right & jolly Miss Richards[4]—& wd. fain send her my blessing on her being so for you. But your little word about Walter [Berry] most rejoiced me; allons, I do believe that when that chapter is closed, conveniently, he will really come round to a better state again. I expect to be able to go up to London for 2 or 3 days on the 9th[5]—tout doucement —to see about an amanuensis person & 2 or 3 other matters. Don't torment yourself about me. I've really arrived at a better basis of comprehension of my affair—& within these 5 or 6 days there has been a good deal of a consequent *détente* for yours all tenderly—& toughly—

Henry James

1. See letter of 3–4 September 1912.
2. Completing *A Small Boy and Others*.
3. An allusion to the Château Barante; see letter of 3–4 September 1912.
4. See letter of 3–4 September 1912.
5. HJ went up to London for two days on 11 September to look at a flat, 21 Carlyle Mansions (see letter of 18 November 1912), as well as to recover Theodora Bosanquet, the substitute amanuensis Lois Barker having proved unsatisfactory.

que . . . comme: that it will be just the same as if I did; *Ayez-en . . . possible:* Have them as much as possible; *doué . . . est:* gifted as he is; *allons:* now then; *tout doucement:* quite quietly; *détente:* relaxation

[DICTATED]   Lamb House, Rye
                                                        18 November 1912

Dear Princesse Rapprochée![1]

But I *must* write, I can't help it, just to express my joy in being again in communication with you: so much the smaller of the two efforts is my seeking the help of this so blest machinery[2] (*so* blest for just these purposes through my long and dismal *crise*)[3]—compared, I mean, with swallowing my fond words! And I haven't had such folichons times this ever so long that it doesn't at once light up the grey scene just to prolong a little the flash of Paris. I'm really glad you're back there[4]—it makes me feel less lonesome. All these weeks' strict tête-à-tête with Herpes Zonalis (I think the proper name of the complaint really *looks* as vicious as the damned thing is!) is a good deal like solitude in the desert, far from any oasis, or passing caravan and with an insatiable tiger prey-ing *all* the while on your vitals. Of course all work has been utterly blasted—and that has appeared but a drop in the bucket of one's woe. I have at last, however, had some light and help in the form of a visit of 24 hours, terminating last p.m., from an admirably kind London friend, Henry Head, F.R.S.,[5] the eminent neurologist and, as it has hap-pened, by a miracle, great and supreme authority on my fell disease, who has bien voulu come down, as an act of pure benevolence and goodwill, and overhaul and enlighten and instruct me. It has been a boon unspeakable, for I had at last come to feeling absolutely *lost* in the wilderness of pain. The situation has put on, thanks to his presence, a different aspect, and I feel myself on the way to relief. Il était bien temps, and I shall have arrears, of the grossest, to make up. As soon as I am quite definitely fit (which you see I now venture to count on) I shall go up to town, and perhaps be there when your visit (which I am ravished to hear of the possibility of) takes place.[6] I have taken (for several years) the lease of a little flat in Chelsea, 21 Carlyle Mansions,

Cheyne Walk,[7] the companion-house to Emily Sargent's, which you may know; and though I can't get into it till some date early in January, it is important I should be in town a while before that, and in fact, says my London authority, from as early a date as my physical condition shall allow. Walter [Berry] I shall in that case be able, I trust, also to welcome to a different tune from the one I had so shabbily to treat him to during his late visit. As for Teddy,[8] I really should have been glad to see him and his car of Juggernaut, for the pure, blest "change" and vivacity of it, *could* my state really have permitted it. But I was literally too wretchedly affected—unfit for *any* approach, however bland and little of an "intellectual strain." I am glad he sent you my letter—I wanted somehow to reach out to you, and my arm felt weak and fell short, and that gently lengthened it.

I most heartily rejoice that Bessy [*sic*] Lodge[9] has accomplished her migration and has you to protect and guide her. A great interest and a great ornament in your life must her presence, with the questions it brings up, now be. Please tell her how I send her my love and benediction—and how fondly I rise to the possibility of seeing her. That certainly we shall manage somehow or other. I hope you are to have her near you—*such* an object in the landscape must so make every centre or standpoint elastic enough to take it in. May Paris shine with all its jolliest lights straight into the consciousness, too, of the innocent babes! But good-bye and à bientôt j'espère. Just a sprig of rosemary— or "rue"—to finish! A letter from "Pussy" Sturgis (Mrs. Julian)[10] the other day quoted to me, from one she had just had from our friend at Quacre: "*Such* a birthday as I haven't had for ages: just Babe and I alone here together! The bliss of it!" After that, somehow the "ladder" must be drawn and we must face the worst. All alternative dreams kind of collapse. But if dear H[oward] is past praying for, please keep it up still for me as hard as you can (for I need and want it yet) and believe me all faithfully yours

Henry James

1. HJ's appropriate adaptation—"the Princess Nearby"—of the title of Rostand's romantic play of 1895, *La Princesse lointaine*, "The Princess Far Away."
2. Dictating to his typist.
3. HJ felt the onset of the attack of shingles (herpes zoster or zonalis)—his

crise or "crisis"—on 30 September; Dr. Skinner's diagnosis was made on 4 October.

4. EW had joined Bernard Berenson and his wife at Avignon early in October and gone with them into Italy. She regained Paris in the first few days of November.

5. Head (1861–1940), a Fellow of the Royal Society, had also read some of HJ's fiction.

6. HJ and EW did not meet until the beginning of July 1913.

7. The unfurnished, L-shaped flat, which Theodora Bosanquet had found for him, boasted (he wrote to Jessie Allen on 9 October) "two 'best' rooms on the river, with an admirable exposure and view," with ample accommodation for cook, maid, and Burgess, and a master bedroom for himself—five bedrooms in all. The rent was £169.8—about $850—yearly.

8. See letter of 10 December 1912.

9. See letter of 5 February 1910.

10. Mary, widow of Julian Sturgis (1848–1904), elder brother of Howard.

folichons: amusing; *bien voulu:* has been willing to; *Il . . . temps:* It certainly was time; *à . . . j'espère:* I hope I'll be seeing you soon

[DICTATED]   Lamb House, Rye
                                              4 [and 9] December 1912
My dear E.W.

Your beautiful Book[1] has been my portion these several days, but as other matters, of a less ingratiating sort, have shared the fair harbourage, I fear I have left it a trifle bumped and bousculé in that at the best somewhat agitated basin. There it will gracefully ride the waves, however, long after every other temporarily floating object shall have sunk, as so much comparative "rot," beneath them. This is a rude figure for my sense of the entire interest and charm, the supreme validity and distinction, of The Reef. I am even yet, alas, in anything but a good way—so abominably does my ailment drag itself out; but it has been a real lift to read you and taste and ponder you: the experience has literally worked, at its hours, in a medicating sense that neither my local nor my London Doctor[2] (present here in his greatness for a night and a day) shall have come within miles and miles of. Let me mention at once, and have done with it, that the advent and the effect of the intenser London Light[3] can only be described as an anti-climax, in fact as a tragic farce, of the first water; in short one of those mauvais tours, so far as results are concerned, that make one wonder how a Patient ever survives *any* relation with a Doctor. My Visitor was charming, intelligent, kind, all visibly a great master of the question; but he prescribed me a remedy, to begin its action directly he had left, that simply and at short notice sent me down into hell, where I lay sizzling (never such a sizzle before) for three days; and has since followed it up with another under the dire effect of which I languish even as I now write. I am of course from this day closing my mouth tight to anything received from his hand, and there will doubtless be, eventually, some "explanation" of the whole monstrous muddle. I shall from this moment shake myself free of *every* form of medicine. I have really been fumbled at these nine weeks (being now in my 10th) with a futility that I can call nothing less than cruel; and my conviction, or intention, is all centred on the simple idea of *escape*, escape from further torment, to take effect about a week hence, at any apparent cost: it's so impossible I should suffer less, in town, on my own hook, than I have up to this moment been suffering here—in a drawn-and-quartered fashion. So much to express both what I owe you—or *have* owed you at moments that at all lent themselves, in the way of pervading balm, and to explain at the same time how scantly I am able for the hour to make my right acknowledgment.

There are fifty things I should like to say to you about the Book, and I shall have said most of them in the long run; but there are some that eagerly rise to my lips even now and for which I want the benefit of my "1st flush" of appreciation. The whole of the finest part is, I think, quite the finest thing you have done; both *more* done than even the best of your other doing, and more worth it through intrinsic value, interest and beauty.

December 9th. I had to break off the other day, my dear Edith, through simple extremity of woe; and the woe has continued unbroken ever since—I have been in bed and in too great suffering, too unrelieved and too continual, for me to attempt any decent form of expression. I have just got up, for one of the first times, even now, and I sit in command of this poor little situation, ostensibly, instead of simply being bossed by it though I don't at all know what it will bring. To attempt in this state to rise to any worthy reference to The Reef seems to me a vain thing; yet there remains with me so strongly the impression of its quality and of the unspeakably *fouillée* nature of the situation between the two principals (more gone into and with more undeviating truth than anything you have done) that I can't but babble of it a little to you even with these weak lips.[4] It all shows, partly, what strength of subject is, and how it carries and inspires, inasmuch as I think your subject, in its essence, very fine and takes in no end of beautiful things to do. Each of these two figures is admirable for truth and justesse; the woman an exquisite thing and with her characteristic finest, scarce differentiated notes (that is some of them) sounded with a wonder of delicacy. I'm not sure her oscillations are not beyond our notation; yet they are all so held in your hand, so felt and known and shown, and everything seems so to come of itself. I suffer or worry a little from the fact that in the Prologue, as it were, we are admitted so much into the consciousness of the man, and that after the introduction of Anna (Anna so perfectly named), we see him almost only as she sees him—which gives our attention a different sort of work to do; yet this is really I think but a triumph of your method, for he remains of an absolute consistent verity, showing himself in that way better perhaps than in any other, and without a false note imputable, not a shadow of one, to his manner of so projecting himself. The beauty of it is that it is, for all it is worth, a Drama and almost, as it seems to me, one of the psychologic Racinian[5] unity, intensity and gracility. Anna is really of Racine and one presently begins to feel her throughout as an Eriphyle [*sic*] or a Bérénice: which, by the way, helps to account a little for something qui me chiffonne throughout; which is why the whole thing, unrelated and unreferred save in the most superficial way to its milieu and background, and to any determining or qualifying *entourage*, takes place comme cela, and in a specified, localised way, in France—these non-French people "electing," as it were, to have their story out there. This particularly makes all sorts of unanswered questions come up about Owen; and the notorious wickedness of Paris isn't at all required to bring about the conditions of the Prologue. Oh, if you knew, how plentifully we could supply them in London and, I should suppose, in New York or in Boston. But the point was, as I see it, that you couldn't really give us the sense of a Boston Eriphyle or Boston Givré, and that an exquisite instinct, "back of" your Racinian inspiration and settling the whole thing for you, whether consciously or not, absolutely prescribed a vague and elegant French colonnade or gallery, with a French river dimly gleaming through, as the harmonious *fond* you required. In the key of this, with all your reality, you have yet kept the whole thing; and, to deepen the harmony and accentuate the literary pitch, have never surpassed yourself for certain exquisite *moments*, certain images, analogies, metaphors, certain silver correspondences in your façon de dire: examples of which I could pluck out and numerically almost confound you with, were I not stammering this in so handicapped a way. There used to be little notes in you that were like fine benevolent finger-marks, of the good George Eliot—the echo of much reading of that excellent woman here and there, that is, sounding through. But now you are like a lost and recovered "ancient" whom *she* might have got a reading of (especially were he a Greek) and of whom in *her* texture some weaker reflection were to show. For, dearest Edith, you are stronger and firmer and finer than all of them put together; you go further and you say mieux, and your only drawback is not having the homeliness and the inevitability and the happy limitation and the affluent poverty, of a Country of your Own (comme moi pour exemple!). It makes you, this does, as you exquisitely say of somebody or something at some moment, elegiac (what penetration, what delicacy in your use there of that term!)—makes you so that, that is, for the Racinian-sérieux;[6] but leaves you more in the desert (for everything else) that surrounds Apex City.[7] But you will say that you're content with your lot; that the desert surrounding Apex City is quite enough of a dense crush for you, and that with the *colonnade* and the gallery and the dim river you will always otherwise pull through. To which I can only assent—after such an example of pulling through as The Reef. Clearly you have only to pull, and everything will come.

These are tepid and vain remarks, for truly I am helpless. I have had all these last days a perfect hell of an exasperation of my dire complaint, the 11th. week of which begins to-day; and have arrived at the point really—the weariness of pain is so great—of not knowing à quel saint me vouer. In this despair, and because "change" at any hazard and any cost, is strongly urged upon me by both my Doctors, and is a part of the regular process of dénouement of my accursed ill, I am in all probability trying to scramble up to London by the end of this week,[8] even if I have to tumble, howling, out of bed and go forth in my bedclothes. I shall go in this case to Garlant's Hotel, Suffolk Street, where you have already seen me; and not to my Club, which is impossible in illness, nor to my little Flat (21 Carlyle Mansions, Cheyne Walk, Chelsea, S.W.) which will not yet, or for another three or four weeks, be ready for me. The change to London may possibly do something toward breaking the spell: please pray hard that it shall. Forgive too my muddled accents and believe me, through the whole bad business, not the less faithfully yours

Henry James

1. EW's novel *The Reef*, completed at Pougues-les-Eaux toward the end of August 1912, and published in New York by Appleton.

2. Sir Henry Head, who with Dr. Skinner continued to treat HJ's attack of shingles; see letter of 18 November 1912.

3. Here is written interlinearly, in a hand other than HJ's, "the London specialist who came down to see him."

4. The following day HJ wrote to Howard Sturgis of EW: "I think she is very wonderful—to have been able to write the exquisite 'Reef' (for I hold that what is finest in The Reef to be really exquisite, & haven't scrupled to try inordinately to encourage her by putting that faith in the most emphatic way)."

5. Jean Racine (1639–1699), French playwright. In his tragedy of 1674, *Iphigénie en Aulide*, Ériphile is the "other" Iphigenia and is the sacrificial victim at Aulis. *Bérénice* is his tragedy of 1670. In his *Portrait of Edith Wharton* (1947), Percy Lubbock illustrates an interesting coincidence of perception by quoting a comment by Charles Du Bos: "Edith lent me the proofs of *The Reef* [in October 1912]. After reading them I told Edith that by the small number of protagonists, the passionate poignancy enhanced by the rigorous restraint of expression, no novel came closer to the quality of a tragedy of Racine. At our following meeting Edith showed me a letter she had just received from Henry James, the letter on *The Reef* written at Lamb House on December 4 1912 ..." (p. 104).

6. The genuine Racinian (accent added in ink by HJ).

7. The hometown, in Kansas, of Undine Spragg and Elmer Moffatt in *The Custom of the Country*.

8. HJ was in any event up in London for New Year's Eve, which he spent with the French writer André Gide (1869–1951) at Edmund Gosse's.

bousculé: jostled; *mauvais tours:* evil turns; *fouillée:* penetrated; *justesse:* accuracy; *qui me chiffonne:* that rankles me; *comme cela:* that way; *fond:* background; *façon de dire:* way of speaking; *mieux:* better; *comme . . . example:* as I have, to be sure; *à . . . vouer:* what saint to devote myself to

[DICTATED]   Lamb House, Rye
                                                 10 December 1912
My dear Edith.

I wrote you belatedly, brokenly and long-windedly but yesterday—in a very limping, floundering fashion; having got out of the couch of pain for an hour (though by no means leaving the pain *in* the couch, but clutching it to my side like a nursing, wailing infant) in order just so to deal with a letter or two by the non-performance of which I was much beset. This a.m. comes your most lucid avertissement about our distracted, and more than ever distracting, friend;[1] who would appear indeed to be much on the loose, judging by a letter (Hotel Majestic, Paris) that I had from him but 3 or 4 days since. This letter, though almost childishly extravagant, portends, fortunately for my decidedly sore and stricken state here, no present movement at all in my direction; but I'm extremely grateful to you for the warning. I shouldn't, as I stand, or rather as I mostly lie, be able at all congruously to receive him. At the same time, as his main purport seemed to let me know how wide a berth he was giving *you,* I to that extent found my account in the picture. Be at your ease, at any rate, so far as mine is concerned; I really feel him fly quite too high over my head—as his present tendency seems to be to do over yours. Howard S[turgis] has acted with the most considerate promptitude on your injunction—so that I also hear from him this morning. He doesn't literally forward me your letter, but repeats to me, apparently, all of it that concerned me, with other, and highly sage (dear Howard *can* be so sage!) reflections of his own. So I am advised all round—and even to the extent of his nobly desiring me to spend Christmas, and even some time before it, "just with him and Babe"—with a possibility of Mildred [Seymour] thrown in! This dazzlement I resist, though I am trying really (as I mentioned to you yesterday) to get up to town by the end of this week; even if I have to be drugged and policed and ambulanced. Such are the resources of civilisation—and such still, I'm sorry to say, remain those of my obstinately and oh so acutely and almost (or say frankly quite) intolerably afflicted state. I am staking all on a throw of the dice. The treadmill and the vicious circle are here—that is now to a certainty proved; therefore the break of the spell (which has been of inordinate length) may well be elsewhere. And when it comes I feel I shall be quite sane and whole and "talented," as you shall see if you'll only still have patience with yours all faithfully

Henry James

1. Teddy Wharton, who was reported to have been cutting capers both in Paris and in Monte Carlo—so extravagantly as to move EW seriously to consider a divorce.

avertissement: warning

> 21 Carlyle Mansions[1]
> Cheyne Walk, S.W.
> 31 January 1913

Dearest Edith.

I saw dear little delicate & delightful Matilda Gay[2] yesterday (looking like a kind of *virtuous* ornament de l'ancienne cour), & we talked of you so long & earnestly & intimately that it brought home to me more poignantly how long my straight (or crooked) silence to you has lasted, *had* somehow to last, even though, heaven knows, I have done little but privately ache with the sense & the shame of that. The case has been that with long physical distress of the scantest kind I have had simply the instinct of keeping in my corner like a sick animal & not crawling out into the middle of the room to bark or caper. I have felt all along that you would perfectly understand this & would know that it was only a question of waiting. Besides, I also felt that you had complications enough on your consciousness—without my piling mine on top of them. For complications, quite merciless, have been my woeful history—from the moment that long weeks & weeks ago, when my accurst Herpes was by the law of Nature beginning to be ready to abate, there took place what I believe often occurs after a bad career of the complaint, the determination of a hideous condition of excruciating pain, horrible chronic sore flatulent distension, produced by the neuralgic poison, in all the neighbouring stomachic & abdominal tract. The effect of this was to redouble all suffering, really quite to an awful point—but all *that* I think I have already told you—in spite of my abysmal *mutisme* my condition is alas that I still suffer too much & am still, though less, under the same harrow. I have to some degree *rallied* & wriggled upwards—but it still all serves quite sufficiently for bad chronic pain. Relief—medical or other—doesn't come in anything like the measure needed; at the same [time] however I am not beaten & arrive at a sort of modus vivendi—till the late p.m. (about 8 o'clk) comes. Then I *am* fairly beaten, & the only thing for me is to tear off my clothes (so aggravating by that time), & tumble straight into early bed—which means bad & long nights; also loss of all time to write letters or notes in however lame a degree. My great *planches de salut* are (1) that I have got back to work,[3] & can put it in from 11 to 1.30, or *1.45,* pretty regularly, & (2) that circulation in the open air in the very largest measure in which I can possibly manage it is directly beneficial to me, almost fully remedial, so does it keep the fiends *comparatively* at bay—for the time it lasts. And this place is excellent for me—of as perfect rightness, though I am as yet installed in it in the roughest & most waiting way—waiting to make it more inwardly decent. I don't care for the decencies, that is for vain appearances one straw yet. My southward outlook on the river is meanwhile simply precious. I try to tell you the good with the evil—deeply & achingly conscious as I am of all the evil with which you are yourself overdarkened & oppressed. Matilda G. told me much, bless her—though I haven't wanted for dismal presumptions & dark imaginations. She will have sent or be showing you Teddy's letter to me[4]—an essentially mad one s'il en fût. I haven't seen the tip of his nose—I had not really at all *incurred* that before he went to the Condamine;[5] & it all (the failure) took place very naturally. Heaven grant he *does* sail in April—he appears to have been in parley for a date. But how his incoherent presence, further off or nearer, must fill for you the ambient air I need no further words from you to say. Only sit tight & have patience—he can only consummately attest his futility! Percy L[ubbock] lunched with me the other day, & was so charmingly redolent of 53 [rue de Varenne] that I both loved & envied him. You did him by your kindness an inestimable service. I hang on the sequences of The Custom[6] with a beating heart & *such* a sense of your craft, your cunning, your devilish resource in the perpetration of them. It's done & archi-done, & it's something to live for if other things do fail. But I really believe my own *barbouillages* will see *me* through too. Oh if I could see you! But I am sunk in *every* abject incompetence. One day perhaps you'll come. Je vous embrasse & am all devotedly yr.

H.J.

1. Under the managerial eye of Fanny Prothero, HJ was installed in his Chelsea apartment on the first weekend of 1913.

2. Wife of the American painter Walter Gay (1856–1937) and a friend of EW's since childhood.

3. On *Notes of a Son and Brother*.

4. See letter of 10 December 1912.

5. La Condamine is the harbor section of the principality of Monaco, north of the Rock.

6. EW's novel *The Custom of the Country* began its serialization in *Scribner's Magazine* this month.

de . . . cour: of the old court; *mutisme:* muteness; *planches de salut:* salvations; *s'il en fût:* if ever there was one; *barbouillages:* daubings; *Je . . . embrasse:* I send you hugs and kisses

[DICTATED]

21 Carlyle Mansions
Cheyne Walk, S.W.
3 February 1913

Dear and admirable Confrère.

I can't possibly not want to thank you on the spot for your so deeply interesting and moving letter, this morning received; and this is the fashion[1] after which I can do so with [the] best economy of time and of my poor *moyens*. The facts you communicate are surpassed in interest only by their dreadfulness; yet, too, I think their dreadfulness really surpassed by their futility, as it were—their general weakness and negligibility. Of course they are superficially sickening—but they don't go down deep—I mean into the soil of Consequence or the fine large substance of the Whole: which may strike you perhaps as an airy way of treating them! But no, it won't, for you will see and feel what I mean—being about the only person who ever does, in general; which fact[2] doesn't, at the same time, prevent me from almost blushing for my incapable situation, my state of inability to contribute by any act of presence or stroke of inspiration to your greater ease. However, you really are all the while and quand même taking care of that yourself, and je conçois bien que vous planez—il n'y a absolument que cela à faire. Planez, planez—to find how one *can* is a magnificent resource. I take the liberty of squeezing the last drop of comfort out of the fact that your gallant kinsman[3] is with you, from N.Y., and that he is taking in hand the great matter[4] in the sense you name. Surely it will be practicable—everything so appears to me to lend itself. I see perfectly how the influence you mention (what types, what cases, what *hideurs*, such situations throw up!) *must* have been needed to work the poor bedevilled brain up to the point of whatever recent performances. But I think with a great longing of the possibility of seeing you. Extraordinarily good would it be for me—if it can only be *actively* anything for you! I bless the image of the beautiful presence from Washington[5]—I cherish the thought of the sweetness of support that may constantly flow from it. Please tell her how this intensifies the sentiment I entertain à son égard. Let me not omit definitely to say that I *have*, and have *englouti*, the second installment,[6] with all sorts of yearning reactions and admirations. It takes care of itself, all, *to* admiration, and one has to the highest and happiest point the sense of a full-orbed muchness to come —the large mass of the orb hanging and looming there, with all the right dimness, in the light actually forecast. Of course I made out for myself—as intelligent readers will, and the others don't matter—that the "good young man" involved some printer's lapse. Don't worry over such mere specks of accidents. I rejoice in what you tell me of Morton [Fullerton], to whom I send the fondest assurances; though I'm not quite clear as to which or what "book" your announcement of a happy finish applies.[7] I seem to make out that there have been questions of others— but unspeakably hope that what you allude to is the Paris. I wallow, by sympathy, in Walter [Berry]'s "hundreds of thousands,"[8] and should like so to see them expressed in the terms of his blest friendly presence. But this must be all in this poor way. À bientôt I do venture grossly to hope! Yours all faithfully

Henry James

1. By a dictated typewritten and therefore "impersonal" letter.

2. HJ wrote in "fact" in ink.

3. EW's Rhinelander cousin Herman Le Roy Edgar (1865–1938), a New York realtor and book collector.

4. The gathering and preparation of evidence of Teddy's adultery (Edgar had just visited him in Monaco) in preparation for divorce proceedings.

5. Bessie (Mrs. Bay) Lodge.

6. Of *The Custom of the Country* in *Scribner's Magazine*.

7. *Problems of Power: A Study of International Politics, from Sadowa to Kirk-Kilissé,* just published by Scribners (see letter of 7 June 1913), and not the book on Paris for which EW and HJ arranged an advance from Macmillan; see letter of 26 July 1909.

8. The estate of Walter Berry's mother was finally settled and Berry came into a substantial inheritance.

moyens: means; *quand même:* in spite of all; *je . . . planez:* I readily make out that you are soaring aloft—that is absolutely the only thing to do. Soar, soar; *hideurs:* hideousnesses; *à son égard:* concerning her; *englouti:* swallowed; *À bientôt:* See you soon

❧ 6 ❧
Entr'acte

EDITH WHARTON QUICKLY ENOUGH RECOVERED from her disappointment at James's scuttling the "American plan" for his seventieth birthday and resumed her motor tour of Italy with Berry. She traveled a great deal during this fifteen-month period, evidently seeking escape from the baleful associations of 53, rue de Varenne. Often her flights brought her to England and to Henry James.

James meanwhile acceded to the "English plan" for his birthday by duly sitting to Sargent for his portrait. There were ten sittings at the Tite Street studio over a period of five weeks in May and June, with James sometimes accompanied by friends—Jocelyn Persse and the American monologuist Ruth Draper (1884–1956) among others—to chat with while Sargent worked. Then, for a week in early July James sat daily to the young sculptor Derwent Wood.

Wharton had arrived in England at the beginning of that month and was briefly James's neighbor down in Chelsea. They dined together and motored with Robert Norton. She was looking for an English residence on a short- or long-term basis; she considered both Hill Hall and Qu'Acre as short-term possibilities and long pondered the purchase of the large property of Coopersale near Hill Hall. Her friends were encouraging about Coopersale, especially James: he involved the architect Edward Warren—who had introduced him to Lamb House—in the enterprise. None of these proved suitable.

James's niece Peggy and nephew Harry arrived in mid-July for a two-month visit; he took them to see the great Russian ballerina Pavlova but then suffered a collapse. Down in Rye he was soon back at work on his autobigraphy, taking walks with Peggy, and driving with Harry. The nephew left at the end of August, the niece at mid-September. Edith Wharton arrived a week later. She had been to Germany with Bernard Berenson in August, a trip interrupted by her brief collapse—like James's a month earlier. In fact, both of them were in dubious health that fall. Nevertheless, Wharton saw her novel *The Custom of the Country* through serialization that year and into publication in October; and James, working better than he had since 1909, mailed off his completed *Notes of a Son and Brother* to the publisher in November.

February 1914 began with James's "momentous interview" with his dentist, followed by six weeks of visits during which most of his teeth were extracted and he was fitted with replacement "machinery." That occupation helped divert his attention from another potentially momentous confrontation—with the talent of Marcel Proust. Wharton sent him the opening volume of *À la recherche du temps perdu: Du Côté de chez Swann* had just been published in November 1913. She later recorded in *A Backward Glance* (1934) sending him the book and noted that he "devoured it in a passion of curiosity and admiration. . . . I look back with peculiar pleasure at having made Proust known to him, for the encounter gave him his last, and one of his strongest, artistic emotions" (chap. 12, sec. 6). That has the ring of truth, but there is no corroborating evidence, and it seems unlikely that James ever read a line of Proust. Perhaps Wharton was recreating the occasion, two decades later, as it *ought* to have happened. For although James's critical faculties were beginning to falter early in 1914, it would have been interesting to have his responses to the great French psychological novelist.

At the end of March Wharton took off with Percy Lubbock for a tour of North Africa. Two weeks later James's nephew Aleck and niece Peggy with her friend Margaret Payson arrived in London. He squired the two girls around town and into the countryside; they had conveniently moved into a flat in Carlyle Mansions and stayed on to the end of July. By that time Wharton had arranged to rent Stocks, the Humphry Wards' country house in Buckinghamshire, occupancy to begin on 10 July. On that date, however, she and Berry abruptly set off for Spain in her automobile.

The Great War erupted at the beginning of August, and James anx-

.iously sought to discover the whereabouts of Edith Wharton. News of the outbreak of war reached her and Berry at Poitiers as they sped back northward. James finally got in touch on 6 August, offering sympathy and comfort, expressing the hope that she could soon cross to England, and announcing accurately "the crash of our civilization."

21 Carlyle Mansions
Cheyne Walk, S.W.
2 May 1913

Dearest Edith.

It is a great relief to my spirit to hear from you as by the whirr of great unresting wings—after the disconnection from further sound or sense that seemed to attend our last exchange of letters. You should have heard from me again before this were it not that my pen refuses each day more & more doggedly to be driven—it is destined, clearly, at some early hour to drop right out of the shafts & lie down flat forever. Wonderful your story now—immense & epic & terrible, even as if all about Gods & Goddesses—Walter [Berry] & Cook certainly a brace of the former & You & She unsurpassed in the ranks, as surely, of the latter.[1] No, I can't tell you from what a *recul* of the far-off & fabulous you come to my constant sofa-side here, where I can touch without a strain my horizon of four brown walls. You light up the place assuredly with the glory of the immortals, & I ask you in my dazzled gladness if you would sit down a bit with me—whereupon you exchange a look & smile, not to say a sigh ("Poor dear thing, isn't his simplicity sweet!") & murmuring that you are due for tea at Castrogiovanni within the five minutes (for you know it's Castrogiovanni that *most* crushes me) you are off over the mountain tops—which have at once become again for me the brown walls of the room. Well, it's magnificent of you, & I don't grudge her a hoot of her pace or a patch of your own purple: I only just lie down flat to take it—I mean the passage over me of the whole—where I can best blubber into the carpet. In that posture I shall lie until you come & pick me up again. Oh & then for the fearful particulars—which I shall insist on even though they kill me.

Less figuratively I delight in your two main facts: that of your definite liberation,[2] signed & sealed (oh blest consummation!) & that of Walter's recovery of happy health. These things do me a world of good—so please, Walter, don't curse my presumption if you happen to have a tummy-ache at the moment my message reaches you. One always feels like the devil at the moment of being congratulated for feeling so well; but believe me, dear Walter, it won't last—the tummy-ache won't—& the grounds for congratulation *will*—& je maintiens le mot. Do come over here again & ask your London Doctor if I haven't reason[3]—for I do so desperately want to see you both. I address this, you see, a bit confusedly & economically—for Edith is my gage of your improvement, just as you are that of her épopée. I hope to stay on here well into June—if not to the very end thereof; so you will have time to find me. You will say, dearest Edith, that I am cool, & that *after* Castro-giovanni—! However, here I am—you know what I mean. And dear old Howard [Sturgis] is so much better that I am tempted to enclose to you a letter about him (as to a part of it) that I have just had from Percy Lubbock, blest creature: though you may be hearing also. I did of course have my fat volume[4] sent to 53 [rue de Varenne], & there it will safely await you if the servants don't rashly forward it. It appears to have been "most kindly received" here—but from America I have had no sign. And about matters here & there I want just to say *this*—I have taken the liberté grande to insert your name (and Walter's too) into the re-enumeration of signers of the loveliest little Birthday letter[5] to me (from Percy's own perfect hand) to whom I address a Letter of Thanks, much less "neat," which appears (a bit belatedly) in a day or two. You can't "contribute" now—that is all over; but you can both come in on the cheap, as if you *had*—& because it was simply not to be borne that you were out. The Golden Bowl is a most charming thing,—& I accepted it with emotion; but I have not accepted the gift of the portrait, & shall in no way possess or retain or enjoy it: I shall simply *sit*—*le reste les regarde*. (I don't say it ungraciously.) And I know the modest value of the (silver-gilt) Bowl; which will have cost my 250 subscribers about 10/ apiece. *That* I shall beautifully have faced. Of the impossibility of my lending myself to the American scheme I will tell you more when we meet—if you will ever so kindly listen. There would have been depths within depths of impossibility—as to the form (the broad form) the movement seemed capable of. A Fifty Pound[6] piece of plate (forgive the vulgar specification) I would radiantly have thanked for—& that is all I have practically thanked for here. Basta! Good night. I am much spent with "acknowledgments," round about me, & the pen now does fall from my hand. Yours, dearest Edith, with constant affection always

Henry James

P.S.   I do plunge up to my neck into your freedom!

1. "She" is the automobile.
2. Her divorce.
3. HJ uses a literal translation of the French *si je n'ai pas raison*—i.e., "if I am not right."
4. *A Small Boy and Others.*
5. A number of HJ's friends in England contributed a maximum of £5 each (the 10 shillings HJ here specifies was perhaps the minimum) to purchase a "Golden Bowl" and to have Sargent paint HJ's portrait. On 15 April the "Birthday letter" announcing these honors and signed by the subscribers was delivered to HJ. Sargent requested his payment go to the young sculptor Derwent Wood for a bust of HJ, now in Lamb House (Sargent's portrait hangs in the National Portrait Gallery, London). HJ's "Letter of Thanks," dated 21 April 1913, was printed by the Chiswick Press, London. See *Letters* 4, 664–68, and *A Bibliography of Henry James*, 3rd ed., ed. Edel and Lawrence (Oxford: Clarendon Press, 1982), 255.
6. That is, £50 (sterling).

recul: realm; *je . . . mot:* I insist on what I say; *épopée:* epic; *le . . . regarde:* the rest is up to them; *Basta:* Enough

21 Carlyle Mansions
Cheyne Walk, S.W.
[7 June 1913]

Dearest Edith.

How can I tell you the pleasure I take in your beautiful letter, which infinitely touches & soothes me?—& particularly in the thought that the "cheekiest" of Small Boys[1] (through his pretention to regale a preoccupied world with the interest of his infinite smallness) has attached you for the passing hour & set the chords of association &c humming. I delight in short in having set in motion the hospitality of your admirable mind, & now feel how greatly I must have enjoyed that séjour. I think I measure what I write now—as to the degree of its achieving form or force—almost only by its seeming happy or right to *you* (which makes me wish so that I wrote, or might write, more. However, I *have* got back to a sort of regular besogne much more steadily than at any time since—awful interval!—1909). The only part of your letter that didn't taste sweet was your account of my not being able to look to have you right here in our little city from one of these near days we have been counting on. I counted on a very near one last night with Mary Hunter,[2] with whom—departing from my quite rigid habit & necessity, in general, of the lonely lamp & book & fireside (this last literally just now), I banqueted at one of her tremendous three-tables affairs—in honour of the singularly ingrat (as he strikes me) Rodin.[3] She announced you, by warrant of having so lately seen you, for the very earliest date, but I didn't at all, I confess, share her sweet assurance. She makes, ever, such large & earnest & expensive preparations for being tremendously wrong. However, she told me of having placed—or being in the act of placing—Hill at your entire & independent disposal (she is going to be only so intensely quiet there from now on herself!) from any moment that you will arrive; & she most kindly stopped to see me this p.m. on her way out to Cobham (or is it Chobham?—Lord Darnley's—for the week-end), in order to see how I was after her pernicious (so awfully *cheffy*) dinner, from which I had fled as soon as we rose from table, & without pretending to go upstairs to the music. She then told me that her letter about your finding a haven of rest at Hill, motoring straight there & making it an ideal headquarters, had gone to you this a.m., & when I said that I shld. be writing you tonight (June 7th 1913) besought me to back that specious picture. This behold I *am* doing—to the exter.t of believing that you would (with Cook's or "Her"[4]—not Mary H.'s— aid) find there, for whatever time, a very firm & large basis of existence—which I also think you might make as free, for coming & going, as le coeur vous en dirait. The only thing is that though I see very well where you would go *from*, I don't see so vividly where you would come *to*; & the case, alas, would have to be that, ravished as I should essentially be with the sight of you here, & as often as possible, I shouldn't be able to go there for more than a sole afternoon, probably, & of necessity without sleeping. The curtain has rung down forever on that possibility, & I have utterly had to scratch from my tablets the fell sign of the country-visit over-night. Do you know that I have never paid one since that adventure of ours last summer at Cliveden; when my sun (not to say my moon) went down in such glory. I spent 3 or 4 hours with poor dear Howard [Sturgis] last Sunday at Quacre (that is I trained it down in time for tea, & came away again just as dinner had ended. That will be the limit of my capacity ever again there). He is gradually on the mend but looks delicate, thin, as if he had been through much—beautifully refined. I think he is really in very good order, but he has known an ordeal & an épreuve that have cost him much of his vitality & won't have left him quite where they found him. He was more intensely *gentil* than ever, & surrounded with Mrs. Maquay & Georgie, & his Nurse (at Dinner); but heaven knows one didn't want the dear thing any *more* thrown back on the resources of the sofa & the work-basket, which were in full operation while I was there—the Eshers[5] being also at tea. What seems to me is that the whole pitch there must find itself now much "lowerer" than in the past—& remain so. Ah, the lower pitches, dearest Edith—I am a lower one, moi qui vous parle, incarnate & beyond all raising! That is my case—even though I find that I in a manner, & with an infinite rich melancholy, adjust myself. The great & difficult thing is to adjust one's friends. But in due course the great adjustment itself will come. What a "full life" you must have, in all your recent gyrations, been having. I should have valued news of Walter [Berry]—but perhaps you will bring some. If you could bring *him* ce serait mieux & plus doux encore. Give him, please, my particular love. Your Oklahoma tribute is a gem of a lustre of verity that we (you & I) pant over, in our yearning for the real, in vain. I quite love the man, & shall be unhappy till I am fitted with a Tiger hat. He doesn't say Tigress, so it must be for the male animal. I leave you the Challenge, as obviously more becoming to your style; so we shall be both suited—especially if you challenge the Tiger. "Sammy Krepps"—better *that*, equal it if you can! You do 200 000 words of Scribner—& he floors you in scarcely more than one! But I deeply share his admiration of Undine,[6] whose whole chronicle "grows upon" me ever so gallantly. It *is*, indeed, the best story Scribner has published for many years—since The House of Mirth in fact. You will have done it again this time—but with a much finer asperity still, & with no end of representative arts & graces that I wonder at—or should if it weren't *you*! But good night—it's now much later than when I began—though it then was late, & I am yours, dearest Edith, all & always

Henry James

P.S.   Sargent is making, I think, a very fine thing—one of his real ones; a full face—or almost—head & shoulders only. I sit for the 6th time—if not 7th—tomorrow.[7] I greatly admire the maîtrise, the brilliant "go" of Morton [Fullerton]'s book;[8] but fear for him a little as for a lost soul of "Journalistic circles," Dantean as it were. Him too how I shld. like to see. Think genially of Hill—Hill not Hell—which it looks like.[9]

1. HJ's *A Small Boy and Others*; see letter of 2 May 1913.
2. At Hill Hall.
3. Auguste Rodin (1840–1917), French sculptor.
4. EW's auto.
5. Lord and Lady Esher; see letter of 7 September 1911.
6. Undine Spragg, heroine of EW's *The Custom of the Country*, still running serially in *Scribner's Magazine*.
7. In fact, the seventh sitting; there would be ten in all.
8. *Problems of Power*: see letter of 3 February 1913.
9. In the manuscript it does.

séjour: sojourn; *besogne:* working; *ingrat:* unpleasant; *le ... dirait:* your heart would bid you; *épreuve:* trial; *moi ... parle:* I who am speaking to you; *ce ... encore:* that would be better and sweeter still; *maîtrise:* mastery

21 Carlyle Mansions
Cheyne Walk, S.W.
11 June 1913

Dearest Edith.

I accept the high philosophy of your view of the abysmal Hill— where even the vision of you at your most recumbent *couldn't* have incited me emulously to m'allonger—even at the most respectful distance from you; so completely do I feel myself for the rest of my vouch-safed days contracted to the compass of my own most intimate gîte. I have become utterly incapable of Hill—dear M[ary] H[unter]'s incapac-ity to se figurer de pareilles choses is fabulous; & I am in no position to wonder at your want of "give"—if not still more of "take." Therefore—therefore—enfin! Yet it *is* very horrible, dearest Edith, that we are so sundered in time & space—& my own poor helplessness as to any remedy makes me blush to the rim of my hat. (That word looks like *plush*—& thick crimson plush may well, in the connection, figure me.) But I should so like one of our fine old-fashioned motor-days— just one; & you must let me dream of this a little. The June roar, the June everything, of London is less, infinitely less of a terror to me than ever before—through the extreme, the utter, simplification of my life by blest disabilities. I practically never dine out (& never, never, never lunch);[1] & that fact itself immensely lowers the pitch. But I like my afternoons, & 2 or 3 friends really quite keep up for me a little hareem of "She's."[2] However, it's for the Gran' Turca herself that I truly yearn—even while I all submissively await her good pleasure. I suppose myself to return to L[amb] H[ouse] on some day between the 1st & the 5th July.[3] All thanks for your news of Walter [Berry]—I hoped his endless "sailings" had ended like those of Ulysses in a definite lotus-land. And he will sail back, I suppose, to Cherbourg, & I shan't see him. But I am more & more gentle—& allow for everything. See how easy it will be to "handle" me, & don't wholly & Undine-like abandon your waiting, wondering, refuge-in-literature-taking, & always funda-mentally infatuated old compagnon de route

Henry James

P.S.   And I do so want news of Bessie Lodge!

1. HJ's diary records two luncheons in May and three in June.

2. Automobiles; "Gran' Turca" is EW's.

3. Unveiling of the Sargent birthday portrait, seven sittings for the sculptor Wood (second week of July), arrival of nephew Harry and niece Peggy, and severe pectoral attacks beginning 18 July, combined to postpone his return to Lamb House until the twenty-second; he was at work again by the twenty-fourth.

m'allonger: stretch out, lie down; *gîte:* lair; *se . . . choses:* to imagine such things; *enfin:* oh well

[DICTATED]   21 Carlyle Mansions
                                                Cheyne Walk, S.W.
                                                28 June 1913

Dear old Friend.

   Your news is better and better, and the idea of having you actually as a cosy neighbour, just round the corner,[1] goes quite to my head; so quite understand if I babble vain sounds for the brief remainder of this —which takes its lurid distinctness of form from the fact that I thus get it off to you literally hours and hours sooner than I should otherwise do. How very very charming and not of this perverse world that R[obert] N[orton] should have a palazzino awaiting you, all complete, just at my (anything but *pointu*) elbow: it's so little the way that things mostly happen to happen! Your presence will fill to repletion all my consciousness and (I insist on saying) all my time from *one o'clock on.* I am already organising a series of amplified luncheons, in your interest, at that hour. Damn immortality, damn style, damn royalties (if there *be* any to damn)—damn everything but your hungry hour. I rejoice to hear about Gilliard [Lapsley] for the Wednesday; and hereby engage you both to dine with me on that evening in the quietest eddy of this whirl-pool that I can find[2] (perhaps you wouldn't mind even the comparatively gentle Berkeley) and go to something frankly low with me (as if there were anything else here!) afterwards. Please consider this as settled. As for the coming down to meet you at Folkestone there is nothing con-ceivable that I should—*tout crûment*—like better; but will you let me wait and wire you definitely about this on Monday?[3] You see (or rather you don't see, and can only do so when you see *me*), I have now and for ever a constant grave handicap in the form of my *chronic* angina pectoris, which the smallest hurry or flurry, acceleration of step or ten-sion of effort brings on very badly indeed; for it is, to be plain, a bad form of the wretched thing, and I have without any sort of intermission to reckon with it. Fortunately mild and careful doings, reliefs from mere immobility, are distinctly good for it; but they require extreme discrimination, the fruit of cruel experience all this past year; and nothing permits me to forget the constant smallness of my margin. I had alas a bad attack yesterday at three o'clock, the consequence of rashly meeting Madame Simone at luncheon in Tite Street[4] (not at Sargent's); and though my pocketsful of nitro-glycerine check the assault up to a certain point, I feel ravaged and shaken afterwards—as you saw me so shockingly feel last summer at Cliveden.[5] I know a thousand times more about the matter now than I did then, and this, with its light on my management of the matter, is a very great help; but confidence fails me for too definite assurances of ability at future hours. I have very little courage or initiative for *that*. All the same, if I go on well again for to-day, to-morrow and Monday, I really hope to be able la veille to wire you that I shall be *somewhere* at Folkestone where you can pick me up. What terrifies me now for any approach to goings forth and travellings is the whole question of catching and meeting and proceeding with the least tension (or emotion!) along docks, railway-platforms, ups or downs of any kind where being *due* at some moment plays a part. If I find positively that le coeur, literally, m'en dit, I shall find means to waylay you, very conspicuously, in front of the Pavilion Hotel—should there seem anything less than the amplest margin, material and moral, for a further advance to your gangway. *With* confidence I shall go tout doucement down by some a.m. train that will permit of this margin. Otherwise, if I have to fail you, it will be in the interest of my intense desire to keep safe and *dispos* to await and meet you *here*. I will in that humiliating event come round to you for half an hour at Norton's on Tuesday p.m. by 9.30, or at any moment you may telephonically designate to me here. But what a long story—! On the spot here, where the plot will, without losing a grain of its beauty, have thinned, on the whole, rather than thickened, I shall not be driven, in your company, to such *lourds* soliloquies. I have already let R.N. know that I will dine with pleasure on Thursday, and I beg you to retain Gilliard as my guest in your very next communication with him. A bientot then at the worst!

Yours all faithfully
    Henry James

P.S.   If it's possible to you to let me know where Cook will put up for his previous night at F., or where be for the hour before your boat arrives, so that I can, if I've time, be picked up by him on his way to you at the Pier, that mild sitting in the car would further my case—if not my appearance of eager gallantry. Since writing the above I have been able to get hold of an A.B.C., an utter stranger to these premises now, and make out that there is no a.m. train to F. *Harbour* that I can at all manageably catch here on the one hand, and that will, on the other, enable me to meet you at the boat. To Folkestone Town (Central), however, there *is* a manageable one, 11 o'cl. hence, arriving Central 1.28; by which I should be able to be *there*, at Central, in a manner to await you (without other than sentimental agitation) on Cook's carrying you from your 1.40 débarquement and finding me, in more or less of an attitude, at said Central entrance. So that the word from you about *his* whereabouts, I mean the mere postcard I was about to suggest, doesn't seem so much to matter. If I *am* able to wire you that I will come it will mean, unless I specify otherwise, that I will come to said Central spot to be, at your convenience, recueilli by you. Ever, again,

Henry James

P.S.   The run to town does, in spite of all, *so* tempt me!⁶

1. EW arrived in England on Tuesday, 1 July, and stayed at Robert Norton's, 211 King's Road, for a day or so, then moved into Rosa Lewis's Cavendish Hotel in Jermyn Street—rather than at "the gentle Berkeley."
2. They dined at the Cavendish.
3. HJ did not go to Folkestone.
4. At the town house of the painter George Percy Jacomb-Hood, M.V.D. (1857–1929), and his wife, Henriette, 26 Tite Street.
5. See letter of 3 August 1912.
6. "P.S." added in ink in HJ's hand.

pointu: sharp; *tout crûment:* quite crudely; *la veille:* the night before; *le . . . dit:* my heart, literally, urges me; *tout doucement:* quite quietly; *dispos:* in good shape; *lourds:* dull; *À bientôt:* See you soon; *recueilli:* picked up

Lamb House, Rye
24 July 1913

Dearest Edith.

Will you do me, by a few of your admirable penstrokes (a very few), a gracious little favour? Two months ago & more I wrote W. M. F[ullerton] a long & genial letter—immediately after reading, with affectionate interest, his brilliant last book.[1] To-day I receive my letter back from the cold Dead Letter Office with "non réclamé" stamped on. I am disgusted at his having had to suffer so long the outrage of my apparent silence, & I do my best to cause the old stale pages to reach him still, with brutal belatedness—that best being to beg you kindly to affix to the enclosed the right address. Evidently there was a vice in my "15 rue du Mont Thabor"—which I *supposed* to be right.[2] (I can't now find a letter of his own with that, as I seem to remember, on it. Or was it properly *14*? Here the small error wouldn't have prevented—!)

Just a word further to say that I am greatly better here—am already in fact a different creature.[3] I was out on foot in green field paths today with my blest companion of a niece for 2 & ½ hours. It was largely the absence of locomotion in London, thanks to the constant conspiracy of the taxi, etc., that had undone me. Yet I regret not one of the hoots with which it bore me to you. Your all-affectionate

H.J.

1. *Problems of Power*; see letters of 3 February and 7 June 1913.
2. Fullerton's Paris address was 8, rue du Mont-Thabor.
3. After almost a week of pectoral distress, HJ resumed work on this date.

non réclamé: not claimed

Lamb House, Rye
30 July 1913

Dearest Edith.

From you I have had a brave little letter & a brilliant postcard (the letter reinforced by all Walter [Berry]'s incomparable presence of mind); & I shld. deplore my not having sooner acknowledged them were it not that I can give you de jour en jour better news. I am in ever so much better form, & my Doctor's tribute to my recuperational powers[1] is more & more justified. I am on my feet—on our gentle grassy field-walks (of which there must be so many at Coopersale),[2] & that is ever so much better for my complaint than panting through the London labyrinth in a taxi-cab that deprives my baffled organs of their necessary gentle exercise. Here they get that, & I am now again on most encouraging terms with them. But no terms are so encouraging as those on which I fondly hope that you're acquiring Coopersale—not perhaps even those on which you are immortalizing Undine.[3] There has been too short a chunk of *her* immortality in this August Scribner than I could have done with; but such as it is je l'ai bien savouré. However, read Katherine Fullerton, in the same no.[4] (about Rhoda Glave—est-ce trouvé, hein, "Rhoda Glave"?) & see what it is to be a real & natural magazinist. I'm so officiously glad for her, & only wish she'd give Morton [Fullerton] a tip. But the great thing is that if the broad acres & the painted chamber do tumble to you you shouldn't let me too long languish in ignorance. I hope your Paris is even $\frac{1}{2}$ as cool & fresh as this. How handsome Bessie L[odge] must have looked[5]—stepping the true goddess—on the level *plage. How* jolly to think that one may see her at C[oopersale]. You see how your engulfing of that morsel makes for the interest of life. I mean of course, unblushingly, of *mine.* Good-night. Yours all & always

Henry James

1. In his diary for 22 July HJ quotes Dr. Des Voeux: "*Very* great powers of recuperation."
2. Coopersale was a property near Mrs. Charles Hunter's Hill Hall, which EW thought of purchasing for its quietness and privacy. When EW learned of the heavy British income tax levied on foreign residents, she decided not to buy.
3. Undine Spragg, heroine of *The Custom of the Country.*
4. Katharine Fullerton Gerould's short story "The Bird in the Bush" (of which Rhoda Glave is the heroine).
5. Evidently with EW on the weekend at Hill Hall.

de . . . jour: from day to day; *je . . . savouré:* I have certainly enjoyed it; *est-ce . . . hein:* is that a find, eh; *plage:* strand

Lamb House, Rye
6 September 1913

Dearest Edith.

I think you must be restored to your Parisian pénates, for I have heard from Howard [Sturgis], bless him, & he had heard from *you*— bless him again! And he had heard from you at *Berlin*,[1] & the moral of this seems to me that with no worlds left to conquer[2] after *that* appropriation, & no impression worth getting thereby remaining to you, doubtless, you must have recoiled & rebounded, charged with booty, upon us mere comparative Latins again. So let this greet you, & let me salaam before you à reculons, while you reintegrate your domicile. I have had a sweet letter from you well before me since the eve of your departure, but have systematically waited till now to thank you for it— these great globe-rushes & vast gyrations of yours lift you so, for me, far above mortal, or Lamb House, ken, & give me such a sense of the rate at which you are living, learning, plundering & pillaging, that the whole adventure makes me crouch in terror or at least in humility, as by its mere side-wind. I kind of feel that your communion with Germany must have been a thing of such power & profit that one couldn't have broken in upon it without being sent about one's business—this however without detriment to my fond confidence that you will hand it over to me, intact, at the very first opportunity. What a big reinforcement of experience you will surely have had, & how glad I am that the golden apple has fallen into the lap of your genius. My sense of that genius had been infinitely quickened today by the perusal of the September "Custom," which, though too short for my appetite, has intensely gratified it. It's an admirable morsel, beautifully done, & you go on being *interesting*, comme on ne l'est pas, without a *défaillance*. You finish on a great coup—but I still hold my breath. Oh the joy of being made a *naïf* reader again—I'm always so ready to be, so yearning, & yet in general never *can*; so that I've only you to thank for it. I've had here some six very good weeks largely by the aid of my admirable niece,[3] giving me, in the most soothing & sustaining way possible, exactly the society that I want & withholding what I don't; so that she has been a peculiar blessing. And her singularly able & delightful brother lately, on his return from the continent, put in a fortnight with us, which we celebrated by considerable motoring; he sailed for N.Y. a week ago—Peggy remains till the 20th. They will have greatly *helped*.

I am happy to say that I am in spite of everything—that is in spite of the settled & seated skeleton at the banquet (who has his eye on me as I have it only on *him*), I am at more general physical ease than for a very long time past. It was a splendid cool rainless August here; this "summer home" has been more than ever a *fester Burg*, as you Berliners say; & in short I have infinitely profited. This will be nothing, however, to the profit of hearing from you—when I may do so at your amplest convenience. One of the drawbacks of the recoils of Alexandrina from the pushing of her frontiers must be the sight of what we call here the hall-table, collapsing with the burden of its postal matter; & as one needn't in fact be an Alexander (even a George),[4] to live up to one's neck in arrears, so I could weep for you & shall be full of indulgence for my hint that I must wait. I shall only permit myself to wonder meanwhile whether you saved enough money at Berlin to be able [to] gratify Coopersale with that £500, that, as I last understood you, they were holding out for. If you didn't I can almost find it in me—that is in my bank-account, to offer to lend them to you. In fine, as you see, I fairly brood upon Coopersale. But al commodo [*sic*] suo. Howard wrote me 10 pages of much recovered equilibrium & of fairly delirious homage to the divine William[5]—no "William*s*," à la Hugo, for him, but that one. The nurse is still with him, however—she too all but divine. It's a regular Olympus. Reposez-vous bien. Your image of Morton [Fullerton] distraught with over-pressure or whatever, at his departure for the U.S., has given me much to think, or at least to groan; but possibly you've had from him some better sign. But I seek my couch—goodnight. Your all-devoted

Henry James

P.S. If only Walter [Berry], too, has made a good cure!

1. EW and Bernard Berenson began a motor tour of Germany; she was taken ill in Cologne due to nervous fatigue after the strain of pushing *The Custom of the Country* to its completion. They reached Berlin on 25 August.
2. HJ's allusion to the story of Alexander the Great weeping at the prospect of no worlds left to conquer is resumed in his feminine coinage "Alexandrina," below, for EW, etc.
3. Niece Peggy and her oldest brother, Harry, arrived in London on 16 July.

4. A playful allusion to Sir George Alexander, who produced and acted in HJ's *Guy Domville* in 1895.

5. Sturgis's companion, William Haynes Smith.

pénates: hearth (household gods); *à reculons:* as I back (ceremoniously) away; *comme . . . pas:* like nobody else; *défaillance:* lapse; *fester Burg:* mighty fortress; *al comodo suo:* at your convenience; *Reposez-vous bien:* Rest well

Lamb House, Rye
10 September 1913

Dearest Edith.

I am twice indebted to you, where even once would be so much! & now I feel you to be ever so much more at my side—*and* so much more (though it's odd enough that shld. be possible!) qualified for a thrilling interest there! There isn't a word of your touching letter that doesn't find in me the fullest comprehension & the deepest response. Weary & worn & derelict you may well indeed have felt when you went forth—& to me it's very dreadful nowadays to think of *having* to go forth, & into strange lands, to escape—more or less fallaciously!—the solitude of one's foyer. But yours will, believe me, be much more calculated to detain you again—& I see you feel that too—as soon as you are back in a more *settled* current of production, especially flowing between big thick green English banks. C'est assez vous dire what a protective virtue & salutary strength I conceive that you may look to Coopersale to fling about you. For "us," & for our genius the act of attestation of the life of the mind & of the play of that genius is by itself a sovereign help, a condition indispensable; & (even if *why* it should be so is a mystery) the most celestial balm flows from it. But one must throw one's self upon it in the most generous trust & without the affront of a single reserve. Well, that's what you will do, I repeat, when once you seat yourself at Coopersale. Have there as many reserves about everything else as you will, but no ghost of one for that act of confidence. Meanwhile, at whatever cost, I will act as you ask of me as to the remainder—that is, begging Elmer Moffat's[1] pardon & the balance—of your epic Serial; I will hold off & await the volume, the nearness of which I rejoice greatly to learn. ("Elmer" is a trouvaille, & your American names in general inspired—though the sympathetic ones, I think, not quite so trouvés as the satiric. But of course they are much more difficult after all.) I like ever so much to hear that you are going down to Bessie Lodge,[2] to whom I send my very best love. May the level, if not quite the lone, sands stretch away for you at Le Touquet as far & as felicitously as they stretched for Ozymandias. Shocked am I, à propos of our friends, to learn what you tell me of poor dear Charles du Bos,[3] whom I think of with infinite sympathy—& whom I should like to write—*after* I have written to beloved & afflicted Percy [Lubbock]. What a blessing it must be to be a good practising "Roman," as they say here, & be able to put up a few sincere masses or light a row of candles bought from an old woman for the benefit of one's struggling friends. It's news to me, & of the happiest, that poor dear Morton [Fullerton], most eminent of these, has been gloriously decorated[4]—since it appears that a glory, or an advantage, s'y attache. I am stupidly vague again as to what the particular nature of his errand *is* là-bas; but a fortnight ago, I was struck with my Nephew Harry's saying to me here, after I had spoken, by chance, with some emphasis, of Morton's *wasted* intelligence, experience &c: "They would give anything for him at the State Department in Washington—he's exactly the kind of man they are looking for & don't get!" And H. doesn't talk in the air & is of a most excellent judgment & observation. If there only shld., or *could* be something *in* that—*for* Morton!—What presses upon me most richly, however, is this possibility that you may be able to take possession for a while of Quacre. That is a most delicious thought. You wd. find there "the bow come 'igh!" as Bourget used never to tire of Jack Gardner's having said, out of his depleted pocket, on joining them in the departing carriage at the Western hotel door—but "oh the difference (or the heartless *in*difference!) to *me!*"[5] Tachez d'arranger ça & think all hopefully of your all devoted

H.J.

1. An important character in *The Custom of the Country* (1913).
2. EW joined Bessie Lodge at Le Touquet-Paris-Plage, on the Channel Coast, an hour's drive north of Boulogne, hence the sandy quotation from the last line of Shelley's sonnet "Ozymandias." See letter of 16 September 1913.
3. Du Bos was suffering from an undiagnosed illness.

4. Fullerton having probably received the Légion d'Honneur, EW wrote to him: "I have post-carded, written & cabled you (congratulations on the Ribbon), to the care of Mr. Lambert" (*EW Letters*, 311). She also quotes to Fullerton the next three sentences of this letter—which suggests that either this letter or EW's is misdated.

5. The quotation from Wordsworth's "She Dwelt Among the Untrodden Ways" seems finally quite inappropriate—"But she is in her grave, and, oh, / The difference to me!"

C'est ... dire: It's enough to tell you; *trouvaille:* find; so *trouvés:* such discoveries; *s'y attache:* is attached to it; *là-bas:* over there; *Tachez ... ça:* Try to arrange that

Lamb House, Rye
16 September 1913

Dearest Edith.

I have been very glad you were struck with my quotation from my Nephew's words about Morton's possibility at Washington;[1] even though it has taken me these 3 or 4 days to tell you so. I lag, palsied age helping, more & more behind my letters; & whenever I seem to you to do so you have only to sweep your glass back along the perspective till it comes to a poor old person pulled up by the roadside, supported against the nearest object & ruefully panting, not to say woefully groaning, while he faces the next "rising ground." I will indeed on one of these 1st days write to my Nephew & ask him to waylay W. M. F[ullerton] if possible—but I don't see, I fear, what *suite* he can very practically give his remark beyond impressing the truth of it on Morton himself & urging *him* to make somehow the application. The thing is for Morton to *look* in that direction, with his own eyes, & realise what there may be there for him, though if Harry can put him in relation with some directly helpful individual, so much the better. Meanwhile the things, exactly, that our friend is doing strike me as much more in the way of *connecting* him & putting him on view, in a general manner, than not. I scarce have a pulse of regret left for such things as his having so (as actually) to occupy himself—*all* my sense being for the dollars, such as they are, that may be in it. If I wanted to be very, *very* sorry, it would be all about that unwritten & now visibly quite forever unwritable book on Paris[2]—he is irrecoverably away from that now, even if he had ever been, by the nature of his competence, really near it—near the right form of it, I mean. He should have *wanted* more to do it—that would have been the sign; wanted so much that the thing somehow would have happened, whatever the curcumstances. And now he won't come back to it—but ne parlons pas de ça. I think H.'s idea was that the State Department would be glad of a man to *keep* there on hand & on tap—& not of such a man as they may give a foreign consulate to, these being much in their view anyhow. It would mean, the bright dream, I shld. suppose, his really taking up with Washington as his scene of work—repatriating & reAmericanizing; & odd though it may seem to you I see more fruitful possibilities in him for just that than for anything more "over here." He is somehow only half, & imperfectly, corrupt—il n'est pas comme nous qui l'avons dans le fond de la nature & jusque dans le sang; thank heaven!—I am sorry to hear of the collapse of Quacre,[3] though I associate Quacre with collapses & it seems to be ever but a more cushiony & more coffeecuppy & Mrs. Leesy House of Usher, of which it still may be laid upon us to write the Fall. No matter, however, if the House of Coopersale will only meantime rise—with all its cracks bouchés & its dark [*sic*] tarns[4] tidied up. Je meurs d'envie to know exactly what point that question has reached & how it actually looks; but I don't in the least press you & *can* wait till the October end, which will have then brought me, I understand, the rounded & bounded Custom[5] too. Apropos of which roundings, not to say boundings, I have ordered Bain to send you Wells's Passionate Friends,[6] just out, a thing of the greatest talent & form & crânerie—he is absolutely the only British *Demon* there is. The book is to me quite demonic, in its way—& not less because it's something of an attempt at the angelic. May it not too much languish [at] rue de V[arenne] while you are at le Touquet.[7] Please renew *there* my fond assurances to Bessie Lodge. Loosen yourself out there well—wallow in the wet sands & let the wavelets—or the surges—trifle with your hair. We are having the rarest, richest September here, up to now; & this place is a daily blessing to me. My Niece, to my great loss, however, leaves me 3 days hence. Do write a *plage* story. There's a fine scrap of a one in Diana of the Crossways.[8] But goodnight, goodmorrow. Ever your

H.J.

1. See letter of 10 September 1913

2. See letter of 3 February 1913

3. The possibility of EW's temporarily occupying Sturgis's house at Windsor; see letter of 10 September 1913

4. HJ continues the Poe theme with a strange misquotation—or perhaps just an anticipation of "tarn," but the manuscript quite clearly has "dark"—from "Ulalume" ("the dank tarn of Auber").

5. Serialization of EW's *The Custom of the Country* concluded with the November *Scribner's*, which would arrive in late October.

6. H. G. Wells's novel *The Passionate Friends* was published this month.

7. See letter of 10 September 1913.

8. George Meredith's novel of 1885. In the central chapter of the book, the twenty-second, the suitor Percy Dacier has a crucial confrontation with Diana Warwick on the "sandy coast" of France—the "plage" (beach) alluded to—just northeast of Caen.

suite: follow-up; *ne . . . ça:* let's not talk about that; *il . . . sang:* he is not like us who have it at the base of our nature and even in our very blood; *bouchés:* filled in; *Je . . . d'envie:* I am dying with envy; *crânerie:* swagger

Lamb House, Rye
9 October 1913

Dearest Edith.

I have been indisposed for a few days in a somewhat acute way (now I am definitely better); or I shouldn't have let this response to your last stand over a single post, and the 1st letter (*after* the little interregnum) that I wanted to write was precisely to dear Gilliard [Lapsley], of which I have now acquitted myself. I am very grateful to you for enabling me, by your *avis*, to do this with a right punctuality. I am so delighted to think of you as administering in these days to Percy [Lubbock] the great emotions & impressions of his quivering young life, bless him—& bless *you*. I shall secure him for a report of them, & of you, to me here at the very 1st propitious hour. Vous avez beau vous moquer de votre banlieue; I'm convinced that it's among the most elegant natural scenes que vous promenez—loin de cacher!—votre bonheur. I am delighted that Percy shall think the elegance of the London banlieue—in the form

of Coopersale—will have nothing to fear from it; & I am so devoted
to believing that Edward Warren[1] *will* be able to throw light on that
question for you that I hear with every satisfaction of your being dis-
posed again to give him a chance. Do give him a really good one. He
will powerfully rise to it. And throw in such a chance for *me* as you
can. It has been admirably beautiful here up to now—the rarest September & initial sequence. I hang hugely on the completed Custom (though
I *have* sneakingly stayed my stomach on the Oct. Scrib.—it *comes!*—&
I wished Undine's experience of la Vieille France—l'ancienne—needn't
perforce to be so sommaire!). But I think too with appetite of the fact
(on the best authority) that Wells has, archdemoniacally, a newer novel
still finished[2] (finished when the P[assionate] F[riends] appeared) & only
awaiting the 1st decent moment. So there's something to live for—while
Benson[3] tarries. (I'm assured by the way that *Arthur* B[enson], who of
course published one the other week, has 4 or 5 finished & up his
sleeve—only making the *queue!*) You all bitterly humiliate your niggling
old slave of the lamp, & of his passion,

H.J.

1. Edward Prioleau Warren (1856–1937), the architect friend of HJ who
helped him find and gain access to Lamb House.
2. H. G. Wells probably had *The Wife of Sir Isaac Harman* (1914) about ready
for publication (see letter of 9 November 1914); he was that summer working
on his science-fiction *The World Set Free* (1914) and had begun *The Research
Magnificent* (1915).
3. Edward Frederic Benson (1867–1940) wrote a number of popular novels
—the Mapp and Lucia series; in the past year he had published only *Mrs. Ames.*
His prolific older brother Arthur Christopher Benson (1862–1925)—master of
Magdalen College, Cambridge, novelist, poet, biographer—had published *The
Child of the Dawn, Paul the Minstrel and Other Stories*, and *Thy Rod and Thy Staff*
in 1912, and *Watersprings* in 1913, "the other week."

avis: advice; *Vous . . . banlieue:* you make fun of your suburb in vain; *que . . .
cacher:* that you parade—far from hide—your happiness; *la . . . l'ancienne:* old
France—of former times; *sommaire:* summary

21 Carlyle Mansions
Cheyne Walk, S.W.
9 December 1913

Dearest Edith.

This is indeed a sorry & a startling tale & a theme for the platitudin-izer about man's (by which of course I mean woman's) "proposing" (for don't women seem to do all the proposing now?). What overcomes me is that your ill case must indeed have reached maximum to make the Firebird[1] fold the iridescent wings she had really begun to spread. A phenomenon like that does speak volumes for the pitch of the Fire-bird's chill, or fever, or combination of both, or whatever it has been that has most waved her back, for the moment, from the great World to the mere Zoo. Most truly must such a dislocation of ripe arrange-ments & blight of noble purposes [have] been an épreuve of the sharpest—& I don't know whether to be most sorry for Trix[2] or for yourself, equally frustrated of your generosity. Really on reflection for you I think—for you have been docked of your fun—while I am sure a plunge into our natal air & concussion there with all the weird ele-ments that now people it would have given you any amount of. There are moments when I myself feel it quite a quickener to think of a friendly week—but *only* a week—there—one would (or at least *you* would), bring such a harvest away. However, as your wings know noth-ing but folding—so gloriously defy anything like clipping, I mean—one must never talk to you of occasions missed. I hope with all my heart that though you've been chained to earth you still have been able to peck a little at the soil around you—not been utterly tucked up, I mean, or too *sensationally* sick or sore. May the better turn have come at any rate & some sort of balm begun to drop on you! I haven't much of that particular extract to send you—save as it may be to you of a little healing help to know that I worry on without the sharper catastro-phes. There are difficulties right & left, & the grey tissue of conscious-ness is woven of them. But they seem to hold it together—"kind of "; & perhaps without them it would shred away to nothing. I had some days ago the very brief visit of Howard [Sturgis] & his young quadri-génaire [*sic*] (they are staying a little in the latter's dark native Nest—that repaire de bandits). Howard was rather capped & shawled & un-corseted; but touching in his gentle optimism (about himself & everything) & fairly heart-wringing in his modesty. The Babe so vert-galant (of aspect, air & detail of conquering dress) as to make me anxious—however, the Nursling is for the time in apparent abeyance. I saw Edward Warren on Friday last—who had been "rung up" very concessionally, he told me, by the Coopersellers[3]—the day before; but he will have let you know of this—if he has learnt you are still in Paris. That business so interests—as *what* peck of the Firebird doesn't, or *what* fine flutter of her genius?—her more than ever faithfully fond old

Henry James

1. HJ's latest nickname for EW, taken from the *Firebird* ballet (music by the Russian composer Igor Fedorovich Stravinsky [1882–1971]; choreography by Mikhail Fokine [1880–1942]), an important cultural event of the 1910 Paris spring season.

2. Still not fully recovered from the nervous tension that plagued her summer and fall, EW felt unable to cross the Atlantic for the wedding of her niece, Beatrix Cadwalader Jones, to Yale history professor Max Farrand (1869–1945), on 17 December. But see letter of 28 December 1913.

3. HJ continues the Qu'Acre group's punning on "Coopersale," which Sturgis hoped EW would soon "Cooperbuy"—near the Hunters' Hill Hall; see letters of 30 July and 9 October 1913.

épreuve: trial; *repaire de bandits:* den of thieves; so *vert-galant:* so much the old Lothario

21 Carlyle Mansions
Cheyne Walk, S.W.
28 December 1913

Dearest Edith.

I have been hideously silent ever since getting your brave little letter, & only with those excuses that are derisive as compared with the noirceur itself. I can only plead a complication of troubles—my upsetting & prostrating (in itself) move up to town[1]—though I am very glad to be here; a state of chronic gout in my left foot, alas—when not more or less in both—such as I haven't had for years; & the fact that I have been swamped in *proof*,[2] which, when attended to, each day, seems to have exhausted my power of attending to anything else. I have been in other words in a *hole*, & now that I have my head up into the air again can of course only wonder how I can have kept breathing below ground. May this at last assure you of my real contrition & affection. If your plan holds of sailing over to Trix's nuptials on one of these next days[3] I can only grovel before the magnificence of the act. It is a very noble, beautiful & generous thing to do, & will be most tremendously appreciated. Likewise it will pay for itself, so [to] speak by the re-consecration to all her good causes that your muse of comedy will get from feeling beneath her feet for a little that vivifying soil. I mean you will come back with a bushel of impressions—though before you use any of them again I want to have a talk with you, & shall soon be capable of coming down to Coopersale, on your return, for the purpose. You don't tell me what you sail in, but I seem to suppose a German liner touching at Cherbourg[4] or something of that sort. Well, may it all be short & sweet & swift, & may you come back to something really achieved here. I have been tempted to ring up Edward Warren & ask him whether to his knowledge anything may not be even now achieved. But I shall probably before long commune with him otherwise. I haven't seen Howard [Sturgis], or any one at all here to speak of yet. My accursed foot keeps me low & weak. But I have read the reprehensive Sally's 2 volumes[5]—which she will in spite of reprehension have sent *you* (as she has done to me, who am but after all an accomplice too); & found them full of interest & pathos. Charles came out of them awfully well I think, & really as a great character. He was more civilized than Undine & even than Moffat;[6] in fact the book is a picture of the going on of a civilization, passive & active, in his field of life—by his effect even after having been in his consciousness—that was probably a case rare & unequalled on this planet during the same years. He stands out, with all takes-off then, a real Figure don't you think? But I put you questions that I don't at all mean to when you are harried & perhaps worried at the last. Goodnight & buonissimo viaggio, felicissimo everything! I enormously applaud & cherish you, & am your all faithfully even when too tacitly fond old

Henry James

1. An indication of HJ's state of health: he had been in London almost six weeks by this time, having come up from Rye on 19 November.

2. For *Notes of a Son and Brother.*

3. EW must in fact have been in New York already.

4. She had sailed on the *France*, as she would return on it at the end of the first week of January 1914.

5. Sara "Sally" Norton (1864–1922) had just published her edition of her father's letters.

6. Undine Spragg and Elmer Moffat of EW's *The Custom of the Country*; a distinctly left-handed compliment to Charles E. Norton.

noirceur: blackness; *buonissimo . . . felicissimo:* have the best of voyages, the happiest

21 Carlyle Mansions
Cheyne Walk, S.W.
16 January 1914

Dearest Edith.

How delightful, how relieving & interesting—nay, how absolutely (as Walter [Berry] would say) rigolo! It's verily with rapture that I think of you as restored to this more credible horizon, though when I think also with what treasures you are freighted[1]—your letter is so rich a flash-out of them!—I lament that the middle distance only as yet possesses you, to the sorry cost of this yearning & aching foreground. You have probably accumulated more spoil of precious substances than whatever bold buccaneer in so brief a raid, & what I want is to have it dumped right down here, on this shabby old carpet, to the last red ruby. However you'll cry me mercy, of course, till you have been able to turn round again—& I therefore breathe upon you all my patience & pray that your rest may be, for as long as you desire, of the most moelleux. Vous l'avez bien gagné—only don't scatter or waste the pearls; treat every one but *us* little better than the beasts of the adage: I say "us" because Gilliard [Lapsley] dined with me 2 nights since & Howard [Sturgis] lunches in a day or two.[2] (The testimony is unanimous as to his, H.'s, being better & better—& Gilliard, who has spent the Xmas-tide, all unwontedly, at Trinity, reports himself quite the same.) Very touching your account of poor dear Minnie,[3] of whose illness I had *not* heard & to whom I shall at once write; & interesting not less your picture of honest Max [Farrand]—whom you will so have placed in the right light. I shall be very glad to know him, & rejoice that they are to give one a chance. But what I most of all feel is how you'll *enlever* New York—when I shall have the bliss of hearing you begin. It's monstrous to ask you a question now—I mean about anything; but here I am—at the "phone," as it were, & only waiting for you to speak. I am wondering if you saw Morton [Fullerton]—but I don't ask you even that. I await your good pleasure & only hope you may *first* find it in lolling after the fashion of one of the fins de rendezvous of the fine Françoise. Tell Walter please, with my love, that to receive his accolade is thereby to rigoler in a manner à nulle autre pareille except by receiving yours! Believe me your devotissimo

H.J.

1. EW's impressions, comparable to HJ's from his visit of 1904–1905 as recorded in *The American Scene*.
2. Lapsley dined on the fourteenth; Sturgis lunched on the nineteenth.
3. Mary Cadwalader Jones.

rigolo: comical; *moelleux . . . gagné:* mellow. You have certainly earned it; *enlever:* satirize; *rigoler:* to laugh; *à . . . pareille:* equal to no other; *devotissimo:* most devoted

> 21 Carlyle Mansions
> Cheyne Walk, S.W.
> 16 February 1914

Dearest Edith.

Yes it is quite too horrid that I should have had to delay these 3 or 4 days to express the joy I have had in hearing from you. But I *have* had to, & to explain my particular slackness (as if my general weren't enough), & dismiss the subject I will mention that I am in the *mauvaise passe* of having my TEETH OUT[1] "for the good of my health," a desperate measure that pectoral & cognate conditions no longer to be endured

have at last determined me to, & that has during the last week in especial steeped me in disqualifying, in demoralizing languors—partly the
result of so much sickening anaesthetic. I have already made sacrifices
sufficient to apprehend the amount of good it is probably going to do
me—I can see that I am already distinctly & directly better; but the
process arrests the flow of soul, arrests the feast of reason almost as
much as any approach to the more vulgar sort—whereby my grasp of
the pen has been as limp as that of the fork. Behold me at any rate for
the time thus awkwardly mumble. Your news is always of the most
vital interest to me, none the less, & I think that no one to whom you
can ever communicate it is formed to understand it better. That you feel
weary & worn comes home to me as the dove to its nest; I *know* how
you feel even as if I had myself drawn up the "specifications" for it in
every detail. Continue to like not to do anything but get over it—&
thus *do* get over it—all at your ease & leisure. If you can but do so by
carrying the war into Africa[2] I shall watch the white dust enshroud your
exploits there with the last luxury of wonder. With Walter [Berry] far
away on the billow & the brave things the rest of you are all doing or
designing, I should feel like a deplorably domestic fowl if I didn't so
hug the barnyard! I find what you say about Walter B. very interesting—as to the effect on him—his spirit—of his lapse of "character,"
so to speak; all the more that the recovery of that value, when it has
lapsed, does take such a lot of doing. And he won't get it back at
Ceylon—though he may mind there less not having it! You offer Percy
[Lubbock] a tremendous chance to let *his* lapse, don't you?—"over there
at Algiers," just when he is supposed to be building it up as hard as
possible at Vienna (how pretty, though too scant & too few, his little
Times articles are!)—but I do quite see everything go to pieces in the
African dust-cloud. I infer from what you say of Morton [Fullerton] that
he is in Paris again, & I rejoice in the image of his *raffermi* state—what
an immense amount of experience & life he must have been taking
aboard with all these things; not one of the values of which, I feel
certain, will have been lost to him. I wish his great round of adventure
could but bring him once in a way to England—the one thing it seems
never to do. Tell him for me, please, that my fidelity is close at his
heels, ever, & hangs over his table, & that, knowing so he doesn't
forget me, I wouldn't he shld. write me for the world. Letting me *see*

him would be another affair!—I have seen Mary Hunter a couple of times lately & found her beset with doctors (her great "they"), plying her with things for her *heart*. She doubts & defies them—& if they could indeed ply her with a less colossally complicated existence it would be more to the point. She is very white & beautiful but rather with les yeux saillants—& with a perfect temper & ability & courage. Don't worry about my temporary ideal[3]—I am certain I am right—& the strongest lights have lately played for me over the subject & determined the step. Pardon my crudity, but when you next see me I shall mumble less. Take it, take everything, easy! Il n'y a que ça. Utterly à vous

Henry James

1. HJ was to have most of his teeth extracted in a series of some nine visits during February (this day saw the fifth) and then fitting of "machinery" in early March; the last visit was 14 March.

2. EW's plans for a tour of North Africa (already well along) with the financially straitened Percy Lubbock, whose employ in Vienna was about to end—see letter of 25 February 1914.

3. HJ evidently meant "ordeal"; the manuscript has quite clearly "ideal."

mauvaise passe: wretched situation; *raffermi:* strengthened; *les . . . saillants:* protruding eyes; *Il . . . ça:* It's the only way; *à vous:* yours

> 21 Carlyle Mansions
> Cheyne Walk, S.W.
> 25 February 1914

Dearest Edith.

The nearest I have come to receipt or possession of the interesting volumes you have so generously in mind is to have had *Bernstein's* assurance, when I met him here some time since, that *he* would give himself the delight of sending me the Proust production, which he learned from me that I hadn't seen.[1] I tried to dissuade him from this excess, but nothing would serve—he was too yearningly bent upon it, & we parted with his asseveration that I might absolutely count on this tribute both to poor Proust's charms & to my own. But depuis lors—!

—he had evidently been less en train than he was so good as to find *me*. So that I shall indeed be "very pleased" to receive the "Schwann" & the Vie & l'Amour[2] from you at your entire convenience. It is indeed beautiful of you to think of these little deeds of kindness, little words of love (or is it the other way round?).[3] What I want above all to thank you for, however, is your so brave backing in the matter of my disgarnished gums. That I am indeed doing right is already unmistakable—it won't make me "well"; nothing will do that, nor do I complain of the muffed miracle; but it will make me mind less being ill—in short it will make me better. As I say, it has already done so, even with my sacrifice for the present imperfect, for I am "keeping on" no less than 8 pure pearls, in front seats, till I can deal with them in some less exposed & exposing conditions. Meanwhile tons of implanted & domesticated gold &c (one's caps & crowns & bridges being *most* anathema to Des Voeux, who regards them as so much installed metallic poison) have, with everything they fondly clung to, been, less visibly, eradicated; & it is enough, as I say, to have made a marked difference in my felt state. That is the point, for the time—& I spare you further details. I greatly rejoice to think that Percy [Lubbock] is with you. I understand but too well the impulse that moved him—& it's so interesting to me that Vienna had sung its song. I like to hear of the limits of joys (the Vienna joy) that I haven't had. I shall perhaps even hear of those of the Algerian joy[4]—& then I *shall* gloat! Yet I want inconsistently to hurry up Coopersale. All love of course to Percy. Yours de coeur

Henry James

1. On 9 February HJ lunched with A. B. Walkley and the French playwright Henry Bernstein, who promised to send him Proust's new novel, *Du Côté de Chez Swann* (which HJ calls "Schwann" below). EW presently sent him a copy—see letter of 2 March 1914—but HJ evidently never read it. For HJ and Proust, see *Letters* 4, 702.

2. By Abel Bonnard (1883–1968), French-Corsican poet.

3. From "Little Things" (1845) by Julia A. Fletcher Carney (1824–1908); HJ has the right order.

4. EW's projected tour of North Africa with Lubbock.

depuis lors: since then; *en train:* in good fettle; *de coeur:* from the heart

[DICTATED]   21 Carlyle Mansions
                                              Cheyne Walk, S.W.
                                              27 February 1914

Dear E.W. and Confrère.

Do come out from under the bed, where I am *so* sorry you have had to take refuge, and if you can't face your dinner at least try to swallow this small epistolary tit-bit.

If everything, literally everything, about Conrad and his situation were not so utterly *cocasse* the cocasserie of Booth Tarkington's appeal would enjoy a glittering pre-eminence;[1] but the whole thing is somehow beyond saying, at least by me in the present circumstances and even with the present admirable aid.[2] I like so Booth's request to you that you should from the Rue de Varenne and "over your signature" testify how much you "rejoice in the man," and in the artless charm of his assurance that Mr. C. "has no part" himself in the flattering movement. However, *I* have not been invited to join in it—I am always coldly neglected in these things altogether; and it seems to me really difficult, so utterly absurd and so peculiarly more queer than I can tell you, is the whole connection anyway! Have you a personal sentiment, by which of course I mean a "realising sense," for poor dear J.C. at all? I have one myself, of a sort, a rum sort, but that is a matter of old history, going back to his having put himself in relation with me years ago, when he had written but his first book or two, and much mixed up with personal impressions since received. And even thus *I* should be hugely embarrassed! Have you read his last book, the "Chance" which has just come out, or have you it at hand? If neither of these advantages are enjoyed by you I will send you the volume at once as the most practical "leg-up" I can give you for scaling the arduous steep. This last book happens to be infinitely more practicable, more curious and readable (in fact really rather *yielding* difficult and charming), than any one of the last three or four impossibilities, wastes of desolation, that succeeded the two or three final good things of his earlier time.[3] If you find yourself able to read "Chance" you may be moved to utterance, but my own sense of your case is that in your place I should be moved to none unless you find it rise in you with something of a gush. That sounds a little as if a steward with a basin might then become your recipients rather than the Tarkington stewardry with only their sheet of paper;

but at any rate I wouldn't so much as trouble to answer them unless after an attempted go at the evidence I thus offer you you do feel the passion work within. I happen myself to have written a word about "Chance,"[4] but not for Booth, only for a different and more mercenary use, which I will send you in due course—that is when it comes out; for which we must wait a little. But meanwhile if Cook will but scrawl a "Send" on your behalf, on a postcard, while you are under the bed, you shall have the work—offered too quite in the hope that it may draw you forth. Forgive this scandalous wriggle out of my responsibility. I *am* glad I haven't your popularity in the U.S.—there are *such* compensations in my obscurity. Truly there is but *us!*—I find in the document you transmit such trills and roulades and refinements of the wood-note wild as baffle all description.

I just revel in Percy [Lubbock]'s revel—please tell him; and also that the situation created by his *fugue* (not to say his fougue,[5] in the Bernstein light, like mine) is almost painful here. Half London society *will* so have it that he has left Vienna for good, or in other words has come to Rue de Varenne for better; while the other half regards the affair but as a "folle équipée" which must have its hour but which will in due course blaze itself out. I side with the former version—but one takes rather, on whichever side, one's life in one's hand. What questions you thus saddle me with—between you! I stagger under them but am none the less your all-faithful & all artful dodger[6]

H.J.

1. The American novelist Booth Tarkington (1869–1946) had asked EW to participate in a *Festschrift* for the Polish-born English novelist Joseph Conrad (1857–1924) to help secure him broader recognition in America.

2. Dictation to typist Theodora Bosanquet.

3. Apparently *A Set of Six* and *The Point of Honor* of 1908, *Under Western Eyes* (1911) and *'Twixt Land and Sea: Tales* (1912) are "impossibilities," and *Nostromo* (1904) and *The Secret Agent* (1907)—and possibly *The Mirror of the Sea* (1906) —are the "good things."

4. In his essay "The Younger Generation," published in the *Times Literary Supplement*, 19 March and 2 April 1914 (see letter of 2 March 1914), and reprinted as "The New Novel" in *Notes on Novelists* (1914).

5. HJ's pun on *fugue* (flight) and *fougue* (mettle, impetuousness) is further

complicated by an additional meaning of *fugue*—the psychological state of momentary flight from reality.

6. HJ wrote in "none" and "& all artful dodger" in ink.

cocasse . . . cocasserie: ridiculous . . . ridiculousness; *folle equipée:* mad frolic

[DICTATED]   21 Carlyle Mansions
                                                   Cheyne Walk, S.W.
                                                   2 March 1914

My dear E.W.

You are very interesting again this morning, in spite of being rather tragic. Your greeps[1] give me the creeps, as they must still more give them to yourself—and even give them most of all to dear Percy [Lubbock], though I see in his predicament too, and can't help seeing, mitigations as well as miseries. We're having here the most wonderful etherial mildness and brightness, and river-god and sun-god conspire together this morning to flood my room with almost blinding and excoriating shafts of light and heat. You are doubtless going several better than this in Paris—as is your way in everything; so it does seem perverse indeed that you should need the duvet par-dessus le marché. If I were only there I think I should really find some way to lift it off you and off dear Percy's smothered programmes of pleasure. But the boundless swing of you—from the Duvet to the Desert! which I suggest as a happy title for your African results when they shall have been gathered in.[2] My results, of so intensely paler a complexion, about which you kindly ask, appear to be destined to come to light, in monstrous form, for *quantity* of remark, in two numbers of Percy's and my favourite organ: the Litt. Supp.; the first of which, however, if I rightly understand, and if the whole undertaking doesn't collapse under my massive weight, will shine forth on the third Thursday of this month, which I compute as the 19th.[3] The queer story of this gratuitous elephantine *gambade*, and of why I am in for it, would amuse you if you were here, but would take more telling in this form than I can just now manage. I almost like you both to be thus deprived of it—in order to create in you that queerness of a Parisian yearning for the literary news of Lon-

don, and thus treat myself to a small revenge for all our general privation and humiliation. So it is at any rate that I have toyed with such
phenomena as "Chance"—on which you reflect in a manner so justly!
—may be ingeniously viewed as presenting when one wants to be awfully benevolent. Gare à vous, Madame, in the same connection, by the
way—save that you will have to wait to vous en garer till Thursday
26th, I fear; when you will be having together such successes at the
hotel at Biskra that, unlike Sarah,⁴ you won't have a ring left on your
fingers lorsqu'ils y auront tous posé leurs lèvres. They will have swallowed them down—at any rate you will, among such Bedouins, and for
your glory, have missed them. Very, very *inénarrable* the Sarah-Rostand
celebration to be sure. What a superb flight the exquisite tribute to
Phèdre, and how one *has* to bow one's head under the accusation! Truly
il n'y a qu'eux! I'm afraid this must be all for the moment save that I
think I am sending you this p.m. (shall be able to) Wells's new volume
of more or less anarchistic world-remarks as such.⁵ I hope you won't
already have laid your hand on it. I shan't yet for a little fall upon Proust
and Co.,⁶ if you don't mind—there are moments when the perusal of
any current fiction becomes to me a thing impossible and je défaillis
before the sight of fatly packed volumes of such, whether in yellow
covers or in red. But I shall keep your kind abundance for a calmer
hour. I shall try to pass a calm one this afternoon on the occasion of
my tenth, if not eleventh, visit to my dentist⁷—where, however, it is if
possible to be the last for the present. You will be glad to know that I
feel my sacrifices to have already done me quite measurable good. And
now how I wish I could at any sacrifice effect your, and Percy's, more
common or garden improvement!

    Yours all faithfully
      Henry James

    1. HJ's Anglicization of the French *grippes* (whims) refers to EW's rather
sudden decision to travel to North Africa and also to take the temporarily
unemployed Percy Lubbock with her as traveling companion—at her expense.
    2. EW did not publish the "results" of this African journey.
    3. The first of two installments of "The Younger Generation"—which included HJ's remarks on Conrad's *Chance* (see letter of 27 February 1914).
    4. Sarah Bernhardt (1845–1923), French actress.

5. Wells's *The World Set Free*.
6. *Du Côté de chez Swann*; see letter of 25 February 1914.
7. The tenth.

duvet . . . marché: down [cushion] into the bargain; *gambade:* caper; *Gare à vous:* Beware; *vous en garer:* to beware of it; *lorsqu'ils . . . lèvres:* when they have all pressed their lips to them; *inénarrable:* hilarious; *il . . . qu'eux:* there is no one like them; *je défaillis:* I grow weak

21 Carlyle Mansions
Cheyne Walk, S.W.
[1 &] 2 June 1914

Dearest Edith.

Yes, I have been even to my own sense too long & too hideously silent—small wonder that I should have learned from dear Mary Cadwal[ader Jones] therefore (here since Saturday night)[1] that I have seemed to you not less miserably so. Yet there has been all the while a certain sublime inevitability in it—over & above those *general* reactions in favour of a simplifying & softening *mutisme* that increase with my increasing age & infirmity. I am able to go only always plus doucement, & when you are off on different phases of your great world-swing[2] the mere side-wind of it from afar, across continents & seas, stirs me to wonderments & admirations, sympathies, curiosities, intensities of envy, & eke thereby of *humility*, which I have to check & guard against for their strain on my damaged organism. The *relation* thus escapes me—& I feel it must so escape you, drunk with magic draughts of every description & immersed in visions which so utterly & inevitably turn their back—or turn yours—on what might one's self have de mieux to vous offrir. The idea of tugging at you to make you look round therefore—look round at *these* small sordidries & poornesses, & thereby lose the very finest flash of the revelation then & there organized for you or (the great thing!) *by* you, perchance: that affects me ever as really consonant with no minimum even of modesty or discretion on one's own account—so that, in fine, I have simply lain stretched, a faithful old veteran slave, upon the door-mat of your palace of adventure, sufficiently proud to give the alarm of any irruption, should I catch it, but otherwise waiting till you should emerge again, stepping over my prostrate form to do so. That gracious act, now performed by you—since I gather you to be back in Paris by this speaking—I get up, as you see, to wish you the most affectionate & devoted welcome home & tell you that I believe myself to have "kept" in quite a sound & decent way, in the domestic ice-chest of your absence. I mix my metaphors a little, comme toujours (or rather comme jamais!) but the great thing is to feel you really within hail again & in this air of my own poor little world which isn't for me the non-conductor (that's the real hitch when you're "off") of that of your great globe-life. I won't try to ask you of this last glory now—for, though the temperature of the ice-chest, the very ice-chest itself, has naturally risen with your nearer approximation, I still shall keep long enough, I trust, to sit at your knee in some peaceful nook here & gather in the wondrous tale. I have had echoes—even, in very faint & vague form, that of the burglarious attempt upon you in the anonymous oriental city³ (vagueness does possess me!) but by the time my sound of indignant participation would have reached you I took up my Lit. Supp. to find you in such force over the subject you there treated⁴ on that so happy occasion that the beautiful firmness & "clarity," even if not charity, of your nerves & tone clearly gave the lie to any fear I should entertain for the effect of your annoyance. I greatly admired by the same token the fine strain of that critical voice from out the patch of shade projected upon the desert sand, as I suppose, by the silhouette of your camel. Beautifully said, thought, felt, inimitably *jeté*, the paper has excited great attention & admiration here—& is probably doing an amount of missionary work in savage breasts that we shall yet have some comparatively rude or ingenuous betrayal of. I do notice that the flow of little *impayables* reviews meanders on—but enfin ne désespérons pas.

[*2 June 1914*] I had to break this off yesterday morning under pressure of complications extreme in proportion to my power to meet *any*. I spent the day (a roaring Bank Holiday) in motoring my 2 young women down to Hill, for luncheon & tea, by one of Mary Hunter's admirably kind & genial (in fact incomparable) prearrangements & felicities.⁵ (One of my young women is my dear & so interesting & conversible niece Peggy, & the other a young cousin of hers, Margaret Payson,

without the smallest interest, but thanks to association with whom &
their halving together of expenses of residence, servants &c, they are
able to be in a very fortunate furnished flat, in the adjacent mansion to
this—which simplifies enormously my dealing with them: though indeed they lead most of the time so independent a life of their own &
are off so much on it those dealings are often for days together reduced
to the minimum.) The hours of Hill (full of a sympathetic little party)
were thoroughly charming, & M.H. herself wonderful for goodness &
grace. Charles & all Daughters propitiously absent. She spoke to me
with simply [sic]⁶ ecstacy of having under your pressure occupied No.
53 [rue de Varenne] for her short time of Paris, & of the beauty &
perfection & interest in which she revelled there & of the extent to
which these *indices* drenched your image with a still deeper radiance for
her. You would have been touched by the pitch of her appreciation &
her homage. I haven't seen Mary Cadwal since Sunday night, when I
dined with her very *learningly* & alone at Symonds's. She is to lunch
with me on Thursday—she is now & till then with the Whitridges⁷ at
Barley End. I am so *wüthened*⁸ at the hideous failure of my fond (my
fondest in that *genre*) dream that she should be benevolently & equitably
"named," to an improving tune, in John Cadwal[ader]'s will that I see
everything connected with her as under black depression—or, frankly,
almost through tears of rage—as of course you do too. But she is admirably gay & droll about it herself—full of courage & resource &
unabated interest in life. These things I am glad you will presently see
for yourself. She tells me to my joy that you are in some sort of *pourparlers* for an Oxfordshire house for the summer.⁹ If so I thrill with
interest, feeling how it's the sort of thing that *vous vous deve₹*—for all its
lights on the question of the Future, the English harbourage in general
&c. When I add to that ce que je vous dois also my interest becomes
of the acutest. M.H. told me nothing of Coopersale but that the people
who were after it a little while back (as appeared from their being seen
there &c) have faded away—but that question seems an abyss into
which I have ceased obscurely to peep. Give me some little inkling
gently, won't you, of your possibilities of advent here in the event of
the right house seeming to meet you? I am in London till July 5th at
furthest¹⁰ & if you were to arrive d'ici là it would intensely gild the
prospect. I am thinking ever so yearningly over Morton [Fullerton] &

his Paris—& shall very soon break out with some hustling "technical" advice to him. Donnez-lui beaucoup (de mon) amour. Let me renew my assurance of the same for your own use, clumsy thing as it is. I have had the dearest note from Percy [Lubbock]—dear in spite of being partly about Vernon.[11] However, it's also partly about you—& that helps; as he manages to keep the right tone on each—without getting you mixed. I think that what I really want most to see you about is that image of 2 traîtresses journées with that curiosity—as to how much of her stuffing comes out &c. But oh dear, I want to see you about everything—and am yours all affectionately & not in the least patiently

Henry James

P.S. And Walter [Berry] donc? his figure "tells" so in my horizon & y fait si bien, even at our mostly so sad distance, that I suffer from the total eclipse.

1. That is 30 May.

2. EW was on her North African tour with Percy Lubbock.

3. At Timgad in Tunisia EW was awakened by a burglar in her room in a lonely inn; she screamed; Cook and her maid Elise Duvlenck rushed to her aid, but the marauder had slipped away. EW lost, as she said later, nothing but her voice.

4. EW's "The Criticism of Fiction," *Times Literary Supplement*, 14 May 1914; reprinted in *Living Age*, 25 July 1914.

5. On Monday, 1 June (the Bank Holiday), with niece Peggy James and Margaret Payson.

6. An apparent slip of the pen for "simple."

7. Lucy (older daughter of Matthew Arnold and cousin of Mrs. Humphry Ward) and her American husband, the lawyer Frederick Whitridge.

8. HJ uses an old form of "wütend" and inserts the penultimate "e" to make the word resemble an English past participle: "infuriated."

9. On 3 June HJ wrote to Gaillard Lapsley that EW intended "to take Sutton Courtney, Oxfordshire, for this summer, & a house in New York for next winter!" But see letter of 5 June 1914.

10. HJ went down to Rye on 13 July.

11. "Vernon Lee," pen name of Violet Paget (1856–1935), an English novel-

ist whom HJ had known for thirty years, lived in Florence. EW and Lubbock
visited her briefly on their return from North Africa.

mutisme: muteness; *plus doucement:* more quietly; *de . . . offrir:* better to offer you;
comme . . . jamais: as usual (or rather worse than ever!); *jeté:* cast; *impayables:*
priceless; *enfin . . . pas:* anyway let us not despair; *indices:* signs; *pourparlers:*
negotiations; *vous . . . devez:* you owe yourself; *ce . . . dois:* what I owe you; *d'ici
là:* in the meantime; *Donnez-lui . . . amour:* Give him lots (of my) love; *traîtresses
journées:* treacherous days; *donc:* then; *y . . . bien:* does so well there

> 21 Carlyle Mansions
> Cheyne Walk, S.W.
> 5 June 1914

Dearest Edith.

    This is only a little "practical" word—very shyly practical—conse-
quent on Mary Cadwal[ader Jones]'s having told me yesterday that she
had let you know of the Humphry Wards' great disposition to let
Stocks.[1] (She lunched with me—M.C. did—& we strolled afterwards,
quite beautifully, in Kensington Gardens & talked of your case. So you
see what you're "missing"!) *But don't at least miss Stocks!*—so much I
feel moved quite crudely & intermeddlingly to say! I don't intermeddle
impulsively or easily—so that this time there may be, or *must be*, something in it. It at any rate occurs to me that it may help you a little to
know that that consecrated retreat of genius & culture—& these things
of the special note so *quite in your line!*—strikes me as really very pleasantly & possibly your affair. You have seen & known it for the passing
hour—I memorably with you!—but the further impression coming
from a few week-ends &c there in the past have determined my good
opinion of its likelihood to "do" for you for three months very sufficiently & amply indeed. It was much modernized & bathroomed some
few years back—not, doubtless, on the American scale; but very work-
ably & conveniently. And it's civilised & big-treed & gardened & library'd & pictured & garaged in a very sympathetic way—& in the
midst of a country of the most pleasing radiations. On top of all this,

further, are the traditions of the house. You write fort bien, but how can 3 months there not kind of inflame to a certain je ne sais quoi that will round it off? So I think—! That is all—I just think. Pardon my hustling tone; but I kind of see you *at rest there* under fine old English umbrage, & that is the happiest possible image to your all-faithfullest

Henry James

1. The Humphry Wards' country house was near Tring in Buckingham-shire—not so close to London as Coopersale but not nearly so far out as the Oxfordshire seat EW was considering. EW did rent Stocks, and took posses-sion at the end of August.

fort bien: very well

Lamb House, Rye
6 August 1914[1]

Dearest Edith.

I have just learned your whereabouts through communication estab-lished, pretty slowly, with White,[2] & though I fear the process of this will be slower still I want to assure you by it of my fondest anxiety for your comfort & sympathy in your, I fear, immediate inconvenience. I have been hoping from day to day to hear from you that your arrival on these shores had been effected—I even believed till a very few days ago that it might already have been, or *was* being, & that the sign would come from Stocks, where I have both written & telegraphed to White (though without answer as yet to my letter). The homely truth is, how-ever, that on hearing from you at the very moment I supposed you were starting for your usufruct of Stocks that you were starting for that of the Balearic Isles, & this with a more than Sandean, a fairly Shan-dean,[3] digressive *allure*, I entered into a state of hébétement on the whole question which has left me bewildered enough for any mistake of cal-culation: the more too that your pictured messages, with Walter [Berry]'s conjoined,[4] only seemed, from day to day, to *bafouer* my thick-ness of wit. So through a whirling cloud of dust denser indeed these last days by the hideous public blackness have I continued to see you.

And now please believe how tenderly I think of you & how worriedly I wonder. Enormous must be your frustration, your dislocation, your painful dividedness—over which I lose myself in desperate conjecture when not in lurid evocation. Ci vuol' pazienza—you *will* get over, by some abatement of the congestion; unless your heart incalculably declares for preference of the whereabouts, the actual, of your body, & you are conscious of greater interests to guard là-bas than here—where White must be so gallantly guarding those that do exist. Mine are intensely in your getting over at the 1st moment you can do it with any comfort, though I call upon you too helplessly, I indeed feel, to make much of a figure as a cherished objective for yourself. If I could only reach out more brilliantly—but I feel all but unbearably overdarkened by this crash of our civilization. The only gleam in the blackness, to me, is the action of the absolute unanimity of this country. I am not here in lonely gloom, entirely; my niece Peggy is with me, & her youngest brother[5]—to the very great & blest mitigation of my solitude, & there can apparently be no question of their early return to the U.S. I only want them moreover to stay on. I have at last extracted from Symonds that Mary Cadwal[ader Jones], bless her, is also hung up near you, & I am writing her by this same "post"—bless *it!* Shall you be able to reach me with a brave word yourself? Try hard, I beseech you, & believe me dearest Edith, your more than ever devoted old

Henry James

1. The First World War had broken out (for Great Britain) two days earlier; HJ's letter to Sturgis on that day explains much of this one to EW: "I am full of anxiety about Edith W., who on the day on which her tenure of Stocks began [10 July 1914] . . . started on a motor-tour to Barcelona, that is to Majorca (!!) with Walter Berry—even like another George Sand & another Chopin. Doubtless you got a picture-card from her . . . the last that reached me was from Poitiers, on the way back to Paris, July 30th."

2. Arthur White, EW's English butler, who had been with her since 1888, had been sent ahead to Stocks with housemaids and footmen to prepare for her coming. He went to France expecting to accompany her to England on July 30, but was sent back on 4 August. EW reached England on 27 August, and dined on that date at Lamb House.

3. Like the erratic, "digressive" narrative of the novel *The Life and Opinions*

of Tristram Shandy (1759–1767) by English novelist Laurence Sterne (1713–1768).

4. EW and Berry sent HJ a series of postcards.

5. Aleck had joined Peggy and HJ in London on 4 July; niece and nephew were away for a few days but rejoined HJ at Rye on 1 August.

allure: gait; *hébétement:* stupefaction; *bafouer:* mock; *Ci . . . pazienza:* That takes patience; *là-bas:* over there

7
"The Distinguished Thing"

AUGUST 1914–FEBRUARY 1916

THE GREAT WAR at first produced a settling and invigorating effect on both James and Wharton. Within two weeks of regaining Paris after her southern jaunt she opened her "*ouvroir*" (workroom) to employ women—principally seamstresses—bereft of income and not eligible for government assistance to dependents of enlisted men. At the end of August she crossed the Channel to take up residence at Stocks; she was there during the Battle of the Marne in September. The inaction and boredom of rural England drove her up to London where she and James spent most of a week together. Then back to Paris to open the American Hostels for Refugees. James confronted the war literally in his own backyard; he opened his ample Watchbell Street studio to Belgian refugees, he accepted the chairmanship in England of the American Volunteer Motor-Ambulance Corps, and his man Burgess Noakes enlisted in the army. But he was soon plagued by coronary annoyances and the return of "food-loathing"; Wharton suffered nervous prostration brought on by serious theft at her *ouvroir* and by Anna Bahlmann's struggle with cancer.

James found some relief in resuming one of his unfinished novels—not *The Ivory Tower*, for which Wharton had arranged the substantial advance, but *The Sense of the Past*. His comment in a November letter explains the choice: "It's impossible to 'locate anything in our time.' . . . It all makes Walter Scott, him only, readable again." *The Ivory Tower* is of "our time"; *The Sense of the Past* about escape therefrom. He also participated eagerly in Wharton's collection of art in various media, published to raise money for war relief, *The Book of the Homeless (Le Livre des Sans-Foyers)*. James's contribution recounts his experience with the wounded in St. Bartholomew's Hospital in London—a tribute to The Soldier, "The Long Wards."

Wharton was actively in touch with the war scene as she and Berry were able to get to the front lines on the eastern border of France early in 1915. James's involvement exposed him to scenes of suffering without the compensation of witnessing heroic battle and retaliation. He grieved the more acutely that Britain fought on without the support of the United States of America. That grief helped lead him to the significant gesture of renouncing his American citizenship and becoming a British subject; he took the oath of allegiance to the British Crown on 26 July 1915. He did so quietly, however: neither his family nor his dear friend Edith Wharton then sympathized with his decision.

By the fall of 1915 James was suffering seriously from heart trouble and eating very little—and in the grip of deepening depression. In October he went down to Rye for the last time and burned most of his remaining papers. Wharton came over to England that month, was herself depressed by James's condition, and arranged with Bosanquet to keep her informed of the Master's health. At the beginning of December the first in a series of strokes afflicted James; he reported to his Rye neighbor Fanny Prothero that it was accompanied by a voice saying, "So here it is at last, the distinguished thing." He rallied, dictated random passages of a Napoleonic autobiography to Bosanquet, and suffered a relapse. Sister-in-law Alice arrived in mid-December. During a lucid interval shortly afterward he was told that he was to be awarded the highest honor England could bestow on a civilian—the Order of Merit. His name was included in the list of honors on New Year's Day 1916.

James's decline was steady, however; Bosanquet sent regular reports to Wharton in France, assuring her that nothing was to be gained by her coming to England. On 25 February James lost consciousness for the last time; on the twenty-eighth at teatime he died.

After the service in Chelsea Old Church, a step westward from Carlyle Mansions, Bosanquet duly informed Wharton. Soon after, Wharton wrote to Gaillard Lapsley: "Let us keep together all the closer now, we few who had him at his best."

Lamb House, Rye
19 August 1914

Dearest Edith.

Your letter of the 15th has come—& may this reach you as directly,
though it probably won't. So I won't make it long—the less that the
irrelevance of all remark, the utter extinction of everything, in face of
these immensities, leaves me as "all silent & all damned" as you express
that it leaves *you*. I find it the strangest state to have lived on & on
for—& yet, with its wholesale annihilations, it *is* somehow life. Mary
Cadwal[ader Jones] is admirably here—interesting & vivid & helpful to
the last degree, & Bessie Lodge & her boy had the heavenly beauty,
this afternoon, to come down from town (by train s'entend), rien que
for tea—she even sneakingly went first to the inn for luncheon—& was
off again by 5.30, nobly kind & beautiful & good. (She sails in the
Olympic with her aunt on Saturday.) Mary C. gives me a sense of the
interest of your Paris which makes me understand how it must attach
you—how it would attach me in your place. Infinitely thrilling & touching such a community with the so all-round incomparable nation. I feel
on my side an immense community here, where the tension is propor-
tionate to the degree to which we feel engaged—in other words up to
the chin, up to the eyes, if necessary. Life goes on after a fashion, but I
find it a nightmare from which there is no waking save by sleep. I *go*
to sleep, as if I were dog-tired with action—yet feel like the chilled
vieillards in the old epics, infirm & helpless at home with the women
while the plains are ringing with battle. The season here is monoto-
nously magnificent—& we look inconceivably off across the blue channel, the lovely rim,[1] toward the nearness of the horrors that are in
perpetration just beyond. I can't begin to think of exerting any pressure
upon you in relation to coming to the "enjoyment" of your tenancy—
your situation so baffles & beats me that I but stare at it with a lack of
lustre! At the thought of *seeing* you, however, my eye does feel itself
kindle—though I dread indeed to see you at Stocks but restlessly chafe.
I manage myself to try to "work"—even if I *had*, after experiment, to
give up trying to make certain little fantoches & their private adventure
tenir debout. *They* are laid by on the shelf—the private adventure so
utterly blighted by the public; but I have got hold of something else, &
I find the effort of concentration to some extent an antidote. Àpropos of

which I thank you immensely for D'Annunzio's frenchified ode[2]—a wondrous & magnificent thing in its kind, even if running too much—for my "taste"—to the vituperative & the execrational. The Latin Renascence mustn't be too much for any by *that*—for which its facile resources are so great. However, the thing is splendid & makes one wonder at the strangeness of the genius of Poesy—that it should be able to pour through that particular rotten little skunk! What's magnificent to me in the French themselves at this moment is their lapse of expression. I hear from Howard [Sturgis]—flanked by Mrs. Maquay & more & more uplifted about William; & I've had some beautiful correspondence with White.[3] Try to want *greatly* to come to him—enough greatly to do it; & then I shall want enormously to urge you. I put here in fact a huge store of urgence—all ready for you the moment you can profitably use it. The *conditions* of coming seem now steadily to improve—though a pair of American friends of ours crossed 9 days ago (or upward) via Dieppe—having come *comfortably* from Paris thither & slept there—in a very tranquil, even if elongated, manner. May this not fail of you! I am your all-faithfully tender & true old

H.J.

P.S. So many, & *such*, things to Walter [Berry] & to Morton [Fullerton].

1. Source of his posthumous essay "Within the Rim" and the collection of war essays with the same title.
2. The "Ode pour la résurrection latine" by the Italian poet and novelist Gabriele D'Annunzio (1863–1938) appeared in *Le Figaro*, 13 August 1914; it boldly chided Italy for hesitating to acknowledge Latin solidarity by taking its place beside France in the war.
3. EW's butler; see letter of 6 August 1914.

s'entend . . . que: understood), just; *vieillards:* old men; *fantoches:* specters; *tenir debout:* stand on their feet

Lamb House, Rye
Sunday P.M.
[30 August 1914]

Dearest Edith.

I am no very grand creature yet, for that state of relapse into the infernal essence of my dismal illness of 1910–11,[1] the temporary insurmountable *sick* rejection of food, only developed further after your evening sight of it,[2] & gave me a particularly damnable 36 hours. However, it has been broken—I mean the worst of it is—& as soon as it *is* broken I begin to mend—though I find the abnormally oppressive heat of today further calculated to sicken. This is poor response to your good word about seeing dear Howard [Sturgis], for which act & which word I bless you. Above all do I bless you for simply being on these shores now— if "simply" it can be called; & I hope with all my heart that with Stocks really spreading its generous umbrage about you, you are feeling something of the balm—if we can talk now of balm!—of that. But I am still full of questions of Walter [Berry][3] & his sister & your maid & the Cooks (so many in all!)—& of wonderment as to actual possibilities. With all my heart do I hope they are making their connections. There is a piece of news[4] in the air which won't be in the papers for 2 or 3 days, but which for a change if valid—as it is generally believed to be —is good—I mean a big operation actually taking place & of which an inkling may have reached yourself: the passing through England in guarded secrecy these last 48 hours of a big Russian contingent shipped from Arcangel [*sic*], landed at Aberdeen & now being injected into France by (presumably) Ostend. It is *much* corroborated—& though I hate premature crowing risk a faith in its making a difference! If it be true, however, we shall know nothing whatever of it until every man has been landed— But I yearn for a small scrap of script from you. I want extremely to know about Walter & Cook!—& that a kind of rest does seem to compass you about. You shall have more from me as soon as I am more completely debout. I am fondly supposing Mary C[adwalader Jones] will have been with you today. This south-coast heat is for the moment abnormal—& to me extenuating—but will probably tomorrow explode. Your all-faithfullest

H.J.

1. Which WJ had diagnosed as a "nervous breakdown."

2. August 27. In a letter to Jessie Allen (1845–1918)—a generous aristocratic friend of HJ's since 1899—dated 28 August, Lamb House, Peggy reported that "Mrs. Wharton dined here last night when she & her servant [Elise Duvlenck] stayed at the Hotel to break their journey." (It was doubtless the George Hotel in the High Street.)

3. Berry was flourishing: his privileged position as president of the American Chamber of Commerce in Paris gave him access to rather large sums of money and enabled him to act as banker for many stranded Americans, and not least EW; he also was able to have her auto shipped across the Channel.

4. A typical example—the "Russian legend"—of wartime rumors (see letters of 1 and 3 September 1914), and indicative of HJ's sharing the common belief that the war could not last more than a very few months.

debout: on my feet

[DICTATED]   Lamb House, Rye
                                                              1 September 1914
Dear E.W.

Cast your intelligent eye on the picture from this a.m.'s Daily Mail that I send you and which you may not otherwise happen to see. Let it rest, with all its fine analytic power, on the types, the dress, the caps and the boots of the so-called Belgians disembarked—disembarked from *where,* juste ciel!—at Ostend, and be struck as I have been, as soon as the thing was shown me this a.m. by the notice-taking Skinner (my brave Dr.!) so much more notice-taking than so many of the persons around us. If they are not straight out of the historic, or even fictive, page of Tolstoy, I will eat the biggest pair of moujik boots in the collection! With which Skinner told me of speech either this morning, or last evening, on his part, with a man whose friend or brother, I forget which, had just written him from Sheffield: "Train after train of Russians have been passing through here to-day (Sunday); they *are* a rum-looking lot!" But an enormous quantity of this apparently corroborative testimony from *seen trains,* with their contents stared at and wondered at, have within two or three days kept coming in from various quarters.[1]

Quantum valeat! I consider the reproduced snapshot enclosed, however, a regular gem of evidence. What a blessing, after all, is our—*our*—refined visual sense!

This isn't really by way of answer to your own most valuable this morning received—but that is none the less gratefully noted, and shall have its independent acknowledgment. I am better, thank you, distinctly; the recovery of power to eat again means everything to me. I greatly appreciated your kind little letter to my most interesting and admirable Peggy, whom you left under the charm. Very painful your report of your evening at Quacre—from which place I have been quite feeling in my bones that some such dire imagery would issue. The worst of it is that it's so horribly consequential and logical; that it was implied and involved as an eventual exhibition, at a given moment, in so many of the things one has had to take kindly and amusedly in the past. The last expression of anything that I myself have lately received thence was, not long since, a characteristic overflow of admiration, at the highest pitch, of the Infant[2] and his peerlessness—"he's such a Man!" However there is, I am convinced, in our poor friend a residuum which would, or even will, play up somehow under final stress! Basta!

My own small domestic plot here rocks beneath my feet, since yesterday afternoon, with the decision at once to volunteer of my invaluable and irreplaceable little Burgess![3] I had been much expecting and even hoping for it, but definitely shrinking from the responsibility of administering the push with my own hand: I wanted the impulse to play up of itself. It now appears that it had played up from the first, inwardly—with the departure of the little Rye contingent for Dover a fortnight ago. The awfully decent little chap had then felt the pang of patriotism and martial ardour *rentrés*; and had kept silent for fear of too much incommoding me by doing otherwise. But now the clearance has taken place in the best way in the world, and I part with him in a day or two. My dependence on such intimate service as he renders me is such that it's like the loss of an arm or a leg,[4] quite literally; but that is completely irrelevant to the matter, and I must make shift as I can. His general *household* use has been precious all along—which is also a fact without bearing!

I do quite hang on your communications with Walter [Berry] and with Cook!⁵—and can't but wish Miss Walter hadn't elected to dangle at Vichy up to such an eleventh hour! However I really back both of those characters, and feel that light will presently break. This is all now, save that I am always yours too much for typists⁶

Henry James

1. For the beginning of this rumored aid see letter of 30 August 1914, and its sad sequel in that of 3 September 1914.

2. William Haynes Smith, usually "the Babe," was occupied with Howard Sturgis's nervous prostration aggravated by the outbreak of war.

3. Noakes enlisted in the 5th Battalion of the Royal Sussex Regiment. His service lasted just over a year.

4. The day before, HJ had written to Lucy Clifford (see letter of 13 October 1914, n. 7): "P.S. My little fifteen-year-long henchman Burgess has just ardently volunteered, under my unreserved benediction. But it's like losing an arm or a leg!"

5. EW's chauffeur, Charles Cook, had accompanied the party to Boulogne and returned to Paris to settle problems over bringing his wife to England. They joined the staff at Stocks at the end of the first week of September.

6. HJ wrote in these last four words in ink.

juste ciel: great heavens; *Quantum valeat:* How valuable; *Basta:* Enough; *rentrés:* strike home

[DICTATED]   Lamb House, Rye
                                                3 September 1914
My dear E.W.

It's a great luxury to be able to go on this way. I wired you at once this morning how very glad indeed I shall be to take over your superfluous young man as a substitute for Burgess,¹ if he will come in the regular way, as *my* servant entirely, not borrowed from you (otherwise than in the sense of his going back to you whenever you shall want him again); and remaining with me on a wage basis settled by me with him, and about the same as Burgess's, if possible, so long as the latter is away. I feel that he will really be of great help to us, and to myself more particularly in view of the several *kinds* of thing, especially in respect to any, however least, bustling use of my arms, and various other odd inevitable motions, that press at once the anginal spring and make *some* intimate personal service indispensable to me. Likewise he will minister very helpfully to Kidd and Joan[2]—and we are on a thoroughly informal accommodating little reciprocal basis together. As I telegraphed, the place is "open" to him at any moment—he will doubtless find the 4.25 from Charing Cross his most convenient; and I will of course fully reimburse him the cost of his journey.

I am afraid indeed now, after this lapse of days, that the "Russian" legend doesn't very particularly hold water[3]—some information I have this morning in the way of a positive sharp denial of the W[ar] O[ffice] points that way, unless the sharp denial is conceivable *quand même*. The only thing is that there remains an extraordinary residuum of fact to be accounted for: it being indisputable by too much convergence of testimony that trains upon trains of troops seen in the light of day, and not recognized by innumerable watchers and wonderers as English, were pouring down from the north and to the east during the end of last week and the beginning of this. It seems difficult that there should have been that amount of variously-scattered hallucination, misconception, fantastication or whatever—yet I chuck up the sponge!

Far from brilliant the news to-day of course, and likely I am afraid, to act on your disposition to go back to Paris; which I think a very gallant and magnificent and ideal one, but which at the same time I well understand, within you, the urgent force of. I feel I cannot take upon myself to utter any relevant remark about it at all; any plea against it which you wouldn't in the least mind, once the thing *determined* for you, or any in favour of it, which you so intensely don't require. I *understand* too well—that's the devil of such a state of mind about everything. Whatever resolution you take and apply will put it through to your very highest honour and accomplishment of service; *sur quoi* I take off my hat to you down to the ground, and only desire not to worry you with vain words.

I have asked Miss Bosanquet for light on the subject of a possible London typist for you, and she kindly says she will send you herself to-day a couple of indications which, she feels practically sure, will meet your case. It's an immense inspiration to myself that you speak of "doing something"; it's so what I myself am trying—when I *can!*—and finding support in[,] in proportion as it at all comes off. If Percy [Lubbock] is with you give him please my fondest assurances; it must be remarkably decent for both of you! I kind of hanker for any scrap of really domestic fact about you all that I may be able to extract from Frederick if he comes. But I shall get at you again quickly in this way, and am your all-faithfullest

Henry James

1. EW sent her footman, Frederic Glyfield—which HJ spelled "Frederick," except in the letter of 2 October 1914—as substitute for Noakes.
2. Minnie Kidd was HJ's housemaid, and Joan Anderson his cook.
3. See letters of 30 August and 1 September 1914.

quand même: even so; *sur quoi:* upon which

Lamb House, Rye
12 September 1914

Dearest Edith.

This is a word to thank you for the exquisite hospitality of your letter—in which the princely note shines out again as from everything that is yours. I almost quake at the grandeur of the installation you promise—I mean you offer, me;[1] & just venture to remind you that it isn't for life—though I wish indeed it were! Peggy & I shall be having "things to do," in the a.m. of Monday,[2] I think, last things of necessity for *her*; & she has two or three friends to lunch with her at the hotel whom she can't otherwise see & with whom I must assist her. But after that—! I don't make out that there is much that presses—from 3.30 or so; & what would be awfully benign of you comes before me as our resorting to you for a small quantity of very plain food in the evening. However—these things at your utter convenience. I shall come to you as soon as her boat-train is off on Tuesday—I think about noon. Deeply interested shall I be in St. André's letter[3]—& I think I remember meeting the Duc de Guiche.[4] Bien des choses to Percy [Lubbock]. Ever your faithfullest old

H.J.

1. As the comparative isolation of Stocks—without telephone—began to tell on EW's nerves, Mrs. Humphry Ward agreed to return to Stocks and give EW her London house at 25 Grosvenor Square, to which EW had just invited HJ. He was with her 15 to 19 September.

2. That is 14 September.

3. Alfred de Saint-André was a friend of EW's from her earliest days in the Faubourg Saint-Germain, a gourmet, and a member of Rosa de Fitz-James's circle.

4. Armand Agénor Auguste Antoine, duc de Guiche, eminent French scientist, was a long-time friend of Marcel Proust.

Bien des choses: All the best

Lamb House, Rye
19 September 1914

Dearest Edith.

I do want you to see this fine little letter of Dick Norton's,[1] on receipt of which this afternoon early I at once wired him to try to see you before his leaving for Paris tonight, in case you shld. have something more to send.[2] Very likely he was out when my wire came, or for other reasons hasn't been able; but here at any rate is the letter—which I am just answering to Paris. I wish we had only thought to send for him to the Grange while I was with you—but I absolutely supposed him in America. What an admirable spirit he exhales—!—My run down here was smooth & I find the comparative "quiet" of the place extreme; but it doesn't make me want to stay—on the contrary! So I am aiming at getting up on Friday.[3] I earnestly pray that I may find you still on the spot. I quite hate your going—even with a lucid understanding of it. Wait, *wait*, WAIT! Ever your

H.J.

P.S.   A good note from Mary Cadwal[ader Jones] written on the last day before reaching N.Y.—the voyage having been dreary but not too abnormal—save for the so *lightless* question!

1. Richard Norton (b. 1872), youngest son of Charles Eliot Norton; an archeologist and director of the School of Classical Studies in Rome, he organized

the American Volunteer Motor-Ambulance Corps and enlisted HJ as its chair-man. See HJ's *The American Volunteer Motor-Ambulance Corps in France* (London: Macmillan, 1914; reprinted in *Within the Rim*—London: Collins, 1919). Norton died of meningitis in Paris, 2 August 1918.

2. Plans were already afoot for EW's return to France on 24 September 1914.

3. HJ did come up to London on 25 September.

Lamb House, Rye
21 September 1914

Dearest Edith.

Reims *is* the most unspeakable & immeasurable terror & infamy[1]— & what is appalling & heartbreaking is that it's *forever & ever*! But no words fill the abyss of it—nor touch it, nor relieve one's heart nor light by a spark the blackness; the ache of one's howl & the anguish of one's execration aren't mitigated by a shade even as one brands it as the most hideous crime ever perpetrated against the mind of man. There it *was* —& now all the tears of rage of all the bereft millions & all the crowd-ing curses of all the wondering ages will never bring a stone of it back! Yet one *tries*, even now—tries to get something from saying that the measure is so full as to overflow at last in a sort of vindictive deluge (though for all the stones that *that* will replace!) & that the arm of final retributive justice becomes by it an engine really in some degree pro-portionate to the act. I positively do think it helps me a little to think of how they can be made to *wear* the shame, in the pitiless glare of history, forever & ever—& not even to get rid of it when they are maddened, literally, by the weight. And for that the preparations must have already at this hour begun: how *can't* they be as a tremendous force fighting on the side, fighting in the very fibres, of France? I think too somehow—[though I don't know *why*, practically—][2] of how noth-ing conceivable could have so damned & dished them forever in our *great art-loving*[3] country! It's at least a drop of balm that you've recovered the money of your caisse & administered the snub to the mistress of the Prussian geste[4]—of which she doubtless thought she had really caught the inimitability. If you go on Thursday[5] I can't hope to see you again for the present, but all my blessings on all your splendid resolution, your courage & charity! Right must you be not to take back with you any of your Englishry—it's no place for them yet. Frederick[6] will hang on your 1st signal to him again—& meanwhile is a very great boon to me. I wish I could do something for White if (as I take it) he stays behind; put him up at the Athenaeum or something. All love & applause to Walter [Berry]—all reiterations to Morton [Fullerton]—& all homage & affection to yourself, dearest Edith, from your desolate & devoted old

H.J.

1. HJ's response to early news of the first bombing of Rheims Cathedral (he used the French spelling)—which somewhat exaggerates the damage. The passion of his response is reflected in the unusually large handwriting of the first three sentences and the vigorous pen strokes throughout. The first seven sentences of the lamentation (ending with "*great art-loving* country!") were translated by EW's friend Alfred de Saint-André, read to a session of the Académie Française on 9 October 1914, and published in the *Journal des Débats*, 10 October 1914. See letter of 17 October 1914.

2. HJ's brackets.

3. It is difficult to tell whether the long stroke in the manuscript is intended to underline these words or to serve as a lengthy dash before the following sentence.

4. Before crossing to England EW had set up in Paris her renowned *ouvroir*, "for employing work women who haven't husbands or sons in the Army & thereby no State assistance, & yet are unemployed in their great sad multitudes," as HJ explained to his niece Peggy in a letter of 20 September. The woman left in control absconded with some $2,000, and the *ouvroir* was near collapse. In view of the context, HJ's calling it a Prussian act (*geste*) is quite understandable.

5. EW left on Thursday, 24 September.

6. The footman EW lent HJ to replace Noakes.

caisse: cash box

Lamb House, Rye

23 September 1914

Dearest Edith.

I cling to you even while I surrender you & bless & back you even while I kind of remonstrate.[1] But I hate to think withal of your dragged-out crossing. There is no hint of an "equinoctial" in these parages today—this & yesterday have been splendid still & sunny specimens. I understand the strong call to you of Paris—it's so hateful to "understand" so—& great glory & honour will she cover you with![2] But for pity's sake—if there *be* any pity in the universe now!—"take care of yourself," as our rich vernacular has it. I don't indeed despair perhaps of breaking out in that medium on some happy pretext seized.—I can't tell you how handsome, how more than magnificent I find your cheque[3] inclosed with so incomparable a geste in the midst of all the bleedings of your balance. It fills me with the most earnest sense of responsibility, & I am saying to myself that I had best not pass it on *en bloc* to any one cause at once, but make 3 or 4 parts of it to meet needs immediately vivid. This is brought home to me by the fact that some 15 or 20 Belgian refugees arrive *here* tomorrow (to be followed by an equal number more), & that I was today waited upon on their behalf by 2 of the ladies of the Catholic community of the place, who seem to me very good & devoted women & to whose charge they come. I have made them over my pretty ample & favorable old chapel-studio[4] for all the time needed, as a gathering-place, living, sitting, letter-writing, newspaper-reading place, for them—bedrooms & vittles being elsewhere provided, & they simple & humble people. Money is wanted to help to run the enterprise—the taking in & keeping on here of a couple of dozen &c; & I will by your leave contribute on your behalf a couple of pounds to begin with—waiting to see what may be, piecemeal or preponderantly, the best use of the rest. I kind of feel that the best use, in one way or another, *is* for the Belgians, unless a pound or two or three should go to the poor wife or mother of a soldier at the front. If you will trust me to place the money cautiously & tellingly I will do so & report to you. But I must now catch the London post, & I am, dearest Edith, more than ever yours to hold on by & *to*,

H.J.

1. HJ refers to EW's decision to return to France on the following day; see letter of 21 September 1914.

2. EW was made a Chevalier of the Legion of Honor in April 1916.

3. EW sent HJ a check for £10 to use for war relief in Rye.

4. At the southwest corner of the Lamb House property, in Watchbell Street—now converted into flats.

parages: climes; *geste:* act

21 Carlyle Mansions
Cheyne Walk, S.W.[1]
2 October 1914

Dearest Edith.

Your letters &c are not only heroic & breathe the most inspiring & inspired *souffle,* but they arrive now with quite normal promptitude. The "&c" above refers to your postcard, which got to me, I think, only some 12 hours or so later than in the old golden age. This a.m., by 1st post, come *together* your deeply interesting 26th & 29th—the latter, you see, almost quite "on time." And most thrilling & uplifting are you—as I confess other signs & portents taken together tend to appear—to my imaginative sense. I am transported this a.m. by the accts. in the papers here (of which I send you the three best), of the landing of the Indian troops of Marseilles—which make me feel that of all the great "epoch-making" spectacles of our (or of any) siècle, it is the one leaving me most heart-broken & deprived not to have assisted at it. The Paris papers will have depicted it—but in a most restricted way, probably. I will send you on papers—for the Hospital English—in general *hence* as freely as I can cause them to be despatched. There can be no doubt that whatever the French are able to do, the English line at the front is being *steadily* re-inforced with real fighting battalions & all the while admirably & imperturbably *fed.* Very wonderful your having assisted at those Tuileries bombs—but what I want of Fate is that the American Ambassador[2] be offered up on the altar of the Union of the 2 (more or less) English-speaking peoples: if a German bomb could but painlessly extinguish him in order to precipitate the American relation to the Kaiser's general undertaking. Such a quite possible incident would magnificently complicate—I see *all* that would follow. I delight in your report of the ouvroir[3]—of Walter [Berry], of Morton [Fullerton], of everything. You are all in your several ways immortalizing yourselves. I haven't yet had your papers for the Belgians[4]—but as regards this *wait*, till you order any extended sending. I want to be clearer as to the growth of the Rye handful. More are expected there on Tuesday next[5]—then I shall learn what their nature & needs may be. I have as yet only given them 40/ of your cheque: it may very well all go to them—as of traceable & measurable action—but only au fur & à mesure as it can be best applied. Therefore the balance awaits its openings. I shall see White again before he leaves—& Frederic [*sic*] has been able to be of some use for him.[6] How interesting indeed must your "thick of it" be! Here too that only augments. It wouldn't take much more to make me *en raffoler*. This is all for the moment. I am beginning now to send you some papers for your hospitals[7]—& will keep it up. Yours arch-devotedly

    Henry James

    1. HJ came up to London on 25 September to escape the "unrelieved solitude" of Rye (as he wrote to niece Peggy on 27 September). He made Lamb House available to the sister-in-law of his Rye neighbor Mrs. Alice Dew-Smith—Mrs. Charles Lloyd, and her two daughters.
    2. William Graves Sharp (1859–1922), ambassador to France (1914–1919) and an advocate of the League of Nations.
    3. See letter of 21 September 1914.
    4. The plan was for EW to send Paris newspapers; but see letter of 5 October 1914, and also that of 13 October 1914.
    5. That is, 6 October.
    6. White was seeing to final details of the EW household's removal to Paris. See letter of 5 October 1914. Frederic, spelled correctly for once, was EW's replacement for Noakes.
    7. That is, London newspapers for hospitalized English in Paris; see letters of 13 and 17 October 1914.

souffle: breath; *siècle:* century; *au . . . mesure:* according; *en raffoler:* dote on it

21 Carlyle Mansions
Cheyne Walk, S.W.
5 October 1914

Dearest Edith.

This is a very short scribble, which I am sending you by White when he goes tomorrow. Frederick has been with him all day helping him to close up No. 25,[1] I believe—while I, to my regret, have had to put in a couple of days in bed again through a temporary collapse, a kick of old liabilities.[2] But I am better tonight—am succeeding in taking food again—or shall, I think, half an hour hence; & I only mention it to plead for the feebleness of my scrawl. I mainly want to say that your Paris papers have beautifully come, but I beg you to stay them now for the present—as up to now the poor Belgians at Rye (*very* few in number) are of such humbleness that they don't understand a *word* of anything but Flemish & the papers are wasted on them. A few more (Belgians) are expected there on Wednesday,[3] I am told, & they may be more doué—but it is a case of very humble folk indeed, I imagine —almost peasants & not à la hauteur. I will let you know if the case improves. All thanks meanwhile—I have made my profit of the *feuilles* —though when I have done with the London I rather falter from beginning on the Paris. It's a rate at which one's style goes to pieces. Forgive this paucity & believe in the fond fidelity of participation & admiration of yours, dearest Edith, ever

H.J.

1. The London House of the Humphry Wards at 25 Grosvenor Place.
2. See letter of 13 October 1914.
3. 7 October.

doué: gifted; *à la hauteur:* up to the mark; *feuilles:* papers

[DICTATED]   21 Carlyle Mansions
                                             Cheyne Walk, S.W.
                                             13 October 1914

My dear E.W.

I am obliged quite utterly, alas, to resort to this,[1] for I am sorry to say I'm having a bad time of it, thanks to my damnable heart complication, with the anginal demon lying in wait at every turn (and *such* turns as the current situation gives it!) and with the heritage of woe of my old illness, in its principal essence, the too constant failure of power to take food, and the consequent weakness and sickness, renewing itself on the slightest pretext. When I fail to feed I of course *have* to collapse into bed, and in short you can see for yourself. Please don't take me as wanting to worry you with this sorry picture, I am only moved to hang it before you for a minute to account for my failure to do much in the way of response, in the way of expression generally, when you so admirably write me. Think of me all the same as resisting much more than giving way; as nursing a demonic art of circumvention, of general and particular counterplotting, so long as life is in me. Only meanwhile I must be thus vulgarly legible if legible at all. Splendid your mention of your own victory over collapse[2] by your resources of action heroically asserted and reasserted. I rejoice more than I can say in the way the ouvroir leaps and bounds and booms, blessings on its head; if I were but capable of physical action I see I should leap and bound and in fact boom almost to a like tune; it's the curse alas of my years and my compromised cardiac state that I can't! I mean to hold out all the same —or if I fall at least to fall gloriously! I send my most affectionate love to W[alter Berry] and to M[orton Fullerton] and, very, very particularly to the sublime Walter Gays,[3] who are clearly winning their immortality. I don't speak of what is happening in Belgium[4]—it's too soon to see or to say; and of the general circumstances of that you know, and above all will know when you get this, as much as we. All thanks for the address of the place to send my English papers to;[5] I shall cause them to be sent as copiously and steadily as possible. Apropos of which let me tell you that your French papers were not in the smallest degree wasted through not being good for poor Rye;[6] they all went as quickly as possible to an excellent lady round the corner here, Miss Partridge, 8 Cheyne Row, Chelsea, S.W., who is in active relation with the arriving refugees, and those in hospital here, among whom they found (as any more sent me for the said distributress here will find) the most acclaimed use. But this is all now.

More faithfully than ever yours
    Henry James

P.S.   But I remember a small and I trust easy service that I have been earnestly requested to ask of you. Mrs. Clifford's[7] younger daughter, Margaret C., is a Red Cross nurse in Paris, a very active and I judge very competent one, at one of the big *hotel* hospitals; I have stupidly forgotten which, but it doesn't matter. She is partly expecting to be called off on duty to Limoges, and is encumbered with a weighty fur motor-coat; which she can take care of in Paris but can't drag after her if she goes elsewhere. The petition is that in the case (perhaps after all improbable) of its being brought to your door, you would just kindly allow it to be hung up or thrust away somewhere for the time, to be called for again. She is wholly at a loss, her mother writes me, where to leave or bestow it; hence this appeal—which I trust won't incommode you.

1. Dictation to a typist.
2. EW was suffering the effects of nervous tension produced by the defection and her pursuit of the original manager of the *ouvroir*, who was soon apprehended; by concern over the health of her secretary, Anna Bahlmann; and by the mounting evidence that a quick ending to the war was unlikely.
3. Gay (1856–1937), American painter, and his wife Matilda, née Travers, a friend of EW since girlhood.
4. The Battle of Ypres (October–November 1914).
5. Evidently the headquarters of the British Red Cross, the Hôtel d'Iéna in Paris; see letter of 17 October 1914.
6. See letter of 2 October 1914.
7. Lucy (Mrs. W. K.) Clifford (d. 1929), English novelist and playwright, early widowed, supported herself and her children by her pen; she was one of HJ's oldest London friends.

[DICTATED]   21 Carlyle Mansions
                                                Cheyne Walk, S.W.
                                                17 October 1914

Very dear old Friend!

Yesterday came your brave letter with its two so remarkable enclo-
sures and also the interesting one lent me to read by Dorothy Ward.[1]
The sense they give me of your heroic tension and valour is something
I can't express—any more than I need to for your perfect assurance of
it. Posted here in London your letter *was* by the Walter Gays, whom I
hunger and thirst for, though without having as yet got more into touch
than through a telephone message on their behalf an hour ago by the
manager, or whoever, of their South Kensington Hotel. I most unfortunately can't see them this p.m. as they proposed, as I am booked for
the long-unprecedented adventure of going down for a couple of nights
to Quacre; in response to a most touching and not-to-be-resisted letter
from its master.[2] G[aillard] L[apsley] and P[ercy] L[ubbock] are both to
be there, apparently; and I really rather welcome the break for a few
hours with the otherwise unbroken pitch of London. However, let me
not so much as name that in presence of your tremendous pitch of Paris;
which however is all mixed, in my consciousness, with yours, so that
the intensity of yours drums through, all the while, as the big note.
With all my heart do I bless the booming work (though not the booming anything else) which makes for you from day to day the valid *car-
apace*, the invincible, if not perhaps strictly invulnerable, armour. So
golden-plated you shine straight over at me—and at us all!

Of the livliest interest to me of course the Débats version of the poor
old Rheins [*sic*] passage of my letter to you[3] at the time of the horror—
in respect to which I feel so greatly honoured by such grand courtesy
shown it, and by the generous translation, for which I shall at the first
possible moment write and thank Saint-André, from whom I have also
had an immensely revealing small photograph of one of the aspects of
the outraged cathedral, the vividest picture of the irreparable ravage.
Splendid indeed and truly precious your report of the address of that
admirable man to the Rheins tribunal at the hour of supreme trial. I
echo with all my soul your lively homage to it, and ask myself if anything on earth can ever have been so blackly grotesque (or grotesquely
black!) as the sublimely smug proposal of the Germans to wipe off the

face of the world as a living force, substituting for it apparently *their* portentous, their cumbrous and complicated idiom, the race that has for its native incomparable tone, such form, such speech, such reach, such an expressional consciousness, as humanity was on that occasion honoured and, so to speak, transfigured, by being able to find (M. Louis Bossu aiding!) in its chords. What a splendid creation of life, on the excellent man's part, just by play of the resource most familiar and most indispensable to him!

This is all at this moment. I am hoping at any minute to get into communication with the Matildas[4] and to settle it that I pass a priceless hour or two with them on Monday. Heaven grant they be here for some days, for they can assuage as won't be otherwise possible the intensity of my yearnings to know. I have still five Pounds of your cheque[5] in hand—wanting only to bestow it where I practically *see* it used. I haven't sent more to Rye, but conferred Three a couple of days since on an apparently most meritorious, and most intelligently-worked, refuge for some 60 or 70 that is being carried on, in the most fraternal spirit, by a real working-class circle at Hammersmith. I shall distil your balance with equal care; and I accompany each of your donations with a like sum of my own. We are sending off hence now every day regularly some 7 or 8 London papers to the Hotel d'Iéna.[6]

Yours all faithfully
Henry James

1. Daughter of Mrs. Humphry Ward.
2. Howard Sturgis.
3. See letter of 21 September 1914. Here and in the following sentence the misspelling must be due to Theodora Bosanquet: HJ spells it "Reims" when he writes, but if he did spell it out correctly, Bosanquet misheard him.
4. Matilda and Walter Gay; see letter of 13 October 1914.
5. See letter of 23 September 1914.
6. Headquarters of the British Red Cross in Paris; see letter of 13 October 1914.

[DICTATED]   21 Carlyle Mansions
                                                     Cheyne Walk, S.W.
                                                     20 October 1914

Very dear old Friend!

Yes, it does keep up communication a bit blessedly that Walter, who dined with me last night, brought me in your touching letter of the 15th, and that something of mine had reached you with a kind of celerity before that. I think meanwhile I must have written you something further that you *hadn't* got by the said 15th.[1] It was a great joy to have an evening of W., who was of the richest and vividest interest[2]—though he gave my unsophisticated spirit a couple of rather dismal chills; as when putting some of the dots on the i's of what is currently meant by the state of things at Bordeaux, and even when speaking from personal observation of some of the idiosyncrasies of the Russian officer. He in fact told me some anecdotes in the course of which the Russian Army was qualified as "mushy" though I take comfort in the reflection that this proceeded probably from some German source (and sauce) that he was more or less derisively quoting, rather than from his own dark mind. His mind was in fact dark only at those two points—it diffused the brightest light for me upon everything else we talked of. He is evidently very well and interestingly occupied here for these next days; but I count on our absolutely meeting again, as he will then probably have "seen," in his magnificent way, more, far more, in the course of the week than I am able to see at all.

I had with me two days since also the dear little Walter Gays,[3] who lunched here and were full of thrilling report and picture. They are indeed an admirable little pair, and my heart goes out to them entirely. They will be able to bring you some small account of me, and they will not depart from the truth if they tell you I showed them how good I wanted them to be able to make it. They go back, I believe, before the end of this week. Yesterday I saw Henry Adams and his two young nieces,[4] the natural and the artificial; in fact I dined with them last night at their hotel, to which they had come from their stay of several weeks at the Cameron-Lindsay place in Dorsetshire—in order to sail for home to-day in some White Star thing of which I forget the name. Henry, alas, struck me as more changed and gone than he had been reported, though still with certain flickers and *gestes* of participation, and a surviving capacity to be very well taken care of; but his way of life, in such a condition, I mean his world-wandering, is all incomprehensible to me —it is so quite other than any I should select in his state. I have had few other private visions—though Mrs. Curtis,[5] "held up" here by various causes, and mainly by that of the fear of Italy's joining of the Allies and the consequent bombardment of Venice by the Austrians, came in to see me yesterday and told me of her being indefinitely quartered with the Charles Hunters at Hill, where are also settled upon them, apparently for all time, Rodin and his never-before-beheld and apparently most sordid and *inavouable* little wife,[6] an incubus proceeding from an antediluvian error, and yet apparently less displeasing to the observer in general than the dreadful great man himself, of whom Mrs. C. entertains a horror and who has Loie [*sic*] Fuller[7] out from town to visit him in much retirement save when she leads him forth as her companion in her car. Mrs. C., who had been lunching with Emily Sargent,[8] further brought me in the dismal news of the death of the so distinguished little French husband of her niece, Violet Ormond's[9] daughter, the Rose-Marie whom Sargent so exquisitely painted a year ago; the said André Michel having been killed in one of these last engagements. But you of course hear nothing but the like all round you. Millicent Duchess[10] is just engaged to be married to a new young soldier—and I can think of nothing else. I don't mean than of that union, but in the way of fag-ends of the smaller matters here. I can't speak of the bigger ones—they are too, too big. Yet I did lunch the other day at 25 Grosvenor Place[11] (where they were up for three or four days); and that in its way was big too. "Are you able to work?" I am asked. "Oh dear no, alas—are you?" "Ah yes—I have already finished half a novel." "That seems to me very wonderful: how *do* you manage?" "Well, you know, it's so preponderantly for America, where they"—*they!*—"mind the War so much less." And then as I, stupefied at the account of the process, but mumbled something about my own lack of *any* recipe, came the triumphant light: "Oh but *I* shouldn't be able to do it in London, you know!" And yet after all I doubt—I think she *would* be able! But this is all just now save that I am probably investing this afternoon One Pound more of your cheque[12] in tobacco for a considerable batch of the Belgian wounded, now at Rye, on whose behalf I have just received thence a Red Cross appeal. I am sending an equal amount from myself (the two sources kept, for your honour, separate)—as I always do when expending for you; so that you do thus double good. I told you in my last of my sending Three Pounds to the Hammersmith Refugees; and now, after to-day's tobacco, there will be Four Pounds left for me carefully to deal out for you. I am going really, I think, to try that precious solution of our friend's:[13] I mean making it, and thinking of it as, so preponderantly for America, where they don't care, that their belle insouciance will infect my condition and perhaps even my style.

Walter tells me that Morton is now positively sailing for the U.S. If this catches him in time please tell him that je l'embrasse bien and feel with him intensely in his errand, and believe that, though the wrench, for interest, of breaking away from Paris must be énorme, the high benefits to him from it, and to the condition là-bas, will admirably justify it. I *see* you from morning till night, and am

Your All Faithful
    Henry James

1. Letter of 13 October 1914.

2. As president of the Chamber of Commerce of America—not yet at war—Berry was able to move with comparative freedom throughout Europe, including Germany, and carry back rumors, gossip, and even news.

3. See letters of 13 October and 17 October 1914.

4. The natural niece was Mabel Hooper La Farge; the artificial one was Aileen Tone.

5. Ariane, née Wormely; the Venetian "perch" of the Daniel Curtises, Palazzo Barbaro, had often been a refuge for HJ.

6. The adjective *inavouable* ("inadmissible" or "shameful") smacks of snobbishness: Rodin had married Rose Beuret, formerly a baker's delivery girl; Rodin was himself of no more exalted social origins. The dedicated Rose cared selflessly for her husband—a sensualist and philanderer though a talented sculptor—until his death.

7. Loïe Fuller (1862–1928), American dancer whose innovations in costume and lighting appealed to the Symbolist poets and Impressionist painters.

8. Emily (1857–1936), sister of the painter John Singer Sargent, and neighbor of HJ in Carlyle Mansions.

9. Violet, née Sargent (1870–1955), Emily's sister; her son-in-law was killed on 13 October, and her daughter would be killed in a German bombardment

of Paris on 29 March 1918. The painting is likely "Rose-Marie" (1912 portrait of her in a white cashmere shawl).

10. Millicent Fanny St. Clair Erskine, eldest daughter of the 4th earl of Roslyn and widow of the 4th duke of Sutherland, was a writer and an old friend of HJ. She would marry Major P. D. Fitzgerald of the British General Staff.

11. The London house of the Humphry Wards.

12. See letter of 23 September 1914.

13. Mrs. Humphry Ward.

gestes: acts; *je . . . bien:* I send him a warm embrace; *là-bas:* over there

> 21 Carlyle Mansions
> Cheyne Walk, S.W.
> 9 November 1914

Dearest Edith.

I have had your good letter & its admirably ministering contents (the cheque for £10.0.0) from the adventurous & invraisemblable Walter,[1] who must have started for his fell (not to say foul—I could apply *any* epithet!) Berlin yesterday, Sunday, a.m. It is very "sporting" & very wonderful his going, & I grasp in a measure the curiosity & the quest of impressions that prompt the enterprise; but the exhibition of such "detachment," such judicial & impartial ease, costs me, I confess, a sort of pang of anguish. I am infinitely redder-hot than I have any right to expect *him* to be—that I recognize; but when I think that he *wants* to go where he will hear this country foully vituperated & vilified without being able (save under great complications) to so much as attenuate perhaps—well, it kind of makes *me* want to cry. But I am doubtless a ridiculous old fanatic—& I find indeed I *am* more fanatical than many persons I have encountered here. I remain to the full as "fiendish" as we were together during those days of Grosvenor Place[2] [*sic*] & of the lady at Symonds's—or rather I am tenfold more so; & moreover I expressed to Walter, who took it with charming mirth, how much I wish he were not so anxious to amuse himself at our expense. Also I admitted that I have a craven terror of what he may have to break to us on his return, & he promises to *horripiler* me to the fullest extent in his power. So our relation on it all is of the candidest & kindest. He will have a rare experience.—I can't talk to you of the public situation—there is so much too much of it for this poor page, & I shift the burden of it off my bowed back in thus writing you even as a poor peasant shifts his pack onto the *borne* near which he rests. I can think of but one thing— of the crying need of this country: raising in more effective ways an immediate further million of men; & as tonight the Ministers declare themselves at the Lord Mayor's Dinner, goodness grant there may be some virtue to communicate to tomorrow a.m.'s papers.—I will with joy apply your offering to the use here of the more & more abounding Belgians. Under your noble reflection on my dribbling of your last I sent the remaining $\frac{1}{2}$ of that to the excellent Hampshire House (Hammersmith) *oeuvre*, in testimony whereof I enclose their receipt. The amt. from *you* was £5.0.0—the 2 more acknowledged were my addition. We are organizing a specific Chelsea relief colony for the Refugees; I attend the meeting that starts it on Wednesday,[3] & I will devote to its work either a part or the whole of your new beneficence.—I broke down utterly with Well's last[4]—found it of a looseness & cheapness scarce credible & sans everything that had made him one's joy before. So I didn't send him over to you. And alas Compton Mackenzie[5] has just sent me an advance copy of a huge 2d vol. of "Sinister Street" which is a deplorable drop from what was best in the 1st—a really rather hopeless & unredeemed mass, the fruit of a most benighted scheme. It's a lamentable mystery of sudden decline—with which his being sick—he has a very bad chronic ailment—& unfit has doubtless something to do. But it's a melancholy lapse—so don't trouble about seeing the evidence. I try myself to get back to work[6]—but it's of a stiffness of uphill—a sheer perpendicular. I crawl like a fly—a more or less frozen fly—on a most blank wall. It's impossible to "locate anything in our time." Our time has been *this* time for the last 50 years, & if it was ignorantly & fatuously so the only light in which to show it is now the light of that tragic delusion. And that's too awful a subject. It all makes Walter Scott,[7] him only, readable again. I don't speak to you of your own grandeur—but am prostrate before it. Think of me as very flat on the ground; it's really the main posture of your all devotedest old

Henry James

1. Berry delivered EW's letter and check on 6 November and added £5 of his own to the fund.

2. In mid-September, when EW was in the Humphry Wards' townhouse in Grosvenor Square.

3. That is, 11 November.

4. *The Wife of Sir Isaac Harman*, published in October, on the theme of sexual jealousy, handled humorously.

5. Edward Montague Compton "Monty" Mackenzie (1883–1972), son of Edward and Virginia (Bateman) Compton, who staged HJ's *The American* in 1890. HJ had praised his first novel, *Carnival* (1912), and pt. 1 of *Sinister Street*, in "The Younger Generation."

6. HJ had sent Theodora Bosanquet down to Lamb House six days earlier to retrieve his manuscript of *The Sense of the Past* (the first two and a half sections) that he might resume work on it. See *Comp. Notes*, 189–91, 502–35; and letter of 1 December 1914.

7. The Scottish romantic poet and novelist (1771–1832) had been the subject of HJ's first published critical essay, "Essays on Fiction" (*North American Review*, October 1864).

invraisemblable: improbable; *horripiler* me: make my hair stand on end; *borne:* milestone

21 Carlyle Mansions
Cheyne Walk, S.W.
24 November 1914

Dearest Edith.

This is a poor word of acknowledgment of your so interesting & vivid letter this a.m. received; which I mean to give to Percy[1] to take for me—when he comes to luncheon tomorrow (as I believe he almost immediately thereafter leaves for your arms & charms). I rejoice for both of you that you are to be reunited, & am even glad that he will be able to bring you fresh personal news of me. I shall charge him with fond messages. Meanwhile your own news is of the highest beauty, & I respond in particular very understandingly, I think, to your remarks about Walter. I had 48 hours ago a telegram from that desperate adventurer, from the Hague, "arrived Berlin, return 25th," which rather puzzled me & which Mrs. Boynton's remarks upon it after I had sent it to her (as he while here had asked me to send anything) have but further obscured. Your letter it is that explains a little—as I didn't know of his having gone through the Belgian ravage, & therefore so wondered at his having *now* only reached the Capital of Civilization[2] that I fairly thought the wire should have read "arrived *from* Berlin" (at the Hague) & "return *London* 25th." I see now that he only left the Hague for Germany days & days later than I had allowed for, & that he must have telegraphed to the American Legation there on the understanding that it shld. be repeated to me—which I take most kindly of him, as I take everything. Ça me fait quelque chose—tout de même—I can't help it —that he should have been able to *shake hands* with ces messieurs & assist at their fond proceedings; still I will forgive him everything if he does come back with his portmanteau bulging, & even bursting, with damnation—such a thrill of joy it is that he *has* found the Belgian horror surpass our dearest hope. Hooray, hooray—it's almost a thing to illuminate for! The rage in his heart, when he exhibits it, will be as sweet to me as the rage in mine—which is saying much; that being the most delicious morsel that has ever diffused its savour there. He will be of course of an entrancing interest, & his having done it all is really of a high & noble beauty. If he does get back to the Hague on this Wednesday[3] he should reach London, I shld. think, on Saturday—or thereabouts; when I count on his gratifying my passion. If he doesn't to the full, then I shall take it hard—but I have every confidence. It's splendid that your genius seems really to leave you no new worlds to conquer.[4] Please find enclosed Five Pounds, a mean little mite toward *your* Belgian beneficence—I mean your Franco American. And also find 2 acknowledgments of your own fine bounty here—excellent local causes each of them, so that I boldly plumped to each half the sum you last nobly sent me.[5] Ever so many of the utterly stranded & denuded are being housed, clothed, fed, companioned & "put up with" in this immediate neighbourhood—with Crosby Hall, transplanted to our riverside, as their magnificent "reading-room" & place of reunion. The Chelsea Arts Club benevolence also seemed to me well worthy of your help. I rub my eyes over my "audition" at the Institut, & am afraid I even not a little stop my ears. Je vous embrasse bien & am your all-devoted

Henry James

1. Lubbock went over to Paris at the beginning of December for a brief visit with EW.

2. Paris.

3. That is, 25 November.

4. At the end of October the influx of Belgian refugees displaced by the battle at Ypres necessitated the founding of a relief organization by EW's French friends—the Foyer Franco-Belge; EW organized the American Hostels for Refugees to furnish a wide variety of succor.

5. See letter of 9 November 1914.

Ça ... même: It does affect me—all the same; *ces messieurs:* those gentlemen; *Je ... bien:* I send you a warm embrace

> 21 Carlyle Mansions
> Cheyne Walk, S.W.
> 1 December 1914

Dearest Edith.

Walter offers me kindly to carry you any word,[1] & I don't want him to go empty-handed—though verily only the poor shrunken sediment of me is practically left after the overwhleming & écrasant effect of listening to him on the subject of the transcendent high pitch of Berlin.[2] I kick myself for being so flattened out by it, & ask myself moreover why I should feel it in any degree as a revelation, when it consists really of nothing but what one has been constantly saying to one's self—one's mind's eye perpetually blinking at it as presumably the case—all these weeks & weeks. It's the personal note of testimony that has caused it to knock me up—what has permitted this being the nature & degree of my unspeakable & abysmal sensibility where "our cause" is concerned, & the fantastic force, the prodigious passion, with which my affections are engaged in it. They grow more & more so—& my soul is in the whole connection one huge sore ache. That makes me dodge lurid lights when I ought doubtless but personally to glare back at them—as under the effect of many of my impressions here I frequently do—or almost! For the moment I am quite floored—but I suppose I shall after a while pick myself up. I dare say, for that matter, that I am down pretty often —for I find I am constantly picking myself up. So even this time I don't really despair. About Belgium Walter was withal so admirably & unspeakably interesting—if the word be not mean for the scale of such tragedy—which you'll have from him all for yourself. If I don't call his Berlin simply interesting & have done with it, that's because the very faculty of attention is so overstrained by it as to hurt. This takes you all my love. I have got back to trying to work—on one of three books begun & abandoned.[3] I have been lately attempting a go at one abandoned—at the end of some "30,000 words"—15 years ago, & fished out of the depths of an old drawer at Lamb House (I sent Miss Bosanquet down to hunt it up), as perhaps offering a certain defiance of subject to the law by which most things now perish in the public blight. This does seem to kind of intrinsically resist—& I have hopes. But I must rally now before getting back to it. So pray for me that I do, & invite dear Walter to kneel by my side & believe your faithfully fond

Henry James

1. Berry joined EW's war relief work in Paris.

2. EW wrote of Berry's report (in a letter of 20 December 1914 to Mary Berenson): "What struck him most was the mass of fresh unused soldiers in every town he went to, & the streams & streams of military trains carrying them *westward* at the very moment when Russia was announcing that German army corps were being transferred to the Eastern front. He was depressed, also, by the undoubted fact that the whole of Germany believes, as one man, the war to have been forced upon it by English ambitions. He thinks it a universally popular war. . . . His account of Belgium was harrowing. . . ." (*EW Letters*, 344).

3. *The Sense of the Past* (see letter of 9 November 1914); *The Ivory Tower* (about one-third finished—see *Comp. Notes*, 466–501) and probably the London Town book for Macmillan (see *Comp. Notes*, 273–80) were the others.

écrasant: crushing

Walmer Castle, Kent
16[, 17] January 1914 [i.e., 1915]

Dearest Edith.

It's too disgusting the way I've not written you—& explanations (if *you* ever required any!) ought to fail me, I suppose, when I've been capable, in the way of an affirmation of my existence, of such an exploit as this—coming down here to spend the week-end with the Prime Minister (& his, ma foi, very agreeable daughter Violet—also, I believe, three or four other persons; the great Winston, I gather, being expected tomorrow).[1] I arrived but an hour ago & have sought retirement till dinner time; so that my only interesting impression as yet is that of having had my tea with Miss Asquith & a mere comparse or two. My point is that you are meanwhile not to imagine that I have conversation to lavish on such as these while withholding it from your adored self. I lavish as little as possible these days & quite never in my one sustained go from Saturday to Monday. I only thought I would cut this particular caper, on the opportunity being very pleasantly pressed upon me, & Frederick[2] spared to see me through, by the chance of some sort of historic or distinguished, of informational or impressional interest in it; the probable failure of which, dreadful cynical pessimistic Mr. J. that I am, I seem already to descry. Your bounties have culminated for me in your blest release of Frederick for these next few weeks; I won't deny that he has become the mainstay of my existence & the apple of my eye. Without him I could never have come here—but fortunately I shall never wish to come again (I am devoutly grateful to you for this extension of his leave—& scarcely less so to the authorities who have curbed their immediate appetite for the young Ormond.)[3] Sometimes I let myself think that I form some sort of approximate image of your great life—& then again I fall back in conscious diminutive impotence; though your vignette of Percy [Lubbock] & you Darby & Joaning it over the evening fire does give me material to work on. Howard [Sturgis] tells me Percy knits—Howard, who blessedly lunched with me yesterday, even described to me the range & variety of Percy's stitches, with illustrative manipulation, as only Howard can. (He seemed extraordinarily well & young & loveable—he has regained much ground.)[4] Whatever other losses his little visits to the "sponging-house"[5] que vous savez may represent. (I never knew what a sponging-house was—but now I grasp the type!) I wish I had some richer effluence from my own life to blow across to you—but it's an intensely selective & simplified life & doesn't break up into specimen morsels. I go on, even without your aids—your aides de camp I mean, great *generalissima* that you are; & to go on is, I find, rather a grand achievement. London is more & more muffled & gathered up. Dick Norton who was lately over from the front for a few days (& who by the way is really magnificent, both as to what he is & as to what he does)[6] noted to me the great change, the increase of stress &c since some weeks before. I find one's only way of life, or *my* only possible one at least, is to take the day in itself, each one as it comes, & treat it as an individual actuality, disconnecting it, living only *in* it, thinking only *of* it, & not recognising any establishment over the way—by which I mean the obscure morrow.

Jan. 17th   I had to break off yesterday to dress for dinner & have had no free moment till now at the same hour. It has been a bright cold day, & this thick-walled machicolated old fortress (it has embrasures 20 feet deep) is virtually a great Terrasse over the channel, where it's a thrill to see the ships of old England going about their business in extraordinary numbers. The sentiment the place makes one entertain in every way for old England is of the most acutely sympathetic, & the good kind friendly easy Asquith, with the curtain of public affairs let thickly down behind him & the footlights entirely turned off in front, doesn't do anything to make it less worth having. It even survived in my breast a bitter cold motor-run this afternoon, round the Isle of Thanet, with him & Viola Tree![7] The car was practically open, but the friendly sight of all the swarming khaki on the roads made up for that. But here comes Frederick again to make me up. I bless you again for him & am with best love to Percy yours all devotedly

Henry James

1. HJ was a guest from 16 to 18 January at Walmer Castle, an old fortress near Deal, Kent, some five miles up the Channel Coast from Dover—an ancient seat of the warden of the Cinque Ports (see *Letters* 4, 734–35)—used in 1914–1915 by Herbert H. Asquith (1852–1928), prime minister from 1908 to 1916, as an informal conference site for government and military leaders. Winston Churchill (1874–1965), then 1st lord of the Admiralty, was one of the guests. Asquith's daughter Violet (1887–1969) married Maurice Bonham Carter (1880–1960), her father's private secretary from 1910 to 1916.

2. Noakes's replacement.

3. Perhaps Rose-Marie, the daughter of Mme Violet Ormond; see letter 20 October 1914.

4. Sturgis had suffered from extreme depression caused by the outbreak of the war.

5. A house kept by a bailiff or a sheriff's officer, formerly in regular use as a place of preliminary confinement for debtors.

6. As director of the American Volunteer Motor-Ambulance Corps.

7. Viola Tree (1884–1938), actress and singer, eldest daughter of Beerbohm Tree.

ma foi: my word; *comparse:* supernumerary; *que . . . savez:* that you know

> Grand Hôtel du Coq Hardi
> Verdun, Meuse
> 28 February 1915

Dearest Cher Maître,

After nearly six months at the same job I felt a yearning to get away for a few days, & also a great desire to find out what was really wanted in some of the hospitals near the front, from which such lamentable tales have reached us.

It took a good deal of démarching and countermarching to get a laissez-passer, for it has always been a great deal more difficult to go East than North, & especially so, these last weeks, on account of the "spies and espions" (as White called them), & also of the movements of troops, more recently. However, thanks to Paul and to Mr. Cambon[1] (the Berlin one) I did, a day or two ago, get a splendid permesso, & immediately loaded up the motor with clothes & medicaments & dashed off from Paris with Walter [Berry] yesterday morning. We went first to Châlons s/ Marne, & it was extraordinary, not more than 4 hours from Paris, to find ourselves to all appearances completely in the war-zone. It is the big base of the Eastern army, & the streets swarm with soldiers & with military motors & ambulances. We went to see a hospital with 900 cases of typhoid, where *everything* was lacking—a depressing beginning, for even if I had emptied my motor-load into their laps it would have been a goutte d'eau in a desert. But I promised to report, & to try to come back with more supplies next week.

This morning we left Châlons & headed for Verdun. At Ste Menehould we had to get permission to go farther, as the Grand Quartier Général can't give it unless the local staff consents. First they said it was impossible—but the Captain had read one of my books, so he told the Colonel it was all right, & the Colonel said: "Very well—mais filez vite, for there is big fighting going on near by, & this afternoon the wounded are to be evacuated from the front, & we want no motors on the road."

About 15 Kmes farther we came to Clermont-en-Argonne, of which you have read—one of the most utterly ravaged places in this region. It looks exactly like Pompeii—I felt as if I must be going to lunch at the Hotel Diomède! Instead, we ate filet & fried potatoes in the kitchen of the Hospice where Soeur Rosnet, the wonderful Sister who stuck to the wounded when the Germans came, gave us a welcome proportioned to the things she needed for the new batch of wounded that she is expecting tonight.—Suddenly we heard the cannon roaring close by, & a woman rushed in to say that we could see the fighting from the back of a house across the street. We tore over & there, from a garden, we looked across the valley to a height about 5 miles away, where white puffs & scarlet flashes kept springing up all over the dark hillside. It was the hill above Vauquois, where there has been desperate fighting for two days. The Germans were firing from the top at the French trenches below (hidden from us by an intervening rise of the ground); & the French were assaulting, & their puffs & flashes were half way up the hill. And so we saw the reason there are to be so many wounded at Clermont tonight.

We went on to Verdun after lunch, stopping at Blercourt to see a touching little ambulance where the sick and nervously shattered are sent till they can be moved. Most of them are in the village church, four rows of beds down the nave, & when we went in the curé was just ringing the bell for vespers. Then he went & put on his vestments, & reappeared at the lighted altar with his acolyte, & incense began to float over the pale heads on the pillows, & the villagers came into the church, &, standing between the beds, sang a strange wailing thing that repeats at the end of every verse:

"Sauvez, sauvez la France,

Ne l'abandonnez pas!"—It was poignant.

To complete our sensations—I forgot to put the incident in its right place—we saw a column of soldiers marching along the road this morn-ing, coming toward us, between a handful of cavalry. Walter said: "Look at their coats! They're covered with mud!" And when they came nearer, we saw the coats were pale grey, & they were a hundred or so

German prisoners, fresh picked from that dark wood where we were to see the red flashes later in the day.

We got here about 4, & presented ourselves at the Citadel, where the officer who took our papers had read me too—wasn't it funny?—& turned out to be Henri de Jouvenel, the husband of Colette Willy!!![2] —He was very nice, but much amazed at my having succeeded in getting here. He said: "Vous êtes la première femme qui soit venue à Verdun"—& at the hospital they told me the same thing. The town is dead—nearly all the civil population evacuated, & the garrison, I suppose, in the trenches. The cannon booms continuously about 10 miles away. Tomorrow we go to Bar le Duc & then back to Châlons & home. I shall come again in a few days with lots of things, now that I know what is needed.

This reads like one of Mme Waddington's letters to Henrietta[3]—but I'm so awed by all I have seen that I can only prattle.—

I shall have to take this to Paris to post, as it takes 8 days for a letter to go from here. I thought my sensations de guerre might interest[4] even in this artless shape.

Your devoted
Edith

9 p.m., & the cannon still booming.

1. Bourget and Jules Cambon (1845–1935), who had been French ambassador to Berlin until the outbreak of war, when he became secretary-general of the Ministry of Foreign Affairs; EW carefully distinguishes him from his brother Paul, French ambassador to London.

2. Sidonie-Gabrielle Colette (1873–1954), French novelist, initially wrote in collaboration with Willy, pseudonym of her first husband, Henry Gauthier-Villars; Jouvenel was her second husband.

3. Mary King Waddington to her mother, Mrs. Charles King, and to her sister Henrietta—*Italian Letters of a Diplomat's Wife* (1905).

4. See HJ's interested response, letter of 5 March 1915.

Cher Maître: Dear Master; *démarch*ing: following procedures (French noun with English gerund ending); *laissez-passer:* pass; *espions:* spies; *permesso:* permit; *goutte d'eau:* drop of water; *mais . . . vite:* but get going quickly; *Sauvez . . . pas:* Save,

save France, / Do not abandon her; *Vous . . . Verdun:* You are the first woman who has come to Verdun; *sensations de guerre:* war impressions

21 Carlyle Mansions
Cheyne Walk, S.W.
5 March 1915

Dearest Edith.

How can I welcome & applaud enough your splendid thrilling letter[1]—in which though it gives me your whole spectacle & impression as unspeakably portentous I find you & Walter somehow of the very same heroic *taille* of whatever it was that gave the rest at the monstrous maximum. I unutterably envy you these sights & suffered assaults of the *maxima*—condemned as I am by doddering age & "mean" infirmity to the poor mesquins *minima*, when really to find myself in closer touch would so fearfully interest & inspire & overwhelm me (as one wants to be overwhelmed). However, since my ignoble portion is what it is, the next best thing is to heap you & Walter on the altar of sacrifice & gloat over *your* overwhelmedness & demand of you to serve me still more & more of it. On this I even insist, now that I have tasted of your state & your substance—for your impression is rendered in a degree so vivid & touching that it all (especially those vespers in the church with the tragic beds in the aisles) wrings tears from my aged eyes. What a hungry *luxury* to be able to come back with things & give them then & there straight into the aching voids: do it, *do* it, my blest Edith, for all you're worth: rather, rather—"sauvez, sauvez la France!" Ah, je la sauverais bien, moi, if I hadn't been ruined myself too soon! Tell Walter, please, that I know I owe him acknowledgment of an exquisite golden letter received from him too many weeks ago—but that if he will now only have a *few* days, or such like, more patience with me! Our case so strikes at certain enfeebled old roots—! Ce-que-c'est for you evidently to find yourself in these adventures, like Ouida[2] "the favourite reading of the military"! Well, as I say, *do* keep in touch with your public! I stupidly forgot to tell Frederick to tell you not to dream of returning me those £6.0.0 (all he wd. take), but to regard them as the contribution I was really then in the very nick of sending to your Belges![3] So I *wired* you a day or two [ago] to that effect, after too much wool-gathering; & to anticipate absolutely any restitution. It made it so *easy* a sending. Well then, à bientôt—Oliver shamelessly (not asks, but) *howls* for more.[4] Yours all devotedlier than ever

Henry James

1. Letter of 28 February 1915.
2. "Ouida," pen name of British novelist Maria Louisa Ramé (1839–1908) —later Louise de la Ramée—whom HJ knew slightly.
3. HJ had sent Frederic, Noakes's replacement, back to EW in Paris. She returned the £6; see letter of 11 March 1915.
4. See end of chap. 2 of the novel *The Adventures of Oliver Twist* (1838) by Charles Dickens (1812–1870).

taille: stature; *mesquins:* shabby; *je . . . moi: I* would certainly save her; *Ce-que-c'est:* What it means; *à bientôt:* see you soon

53, rue de Varenne
11 March [1915]

Cherest Maître,
    Your letter of the 5th, which I found here on my return last night, demands such moving incidents that the chronicle I have to send this time is not à la hauteur. The second trip was like all sequels—except that it certainly wasn't a mistake! But it was less high in colour than the first adventure, & resulted in several disappointments, as well as in some interesting moments—indeed, once within the military zone *every* moment is interesting.
    We left 5 days ago & went straight to Verdun in a bitter rain, dropping bundles of shirts & boxes of fresh eggs & bags of oranges at the various ambulances I told you of. At Verdun we looked up our médecin en chef, who had promised to take us to see an ambulance on the first line, in the Hauts de Meuse, but, alas, it had been moved nearer to Les Eparges, where there was such hard fighting that we couldn't be allowed to go. However, thanks to a lucky laissez-passer we *did* get, with him & the Director of the Service de Santé of that region, to an ambulance

on the Meuse, within about 7 Kmes of Les Eparges—a hamlet plunged to the eaves in mud, where beds had been rigged up in two or three little houses, a primitive operating-room installed, &c. Picture this all under a white winter sky, driving great flurries of snow across the mud-&-cinder-coloured landscape, with the steel-cold Meuse winding between beaten poplars—Cook standing with Her[1] in a knot of mud-coated military motors & artillery horses, soldiers coming & going, cavalrymen riding up with messages, poor bandaged creatures in rag-bag clothes leaning in the doorways, & always, over us & about us, the boom, boom, boom of the guns on the grey heights to the east. It was Winter War to the fullest, just in that little insignificant corner of the immense affair! And those big summing-up impressions meet one at every turn. I shall never forget the 15 mile run from Verdun to that particular ambulance, across a snow-covered rolling country sweeping up to the white sky, with no one in sight but now & then a cavalry patrol with a blown cloak struggling along against the wind.

Then we went to another village on the west bank of the Meuse, where there is a colony of *1500* "éclopés"[2] waiting to pick up strength enough to be shipped on to the next dépôt d'éclopés in the rear. Here also the church—a big dreary disaffected one—is full to the doors, but it is not a hospital but a human stable. The poor devils sleep on straw, in queer little compartments made of plaited straw screens, in each of which compartments a dozen or so are crammed, in their trench clothes (no undressing possible)—with nothing that I could see to be thankful for but the fact that they were out of the mud, & in a sort of fetid stable-heat. It was *awful*—and the Directeur du Service de Santé was so complacent!

In other places, of course, we saw things better done—but for a Horror-of-War picture, that one won't soon be superseded. At least I hope not!

I had everywhere le meilleur accueil from the Drs. & the Service de Santé, & came back with a long list of wants. We had hoped to get to Nancy & Gerbevillers [*sic*], but at Ligny en Barrois we came across a sulky commandant who kept us waiting 4 hours & then refused the permit—so we had to turn back to Châlons! We got there at about 7 p.m., on the coldest day imaginable, "only to learn" that *every* hotel, even to the lowest of the "garnis," was absolutely full. We applied for a permit to go on to Epernay (20 Kmes), but were politely éconduits, as motors can't circulate in the war zone après la tombée de la nuit. We went back to the hotel where we were known, & the land-lady told us she had two rooms, requisitioned by the Grand Quartier General, which had not been called for that night, & which we might get. In the restaurant, where we went to dine before making our appeal to the Quartier Général, we met our friend Jean Louis Vaudoyer,[3] who is attached to the Q. G.—He gave us little hope, but said we could go & try! So after dinner we got into the motor again & went through the pitch black icy streets to the Hotel de Ville, where I sent in my papers & my appeal. A polite officer came out, & was désolé—but it was against the rules! I tried to harrow him, but in vain. Finally he suggested giving us a permit to go back to Paris—a 7 hours' run on a dark night, with the strong probability of being turned back at the first railway crossing, as experience had convinced us that hardly any of the sentinels can read!! —We went back to the motor, & Vaudoyer very kindly suggested that we might camp for the night in a little flat he has in a maison bourgeoise, which he uses only in the day time—*if* we found the landlady still up, or could wake her! He couldn't go with us, as he was on duty, & it was past the hour (9.30) when one is allowed to be in the streets. And as we stood in the pitch-blackness of the deserted street, & he whispered: "C'est au no. 9, rue de l'Arquebuse—si l'on vous arrête, le mot est 'Jéna,'" I suddenly refused to believe that *any* of it was true, or happening to *me*, or that a nice boy who dines with me & sends me chocolates for Nouvel An, was whispering a *pass-word* to me, & adding: "Quand vous le dites au chauffeur, prenez garde qu'une sentinelle ne vous entende pas"—It was no use trying to keep up the pretense of reality any longer!

Luckily his rooms *were* real, & the landlady was awake, & made fires—but Cook slept in the motor, wrapped in Red Cross dressing-gowns & pillowed on gauze pads!—And so we got through the night —& yesterday morning, when we left for Paris, we understood why Châlons was so crowded, for the cannon was crashing uninterruptedly, & seemingly much nearer than usual, & troops were streaming through the town in the direction of Suippes in a long unbroken train—the biggest lot of them we had yet seen.

We lunched at Meaux, & went to see the Bishop, who took us over his hospital, & a splendid dépôt d'éclopés he has organized, with library, games, douches, & all kinds of blessings—& here I am again, & must go back to work instead of telling you more adventures. I hope to get off again in 10 days—but one can't be sure of permits nowadays,

> Yours devoted
> Edith

No, no, you must keep the £6 for English needs—bless you![4]

1. EW's automobile.
2. In *Fighting France* (1915) EW defines *éclopés* (lit. "lame") as "the unwounded but battered, shattered, frostbitten, deafened and half-paralyzed wreckage of the awful struggle" (49–50).
3. Vaudoyer (1883–1963), a young French writer whom EW knew in Paris.
4. See end of letter of 5 March 1915.

à la hauteur: up to the mark; *médecin en chef:* head doctor; *laissez-passer:* pass; *Service de Santé:* Health Service; *le ... accueil:* the best welcome; *garnis:* furnished; *éconduits:* shown out; *après ... nuit:* after nightfall; *désolé:* dreadfully sorry; *maison bourgeoise:* a substantial residence that lets apartments; *C'est ... Jéna:* It's at no. 9 Arquebuse Street—if you are stopped, the word is 'Jéna.' "; *Nouvel An;* New Year's; *Quand ... pas:* When you tell it to the chauffeur, be careful that a sentinel doesn't hear you; *douches:* showers

[DICTATED]   21 Carlyle Mansions
                                                   Cheyne Walk, S.W.
                                                   23 [–24] March 1915

Chère Madame et Confrère!

Don't imagine for a moment that I don't feel the full horror of my having had to wait till now, when I can avail myself of this aid,[1] to acknowledge, as the poor pale pettifogging term has it, the receipt from you of inexpressibly splendid bounties. I won't attempt to explain or expatiate—about this abject failure of utterance: the idea of explaining anything to *you* in these days, or of any expatiation that isn't exclusively that of your own genius upon your own adventures and impressions! I think *the* reason why I have been so baffled, in a word, is that all my powers of being anything else have gone to living upon your two magnificent letters, the one from Verdun, and the one after your second visit there;[2] which gave me matter of experience and appropriation to which I have done the fullest honour. Your whole record is sublime, and the interest and the beauty and the terror of it all have again and again called me back to it. I have ventured to share it, for the good of the cause and the glory of the connection (mine), with two or three select others—this I candidly confess to you, one of whom was dear Howard [Sturgis], absolutely as dear as ever through everything, and whom I all but reduced to floods of tears, tears of understanding and sympathy. I know them at last, your incomparable pages, by heart—and thus it is really that I feel qualified to speak to you of them. With the two sublimities in question, or between them, came of course also the couple of other favours, enclosing me, pressing back upon me, my attempted contribution to your Paris labour: to which perversity I have had to bow my head. I was very sorry to be so forced, but even while cursing and gnashing my teeth I got your post-office order cashed, and the money *is*, God knows, assistingly spendable here! Another pang was your mention of Jean du Breuil's death,[3] with its bearing on poor dear B[essie] L[odge]'s history. It can't have been sweet having to write that letter to her—any more than there can be any great other douceur in her life now! I didn't know him, had never seen him; but your account of the admirable manner of his end makes one feel that one would like even to have just beheld him. We are in the midst, the very midst, of histories of that sort, miserable and terrible, here too: the Neuve Chapelle business,[4] from a strange, in the sense of being a pretty false, glamour at first flung about which we are gradually recovering, seems to have taken a hideous toll of officers, and other distressing legends (legends of mistake and confusion) are somehow overgrowing it too. But painful particulars are not what I want to give you—of anything; you are up to your neck in your own, and I had much rather pick my steps to the clear places, so far as there be any such! I continue to try and keep my own existence one, so far as I may—a place clear of the last accablement, I mean; apparently what it comes to is that it's "full up" with the last but one.

Wednesday, 24th. I had to break this off yesterday—and it was time, apparently, with the rather dreary note I was sounding; though I don't know that I have a very larky one to go on with to-day—save so far as the taking of the big Austrian fortress, which I can neither write nor pronounce, makes one a little soar and sing. This seems really to represent something, but how much I put forth not the slightest pretension to measure. In fact I think I am not measuring anything whatever just now, and not pretending to—I find myself, much more, quite consentingly dumb in the presence of the boundless enormity; and when I wish to give myself the best possible account of this state of mind I call it the pious attitude of waiting. Verily there is much to wait for—but there I am at it again, and should blush to offer you, in the midst of what I believe to be your more grandly attuned state, such a pale apology for a living faith. Probably all that's the matter with one is one's vicious propensity to go on feeling more and more, instead of less and less— which would be so infinitely more convenient; for the former course puts one really quite out of relation to almost everybody else and causes one to circle helplessly round outer social edges like a kind of prowling pariah. However, I try to be as stupid as I can, and perhaps it was an effort in that direction that led me to lunch yesterday with Mrs. Maguire, along with Mrs. John Astor and the Gifford Pinchots,[5] both of whom I find quite "real people," and animated with a flame (oh how I hug the flame when I find it burn really clear!) of which her beautiful hair seemed to give me the note. And then there was an interesting gentleman who repeated to me his son's (an officer in the Guards) terrific account of that extraordinary battle of the "brickfields," which the British, the said Guards, I believe, almost altogether, sprang upon the enemy some months ago and which I but imperfectly grasped at the time. This worthy's (a very nice vivid veracious worthy I found him) reproduction of his young man's report of the overwhelming fury of the onset, preceded by a quarter of an hour of cannonade not intermitted for a single second and that was exactly like the playing, all along the line, of a colossal hose of fire—this did me a kind of unholy hideous good; especially the part about the *instantaneous* rush in of the infantry on the quarter of an hour ending to the second, with the huge hose deflected for them to go and spending itself during the next minutes upon the immediate near ground. It appears to have been an absolute massacre for our advance, the Germans surprised, fleeing, hiding terrified in every corner and cavity offered by the big bricky place; it overwhelmed and annihilated, to an appalling tune of numbers, while our losses were "comparatively" small and the big bricky place has never again been filched from us. I declare it quite wreathes me in smiles again—"comparatively"—to repeat it to you; so that perhaps I *shall* under the recovery of glow, be able to face the privilege just telephoned at me by Mary Hunter: that of assisting this afternoon at a vocal recital by a Belgian baritone, patronised and presided over by Réjane,[6] and with the Prince Victor Napoleon and Princess Clémentine[7] due at 5.30 sharp; which performance narrates with premeditated art, and an effect guaranteed by Réjane to drown us all in tears, the manner in which he *sang* himself out of captivity in Germany, bribing his captors by the beauty of his gift, and from one acute danger of being hung or shot for a spy to another, to get on, to go free, a little further and further, till he at last escaped altogether. He has arranged the story as a musical monologue, I believe; thirty people are to be present, and hang it if I don't go, after all, to prove to you that, like vous autres, I *am*, we all are, in tune and à la hauteur.

All the while, with this, I am not expressing my deep appreciation of your generous remarks about again placing Frederick at my disposition. I am doing perfectly well in these conditions without a servant; my life is so simplified that all acuteness of need has been abated; in short I manage—and it is of course fortunate, inasmuch as the question would otherwise not be at all practically soluble. No young man of military age would I for a moment consider—and in fact there *are* none about, putting aside the physically inapt (for the Army)—and these are kept tight hold of by those who can use them. Small boys and aged men are alone available—but the matter has in short not the least importance. The thing that most assuages me continues to be dealing with the wounded in such scant measure as I may; such, e.g., as my having turned into Victoria Station, yesterday afternoon, to buy an evening paper and there been so struck with the bad lameness of a poor hobbling khaki convalescent that I inquired of him to such sympathetic effect that, by what I can make out, I must have committed myself to the support of him for the remainder of his days—a trifle on account having sealed the compact on the spot. It all helps, however—helps *me*; which is so much what I do it for. Let it help *you* by ricochet, even a little too. And if it can do the same just a tiny trifle for W[alter] B. also, en attendant that I do really grapple with him, the case will really be a most fortunate one.

There's another thing—but it haunts me too much, positively, for me to be able to touch on it. If this weren't so I should mention how it breaks my heart to have learnt from you that W. M. F[ullerton] hasn't done well in America and is coming back on that collapse. This is quite a hideous little pang, leaving one afresh as it does, bang up against that exquisite art in him of not bringing it off to which his treasure of experience and intelligence, of accomplishment, talent, ambition, charm, everything, so inimitably contributes. If he comes through London, as I don't see but that he must, I do hope he won't have the infamy to pass without letting me know. But when a person is capable of *such* things—! At any rate good-bye for now, and believe me less gracelessly and faithlessly than you might well your would-be so decent old

Henry James

1. Dictating to a typist.

2. See letters of 28 February and 11 March 1915. The chapter "In Argonne" of EW's *Fighting France* does not distinguish between these two Verdun sorties but presents them as a single experience.

3. Lieutenant Jean du Breuil de Saint-Germain, a distinguished cavalry officer, sociologist and traveler, killed in action on 22 February 1915 near Arras. See EW's obituary essay in the *Revue Hebdomadaire* of 8 May 1915.

4. Field Marshal Sir John French decided to attack the small German salient into the British front line at the village of Neuve-Chapelle, some ten miles west of Lille, on 10 March—without French or Belgian support. General Douglas Haig's 1st Army captured the village but was unable to gain the Aubers ridge that dominates the plain leading to Lille. The attack was stalled by insufficient planning for bringing up reserves and ineffective communication between infantry and artillery; the Germans were able then to regroup, reenforce their troops, and halt any further British progress. Haig withdrew his troops on 14 March. It was an ill-advised venture and a costly learning experience for the British.

5. Ava Lowle Willing (1870–1958) in 1891 became the first wife of John Jacob Astor IV (1864–1912). Gifford Pinchot (1865–1946) was head of the National Conservation Commission and founder of the Yale School of Forestry.

6. Gabrielle Charlotte Réjane (1856–1920), a leading French comedienne between 1880 and 1915.

7. The Belgian Prince Victor Napoleon (1862–1926), grandson of Napoleon I's youngest brother and the recognized Bonapartist pretender since 1891, in 1910 married Princess Clémentine (1872–1955), third daughter of King Leopold II of Belgium.

douceur: sweetness; *accablement:* encumbrance; *vous autres:* the rest of you; *à la hauteur:* up to snuff; *en attendant:* until the time

53, rue de Varenne
26 March [1915]

Dearest Cher Maître,

I never expected such a rich reward for a letter without a battle in it! Your chronicle of the Brickfield[1] is so magnificent that the only response I can make is to send you two articles from the Revue des Deux Mondes, called "Dixmude,"[2] which may have escaped you, & which seem to me the one bit of good literature (except our letters!) that the war has produced.

Yes—I suffer as you do from the inability to communicate with people who are not vibrating to tune. They are far fewer here, however, than in London, I imagine. Even Walter [Berry] vibrated—though he preferred to do it at the Ritz! In fact, it's not a little rift but a little ritz that's between us just now—for I can't stand that scene of khaki & champagne. The British officer here isn't as sympathetic as in the brickfield.

Robert Norton was here for two days last week, & I heard from him what a ghastly blunder Neuve Chapelle was. One rather understands why the French think that the English are heroes, but not professional "militaires." The Dardanelles attack looks a good deal like another muddle, & I heard it criticized as such here on the first day, when we all thought they were going to week-end at Byzantium!

We jog on as usual meanwhile, & people are waking up a little to the small humours of the hour. The Balkanics are called "La Triple

Attente," & Barrès "Le Littérateur du Territoire"—in remembrance of Thiers' title, "Le Libérateur du &c."—[3]

I haven't heard yet from my poor Bessy [*sic*] [Lodge], but I had the other day a letter from Jean du Breuil's best friend, the Comte de Séguier,[4] which seems to me one of the noblest things I ever read. Séguier is a captain of artillery, in a very important post at the front.

Another great friend of mine, Georges Rodier, whom you have very probably seen in London, revealed himself as having all kinds of unsuspected qualities when war broke out, hired de ses deniers a "summer hotel" in Brittany, turned it into a Red Cross hospital, & has devoted himself to the work uninterruptedly since September. About six weeks ago he caught an infectious fever there, followed by pneumonia, was moved up to Paris last week, & has had another relapse. So I don't feel particularly gay just now!

I had a wonderful letter from Howard as the result of meeting you at the great Rhoda's![5] How I wish we could compare notes over him, & things in general. I must come & see you soon.

Je vous embrasse tendrement,
  Edith

1. See letter of 23 March 1915.
2. "Dixmude—A Chapter in the History of the Fusiliers-Marins" in the *Revue* of 1 and 15 March by the Breton writer Charles Le Goffic (1863–1932) tells of the fierce battle for the Belgian city Dixmude in the autumn of 1914; in spite of the vigorous defense by the marines under Admiral Ronarc'h and a Belgian brigade, Dixmude fell to the Germans on 11 November.
3. "The Triple Expectation," a pun on La Triple Entente, an informal understanding among Britain, France, and Russia; Louis Adolphe Thiers (1797–1877), president of France, 1871–1873; Maurice Barrès (1862–1923), French novelist and politician.
4. See app. C.
5. Rhoda Broughton (1840–1920), popular Victorian novelist whom HJ had known since the mid-seventies.

de ses deniers: with his (own) money; *Je ... tendrement:* I embrace you tenderly

21 Carlyle Mansions
Cheyne Walk, S.W.
3 April 1915

Dearest Edith.

Bounties unacknowledged & unmeasured continue to flow in from you, for this a.m., after your beautiful letter enclosing the copy of M. de Séguier's so extraordinarily fine & touching one, arrive your 2 livraisons of the Revue containing the Dixmude of which you wrote me.[1] It is quite heartbreakingly noble of you to find initiative for the rendering & the remembering of such services & such assurances, for I myself gaze at almost *any* display of initiative as I should stare at a passing charge of cavalry down the Brompton Road—where we haven't come to that yet, though we may for one reason & another indeed soon have to. One is surrounded in fact here with more affirmations of energy than you might gather from some of the accounts of matters that appear in the *Times*, & yet the paralysis of my own power to do anything but increasingly & inordinately *feel*, feel in a way to make communication with almost all others impossible, they living & thinking in such different terms,—& yet that paralysis, dis-je, more & more swallows up everything but the sore & sterile & unresting imagination. I can't proceed upon it after your sublime fashions—& in fact its waking life is a practical destruction of every other sort, which is why I call it sterile. But the extent, all the same, to which one will have inwardly & darkly & drearily & dreadfully lived!—with those victims of nervous horror in the ambulance-church, the little chanting country church of the deadly serried beds of your Verdun letter,[2] & those others, the lacerated & untended in the "fetid stable-heat" of the other place & the second letter[3]—all of whom live *with* me & haunt & "inhibit" me. And so does your friend du Breuil, & *his* friend your admirable correspondent (in what a nobleness of blest adequacy of expression *their* feeling finds relief!)—& this in spite of my having neither known nor seen either of them; Séguier creating in one to positive sickness the personal pang about your friend & his, & his letter making me feel the horror it does himself even as if my affection had something at stake in that. But I don't know why I treat you thus to the detail of one's perpetually renewed waste. You will have plenty of detail of your own, little waste as I see you allowing yourself.—I haven't yet had the hour of reading your Dixmudes, which I am momentarily reserving, under some other pressure, but they shall not miss my fond care—so little has any face of the nightmare been reflected for me in any form of beauty as yet;—your Verdun letters excepted. This keeps making mere blue-books & yellow-books & rapports the only reading that isn't, or hasn't been, below the level; through their not pretending to express, but only giving one the material. As it happens, when your Revue came I was reading Georges Ohnet[4] & one of the 3 fascicules of his Bourgeois de Paris that have alone, as yet, turned up here!—& reading him, ma foi, with deep submission to his spell! Funny enough to be redevable at this time of day to that genius, who has come down from the cross where poor vanquished Jules Lemaître long ago nailed him up,[5] as if to work fresh miracles, dancing for it on Jules's very grave. But he is in fact extraordinarily vivid & candid & amusing, with the force of an angry little hunchback & a perfect & quite gratifying vulgarity of passion; also, probably, with a perfect enormity of *vente*—in which one takes pleasure.—Easter has operated to clear London in something like the fine old way—we would really seem to stick so much to our fine old ways. I don't truly know what to make of some of them—& yet don't let yourself suppose from some of such appearances that the stiffness & toughness of the country isn't on the whole deeper than anything else. Such at least is my own indefeasible conviction—or impression. It's the queerest of peoples—with its merits & defects so extraordinarily parts of each other; its wantonness of refusals—in some of these present ways—such a part of its attachment to freedom, of the individualism which makes its force that of a collection of individuals & its voluntaryism of such a strong quality. But it won't be the defects, it will be the merits, I believe, that will have the last word. Strange that the country should need a still bigger convulsion—for itself; it does, however, & it will get it—& will act under it. France has had hers in the form of invasion—& I don't know of what form ours will yet have to be. But it will come—& then *we* shall; damp & dense, but not vicious, not vicious *enough*, & immensely capable if we can once get *dry*. Voilà that *I* am, however; yet with it so yours

H.J.

1. See letter of 26 March 1915.
2. See letter of 28 February 1915.

3. See letter of 11 March 1915. For a fuller account, see *Fighting France*, 78–80.

4. The *Journal d'un bourgeois de Paris* by Georges Ohnet (1848–1918), French novelist and playwright, was a series of fascicles published at irregular intervals (originally promised to be once a fortnight) beginning in the autumn of 1914; it offered a running commentary on the progress of the war, supported by excerpts from private journals, eyewitness accounts, letters, etc.

5. Lemaître had published a scathing review of Ohnet in the *Revue Politique et Littéraire (Revue Bleue)* of 27 June 1885.

livraisons: installments; *dis-je:* I say; *ma foi:* my goodness; *redevable:* indebted; *vente:* sales; *Voilà:* You see

Grand Hotel
Place Stanislas
Nancy
14 [–15] May 1915

Dearest Cher Maître,

I don't dare write you except when I'm scaling heights or exploring trenches, & as I'm yearning for news of you I've asked—& obtained —a permit for the front in Lorraine & the Vosges.—Walter [Berry] & I started out three days ago, first going to Châlons, & then through the ravaged & wiped-out-towns of Sermaize-les-bains, Pargny, & several others, to Commercy, where the cannon was thundering. But life seemed fairly normal. Then we came on here the day before yesterday, armed with a letter for General Humbert, in command of the army of Lorraine. As luck would have it, I found out just as I was leaving Paris that a great friend of mine, Raymond Recouly,[1] is one of his aides-de-camp, so we were received with the greatest kindness, & have almost been allowed to play in the Boche trenches. Yesterday we were to see the incredibly destroyed Gerbéviller,[2] where we spent a very interesting hour with M. Liégeay, who acted as mayor during the German invasion, & who took us over the lamentable ruins of what must have been his once charming old house, with a terraced garden overhanging the valley, & told us the tale of his three days in his cellar, with wife & other womenkind, their house blazing above their heads, & the Germans shooting & torturing people all through the town—the details are fantastic—but I must hurry on to our trip today. We lunched at the Quartier Générale with Genl Humbert & his staff, & then started in an army motor with Recouly to make the tour of the Grand Couronné de Nancy, ending up at Mousson & Pont à Mousson, within about a mile of the German trenches, which were in full view. Very few people have been allowed to go to Mousson, as it is bombarded almost daily, & only last Friday a number of people were killed there. Luckily today they didn't happen to be firing, so we got there. We went to the Military Hospital, which lies on the Moselle, directly under the Bois le Prêtre, where there has been very violent fighting these last days, & from which the Germans were driven (to the next ridge) only the night before last.

We could see, from the garden of the Hospital (which is all ploughed up with shells) the deadly slope they have left, & all the other ridges from which they still rake the town. But far more interesting is Mousson, a ruined castle & hamlet on a sharp cone (like an Italian hill-town) high above the river. We could only motor up about a third of the way, for beyond that the motor wd have been seen, & the slope is swept by German batteries. From there we walked to the top, & Recouly would not even let us stop to look at the view lest we shd be reperés. Once on top we were safe in the lee of the castle, & creeping around it we climbed through a series of wattled trenches to the chapel on the summit, which is an artillery observation post. The view is magnificent, & in clear weather Metz is clearly visible, about 18 miles off.—Today was cloudy, & we could just make it out in a blur. Near by, just across the valley, was the hill called "Le Yon," trenched to the top & facing the hills held by the enemy. Below the Yon, & between it & Pont à Mousson, the whole river valley up to the gates of Pont à Mousson, almost, is held by the Germans also. We looked across with glasses at the farm of Belair, which is hardly a mile from where we were, & where they are strongly planted. In trying to show me something, Walter put his hand (not his arm, only *his hand*) through the window of the chapel, & instantly one of the artillery officers pulled him back & said: "Prenez garde, Monsieur. On pourrait vous voir!" & you may imagine the sense it gave us of almost feeling their breath in our faces. Walter, who has fewer thrills than course through my ardent old bones, pretends he didn't feel them as near as at Vauquois, where we saw the flame of their guns in that Dantean wood, but the fact of having to *hide* from their invisible eyes gave me an even acuter sense of being in the very gates of Hell.

May 15   Today Recouly is taking us off again to see other military scenes inaccessible to the civilian. When Barrès was here about 10 days ago Recouly took him over the same ground, but they were unable to get to Pt à Mousson, as it was being bombarded; so we were in luck yesterday.—And now I must break off to go about some Red Cross business in Nancy.

I'm going over to see you next month if I can possibly get away.[3]

Your devotedest
     Edith

We go on from here all through the Vosges to Belfort, then home.

1. Cosmopolitan journalist, fourteen years EW's junior.
2. See letter of 11 March 1915, and "In Lorraine and the Vosges," *Fighting France.*
3. EW did not get over to England until October 1915.

repérés: spotted; *Prenez . . . voir:* Be careful, Sir. You might be seen!

21 Carlyle Mansions
Cheyne Walk, S.W.
23 May 1915

Dearest Edith.

In what a serried row you & Walter, & I suppose Cook, do seem to advance,[1] what wondrous wafts of the real right thing the post gathers from you à mon adresse, & how these, reaching my comparatively dim corner here, move me to admiration & gratitude & the sense of being unsurpassably distinguished! You're magnificent & I am thrilled, & can't sufficiently rejoice in you & be proud of you. The only thing is that you make my life on these dim terms of my own not worth the living, when there are such possibilities of vision, moyennant Her[2] & a few other matters, & I languish here without them. I do find myself intensely enough in presence, I profess—in presence of the whole monstrosity—till I hear from you, & then I shrink to nowhere & to nothing, learning from you what it really is to live. Well, you have still gone on living at that pitch, I take it, these days since, & raking in impressions in such handfuls that there will never be any room more for any others—others, I mean, that are not of this heroic breed. As if you will want these last however, poor old spectre of a bygone fashion impossible to revive—& with the present pattern stretching certainly as far into the future as ever the strained eye can reach. You have, it seems to me, great bonheurs & romantically happy chances with all the affil- iated paladins that spring up in your path—in addition to all the magic passwords or open-Sesames that you manage to start out with. I myself have no adventure of any sort equal to just hearing from you of yours —apart I mean from the unspeakable adventure of being alive in these days, which is about as much as I can undertake at any moment to be sure of. *That* seems to go on from day to day, though starting fresh with each *aube* & getting under way in fact always with such difficulties, such backings & toughings & impossible adjustments, as if I were that gentleman of legend who attempted to drive the horses of Phoebus Apollo. I stagger out of my dusk to follow the path of the hours, & I *have* followed them, I suppose, when I flop back to my intersolar swoon again—though with nothing whatever to show for them but that sad capacity to flop. However, one surmounts, one surmounts by this ex- traordinary & incredible extension of *use*, even to the very abuse of it, the inability itself to surmount, & gasps along in amazement at what one takes for granted. I am learning to take for granted that I shall probably on the whole *not* die of simple sick horror—than which noth- ing seems to me at the same time more amazing. One aches to anguish & rages to suffocation, & one is still there to do it again, & the occasion still there to see that one does. *Every one* is killed who belongs to any one here, & one looks straight and dry-eyed, hard & arid, at those to whom they belonged. I have just spent a pair of hours of talk with a friend, a "lady-friend" with a huge black welt across her face, who has survived from the Lusitania, with the effect of my feeling, thanks to the so appallingly particularised truth of her slow water-logged recital, that I had been living through the horror, & at last been saved myself—but only saved for the same sterile soreness of woe. I lunched today with two American officials—that is an official & an amateur (close friend & practical emissary of the President),[3] & got from them the impression that though they find no positive forecast of the German answer to the American Note possible, this apprehension doesn't exclude a virtual flouting of the same—such a flouting as will test the President's true sticking up at the pitch at which the Note so admirably placed him. I can't be sure they are sure he *will* stick—they stick so themselves, up, up, up! (It's of an enormous effect for them to be here, & to have been in France—& in Germany!) But I may do them (or the President himself) injustice, & am only afraid Germany may not flout us *enough*. If she only will, if she only will!—that is my perpetual pious prayer. And I'm kind of thinking now of Italy, & of the other 2 Balkan States, & of Greece, *and* of the sweet country que vous savez, *all together*—& it's about the only good time I have; save when I think of *you*. I was rather lately with Howard just for one afternoon & found him of a more *arrested* deliquescence than seemed possible a while back. Percy was with him—but Percy has now (as you will know) gone off to Alexandria on that identification job—it's already so wanted there. People go to the most prodigious places at the most momentary notice, as they would go round the corner. Do very kindly, if you shld. nobly write me another sublimity from Paris, tag on with it a mere mortal word about what in the name of the unthinkable has ever become of W. M. F[ullerton] & his campaign, his everything, his anything. The noncontinuation of him! Je vous embrace [*sic*], je vous vénère! Ever your

H.J.

1. See letter of 14 May 1915.

2. By means of EW's automobile.

3. Colonel E. M. House (1858–1938), special representative of Woodrow Wilson (1856–1924; U.S. president, 1913–1921) to European governments during World War I, and his wife Loulie, née Hunter. A discrepancy: HJ's diary for 22 May notes "Lunch with Col. & Mrs. House."

bonheurs: strokes of good fortune; *aube:* dawn; *que . . . savez:* that you know; *Je . . . vénère:* I embrace you, I venerate you

21 Carlyle Mansions
Cheyne Walk, S.W.
25 June 1915

My dear Edith.

This will introduce to you my old & admirable friend Dr. J. W. White[1] of Philadelphia, never so admirable, as indeed also never so little "old," as during the magnificent campaign on behalf of our cause that he has been waging in the U.S., since the War began, by pen & voice, by the most invincible ability, & which has constituted the most triumphant efforts in our interest achieved by any one mind & hand, any individual maneuverability. However, you will know, without my reminder, his immensely circulated Primer & Text Book, & will connect him with them to his glory & his benefit. Recognition of these things has just been flooding him here but he goes over to a Paris,[2] with as little further loss of time as possible, in charge of a splendid hospital relay, from the University of Pennsylvania, but of his own organizing & recruiting, for our establishment at Neuilly. Extend him the hand of fellowship as one great worker does to another, & you will find yourself but the more interested & inspired. You have a great common association in your equal friendship with Theodore Roosevelt, of whom he will bring you the latest news. He will report to you not less faithfully moreover of your entirely devoted old

Henry James

1. Dr. J. William White (1850–1916), eminent Philadelphia surgeon of international reputation, had lent his services to the American Volunteer Motor-Ambulance Corps. See HJ's *Within the Rim and Other Essays 1914–15* (1919), and letter of 19 September 1914. In 1914 White published *A Primer of the War for Americans*; in 1915 a fourth edition of the *Primer*, "revised and enlarged," was published as *A Text Book of the War of Americans*.

2. James here seems to have failed to complete the construction "over to a Paris that. . . ."

[DICTATED]   21 Carlyle Mansions
                                                        Cheyne Walk, S.W.
                                                        19 July 1915

Dear and unsurpassably distinguished old Friend!

I am writing you in this monstrous manner[1] exactly because, M.C.J. having delivered me yesterday the various elements of your inspiring appeal,[2] I am preparing myself to act on it with as little delay as possible, and because such action seems likely to land me in such a wealth of verbiage that I am just catching Remington by the forelock. In fact I see I must ride him, so caught, as hard and as far as my poor old heels will help me to jab into his sides; which means, less hyperbolically, that I will pass on your earnest prayer at once to the individuals you name, and back it up with my own—and also that I will of course, with the greatest pleasure, try to knock something into shape for you myself— at the same time that I promise to forge for you such a simulacrum of my script as will successfully pass in the New York market for the copy sent to the printer. I can't do or say fairer than this—even if I am a little afraid that some of the eminent persons you direct me to may prove rather arid. I haven't for instance much hope of Conrad, who produces by the sweat of his brow and tosses off, in considerable anguish, at the rate of about a word a month. But I will try, I will do my best. Of course my own incorrigible habits in the tossing-off way will bring me on with an inimitable dash.

This is all just now, for the private and confidential must await a better occasion. I spent long hours yesterday with your messenger, had luncheon with her and then took her to Kensington Gardens and to tea; all of which made for full communication, and to say that she was interesting and thrilling and overwhelming about you is barely to effleurer the fact. I shall be more private and more confidential, less mean and bare, after I have a little worked your will. I am meanwhile prostrate before the glory of your greatness, and am your devotedest old

Henry James

P.S.   I am sending you today a copy of the Book of France, and one of Oliver's Ordeal of Battle,[3] which our friend mentioned you would like to see, and which je tiens that you should have from my hand only.

It's a work of brilliant ability. The B. of F. doesn't amount to much (these things, con rispetto parlando, never do!) but the best thing in it, to my sense, is Mrs. Woods' translation of Mme de Noailles,[4] which I really find remarkable and superior as a verse equivalent, making an English poem at least as fine as the original and less rhetorical and asservie to the alexandrine. I didn't find much inspiration in the little Barrès morsel to which I was applied. But à la guerre comme à la guerre. Please give on your first opportunity my very best love to W. M. F[ullerton], of whose return from America, and whose bereavement, I was entirely unaware till now—I had my benighted impression that he was still là-bas. However, I won't for the present otherwise assault him.

1. Dictation to a typist.

2. Mary Cadwalader Jones, acting as "messenger," brought EW's plans for a volume comprised of contributions from writers and artists to raise funds for her charitable warwork, asking HJ's aid with possible contributors in England and inviting a contribution from him. See letter of 26 July 1915.

3. Frederick Scott Oliver (1864–1934), Scottish-born barrister and prolific political scholar. His *Ordeal by Battle* (1915) is a thorough canvassing of the causes of the war and a recommendation for military conscription. *The Book of France in Aid of the French Parliamentary Committee's Fund for the Relief of the Invaded Departments* (1915) included HJ's essay "France" (reprinted in *Within the Rim*) and his translation "The Saints of France" of "Les Saints de la France" by Maurice Barrès.

4. British poet and novelist Margaret Louisa (Bradley) Woods (1856–1945).

effleurer: graze; *je tiens:* I maintain; *con . . . parlando:* if you will excuse my saying so; *asservie:* subservient; *à . . . guerre:* when at war do as war demands; *là-bas:* over there

[DICTATED]   21 Carlyle Mansions
                                          Cheyne Walk, S.W.
                                          26 July 1915

Dear Redactress-in-Chief.[1]

I have had the enclosed from the grim Rudyard,[2] which is very much what I took for granted. I was pretty sure there would be no hope of him. Also the enclosed from Conrad, who I *fear* will also fail us; especially if I write to him of the early date for which you want his contribution—as I naturally must. From Sargent and from Hardy I have heard nothing—and don't think me a prophet of woe if my expectation of Hardy is small. He is aged, newly married, without facility or current inspiration, I think; and it is many a year since I've seen anything from him anywhere at all of the occasional nature—if indeed I've ever seen it. I think it probable Sargent will favour us with something, and if I don't hear from him in a day or two more I will assault him again. I say *probable*, mind you, but somehow don't feel moved to answer for him. Very numerous are the publications of sorts on behalf of which such appeals have been made, and are being made, here. The little demon of an Elizabeth Asquith[3] detains in her clutches a small piece which I sent her several months ago, under her extreme urgency, for a Book of her own—which up to now has never come out. Thus she neither uses it nor returns it; if she would but do the latter it would be just the thing to send to *you*, even though now a little belated in date. However, I promise you something as soon as I am better of a most tiresome attack of sickness that has now gone on for me, in a most blighting way, these several days. I have likewise another confession for you. I haven't written on your behalf to H. G. Wells[4]—for reasons I can't now go into, but which make correspondence with him disagreeable and in fact impossible to me. So I fear you will have to appeal to him directly, it is really a matter in which I am of no use. This, I feel, is a lame story—I wish it were a livelier one. What it comes to is that I'm *sure* only of sending you something or other, a poor thing but mine own, my broken-down old self. Voilà. I sent you the other day Oliver's Ordeal of Battle,[5] desiring you to have it from *my* hand; whereby I hope it has safely reached you. I also sent you a copy of The Book of France,[6] thinking it perhaps isn't kicking much about Paris. I found the Barrès morsel I was invited to translate a fairly thin scrap. M[ary] C[adwalader] J[ones], whom I spent yesterday afternoon with, partly at Mrs. Phipps's, tells me she is writing you; on behalf of an offer of the Whitridge's [*sic*] to lend you a servantless Barley End for a part of next month, among other things. This would be delicious from points of view, but I somehow don't see you saddled with the working of a ménage there. My poor little Burgess-servant is out of hospital now[7] and at his regimental depot; but with his hearing so almost completely gone that I can't believe they will send him back to the Front for the destruction of the small remnant that remains; can't believe in fact that they can in common humanity do anything after a bit but discharge him. In this case I shall have him back on my hands for practically deaf-and-dumb ministrations; which, however, I think I should prefer to none at all. This is all now.

Yours most ruefully
        Henry James

P.S.   Don't return the notes!

1. EW was editing *The Book of the Homeless* (1916). See letter 19 July 1915.

2. Rudyard Kipling (1865–1936), British poet and novelist, did not participate. Joseph Conrad, John Singer Sargent, and Thomas Hardy (1840–1928), British novelist and poet, all contributed. HJ's contribution was "The Long Wards," reprinted in *Within the Rim*.

3. Elizabeth Asquith (1898–1945), daughter of Prime Minister Herbert H. Asquith (1852–1928), retained HJ's essay "Within the Rim" and published it with her own introduction in the *Fortnightly Review* for August 1917. It was reprinted in *Within the Rim*.

4. On 5 July 1915 HJ received at the Reform Club a copy of Wells's *Boon: The Mind of the Race, The Wild Asses of the Devil, and The Last Trump*; it contained a section entitled "Of Art, of Criticism, of Mr. Henry James," which cruelly mocked and parodied HJ. *Boon* led to an exchange of letters and the end of their friendship. See *Henry James and H. G. Wells: A Record of Their Friendship, Their Debate on the Art of Fiction, and Their Quarrel*, ed. Leon Edel and Gordon N. Ray (Urbana: University of Illinois Press, 1958).

5. See letter of 19 July 1915.

6. See letter of 19 July 1915.

7. Burgess Noakes had been wounded in action in late spring—peppered with shrapnel and deprived of hearing—and hospitalized in Leicester. He would rejoin HJ in the autumn and finally regain much of his hearing; see Theodora Bosanquet's report in the letter of 4 November 1915 in app. B.

Voilà: There you are; *ménage:* household

53, rue de Varenne
10 August 1915

Dearest Ch. M.,[1]

I enclose some more notes to be kindly passed on. Please excuse their being sealed, as I machinalement prepared to post them!—I have written Hardy a line to say that I was very grateful to him for so much as considering the possibility of letting me have a few words; & to Wells to ask him for "one page."[2] He was expected here last week, but never turned up, & I don't know his home address.

I send you the portraits of some of our infants, & also an up to date circular[3] to show you what a proud list we're getting!—

Mr. Sargent has been perfect.

Best love from
    Edith

1. Cher Maître.
2. Hardy and Wells did contribute to EW's *Book of the Homeless*.
3. See app. C.

machinalement: mechanically

53, rue de Varenne
11 August [1915]

Dearest Rédacteur,[1]

Thank you again & again, & de tout coeur, for everything—including the jolly Hardy malediction, just come by the same post as your letter. What a splendid script, & *how* good of him!—And yesterday Joffre[2] sent me word that he would give me "une page" too.

As for your blessed self, of course you'd much better send your contribution[3] direct to Scribner, REGISTERED. I will announce its arrival in the letter I am sending him today.

Thank you also for your pamphlet, which I had not-yet-seen, & with which I shall delect myself the day after tomorrow en route to Alsace.[4]

I shall hand it on later to Morton, who has quite completely abandoned me. All through Anna's severe operation & illness[5] he never even telephoned to ask for news of her—or of me—& it must be six weeks since I have seen him. He will turn up again when I can be of use to him.—Enfin!—

Your ever grateful
Edith

1. EW returns the courtesy of HJ's salutation in the letter of 26 July 1915 by calling HJ "Editor."
2. Joseph Jacques Césaire Joffre (1852–1931), marshal of the French army.
3. "The Long Wards"; see letter of 13 August 1915.
4. See "In Alsace," Fighting France, for an account of this sojourn.
5. Anna Bahlmann had been operated on for cancer.

de . . . coeur: with all my heart; Enfin: So there

21 Carlyle Mansions
Cheyne Walk, S.W.
13 August 1915

Dearest Edith.

I do then send my poor Copy straight to the Scribners[1] with a little supplementary word. It is quite inoffensive. And I have sent on the 3 last letters (yours) to their destinataires & will today assault Yeats[2] with a blandishment, of some sort, of my own.

I find your account of W.M. F[ullerton]'s dissociation[3] too lurid. Qu'est-ce que ça veut bien dire? He is the most inscrutable of men—he will never pose long enough for the Camera of Identification—unlike you, who fatigue a thousand Cameras by the defiant finality of each of your thousand simultaneous attitudes & actions! Que la vie est étrange! as A. Daudet[4] said to me here, years ago, when I told him that Florence Bell, from whose hand he was feeding, was the daughter of Sir J. Oliffe whom Le Nabab had caricatured as le Docteur Jenkinson, author of the stimulating pillules à base arsénicale [sic]—& that she had never read the fiction! However, we are beating all étrangetés, as I feel when I think that this may possibly dangle after you to Alsace[5]—or even to Silesia or Galicia at once. I am prostrate before your incomparable magnificence—& yet love you, venture to, as much as if I could take you in my hand. In that case I would take Walter in the other, please tell him —& so would become myself a case for the Camera. I keep a clutch of you, a breathless one, at any rate, on your wondrous way, & am yours ever so constantly

Henry James

1. See letter of 11 August 1915.
2. William Butler Yeats (1865–1939), Irish poet and playwright, contributed the lyric "A Reason for Keeping Silent" to *The Book of the Homeless*.
3. See letter of 11 August 1915.
4. Alphonse Daudet (1840–1897), French novelist and a friend of HJ's since the seventies; his novel *Le Nabab* was published in 1877. Florence Eveleen Eleanore Oliffe (1851–1930), novelist and playwright in French and English, in 1876 married the wealthy Yorkshire colliery owner Hugh Bell (1844–1931); she was a close friend of HJ's during the nineties.
5. After a brief run northeast to Rheims, EW traveled southeast again near to the German lines (Colmar, Belfort). It was during this foray—recounted in "In Alsace," *Fighting France*—that she had her mule ride up the mountain and discovered an old boundary stone with *F* on one face and *D* on the other: "... on what, till a year ago, was the boundary line between Republic and Empire" (198).

Qu'est-ce . . . dire?: What on earth does that mean?; *Que . . . étrange:* How strange life is; *pilules . . . arsenicale:* pills with an arsenic base; *étrangetés:* strangenesses

21 Carlyle Mansions
Cheyne Walk, S.W.
21 August 1915

Dearest Edith.

This is just to report to you of 2 more successful recruits to the Book[1]—one of whom Eddie Marsh, the late Rupert Brooke's literary executor, will himself have written to you of my having appealed to him, & have sent you straight a very charming little inédit lyric of Rupert's, which is to appear eventually in a new vol. of his poems, but of which the Book enjoys meanwhile the usufruct. W. D. Howells, dear man, has sent me from York Harbour, Maine, also a lyric de sa façon, a fine & forcible & most feeling one called "The Children," really grim & strong & sincere, which I am sending straight to Scribner & your Editors for you. It seems best at this crisis not to make things travel more than need be—& I am only afraid alas that *my* contribution to your pages will have gone down by this foul ferocity of the sunk Arabic.[2] I shall in this case have to do it over again, the wretched affair— from a rough 1st draft which I fortunately have. I shall probably be able [to] learn tomorrow definitely whether it *did* go by the Arabic; but I rather fear the worst. Rupert B. should of course be cited as the *late* R.B.

Truly this is all now—so blankly do I, am I only able to, gape at your latest feat of arms,[3] Generalissima that you are. The foregoing is only that you should know, & also that I wrote to Yeats for you.[4] No answer yet. Yours all bustlingly

Henry James

1. *The Book of the Homeless.* Edward Marsh (1872–1953), secretary to Winston Churchill and then attached to Prime Minister Asquith's office, played a strong role in aiding Asquith to get the Order of Merit for HJ in January 1916. The young English poet Rupert Brooke (1887–1915), whom HJ met in Cambridge in June 1909, had died in April aboard a French hospital ship in the Aegean. HJ's last piece of writing was the preface for Brooke's *Letters from America* (1916).
    2. It had not; see letter of 27 August 1915.
    3. Probably her visit to the Front in Alsace; see letter of 13 August 1915.
    4. See letter of 13 August 1915.

inédit: unpublished; *de sa façon:* after his fashion

21 Carlyle Mansions
Cheyne Walk, S.W.
27 August 1915

Dearest Edith.

I *do* so like to hear from you, as this a.m. by your beautiful letter with Raymond Recouly's blest extract (I so thank you for that!) and also as by your & Walter's postcards from Belfort testifying to the vitality of the animal[1] (& thereby to that of your fond zoologist), whom a doubtless too superficial report had characterized as dead. I affectionately thank Walter for having so promptly grasped & publicly proclaimed the truth of the case. We are even now wagging, at intervals, a considerable tale. Apropos of which it's a blessing to be able to feel pretty sure that my contribution to the Book *didn't* probably after all go down in the Arabic[2]—but travelled to all appearance by the American liner of the Saturday before the Arabic's fatal Wednesday—for such a ship sailed on that 14th [Saturday], & my copy, as I now apprehend, was posted on the 13th. It's a relief to be able to believe this—in which case its having arrived in N.Y. will be confirmed to us. I rejoice with you in the way all your Marionettes have played up—& am not even disconcerted by Howells's having just written to me to "withdraw" his fine & brave little piece (as being too crude & imperfect in form). I am going, in respect to that, to *passer outre*—to write to him tomorrow that he is utterly deluded, that we greatly admire it & in fine decline to give it up.[3] I shall play *you* on the subject for all you are worth—& in short know just what to write him.—The passage from your letter from the front heartens me exceedingly; one gets here today such an impression of the enormous numbers of soldiers in training that it's a solid support to know of their reaching France proportionately & making so good an impression on the expert judgment there. What an impression, in this connection, you & Walter must have made in Alsace—& how uplifting some echo of it would be: which if I bide my time in patience, however, I feel I shall publicly have! M[ary] C. J[ones]'s mention of the 11 miles you marched to the front gives me the measure—of your foot. Incomparable redactress! M.C.J. goes to you, I think, on Sunday—greatly to be missed of *me*, alas, till Oct. 1st, when she promises me to return. This boy stands on the burning deck—which fortunately doesn't burn very fast—for an indefinite time to come.—What a tragic laideur indeed your brother H.'s definite defection[4] at such a time as this—when everything shld. have prompted him to rally to you! The horrible enchaînement of our past acts—in what monstrosities of the present they land us! He makes me feel—that is he would make me write!—like George Eliot. I feel deeply all it must do to you. But only increases, dearest Edith, the attachment of your devoted old

Henry James

1. A feature of their visit to Alsace was a ride on muleback up a mountain to the German border; see letter of 13 August 1915.

2. See letter of 21 August 1915.

3. HJ succeeded; Howells's poem remained.

4. The original breach between EW and brother Harry, occasioned by his belief that she disapproved of his irregular union with his Russian countess, Tecla, dated from his nasty letter of denunciation to his sister in January 1913.

passer outre: move beyond; *laideur:* ugliness

[DICTATED]   21 Carlyle Mansions
                                                  Cheyne Walk, S.W.
                                                  22 September 1915

Dear old Friend.

See how I have to thank you for your beautiful little Brittany letter[1] this morning received—and be glad to deal with it even in this rude form. I grieve to say that I have for all these weeks, ever since the end of July, been having the most damnable difficulties of physical condition (an interminable gastric crisis of the most vicious and poisonous order); and though I believe I have at last practically surmounted it—all by fighting my lone battle myself, day by day and hour by hour—the apparently retreating shadow of it is still upon me, and I am even now (as for that matter you must have seen by my various scrappy communications these two months) very imperfectly articulate. I *can* hint to you, all the same, that it has been a joy to know of your having got off to such another set of scenes and impressions as you mention, and achieved, as I seem to make out, something of a tonic draught of the more or less restorative cup. I myself feel almost as abject in my ignorance of that land as I have lately felt in my disgraceful, my humiliating state of unfitness; but I had always rather your sensorium, instead of mine, were exposed to any of the forces of nature, or art, or life—so just as much, virtually, do I sooner or later gain by it, with the comfort added that you don't lose. Do come over with M[ary] C. J[ones], accordingly, if it is at all decently possible to you, and tell me everything about everything, to the very last kick of the record. It will be unutterably good to see you, and I shall do my best to be by that time less of a mere cumberer of the ground. I'm inexpressibly with you and with M. Rodier, as to the sole sort of consciousness that makes our situation bearable; only I have, alas, to hang on to that consciousness as a mere yearning ghost of a theory, whereas your magnificent time of life and force of activity keep putting into your hand every anodyne of energy. Treat it then simply as one of these, as a charitable pause by the pallet of one of the prostrate, to push over to us for a few days and breathe upon us your heroic souffle. Take well home that I haven't had a single day's "holiday," as people keep so queerly saying, since I left you in Grosvenor Place,[2] not much later than this last year (in order to come hither), and let the mere monotony of that plead for me a little.

I greatly like your having found such gallant goodness in Edith Fairchild,[3] and heartily feel that she has earned the benevolence of your visit. And in the glitter, the prospective, of the Book,[4] I take the greatest interest—surely it *will* coruscate as no like constellation has ever done before. How M.C.J. must indeed be backing you up at home! It's splendid to think of—and of how I shall welcome all *her* histories. I shall bless your news of dear John Hugh [Smith], and I am your all-battered but all-affectionate old

Henry James

1. EW had probably gone to visit a Red Cross hospital: see letter of 26 March 1915.

2. The Wards' townhouse in Gosvenor Square, where EW stayed briefly in mid-September 1914; see letter of 12 September 1914.

3. Howard Sturgis's cousin; see letters of 7 and 13 September 1911.

4. *The Book of the Homeless*; see letter of 26 July 1915.

souffle: breath

Appendix A

JAMES WAS UNABLE to accept Edith Wharton's invitation to accompany her and Walter Berry on a motor trip to Italy (see chap. 4, letter of 27 September 1911). They sent him a series of postcards, one every couple of days; of those, the earliest that survives is from Wharton alone—see chap. 4, postcard of 9 October 1911. The handwriting on the four included here is Berry's; the verses may be principally his.

Bologna
11 October 1911

Henry James
Lamb House[1]

Without the Worm the Beaks are growing starker,
The more so in This Room; and if Petrarca
Could live again he'd sing: "We want the aura
Of Henry more than all the lure of Laura"!

W.B.
E.W.

Arquà [Petrarca][2]

1. The card is postmarked "Rye Oct 14" and readdressed in ink to HJ at the Reform Club, London.
2. Site of Petrarch's death in 1374, on his seventieth birthday.

Ravenna
13 October 1911

Henry James
Lamb House

> *In such a place, in ties unholy,*
> *How could he live with La Guiccioli?*[1]
> *Between Syarchate*[2] *& Guiccioli*
> *Compelled to make a choice, oh which shall he*
> *Forsake forever?—No less grave*
> Our *problem by this sad sea wave:—*
> *Th'Italian accent's wilful truancy*
> *Is such a check upon our fluency!*

    E.W.
    W.B.

    Ravenna

1. Teresa Gamba Ghiselli (1800–1879) married Count Alessandro Guiccioli (1761–1840) in 1818; that year she met Byron and became his mistress—his last—until 1823.

2. Is this a slip for "Segati"? Marianna Segati was another of Byron's mistresses in Italy.

Firenze
15 October 1911

Henry James
Lamb House[1]

> *A flashing word to mark the giro's gesta*[2]
> *Merced-ing through the land of Malatesta,*[3]
> *Hoping the Trin will not forget the Gemini*[4]
> *But send a counter-thought from Rye to Rimini.*

    W.B.   E.W.

1. The card is postmarked "Rye   Oct 19" and readdressed in ink to HJ at the Reform Club, London.

2. The spin's action; i.e., the action of the motor tour.

3. Going by Mercedes (EW's automobile). The Malatestas were a family of great temporal power in northern Italy from the middle of the thirteenth century; Malatesta da Verruchio was its first important head and leader of the Guelph party. The Malatesta rise to power began and was centered in Rimini —hence the last line of the poem—on the Adriatic, some twenty-five miles south of Ravenna.

4. The third of the trinity may not forget the other two—the twins (Gemini).

Firenze
17 October 1911

Henry James
Lamb House[1]

> *Climbing hills & fording torrents*
> *Here we are at last in Florence,*
> *Or rather perching on the piano*
> *Nobile, at Settignano.*[2]
> *Doing picture galleries? No, sir!*
> *Motoring to Vallombrosa,*
> *Pienza, Siena, tutte quante,*
> *High above the Dome of Dante;*
> *Then (compelled by the busy lawyer),*
> *Back to France by a scorciatoia.*

E.W.—W.B.—

1. The card is postmarked "Rye   Oct 20" and readdressed in ink to HJ at the Reform Club, London.

2. On the main floor—actually of Berenson's Villa I Tatti, Settignano.

tutte quante: the whole lot; *scorciatoia:* short cut

Appendix B

EDITH WHARTON'S PLANS to have Theodora Bosanquet report to her on James's health began with his suffering from "stomachic collapse" and "food-loathing," as he termed it, in January 1910. Plans were resumed with his attack of shingles late in 1912 and on into 1913, when he was further threatened with the temporary loss of Minnie Kidd, whose mother had fallen ill; they were resumed again in the autumn of 1915, when his "pectoral" difficulties were acute. In mid-October Wharton asked Bosanquet to send regular reports if James's condition worsened. It did. With the strokes of 4 December 1915, Bosanquet began frequent despatches to Wharton, who sent as frequent replies, first from the South of France (where she was visiting the Bourgets) and then from Paris—mainly to discover whether it would be useful for her to come to England and offer her assistance. Members of James's family arrived in mid-December and early in the new year. Bosanquet was brusquely relieved of her responsibilities yet still managed to send reports to Wharton from her own adjacent Chelsea flat (although some of her last reports are on stationery of 21 Carlyle Mansions). Wharton consequently offered Bosanquet a post as her secretary; she declined.

Lamb House,
Rye, Sussex
23 January 1910

Dear Mrs. Wharton

I'm delighted to be able to tell you—in response to your letter—that Mr. Henry James' doctor, whom I interviewed this morning, states emphatically that there is no cause for any anxiety about his condition which is really improving.[1] It is only since yesterday that he has given himself over into the hands of the doctor and a nurse. Up to then, as you very likely know, he had been diagnosing and treating his own case—allowing the doctor to look on.

I think this is really the cause of the puzzling and distressing relapses he has had. *His* method, you see, was to go immense walks whenever he felt a little better—all the time eating little or nothing. Now he stays in his bed and is fed every two hours—and the improvement is already marked.

In case you want any further independent news of his condition the doctor in charge is Doctor Skinner, Mountsfield, Rye. I shan't be here myself, I'm afraid, after the middle of the week—as Mr. James doesn't want an amanuensis for the next few months. (This isn't on account of his illness—he had meant to work by himself for a bit in any case.)

The doctor thinks that for the present he will be best left alone—to rest absolutely for a week or two— So there seems to be nothing anyone can do for him—I only wish there were!

Believe me, dear Mrs. Wharton
Yours very truly
    Theodora Bosanquet

1. See Chap. 3, letters of 17, 21, and 23 January 1910.

                                                    53, rue de Varenne
                                                    25 January [1910]

Dear Miss Bosanquet,

Thank you very much for writing me so fully & reassuringly about Mr. James's condition. I am so glad that he has decided to submit to the Doctor's orders & especially to have a nurse.

Thank you also for giving me Dr. Skinner's address, so that I may write him for news after you have left.[1]

Believe me

Yours very truly
    Edith Wharton

1. See previous letter.

53, rue de Varenne

15 December [1912]

Dear Miss Bosanquet,

You could not have done me a greater kindness than in sending me news of Mr. James. I had stupidly forgotten Dr. Skinner's name, & I did not know you had been with Mr. James during his illness, or I should have written you long ago.

I have been extremely anxious, & yet unwilling to go to Folkestone & run over from there to Rye, lest my doing so should worry him.[1]

I am indeed glad that he has reached London & that he is able to be out. It would be most kind if you would send me a line now & then to tell me how he is getting on.

Thank you so much, also, for telling me you like The Reef.[2] I am deeply dissatisfied with it, as it missed the final revision which I like to give at leisure, owing to the fact that the proofs were lost for nearly a month on their way to me.

I hope Mr. James will be able to get to work soon, & I am sure that being in his own flat next month[3] will help him toward recovery.

Excuse my having to dictate this,[4] & believe me

Yours very sincerely
      E. Wharton

1. Exactly the sentiment EW expressed in her letters during HJ's final illness; see letter of 4 December 1915 et seq. in app. B.

2. For HJ's glowing response to *The Reef*, see chap 5, letter of 4 [and 9] December 1912.

3. HJ moved into 21 Carlyle Mansions, Chelsea, on the first weekend of January 1913.

4. The letter is handwritten, however, not typed.

53, rue de Varenne

Friday, 14 February [1913]

Dear Miss Bosanquet,

Thank you so much for writing! I am so glad a definite reason for Mr. James's mysterious attacks of pain has at last been found;[1] I am still naturally anxious, in spite of your encouraging report, & am telegraphing now to ask for today's news.

I am longing & hoping to get over to London tomorrow, but there is little prospect of it, as I am likely to be detained by business; still, if it is at all possible, I will come. Meanwhile I am making all my arrangements to come in about ten days if I am prevented now. And I want to ask you to telegraph me *at once* if he is less well, or even if he is nervous about himself & expresses a great desire to see me.

In that case I should simply rush over for two or three days at once. I'm sure I can count on your doing this, Dear Miss Bosanquet.

I'm sorry Kidd is away, but if her move was needed, & the nurse is obliging, perhaps it's not a serious inconvenience.[2] And I'm so glad to know you are there, for I know his regard & affection for you, & can understand how helpful you must be now.

Yours very sincerely
    Edith Wharton

1. The inactivity imposed on HJ as a result of his severe bout of shingles resulted in an accumulation of fluid in his lungs that made breathing difficult and painful; the condition was not immediately diagnosed. See chap. 5, letter of 31 January 1913, and letter of 16 February 1913 in app. B.

2. Minnie Kidd's mother had fallen ill. EW soon provided a nurse to look after the mother and allow Kidd to return to care for HJ.

53, rue de Varenne
Sunday, 16 February [1913]

Dear Miss Bosanquet,

Thank you so much for your letter of yesterday. I should be very grateful if you wd. send me a daily post-card while Mr. James's condition continues unsatisfactory; & please, *please* telegraph me at any moment if you are in the least anxious; & ask the doctor to let you know, so that you may send me word as promptly as possible.

Of course I can't but feel worried at this condition of the lungs coming after so long & exhausting an illness. Can't you have, on my behalf, a private talk with the doctor, asking just what he thinks of the case in general?

I venture to be a little insistent because, in the absence of Mr. James's family, I think the Dr. should know that there is someone to whom the exact facts should be reported—& you can explain to him who I am, & how old & intimate a friend of Mr. James's.

And now about Kidd; it seems to me essential that she should be got back at once, & your idea of writing to the curate was an excellent one. But if another sister cannot be induced to come, will you not propose to Kidd (on the understanding, of course, that it is kept *absolutely secret* from Mr. James) to let me pay for a good nurse for her mother, for as long as is necessary? No doubt the excellent Dr. at Rye,[1] if he is attending Kidd's mother, wd. arrange this promptly & effectually, & I have known Kidd so long that I'm sure she will understand why I suggest the arrangement in the present emergency.

I do believe this might be managed, & I will send Kidd the money at once, if you can settle the matter with her.

Thank you again, Dear Miss Bosanquet.

Yours ever sincerely
E. Wharton

1. Dr. Ernest Skinner.

Brest
16 September [1915]

Dear Miss Bosanquet,

I was just leaving Paris, horribly tired out, for a few days' rest in Brittany, when your letter came, & had only time to send a telegram of enquiry, your answer to which overtook me yesterday.

I was *so* relieved to hear that Mr. James was so much better. I was sure he was improving, as Mrs. Jones[1] received his cheerful dictated letter just as I was leaving Paris; but it is a great relief to know from your telegram that the improvement continues.

If he had not made such progress I should have gone to London early next week to be with him; & I can still arrange to come at any time if you think his condition less satisfactory.

I want to tell you how much I appreciate your writing me so fully about him. I hope you will always do so, & always feel that whatever

I am doing, I may be telegraphed for at any moment, & will manage to come.

I am sorry Mr. James had to have a new doctor,[2] for I think any doctor who does not know him wd. find it difficult to judge his case at first, & might be more alarmed than circumstances justified.

I quite agree with you that the responsibility is far too serious for Kidd, & I think we shd. all try to induce Mr. James to get a really efficient elderly man servant.

Mrs. Jones will be in London again by Oct 1st & I may come with her—I certainly will if there is any further cause for anxiety.—Meanwhile, please feel that you can telegraph me (to 53 rue de Varenne) *at any time.* I am away motoring for 8 days, but a telegraph will be forwarded.

Next week I shall be at the

Villa des Feux
Houlgate
Calvados,

& shd. be so glad if you would send me a line there with a further report.

Yours very sincerely
E. Wharton

1. Mary Cadwalader Jones.
2. Harrison.

Villa des Feux
Houlgate (Calvados)
27 September 1915

Dear Miss Bosanquet,

So many thanks for your kind & reassuring letter, which followed me here.

I am *so* glad there is such a decided improvement.—I expect to be in London on the 1st or 2d of Oct., & hope certainly to see you this time.[1]

The idea of going back to Rye seems to me excellent for Mr. James,[2] but what a pity he has not been there all this month.

Yours very sincerely
E. Wharton

I return to Paris today.

1. EW was in London at the beginning of October 1915, and invited Bosanquet to her rooms in Buckland's Hotel, Brook Street, to persuade her, in person, to continue to report on HJ's health.
2. At the middle of October HJ went down to Rye for a week with Noakes, Minnie Kidd, and Joan Anderson. Ill health—heart trouble—gave him three wretched days and nights. See letter of 4 November 1915 in app. B.

10 Lawrence Street[1]
Cheyne Walk, S.W.
4 November 1915

Dear Mrs. Wharton,

I think that you will perhaps like to have a report of Mr. James's state pretty well up to date, and this seems rather a good time to be making it, because he has, I very much hope, really begun to get better again after a very bad phase.[2]

In one sense his visit to Rye last month[3] did him no good at all, though he was able to see to the packing of books and bookcases for London, which will make his flat here a much more homelike and liveable-in place. He was only there a week, and for three out of the seven nights didn't go to bed at all on account of his breathing difficulties being so great. Naturally he called in Dr. Skinner, and thanks to his outspoken diagnosis Mr. James began to realise that it was his heart rather than his digestion that was causing his trouble. So that was to the good, for neither of the doctors he had recently seen in London had told him there was anything the matter with his heart, and he was pursuing a will-o'-the-wisp in trying to track each discomfort to indigestible food. He came back to London and saw Sir James Mackenzie, who very greatly cheered and reassured him about his heart, though quite pronouncing it to be out of order, and prescribed digitalis, which is apparently having the best effects. Another doctor (Des Voeux) is administering the drug and generally pulling Mr. James round towards something like his normal health again, but he has had a really horrid time lately, complicated by a sort of gastric chill and sleeplessness. But for the last few days he has been getting fairly steadily better and yesterday went out, for the first time since he came back from Rye. It speaks well for his reserve of strength that he was able to walk back to Chelsea from Pall Mall after having tea at the Athenaeum, and afterwards to dine with Miss Sargent—all on the first day.[4]

Burgess is still with him, living on extensions of leave. We hope he may get his discharge, though he seems to me to have recovered so much of his hearing now that I shouldn't have thought his military value was gravely affected.[5] However, it will be a blessing if they do consider him sufficiently damaged to be set at liberty and will make all the difference to poor Kidd.

I will write again in a few weeks—or sooner if Mr. James doesn't get better, as I quite hope he will now. Please don't think of troubling to acknowledge this, dear Mrs. Wharton, and believe me

Yours very sincerely
Theodora Bosanquet

1. Bosanquet's flat in Chelsea, near 21 Carlyle Mansions.
2. HJ's apparent recovery was short-lived: see letter of 6 December 1915 in app. B.
3. 14 October 1915.
4. The final sentence of the paragraph is underlined in red ink, and opposite it in the left margin, written in a hand very like EW's: "Result of returning to Mrs. Page"—perhaps the wife of the American ambassador to England, Walter Hines Page.
5. Burgess Noakes had been wounded in action in the late spring of this year and had lost his hearing; see chap. 7, letter of 26 July 1915.

53, rue de Varenne
6 November 1915

Dear Miss Bosanquet,

I have been expecting to hear from you, for Mrs. Hunter wrote me the other day about Mr. James's bad time at Rye, which I had suspected from his complete silence.

I am thankful he is back in town, & above all that Sir James Mackenzie has him in charge, & has exploded the indigestion theory, which is really much more harmful to him than knowing the truth.

I am very much touched by your thoughtfulness in writing, & I know I can count on your doing so whenever things go wrong.—

Yes, I do hope Burgess will be left, as much on Kidd's account as Mr. James's.

Thank you for your promise to write again later, & believe me, dear Miss Bosanquet,

Yours gratefully & sincerely
E. Wharton

Costebelle Hotels
Hyères
4 December 1915 [Saturday]

Dear Miss Bosanquet,

I was sent down here ten days ago for a rest of two or three weeks, & your telegram has just been forwarded to me.

I can't tell you how I feel—I am in despair at being so far off. I am telegraphing you today to ask if you think I had better come; but I am almost sure you will say no, for the present at any rate, for it probably would not be well to have Mr. James think I had rushed over on account of his illness, & every one knows that people don't come & go nowadays between England & France without a special reason. If this dreadful thing had to happen, how I wish I could have been in England at the time![1] I am also writing Mrs. Charles Hunter to let me know what she thinks. I shall wait here, at any rate, till I hear more, so please write & wire me *here*—I am thankful Burgess was with Mr. James, & above all that he was not at Rye. It is all so unforeseen—I had expected a sudden heart-attack at any time, but never had thought of this far worse thing.

Of course in some cases of partial paralysis, even at Mr. James's age, complete recovery takes place. I have known such instances. But with his weak heart that seems improbable.

I shall be so thankful when you have time to write the details—I suppose you have cabled his people? Surely some one will come from America.

Thank you again, dear Miss Bosanquet, for always remembering to let me hear when there is any cause for anxiety.

Above all, tell me quite frankly what you think I had better do.

Yours very sincerely,
    E. Wharton

If you think I had better not come for the present, please let me know when I can write to him—if it is advisable to write—& how much I can appear to know.

    1. See the following two letters.

                           21 Carlyle Mansions
                           Cheyne Walk, S.W.
                           6 December 1915 [Monday]

Dear Mrs. Wharton,

I was so greatly relieved to get your telegram this morning and know definitely that you had had one at least of mine. I'm afraid the second Friday telegram will have alarmed you, but I hope you will have had the third, more reassuring one, by this time. On Friday we were all really expecting the end to be not far off, as Mr. James seemed to be passing into unconsciousness; but he has rallied considerably since, and Dr. Des Voeux tells me now that he will pull through now unless he has another stroke. One doesn't know, at this stage, how far he can really recover—the doctor is dubious about anything like complete recovery of movement, and considers the injury to the brain certain to leave it much impaired, and under these circumstances one can hardly wish his life to be much prolonged. Mr. James isn't himself aware of the seriousness of his illness. He knows that he had the slight stroke on Thursday [2 December] morning, but not of the following one during the night, and he talks of work again. His mind seems very clear, considering the difficulties it must have to contend with. He even saw three people yesterday, but Dr. Des Voeux has forbidden him to see any more, which is a very good thing. It is really too much effort for him to talk. I try not to go into his room myself unless he asks for me very insistently, because seeing and hearing me only troubles his mind with thoughts of his work and the people he wants me to write to. Of course we cabled to his nephew in New York[1] at once, and I hear from him today that his mother has already sailed for England. Probably Peggy will follow her as soon as she can. I shan't let Mr. James know that Mrs. James is on her way—the thought of her lonely crossing would worry him, but he will like to see her when she is here, and it will be the greatest relief for the household to be able to pass over the responsibilities that the situation produces such a large crop of to authoritative hands.

I don't really think it would be worth your while to come over now[2]—Mr. James can't see any one for long, and though it is always the greatest pleasure he can have to see you, I think he would be dreadfully worried to think that you had come such a distance for such a very few moments of talk.

Please be assured, dear Mrs. Wharton, that I will always let you know immediately if there is any serious change, and will transmit any message Mr. James may want to send (at present he thinks that he will be well in a few days and that people won't have heard much of his illness and he certainly wouldn't worry you by sending any direct news from himself) and believe me

Yours very sincerely
Theodora Bosanquet

1. Harry.
2. On this date EW cabled from Hyères and Mrs. Mary Hunter telephoned (at EW's request) from Hill Hall to see if EW should come over to England and offer assistance.

21 Carlyle Mansions
Cheyne Walk, S.W.
8 December 1915 [Wednesday]

My dear Mrs. Wharton,

Your so beautifully considerate letter[1] came this morning, and since then Mrs. Hunter has been round to see me. She had heard nothing at all till today, as she was in Norfolk and the letter I wrote to Hill was waiting for her in London with yours. She is immediately telegraphing you not to come, but I feel sure that you probably aren't thinking of doing so at present. I do so understand and sympathise with your wish to have been here when this thing happened; but now that it *has* happened the only thing to be done is to keep Mr. James as quiet as possible. I had a letter from Mr. Howard Sturgis this morning begging me most earnestly that visitors should be kept from Mr. James, and we are really keeping everyone away until he demands to see them, which I hope won't be for some time yet.

But do write to him—your letters are always a great joy to him. I think you may quite safely seem to know that he has had a slight stroke (he knows about the first one, but not that it was followed by a second)—he told Mrs. Prothero to tell his intimate friends that, and said at the time that it always made complications not to tell the truth. But I think, if you don't mind, that it would perhaps be as well if you didn't say anything about having heard it from me. No—on second thoughts I don't think it will matter if he does know—I only thought for the moment that it might lead him definitely to forbid my worrying you, as he might think it, in future; but I don't really think he will mind.

Yesterday when I saw him he seemed ever so much clearer in his mind, and quite ready to be mildly interested in the messages of affection and sympathy from his various friends. He was particularly himself in regard to a letter from Mr. Gosse, and told me to say in my reply that his powers of recuperation were infinite![2] He also composed a perfectly characteristic phrase for me to cable to New York. He was very sleepy all this morning, and didn't send for me till nearly luncheon time, when I was very sorry to find him quite oblivious of everything but the effort to give expression to the sensations of illness and convalescence. That isn't very clear. What I mean is that he was intent on dictating several laboriously composed sentences, quite long and punctuated, describing his state of mind at the moment in regard to his illness. That seems to me to be about the worst thing possible for his brain, but it isn't possible, nor indeed desirable, to stop him, for he only goes on worrying about the phrases and it must be some relief to have them spoken and taken down and done with. But I'm very sorry his mind is trying to force itself to such activities.

This is all there is to tell you today—and no doubt Mrs. Hunter is writing too. She tells me she knows of an excellent male nurse and is going to find out about him. I am sure Mr. James won't submit to his present female ministrants much longer!

Yours very sincerely
　　Theodora Bosanquet

1. Of 4 December, from Hyères, app. B.
2. He was recalling Dr. Des Voeux's comment on his recovery from the collapse in the summer of 1913, recorded in his diary for 22 July—"*Very* great powers of recuperation"—and repeated in his letter of 30 July to Mrs. Wharton, Chap. 6.

Costebelle Hotels
Hyères
8 December 1915 [Wednesday]

Dear Miss Bosanquet,

Your letters of the 2d & 3d[1] came yesterday, & your telegram saying "improvement maintained." If there have indeed been two strokes the end may not be far off. It is what I hope for! That one phrase of yours—"mind confused"—is beyond bearing!

Thank you again with all my heart for writing so promptly & fully. I suppose Mr. Harry James will surely come; but steamers are slow & infrequent now, & if in the interval I am needed, or if you think my presence wd. be any comfort to Mr. James, or any help to the household, don't hesitate to telegraph me, *please.* I expect to stay here till the 17th,[2] unless you send for me; but I can leave at any time, & you know how gladly I would come.

Yours ever sincerely
　　E. Wharton

1. These have not survived.
2. See EW's letter of 11 December 1915 in app. B.

21 Carlyle Mansions
Cheyne Walk, S.W.
11 December 1915 [Saturday]

Dear Mrs. Wharton,

There's very little more to tell you than the telegrams have already made you aware of. Yesterday morning he was much worse—had a temperature of 101° and pain in his right side. Dr Des Voeux was uncertain about the cause till the evening when he said it was certainly pneumonia. Today he knows enough more to be able to diagnose it as embolic pneumonia—which you will understand all about from the term itself. He wasn't conscious most of yesterday—and today, though his temperature isn't very high (99.6) he is quite delirious. The paralysis seems much less—up to today he hasn't been able to move his eyes or really see anything—but when I went into his room a few moments ago he certainly saw and recognised me. I feel very sorry now that you aren't here—but *this* complication was so entirely unforeseen. He was speaking about you on Thursday—his last conscious day—and I told him then that you were ready to come at once if he wanted you—I gave him the message as received through Mrs. Hunter and told him that Mrs. Hunter wanted him to know she had taken it upon herself to wire you not to—and he said immediately that she had done quite right—he couldn't bear the thought of your being "dragged across the seas," especially from such a distance—he quite realised where you were.

There's no more to tell you today—I'll write again tomorrow.

Yours ever sincerely
Theodora Bosanquet

Hotel Costebelle
Hyères
11 December 1915 [Saturday]

Dear Miss Bosanquet,

Your letter of the 6th has this moment come, & I am so relieved to have this full account from you, & especially to know that Mrs. James is on the way. You must be overwhelmed with care & anxiety, & I am glad indeed that some member of the family will soon come to relieve you.

It would have been a real comfort to me to see Mr. James, even if only for a few moments; but it would be a mistake[1] for me to go at present, & I hope with you that the Dr. will firmly keep every one from his room.

I am returning to Paris on the 16th,[2] so your next telegram or letter had probably better go there, as you see it takes five days for a letter to get from London here.

I wish the end could have come that first night!—

With all gratitude for your kindness in finding time to write,

Yours very sincerely
E. Wharton

1. EW wrote "a great mistake" and then crossed out "great."
2. See letter of 15 December 1915 in app. B.

21 Carlyle Mansions
Cheyne Walk, S.W.
12 December 1915 [Sunday]

Dear Mrs. Wharton,

Your letter of the 8th., came last night. You will have had three other letters and at least two telegrams from me since, and I know Mrs. Hunter is telegraphing and writing as well. I wrote yesterday, or was it the day before?[1] fully convinced that the end was very near indeed. But apparently it isn't, and I'm glad for Mrs. William James's sake, at any rate, that he will probably live now at least till after she arrives tomorrow. Did I tell you that she was coming in response to my cable of

Friday week?[22] I think it's very fine and spirited of her to set off, at her age and practically alone (a friend did happen, fortunately, to be crossing by the same boat) across the winter Atlantic, at not more than 24 hours' notice. Why Harry James isn't coming himself I can't imagine. I suppose he must have the very best of reasons for not being able to do so, in the face of the very urgent and personally addressed cable Miss Lily Norton and I sent him last Sunday. I wasn't sure about whether Mr. James wouldn't be greatly disappointed by the arrival of his sister-in-law instead of his nephew, but when Mrs. Hunter told him this morning that she was coming he seemed to be very much pleased. I hope the fact will just drop into his mind enough for it to be no shock when she comes. At present he is perfectly capable of taking in who is talking to him or being spoken about but has no consciousness of where he is —or rather he has a consciousness that he isn't in London, but is in an hotel somewhere, we can't make out where. But Mrs. Hunter will be telling you about her talk with him.

What I want to tell you particularly is the exact nature of the disease, which the doctor has now been able to establish quite conclusively to be due to the heart condition. Two clots have been formed within the last ten days—the first affected the right side of the brain and the second the base of the right lung, setting up embolic pneumonia. This is better today, and I suppose will get better still. Dr. Des Voeux considers there is no reason now why he shouldn't pull through. But he has very little hope that the paralysis will ever be any better. Paralysis due to clotting is, he tells me, much less likely to disappear than that due to the breaking of a blood-vessel in the brain. Since this is the case, and there is so little hope of either the paralysed part of the body recovering or the brain not being seriously damaged for future mental activity, my own hope is that there will soon be some further complication which he won't survive. I can't bear to contemplate any dragging out of life for him under such conditions. As it is it's almost more than I can bear to go into his room (as he so often wants me to do) to take down from his dictation fragments of the book he imagines himself to be writing. At the same time that it is a heart-breaking thing to do, though, there is the extraordinary fact that his mind *does* retain the power to frame perfectly characteristic sentences—even whole pages of pure "Henry James" prose composition. At first I thought it might be bad for him, but I believe now that it really helps him to hear it being ticked off on the typewriter. He remains conscious of having done it and goes more easily to sleep afterwards. And the fragments he dictates do, in the queerest way, hang together—they seem to form part of a book he is writing in his mind about Bonaparte. He leaves huge gaps undictated, but everything somehow fits into the scheme. It's the most extraordinary thing to watch the bits falling together.

I shall always remember, dear Mrs. Wharton, that I can send for you at once if Mr. James wants you, and it's ever so kind of you to say you would come over to be a help to us all if needed. But I shan't dream of asking you to leave Hyères unless Mr. James wants to see you, though please be assured that I shall at once then.

Everyone is being so wonderfully kind. Mrs. Hunter has been the greatest support since she came up to town. And Mr. Percy Lubbock came in to see me the other day[3] and was very helpful about the notice for the papers. I had heard that there was already something in the New York papers, so I thought we had better put something in the English "Times" ourselves instead of letting them get it in a roundabout way.

This is all till my next report,

Yours most sincerely and gratefully
    Theodora Bosanquet

1. Yesterday; see Miss Bosanquet's letter of 11 December 1915.
2. That is, 3 December.
3. Lubbock visited on 9 December.

                        21 Carlyle Mansions
                        Cheyne Walk, S.W.
                   14 December 1915 [Tuesday]

Dear Mrs. Wharton,

The bulletin today is fairly favourable—"condition slightly improved." The chief event has been Mrs. James's arrival. She got to London very late yesterday evening, not till nearly twelve o'clock, so she very sensibly went straight to her hotel and came on here this morning.

Unfortunately Mr. James had not only been told (most tactfully and reassuringly by Mrs. Hunter) that she was coming, but had also been told, by a different person, that she was coming within a certain time, by train. It isn't to be wondered at, therefore, that when she didn't turn up last night he grew restless and uneasy. In fact he had a very bad night and is weak and tired today in proportion. But the pneumonia is clearing off and the doctor has ordered a little food for the first time for many days. The meeting with Mrs. James went off very well, and he has been much happier and quieter ever since, and not in the least worried about her voyage. He is perfectly clear now about personal identities but still refuses to entertain the idea that he is anywhere himself but in a third-rate hotel in Ireland. Thank goodness it might be a much worse delusion, and it will clear away as the pneumonia goes. It's the ordinary type of feverish idea, not a bit like the distressing mental condition he was in last week. And his speech is quite clear now, so that there can't be much facial paralysis. The doctor thinks too, and the type of stuff he has been dictating in his delirium quite bears out his theory, that the "intellectual" centers aren't much, or even at all, damaged. And if that is the case he may yet have a great deal to live for. That's the best hope we can have if he *is* going to live. But my own belief is that he won't live very much longer, and I think that is the opinion of his nurses.

In any case Mrs. James will stay near him now till the end, and probably Peggy will come out to join her within a very short time. It's a great relief to have her here and not feel responsible for practically everything any longer. I don't mean that the nurses and the servants haven't been angels of kindness and consideration, because they have; but I did feel very strongly that there should be someone more than a mere hireling of a secretary (however devoted) to apply to in emergencies of so grave an importance.

I'll write or telegraph again, of course, immediately if there is any change for the worse; and in any case will send you a further report before long.

Ever yours sincerely
Theodora Bosanquet

Costebelle
[Hyères]
15 December [1915, Wednesday]

Dear Miss Bosanquet,

Again all my thanks for your last letter & telegrams. The news is so conflicting that I feel the uselessness of writing, since each day brings a different message. The day before yesterday your two telegrams, & Mrs. Hunter's, made me feel the end had come; & yesterday early came Mrs. Hunter's message speaking of a marked improvement! How I wish now I had written Mr. James the first day I heard of his illness. I did not dare to, as I thought it might agitate him if I sent it directly to him, & involve you in difficulties if I enclosed it to *you*. Now, however, I send a line for him, which you can give him if an opportune moment comes, or which you can open and *read* to him if it seems better. If it is not possible to give Mr. James my letter, do, at least, if you can, give him a little message of love from me, telling him I have known of his illness & have refrained from writing in order to spare him the trouble of answering.

I have said that I heard of his illness through Mrs. Hunter, as that puts you quite hors de cause.

I hope so much Mrs. Wm. James has arrived. I am anxious for another letter from you telling me of this sudden & unexpected rally.—I shall be in Paris on the 17th, so please write to 53 rue de Varenne.

Yrs ever sincerely
E. Wharton

hors de cause: free of responsibility

21 Carlyle Mansions
Cheyne Walk, S.W.
17 December 1915 [Friday]

Dear Mrs. Wharton,

I found your letter of the 15th., enclosing a note for Mr. James, when I got here this morning. I will guard the enclosure until he is either well enough to read it himself or would like it read to him, and in the meantime I will take the first opportunity of giving him your message. That will be a comfort and pleasure to him, and won't be the perplexity that messages from London friends are apt to prove. He is still in the same state of confusion as to locality which I wrote of two days ago,[1] and doesn't like any suggestion that these people are really in London. That will probably clear with time—he must be pretty weak after ten days of starvation and several of fever, and one can't expect his mind to be itself at once. As to the general condition, the doctor seems to be satisfied and there are no fresh complications. Recovery, to whatever extent it may be looked for, is bound to be a long, dragged-out process and I'm afraid a terribly difficult one for him to bear. One can't look far ahead or see much ground for hopefulness—at least I can't. Mrs. James seems much better able to perform the act of faith; but I'm still too sorry that it didn't all end quickly and completely.

There was a most beautiful surprise waiting for me when I got home yesterday, in the shape of your "Fighting France," from Macmillans [*sic*]. I can't at all adequately tell you, dear Mrs. Wharton, how greatly I appreciate your kind thought in sending me a copy. Appreciation of its contents will begin at the first available moment; and I quite hope, thanks to the relief of Mrs. James's responsible presence here now, to be having available moments fairly soon again.

Ever yours sincerely
Theodora Bosanquet

1. That is, three days ago, Tuesday, 14 December; see letter of that date.

53, rue de Varenne
Sunday night 19 December [1915]
Dear Miss Bosanquet,
I got back two days ago, & have not had a quiet moment till now. I have to thank you for your two admirable letters, of the 12th & 14th, which at least brought me the comfort of knowing that, if he must live, it will not be with an impaired brain. But real rest from *everything* would be so much better.
I am unspeakably glad that Mrs. James has come. It was being plucky

of her to rush over at such short notice; & how fortunate that Mr. James took her arrival quietly! I am so relieved to know that the great strain is taken from you; & I hope Miss [Peggy] James may soon come too.

As I have not heard from you or Mrs. Hunter since your letter of the 14th I suppose there is no change. I am prepared to go to England at any moment that he may express the wish to see me, & that my coming may not be thought too disturbing. I hope you were able to give him, or read him, the few lines I sent you from Costebelle.[1]

If you can manage to let him know that I am in Paris again (supposing that he improves enough to make my coming possible) perhaps he would of himself express a wish to see me. I would rather never see him again than run the least risk of exciting or troubling him—need I say it! But I shall let nothing interfere with my coming if I may come without the possibility of such consequences.

Yours with sincere gratitude,
    E. Wharton

Every detail you give me is precious, & I appreciate so much your finding time to tell me so much

Will you be kind enough to hand Burgess & Kidd this small Xmas present of £1 for each?

1. For an account of HJ's response to EW's message of 15 December 1915 (app. B), see Miss Bosanquet's letter of 22 December.

21 Carlyle Mansions
Cheyne Walk, S.W.
20 December 1915 [Monday]

Dear Mrs. Wharton,

I don't know whether you'll think I'm doing right in not sending you another wire today—Mr James has had a bad relapse and there is another clot on the lung which is giving rise to a fresh pneumonic patch. But it doesn't seem much use to worry you with telegrams of worse and better states which seem to be only temporary. If I could have got to an office yesterday I should have wired, but today there is again a rally—Dr. Des Voeux quite thinks the prognosis is fairly hopeful, unless or until there is a fresh complication. He is frankly rather puzzled by this recurrent clotting condition and inclined to suspect a diseased blood vessel somewhere which releases solid fragments into the stream. But this doesn't account for the clots appearing in two different systems of circulation. His opinion is, I imagine, that it can only be a question of time now, and that it's just a lingering on till one of these attacks is fatal. *This* attack he will probably in some measure recover from. He had a wretchedly painful day yesterday; but had morphia injections in the evening and again in the night, which gave him some sleep. He seems to be quite conscious today, though chiefly conscious of feeling miserably ill—and no wonder!

I will write again very soon.

Yours very sincerely
Theodora Bosanquet

21 Carlyle Mansions
Cheyne Walk, S.W.
21 December 1915 [Tuesday]

Dear Mrs. Wharton,

There is nothing fresh exactly, no new complication or great change of condition today. There is the conflicting evidence of the nurses and the doctor—the nurse thinks Mr. James a good deal weaker, the doctor reports the symptoms of the last pneumonic state to be abating. One can only think that he isn't really worse, though this extreme weakness will make it difficult for him to get over the attack. I'm afraid the whole struggle is just the prolonged lingering of a naturally strong man—for his constitution is certainly strong and his recuperative powers have always been great.

Mrs. James is equal to every emergency, though the strain and worry tell on her. I think she had a very assured hope of his recovering enough to enjoy life for several months, if not years, more when she arrived, and it has come as a renewed shock to her that he probably won't recover even partially. Peggy and possibly the eldest son, Harry, will sail on Friday [24 December], and that will be a good thing for their mother, even if Mr. James can't take any pleasure in seeing them. I gave him your message, which greatly touched and pleased him, but he isn't able to have the note yet.[1] Yesterday his mind was fairly clear in the evening, but today he is wandering a good deal. Of course I will report again very soon.

Yours ever sincerely
    Theodora Bosanquet

1. See letters of 15 and 22 December 1915 in app. B.

10 Lawrence Street
Cheyne Walk, S.W.
22 December 1915 [Wednesday]

Dear Mrs. Wharton,

Yesterday evening Dr. Des Voeux told us that there was some fluid at the base of the right lung, which adds a further complication to a case already pretty thoroughly involved in various directions. I think the nurse had suspected pleurisy for a couple of days, but there wasn't any certainty till yesterday. The worst of the pain is over; he really sleeps most of the time, and if he does seem restless and in pain he has an injection of morphia which relieves him very quickly.

I saw Mr. James last night at about 10 o'clock for a few minutes. He was pretty clear in his mind, except for a worry about the strange place in which he found himself. And he asked me if I were in any sort of communication with any of his friends. I repeated your message to him, and told him there was a letter from you for him to read or have read to him when he felt a little stronger.[1] He asked me to thank you very much. I can't give you the absolutely exact verbatim report, but he said something very much like this. "Please tell Mrs. Wharton that I thank her very much, and that for the present, among these strange and difficult conditions, I leave the answering of her enquiries to you. But tell her that I hope very soon to get into a closer relation with her." He had already asked, when I told him of having had a letter from you, if I thought you were aware of his state. It was a great comfort to him to know that you were and that you had written, and I shall repeat it to him if I have another chance, because he doesn't remember for long.

Now I will go across again. I went before breakfast and had the night nurse's report—a restless wakeful night till 3 o'clock, when she gave him morphia. He was asleep when I looked in.

I will add the doctor's latest bulletin to this over there.[2]

11 o'clock   Dr. Des Voeux says there is no increase of fluid and that unless some fresh conditions appear there is no reason why Mr. James should not recover from this last attack— It doesn't *look* possible, but he has such a reserve of strength that I suppose any miracle may happen.

> Yours ever sincerely
> Theodora Bosanquet

1. See previous letter.
2. The James family's resentment, and especially Mrs. WJ's—not simply of Bosanquet's "interference" but particularly of her communicating with EW (of whom Mrs. WJ disapproved)—meant that she was now increasingly excluded from affairs at 21 Carlyle Mansions, "over there." The balance of the letter, beginning with "*11 o'clock*," is in ink in Bosanquet's hand.

> 10 Lawrence Street
> Cheyne Walk, S.W.
> 23 December 1915 [Thursday]

Dear Mrs. Wharton,

Mr. James had an easier night last night than he has had for a long time, and has passed what seems like the most conscious day he has had since his stroke, nearly three weeks ago. I haven't seen him to speak to—he was asleep both the times I looked into his room—but the doctor and the nurse and Mrs. James and Kidd all report that he realises his condition and his surroundings much more fully than he has hitherto done. That the realisation is unspeakably bitter is inevitable. Whether he will think life, even under such maimed conditions, worth while when he is stronger and better one can't tell yet. It seems as if death would have been so infinitely more merciful. It may easily, of course, come even now. This is the third time Mr. James has rallied from what looked like an almost certain dying condition (no man could have looked worse than he did even so lately as last night when I was in his room) and I don't think even his constitution can pull him through any further attack. This last one has terribly weakened him, and his face is very much wasted. He will probably take comfort in the wastage of his body when he realises it! As for the actual facts of his case—Dr. Des Voeux says the lung is clearing satisfactorily and the blood flowing so well that there is no probability of another clot forming at present.

I've begun with my bulletin, and now pass on to your letter of the 19th. [Sunday], which came last night. I gave the little packets to Kidd and Burgess,[1] and both are intending to write their thanks for your kind remembrance of them as soon as ever they have a moment to do so. But their moments are very few, for they're both quite invaluable in the sick room. Kidd seems to be the only person whose suggestions of food Mr. James doesn't feel impelled to contradict, and Burgess is called upon at all hours of the day and night to help to move his master into an easier position, or even to get him right out of bed. I'm afraid there is no real sign of a return of power in the paralysed limbs. Luckily the nurses have both managed to adapt themselves to their patient in a way that does real credit to their intelligence, and I don't think he dislikes either of them now.

I suppose, even at the best, it must be a long time before he can have much intercourse with friends, but I feel quite sure that when he *is* allowed to it will be the greatest pleasure for him to see you. I remember how much he looked forward to the vague possibility of your coming over when he had had that touch of pleurisy two winters ago.[2] And I hope you'll feel always quite sure that I will let you know the very moment it seems advisable for you to come—for I certainly will.

Yours ever sincerely
Theodora Bosanquet

1. Miss Bosanquet recorded in her journal for 22 December 1915: ". . . touching letter from Mrs. Wharton, enclosing Christmas boxes for Kidd and Burgess. She really has shown the most perfect and tender consideration for everyone, and especially for Mr. James, and really comes through with a perfect crown of glory."

2. In February 1913, as a side-effect of his attack of shingles, HJ suffered the touch of pleurisy but made no specific mention of it in his letter of that month to EW.

53, rue de Varenne

23 December [1915, Thursday]

Dear Miss Bosanquet,

Your letter of the 20th has only just come, & as there has been no telegram since I conclude the weary struggle is going on.

I can't tell you how happy I should be if I could be helping you; but to be in London simply hanging on the telephone would be dreadful— & that would probably be my fate if I were there! Mrs. Hunter is very sensible, & she advises me strongly not to come. Still, I have written to ask Mr. Asquith[1] for a laissez passer, as I am told it is almost impossible now for neutrals to get permission to go to England at all!—

Thank you for your promise to write again soon. All Mr. James's friends are touched by your thoughtfulness in keeping them informed, & appreciate it so much; & we are all so thankful that you are with him.

Will you accept this little Christmas card in the shape of a collar embroidered by one of the poor refugee women whom we are teaching to sew?—It brings you my friendliest wishes & my sincere gratitude.

E. Wharton

1. Herbert H. Asquith, prime minister, 1908–1916.

21 Carlyle Mansions

Cheyne Walk, S.W.

26 December 1915 [Sunday]

Dear Mrs. Wharton,

I haven't written for a day or two just because there hasn't been anything fresh to tell you. Mr. James has slept a great deal in the day, under the influence of sleeping draughts and morphia injections which all take effect during the wrong part of the 24 hours, and has passed miserably restless nights. I haven't seen him to speak to since the night he gave me that message for you.[1] The only at all hopeful sign about his condition now is that there have been signs of movement, voluntary movement, in the fingers of the left hand. He does get a little stronger every day, and takes a little more nourishment in the shape of eggs and milk and meat juices. But as he slowly begins to realise his condition (I don't think he is very continuously conscious of it or his surroundings yet) he becomes more unhappy and creates more insuperable difficulties for his nurses and other surrounding people, which must, I'm afraid, almost inevitably increase rather than diminish as time goes on. If he goes on living he will have to face such terribly altered circumstances that it's really not possible to believe (not possible for me anyhow) that he can ever reconcile himself to them. He has been wheeled into the dining-room today, under the doctor's supervision, and is there now. When he has restless fits he wants to be lifted out of bed onto a chair every few minutes and the physical strain on the nurse and Burgess is very great.[2] They hope that this more complete change may soothe him for a longer time.

I wish there were anything better to tell you, and I shall very gladly write at once when there is. But just now things look very black. This increase of physical strength doesn't seem to be accompanied by a corresponding return of mental power. The delirium, during which he wanted to do literary work,[3] is over, and his mind is entirely occupied by the misery of the state in which he finds himself. In *that* condition it isn't clear. He doesn't take in or remember anything that is said unless it is often repeated and even then it's all wiped out in five minutes. But this too may, and probably to some extent will, pass.

Mrs. James is looking absolutely worn out with the strain. She is up much too much in the night, and can't rest in the day. I shall be very glad when Peggy is here to relieve her.

If I don't write for some days please take it that there isn't any change. It's only our opinions that fluctuate from day to day, and we haven't enough data yet to form any very solid ones.

Yours ever sincerely
    Theodora Bosanquet

1. That is, 22 December; see letter of that date in app. B.
2. See following letter.
3. See Miss Bosanquet's letter of 12 December, and *Comp. Notes*, 581–84.

21 Carlyle Mansions
Cheyne Walk, S.W.
28 December 1915 [Tuesday]

Dear Mrs. Wharton,

I was fortunately prevented from yielding to the impulse to write to you yesterday, immediately after receiving your own letter of the 23rd., with its enclosure of the charming Belgian-worked collar[1]—a decoration I shall wear with great pride and for which I thank you very much. When your letter arrived I had just been writing to Mrs. Hunter and Mr. Sturgis and a third report must have been couched in the same overwhelmingly gloomy terms as theirs were. It's difficult to keep one's judgment at all steady in the middle of the daily fluctuations of Mr. James's state and other people's opinions of it, and I haven't seen him myself, awake, since last Wednesday, I think it was. The day before yesterday was so bad—he was in such a difficult mental state and needed such unceasing physical motion (constant lifting from one chair to another) that the nurses and entire assisting househeld had completely collapsed by the evening and I'd found Kidd and Burgess each stretched almost flat in the kitchen and the nurse nearly hysterical and Mrs. James convinced that he could never be anything but a perfect wreck of his former self, mentally and morally, again. But that state didn't last. He had a fairly quiet day yesterday and a moderately quiet night, and this morning they have wheeled him into the sunny dining-room which is ever so much pleasanter a room than his dark northward looking bedroom. He is so strong physically, in spite of all these attacks, that it doesn't seem to tire him sitting up in a chair for the greater part of the day. The nurses tell me, too, that there are better signs of returning power in the left hand and leg, which is all to the good. His ideas are still a good deal confused, and I don't think he quite realises where he is, but that may very well be partly due to the morphia he has been having till within the last day or two. In any case we can only wait and hope that mental power will slowly return. The doctor thinks it will return, and that is the great thing. I don't think it would be a bit of good for you to come over yet—he isn't seeing anyone and hasn't been expressing any desire to see anyone beyond the circle of nurses and doctor and general household ministrants. He has quite stopped thinking about literary work, and with the cessation of that preoccupation has, naturally, stopped wanting to see me at all. In fact I feel extremely functionless just at present. I suppose that until Peggy is over here and established I'd better go on hanging round, but after that I shan't be anything but a quite useless expense. I imagine that she and Mrs. James will both settle down in Chelsea for the rest of Mr. James's life, and they are more than sufficient to manage everything. It's almost too much even to hope that he can ever write anything again—his powers of doing that had been failing for some time before these attacks, and even if he does ever want to his niece is quite a practised typist and entirely capable of doing the very small amount of amanuensis work that would be needed. However, that question will very likely solve itself easily and naturally in the course of the next week or two when we know better how much recovery can be hoped for. It is quite obvious that there will have to be a permanent addition to the staff in the shape of a good strong nurse, if not two nurses.

With ever so many thanks, dear Mrs. Wharton, again, for your Christmas gift, and your so much too kind letter—I wish I could tell you better how great a help your letters and the constant knowledge of your consideration and sympathy has been.

Yours ever sincerely
Theodora Bosanquet

1. Bosanquet's journal entry for 27 December 1915 specifies that the collar was "worked by one of her [EW's] Belgian refugee women."

53, rue de Varenne
17 January 1916 [Monday]

Dear Miss Bosanquet,

Your letter of the 15th[1] has just come, & sad as it is I take comfort from the phrase: "The end may come soon."

I want to tell you again how much I feel for you in your present loneliness & your sense of being of no use. Whatever Mr. James's relatives may think—& perhaps they are more appreciative than they appear to be—all his friends owe you a deep debt of gratitude for the promptness with which you kept them informed of his condition in those first harassing weeks, & for your perfect understanding of what they felt & of all they longed to be told.

I should have been so glad to have you come here for a short rest of a week or ten days, & I wrote Mr. [Howard] Sturgis about it; but he tells me that, very naturally, you don't want to go away even for a day.

I wonder if, later, there wd. be a chance of your coming to me as a secretary? There are three difficult conditions.

1. Living in Paris, where you wd. probably be lonely at times.

2. Speaking & writing French easily—do you?

3d. Having to begin work at 9 a.m.—& having to do queer odds & ends of things for me—a muddle of charity, shopping & literature—! Perhaps you don't think the picture tempting. (The muddle of things is of course due to war time, & is *not* the habitual duty of my secretary!)

It would be very pleasant to have you undertake the task, if only for a few months; & perhaps we might arrive at some kind of compromise even if you haven't the habit of writing French. It *would*, of course, be necessary that you should speak it enough to get about, & to communicate with the natives.[2]

I am going away in about a month for another rest of six weeks or more, & this wd. be a project for the spring, after my return.

Yours very sincerely
E. Wharton

1. It no longer exists.
2. See the following letter on Bosanquet's refusal of the offer.

53, rue de Varenne
26 January 1916

Dear Miss Bosanquet,

Yes, of course I understand all your reasons,[1] & I think you quite right in deciding as you do. Moreover, at this moment, very fluent French *is* absolutely necessary for the work I am doing.

I hope you may be able to get away to the country soon & write; but for the present I can well imagine your reluctance to put any distance between yourself & Carlyle Mansions.

This news of returning physical strength is too dreadful—

Yours ever sincerely
    E. Wharton

Let me know when there is any change, won't you?

1. For refusing EW's offer of a position as her secretary; see previous letter.

53, rue de Varenne
1 March [1916]

Dear Miss Bosanquet,

It was very kind of you to telegraph, & I need not say what relief your news brought ... I was so glad to know the end was quiet & unconscious.[1]

You will be feeling a great void now; but you will have happy & dear memories of the long years of your collaboration with one of the wisest & noblest men that ever lived. We who knew him well know how great he would have been if he had never written a line.

I send you my deepest sympathy, & I hope you will now go off quietly to the country to rest & think of your own work—[2]

Thank you again for your kindness in always remembering my longing for news.

Yours very sincerely,
    Edith Wharton

I hope you will let me hear from you sometimes.

1. HJ's death on 28 February 1916.
2. As writer and editor.

Appendix C

THE LETTER from the Comte de Séguier, captain of artillery, is a response to Wharton's letter of condolence on the death of Lieutenant Jean du Breuil de Saint-Germain in action (see chap. 7, letter of 23 March 1915). She sent this letter to James in hers of 26 March 1915. In her letter of 10 August 1915, she sent James this current prospectus for *The Book of the Homeless*.

The Army[1]   10 March 1915   Division Park   Postal Section 101
Dear Madam,

Thank you for writing to me. You have done me some good, all the good, alas! that anyone can do me. Had you any idea how much I loved him? I didn't know it myself: I learned it on the day when I got the frightful news, and when my heart suffered a shock it had not known before.

I stupidly thought, if you can imagine, that he would be spared, and that all these brutalities unleashed by civilization and human progress would treat him gently, him who represented in my view all that is finest and most sincerely human; and death, which claims to be blind, went to seek out at this front flooded with men the one who most closely touched my soul!

My sadness, I confess, remains indifferent to what is called the glory of his dying. His personality alone was in my eyes sufficient to crown him with glory, and those who honor him today do not know his value of yesterday. They did not know all the resources of that constant and discreet affection of his or that admirable mixture of intelligence and wit that raised his conversation well above the ordinary. They did not know that imagination, so delicate and independent, that judgment accessible to all right reasoning, that tireless and reliable generosity, that moral countenance so open and so engaging— And I, whom this war could please only by certain results, I see the war refuse me the one consolation it might have offered me, that of dying at his side or at least clasping him in my arms, catching his last words, and closing his eyes.

For a long time yet tears will come to my eyes when I think of him. I cannot believe that I will ever forget him.

You were one of those he valued most and highest. It is thanks to him that I have known you: and, beyond all considerations of sympathy, to remain faithful to you will be to render further homage to his memory. I will not fail in that.

Most respectfully and sadly yours
    Séguier[2]

1. Just below this EW wrote "don't return."
2. My translation.

THE BOOK OF THE HOMELESS

(Le Livre des Sans-Foyers.)

To be sold for the benefit of the American Hostels for Refugees and the Children of Flanders Rescue Committee, founded in Paris by Mrs Wharton (in Nov. 1914 and in April 1915), and chiefly maintained by American subscriptions.

The Book of the Homeless is to be published simultaneously in New York and London, in October 1915.

It is to consist entirely of *original and unpublished* contributions from Belgian, French, English, Italian and American authors, painters and composers. Each of the articles contributed will be printed in its original language, and the French and Italian articles will be translated into English.

As far as possible, the painters invited to contribute will be asked to give us portraits of the authors who have consented to give us articles, or else original sketches. The original sketches and autograph articles or musical scores contributed will be sold by auction, in New York, after the publication of the book, for the benefit of the same charities.

Authors are therefore earnestly requested to give their manuscripts for this purpose.

Mr. Roosevelt has been asked to write an introduction.

The volume will be sold entirely for the benefit of the two charities above-named.

List (in alphabetical order) of authors artists and composers invited to contribute: (the names of those who have already accepted are marked with an asterisk).

Authors

Mr D'Annunzio

Mr Maurice Barrès*

Mr René Bazin

Mr Jacques Emile Blanche*

Mr Paul Bourget*

Mr Claudel*

Mr Jean Cocteau*

Le Prof. Benedetto Croce

Mme Eleonora Duse

Mr André Gide*

Mr Paul Hervieu*

Mr Francis Jammes*

Mr Pierre Loti

Mr Maeterlinck*

Comtesse de Noailles*

Mr Marcel Proust

Mr Henri de Régnier*

Mme Henri de Régnier*

Mr Rostand*

Mr André Suarès*

Mr Emile Verhaeren*

Mr Arnold Bennett

Mr Max Beerbohm

Mr Laurence Binyon

Mr W. C. Brownell

Mr John Galsworthy

Mr Edmund Gosse

Judge Robert Grant*

Mr Thomas Hardy*

Mr W. D. Howells

Mr Rudyard Kipling

Mr E. S. Martin

Mr Masefield

Mrs Meynell

Mr Paul Elmer More

Miss Josephine Preston Peabody

Miss Edith M. Thomas

Mr Herbert French*

Mrs Humphry Ward

Mr H. G. Wells

Le Prof. Barrett Wendell

Mrs Woods

Mr W. B. Yeats

Painters and Sculptors

Mr Bakst*

Mr J. E. Blanchet*

Mr Dagnan Bouveret*

Mr Jean Cocteau*

Mr Forain

Mr Walter Gay*

Mr Maxfield Parrish

Mr Picasso

Mr Renoir*

Mr Rodin*

Mr John Sargent, R.A.*

Mr Van Rysselberghe*

Musiciens

Mr Debussy   Mr Vincent d'Indy*
Mr Fauré   Mr Stravinsky*

Contributions should be sent to Mrs WHARTON
53, Rue de Varenne, Paris
avant September 1st

* have accepted.

Index

About the Author

LYALL H. POWERS was born and raised in Canada and educated at United College (now the University of Winnipeg), the University of Manitoba, l'Université de Paris, and Indiana University. In 1944–45 he served with the RCAF and the Canadian army. He has taught at the University of Manitoba, Indiana University, the University of Wisconsin, the University of British Columbia, the American School in Rome, the University of Göttingen (West Germany), and the University of Hawaii in Manoa; he is now professor of English at the University of Michigan. He was a *boursier* of the French government and has held fellowships from the Royal Society of Canada and the Guggenheim Foundation. Among his publications are books and articles on English, American, Canadian, and French literature, including *A Guide to Henry James, Henry James and the Naturalist Movement, Henry James: An Introduction and Interpretation, A Bibliography of American Periodicals 1850–1910,* and *Faulkner's Yoknapatawpha Comedy;* he has edited *The Portable Henry James* (revised), *Studies in "The Portrait of a Lady," Henry James's Major Novels: Essays in Criticism,* and *Leon Edel and Literary Art,* and, with Leon Edel, *"Henry James and the Bazar Letters"* and *The Complete Notebooks of Henry James.* He is a member of the editorial board of *The Henry James Review* and treasurer of the Margaret Laurence International Society. In 1986 he was elected a Fellow of the Royal Society of Arts. Currently he is preparing a literary biography of the eminent Canadian novelist Margaret Laurence.

Lamb House
Rye
Sussex

September 21st 1914

Dearest Edith.

Reims is the...

unspeakable & immeasu...

horror & "infamy"... or wha...

appalling & heartbreak...

...it's for...

meet me at Ea...
Jagel the 15th me...
that particul...
a snow-covered...
sweeping up to th...
no one in sight...
a cavalry par...
hun cloak...
against the wind...
Then we went to...
the meat back...
where there is a ca...
"éclat..."